The NATO Intervention in Libya

This book explores 'lessons learned' from the military intervention in Libya by examining key aspects of the 2011 NATO campaign.

NATO's intervention in Libya had unique features, rendering it unlikely to serve as a model for action in other situations. There was an explicit UN Security Council mandate to use military force, a strong European commitment to protect Libyan civilians, Arab League political endorsement and American engagement in the critical, initial phase of the air campaign. Although the seven-month intervention stretched NATO's ammunition stockpiles and political will almost to their respective breaking points, the definitive overthrow of the Gaddafi regime is universally regarded as a major accomplishment.

With contributions from a range of key thinkers and analysts in the field, the book first explains the law and politics of the intervention, starting out with deliberations in NATO and at the UN Security Council, both noticeably influenced by the concept of a Responsibility to Protect (R2P). It then goes on to examine a wide set of military and auxiliary measures that governments and defence forces undertook in order to increasingly tilt the balance against the Gaddafi regime and to bring about an end to the conflict, as well as to the intervention proper, while striving to keep the number of NATO and civilian casualties to a minimum.

This book will be of interest to students of strategic studies, history and war studies, and IR in general.

Kjell Engelbrekt is Associate Professor of Political Science at the Swedish National Defence College and member of the Royal Swedish Academy of War Sciences.

Marcus Mohlin is a Commander in the Swedish Navy. He also holds a Ph.D. in Military Sciences and is currently a Researcher at the Swedish National Defence College.

Charlotte Wagnsson is Professor of Political Science at the Swedish National Defence College; she received her Ph.D. in Political Science from Stockholm University.

Contemporary Security Studies
Series Editors: James Gow and Rachel Kerr
King's College London

This series focuses on new research across the spectrum of international peace and security, in an era where each year throws up multiple examples of conflicts that present new security challenges in the world around them.

NATO's Secret Armies
Operation Gladio and terrorism in Western Europe
Daniele Ganser

The US, NATO and Military Burden-sharing
Peter Kent Forster and Stephen J. Cimbala

Russian Governance in the Twe rst Century
Geo-strategy, geopolitics and governance
Irina Isakova

The Foreign Office and Finland 1938–1940
Diplomatic sideshow
Craig Gerrard

Rethinking the Nature of War
Edited by Isabelle Duyvesteyn and Jan Angstrom

Perception and Reality in the Modern Yugoslav Conflict
Myth, falsehood and deceit 1991–1995
Brendan O'Shea

The Political Economy of Peacebuilding in Post-Dayton Bosnia
Tim Donais

The Distracted Eagle
The rift between America and Old Europe
Peter H. Merkl

The Iraq War
European perspectives on politics, strategy and operations
Edited by Jan Hallenberg and Håkan Karlsson

Strategic Contest
Weapons proliferation and war in the Greater Middle East
Richard L. Russell

Propaganda, the Press and Conflict
The Gulf War and Kosovo
David R. Willcox

Missile Defence
International, regional and national implications
Edited by Bertel Heurlin and Sten Rynning

Globalising Justice for Mass Atrocities
A revolution in accountability
Chandra Lekha Sriram

Ethnic Conflict and Terrorism
The origins and dynamics of civil wars
Joseph L. Soeters

Globalisation and the Future of Terrorism
Patterns and predictions
Brynjar Lia

Nuclear Weapons and Strategy
The evolution of American nuclear policy
Stephen J. Cimbala

Nasser and the Missile Age in the Middle East
Owen L. Sirrs

War as Risk Management
Strategy and conflict in an age of globalised risks
Yee-Kuang Heng

Military Nanotechnology
Potential applications and preventive arms control
Jürgen Altmann

NATO and Weapons of Mass Destruction
Regional alliance, global threats
Eric R. Terzuolo

Europeanisation of National Security Identity
The EU and the changing security identities of the Nordic states
Pernille Rieker

Conflict Prevention and Peacebuilding in Post-War Societies
Sustaining the peace
Edited by T. David Mason and James D. Meernik

Controlling the Weapons of War
Politics, persuasion, and the prohibition of inhumanity
Brian Rappert

Changing Transatlantic Security Relations
Do the US, the EU and Russia form a new strategic triangle?
Edited by Jan Hallenberg and Håkan Karlsson

Theoretical Roots of US Foreign Policy
Machiavelli and American unilateralism
Thomas M. Kane

Corporate Soldiers and International Security
The rise of private military companies
Christopher Kinsey

Transforming European Militaries
Coalition operations and the technology gap
Gordon Adams and Guy Ben-Ari

Globalization and Conflict
National security in a 'new' strategic era
Edited by Robert G. Patman

Military Forces in 21st Century Peace Operations
No job for a soldier?
James V. Arbuckle

The Political Road to War with Iraq
Bush, 9/11 and the drive to
overthrow Saddam
Nick Ritchie and Paul Rogers

Bosnian Security after Dayton
New perspectives
Edited by Michael A. Innes

Kennedy, Johnson and NATO
Britain, America and the dynamics
of alliance, 1962–68
Andrew Priest

Small Arms and Security
New emerging international norms
Denise Garcia

The United States and Europe
Beyond the neo-conservative
divide?
Edited by John Baylis and Jon Roper

Russia, NATO and Cooperative Security
Bridging the gap
Lionel Ponsard

International Law and International Relations
Bridging theory and practice
Edited by Tom Biersteker, Peter Spiro, Chandra Lekha Sriram and Veronica Raffo

Deterring International Terrorism and Rogue States
US national security policy after 9/11
James H. Lebovic

Vietnam in Iraq
Tactics, lessons, legacies and ghosts
Edited by John Dumbrell and David Ryan

Understanding Victory and Defeat in Contemporary War
Edited by Jan Angstrom and Isabelle Duyvesteyn

Propaganda and Information Warfare in the Twenty-First Century
Altered images and deception operations
Scot Macdonald

Governance in Post-Conflict Societies
Rebuilding fragile states
Edited by Derick W. Brinkerhoff

European Security in the Twenty-first Century
The challenge of multipolarity
Adrian Hyde-Price

Ethics, Technology and the American Way of War
Cruise missiles and US security policy
Reuben E. Brigety II

International Law and the Use of Armed Force
The UN charter and the major powers
Joel H. Westra

Disease and Security
Natural plagues and biological weapons in East Asia
Christian Enemark

Explaining War and Peace
Case studies and necessary condition counterfactuals
Jack Levy and Gary Goertz

War, Image and Legitimacy
Viewing contemporary conflict
James Gow and Milena Michalski

Information Strategy and Warfare
A guide to theory and practice
John Arquilla and Douglas A. Borer

Countering the Proliferation of Weapons of Mass Destruction
NATO and EU options in the Mediterranean and the Middle East
Thanos P. Dokos

Security and the War on Terror
Edited by Alex J. Bellamy, Roland Bleiker, Sara E. Davies, Richard Devetak

The European Union and Strategy
An emerging actor
Edited by Jan Hallenberg and Kjell Engelbrekt

Causes and Consequences of International Conflict
Data, methods and theory
Edited by Glenn Palmer

Russian Energy Policy and Military Power
Putin's quest for greatness
Pavel Baev

The Baltic Question during the Cold War
Edited by John Hiden, Vahur Made and David J. Smith

America, the EU and Strategic Culture
Renegotiating the transatlantic bargain
Asle Toje

Afghanistan, Arms and Conflict
Armed groups, disarmament and security in a post-war society
Michael Bhatia and Mark Sedra

Punishment, Justice and International Relations
Ethics and order after the Cold War
Anthony F. Lang, Jr.

Intra-State Conflict, Governments and Security
Dilemmas of deterrence and assurance
Edited by Stephen M. Saideman and Marie-Joëlle J. Zahar

Democracy and Security
Preferences, norms and policy-making
Edited by Matthew Evangelista, Harald Müller and Niklas Schörnig

The Homeland Security Dilemma
Fear, failure and the future of American security
Frank P. Harvey

Military Transformation and Strategy
Revolutions in military affairs and small states
Edited by Bernard Loo

Peace Operations and International Criminal Justice
Building peace after mass atrocities
Majbritt Lyck

NATO, Security and Risk Management
From Kosovo to Khandahar
M. J. Williams

Cyber Conflict and Global Politics
Edited by Athina Karatzogianni

Globalisation and Defence in the Asia-Pacific
Arms across Asia
Edited by Geoffrey Till, Emrys Chew and Joshua Ho

Security Strategies and American World Order
Lost power
Birthe Hansen, Peter Toft and Anders Wivel

War, Torture and Terrorism
Rethinking the rules of international security
Edited by Anthony F. Lang, Jr. and Amanda Russell Beattie

America and Iraq
Policy-making, intervention and regional politics
Edited by David Ryan and Patrick Kiely

European Security in a Global Context
Internal and external dynamics
Edited by Thierry Tardy

Women and Political Violence
Female combatants in ethno-national conflict
Miranda H. Alison

Justice, Intervention and Force in International Relations
Reassessing just war theory in the 21st century
Kimberley A. Hudson

Clinton's Foreign Policy
Between the Bushes, 1992–2000
John Dumbrell

Aggression, Crime and International Security
Moral, political and legal dimensions of international relations
Page Wilson

European Security Governance
The European Union in a Westphalian world
Charlotte Wagnsson, James Sperling and Jan Hallenberg

Private Security and the Reconstruction of Iraq
Christopher Kinsey

US Foreign Policy and Iran
American–Iranian relations since the Islamic revolution
Donette Murray

Legitimising the Use of Force in International Relations
Kosovo, Iraq and the ethics of intervention
Corneliu Bjola

The EU and European Security Order
Interfacing security actors
Rikard Bengtsson

US Counter-terrorism Strategy and al-Qaeda
Signalling and the terrorist world-view
Joshua Alexander Geltzer

Global Biosecurity
Threats and responses
Edited by Peter Katona, John P. Sullivan and Michael D. Intriligator

US Hegemony and International Legitimacy
Norms, power and followership in the wars on Iraq
Lavina Lee

Private Security Contractors and New Wars
Risk, law, and ethics
Kateri Carmola

Russia's Foreign Security Policy in the 21st Century
Putin, Medvedev and beyond
Marcel de Haas

Rethinking Security Governance
The problem of unintended consequences
Edited by Christopher Daase and Cornelius Friesendorf

Territory, War, and Peace
John A. Vasquez and Marie T. Henehan

Justifying America's Wars
The conduct and practice of US military intervention
Nicholas Kerton-Johnson

Legitimacy and the Use of Armed Force
Stability missions in the post-Cold War era
Chiyuki Aoi

Women, Peace and Security
Translating policy into practice
Edited by Funmi Olonisakin, Karen Barnes and Ekaette Ikpe

War, Ethics and Justice
New perspectives on a post-9/11 world
Edited by Annika Bergman-Rosamond and Mark Phythian

Transitional Justice, Peace and Accountability
Outreach and the role of international courts after conflict
Jessica Lincoln

International Law, Security and Ethics
Policy challenges in the post-9/11 world
Edited by Aidan Hehir, Matasha Kuhrt and Andrew Mumford

Multipolarity in the 21st Century
A new world order
Edited by David Brown and Donette Murray

European Homeland Security
A European strategy in the making?
Edited by Christian Kaunert, Sarah Léonard and Patryk Pawlak

Transatlantic Relations in the 21st Century
Europe, America and the rise of the rest
Erwan Lagadec

The EU, the UN and Collective Security
Making multilateralism effective
Edited by Joachim Krause and Natalino Ronzitti

Understanding Emerging Security Challenges
Threats and opportunities
Ashok Swain

Crime-Terror Alliances and the State
Ethnonationalist and Islamist challenges to regional security
Lyubov Grigorova Mincheva and Ted Robert Gurr

Understanding NATO in the 21st Century
Alliance strategies, security and global governance
Edited by Graeme P. Herd and John Kriendler

Ethics and the Laws of War
The moral justification of legal norms
Antony Lamb

Militancy and Violence in West Africa
Religion, politics and radicalisation
Edited by Ernst Dijxhoorn, James Gow and Funmi Olonisakin

Mechanistic Realism and US Foreign Policy
A new framework for analysis
Johannes Rø

Prosecuting War Crimes
Lessons and legacies of the International Criminal Tribunal for the former Yugoslavia
Edited by James Gow, Rachel Kerr and Zoran Pajić

The NATO Intervention in Libya
Lessons learned from the campaign
Edited by Kjell Engelbrekt, Marcus Mohlin and Charlotte Wagnsson

The NATO Intervention in Libya

Lessons learned from the campaign

Edited by Kjell Engelbrekt,
Marcus Mohlin and Charlotte Wagnsson

LONDON AND NEW YORK

First published 2014
by Routledge
2 Park Square, Milton Park, Abingdon, Oxfordshire OX14 4RN

and by Routledge
711 Third Avenue, New York, NY 10017

First issued in paperback 2015

Routledge is an imprint of the Taylor & Francis Group, an informa business

© 2014 selection and editorial material, Kjell Engelbrekt, Marcus Mohlin and Charlotte Wagnsson; individual chapters, the contributors

The right of the editors to be identified as the authors of the editorial material, and of the authors for their individual chapters, has been asserted in accordance with sections 77 and 78 of the Copyright, Designs and Patents Act 1988.

All rights reserved. No part of this book may be reprinted or reproduced or utilized in any form or by any electronic, mechanical, or other means, now known or hereafter invented, including photocopying and recording, or in any information storage or retrieval system, without permission in writing from the publishers.

Trademark notice: Product or corporate names may be trademarks or registered trademarks, and are used only for identification and explanation without intent to infringe.

British Library Cataloguing in Publication Data
A catalogue record for this book is available from the British Library

Library of Congress Cataloging in Publication Data
The NATO intervention in Libya : lessons learned from the campaign / edited by Kjell Engelbrekt, Marcus Mohlin, and Charlotte Wagnsson.
    pages cm. – (Contemporary security studies)
    Includes bibliographical references and index.
    1. Libya–History–Civil War, 2011–Participation, European.
2. Libya–History–Civil War, 2011–Participation, American.
3. North Atlantic Treaty Organization–Armed Forces–Libya.
4. Military assistance, European–Libya. 5. Military assistance, American–Libya. 6. Regime change–Libya. 7. Intervention (International law) I. Engelbrekt, Kjell, author, editor of compilation. II. Mohlin, Marcus, 1965– author, editor of compilation. III. Wagnsson, Charlotte, editor of compilation.
DT236.N38 2013
961.204'2–dc23   2013016382

ISBN 13: 978-1-138-92268-6 (pbk)
ISBN 13: 978-0-415-70549-3 (hbk)

Typeset in Baskerville
by Wearset Ltd, Boldon, Tyne and Wear

Contents

List of illustrations	xiii
Notes on contributors	xiv
Foreword	xvi
JOHN ANDREAS OLSEN	
Acknowledgements	xix

Introduction   1
KJELL ENGELBREKT AND CHARLOTTE WAGNSSON

PART I
The law and politics of intervention   15

1   Able but not willing: a critical assessment of NATO's Libya intervention   17
JEFFREY H. MICHAELS

2   Why Libya? Security Council Resolution 1973 and the politics of justification   41
KJELL ENGELBREKT

3   A legal view on NATO's campaign in Libya   63
FREDRIK A. HOLST AND MARTIN D. FINK

PART II
The military campaign   101

4   Executing strategy from the air   103
ANDERS NYGREN

5	Naval assets: not just a tool for war CHRISTIAN WOLLERT	128
6	Fragments of an army: three aspects of the Libya collapse KARL SÖRENSON AND NIMA DAMIDEZ	151

PART III
Auxiliary measures and arrangements 169

7	Managing perceptions: strategic communication and the story of *success* in Libya RIKKE BJERG JENSEN	171
8	Cloak and dagger in Libya: the Libyan *Thuwar* and the role of Allied Special Forces MARCUS MOHLIN	195
9	Conclusion: lessons and consequences of Operation Unified Protector ROBERT EGNELL	221

Select bibliography 236
Index 242

Illustrations

Figures

3.1 Overview of the legal aspects   65
3.2 Example of leaflet distributed in Libya   83

Tables

6.1 Status of Libyan Armed Forces, 2010   158
8.1 Special Forces core activities   200
8.2 Strategic goals and operational tasks   209

Contributors

Rikke Bjerg Jensen is a Ph.D. candidate at the Communication and Media Research Institute, University of Westminster (London), working on a dissertation devoted to strategic communication.

Nima Damidez is an instructor at the Swedish Armed Forces Language School; he is also affiliated with the Swedish National Defence College.

Robert Egnell is Lecturer in War Sciences at the Swedish National Defence College, and presently affiliated with Georgetown University (Washington D.C.).

Kjell Engelbrekt is Associate Professor of Political Science at the Swedish National Defence College and member of the Royal Swedish Academy of War Sciences.

Martin D. Fink is Lecturer in Law at the Netherlands Defence Academy and has held several appointments as a legal officer in the Royal Netherlands Navy.

Fredrik A. Holst is a Ph.D. candidate at the International Law Centre at the Swedish National Defence College, as well as a Lieutenant-Colonel and part-time legal adviser with the Swedish Armed Forces.

Jeffrey H. Michaels is Lecturer in Defence Studies at King's College London, and presently based at the Joint Services Command and Staff College (Shrivenham).

Marcus Mohlin is a Commander in the Swedish Navy. He also holds a Ph.D. in Military Sciences and is currently a Researcher at the Swedish National Defence College.

Anders Nygren is a Lieutenant-Colonel and has held several postings in the Swedish Armed Forces HQ; he currently serves as Instructor in Joint and Air Operations at the Swedish National Defence College.

John Andreas Olsen is an active serving Colonel in the Royal Norwegian Air Force and a Visiting Professor of Operational Art and Tactics at the Swedish National Defence College.

Karl Sörenson is a Ph.D. candidate in Philosophy at the Royal Institute of Technology (Stockholm), working on a dissertation devoted to game theory and asymmetric conflicts; he is also affiliated with the Swedish National Defence College.

Charlotte Wagnsson is Professor of Political Science at the Swedish National Defence College; she received her Ph.D. in Political Science from Stockholm University.

Christian Wollert is a Commander in the Royal Swedish Navy, and presently serves at the Swedish National Defence College as Instructor in Naval Operations.

Foreword

John Andreas Olsen

The Arab Spring – with its various waves of mass demonstrations, armed uprisings and civil wars – has played out differently for each of the Arab states. Nowhere did the international community react more cohesively and decisively than in the Libya case. As clashes between forces loyal to Colonel Moammar al-Gaddafi and the rebel opposition seeking to oust his regime escalated, the UN adopted resolution 1973 on 17 March 2011 authorizing 'all necessary measures' short of foreign occupation to protect civilians. American, British and French air power spearheaded military action, and within the next few days NATO 'answered the call' by initiating Operation Unified Protector. The extensive air campaign came to an end seven months later, with the capture and death of the man who had ruled Libya with an iron fist since 1969.

The NATO Secretary General announced from Tripoli that Unified Protector was 'one of the most successful missions' in the history of the Alliance. EU leaders welcomed the fall of the old regime and urged the transitional authorities to build a democratic country. The Obama administration stated that the death of Gaddafi marked 'the start of a new era' for the people of Libya.

At first sight the Libya case seems to offer a model for the future: testimony to constructive and resolute statecraft in which politics and military action combined on solid legal grounds. This triad of force – political, military and judicial – offers an exemplar for how to deal with regimes that conduct large-scale crimes against humanity, but the first rule for seeking valid conclusions from the campaign is to distinguish the unique features of the situation from general, enduring maxims. In acknowledging that an unusual convergence of international relations made the intervention possible, this book takes a close look at repercussions of the choices made, and their implications for the future. Drawing on instant history and the first wave of scholarship available on the Libya intervention, the authors offer insight well beyond sorties flown, bombs dropped, targets destroyed and vessels hailed.

Turning a mission originally designed to protect civilians into an operation to bring about regime change is controversial. When Russia and

China withheld their veto on resolution 1973, they did so with the understanding that the mission focused only on civilian protection. Gaining their passive consent in a similar future scenario – as Syria already has demonstrated – may prove exceedingly difficult. While most Western countries may conclude that the model often referred to as Responsibility to Protect, or R2P, is adaptable for handling other recalcitrant regimes, Russia and China may well come to different conclusions, insisting even more on the principle of absolute state sovereignty.

Although the Libya episode in some aspects resembles previous NATO-led interventions, most notably Operation Deliberate Force in 1995 and Operation Allied Force in 1999, a series of distinctive feature sets it apart from all other campaigns. Looking behind the curtain clearly reveals that the 28 NATO heads of state were far from unanimous about how to deal with the Libyan situation. Despite agreeing to 'answer the call' of resolution 1973, they had different opinions and interpretations of ends, ways and means. The result was that a 'coalition' within the Alliance, in partnership with several Arab countries, contributed significantly more than other NATO members. Some of the larger NATO countries remained reluctant supporters of the air and maritime operations, while some of the smaller countries showed an unprecedented political and military commitment. While NATO ruled out troops on the ground, some member states provided Special Forces that at times played a crucial part in the air-land interface. Furthermore, NATO personnel trained and advised the rebels, enabling the poorly organized and modestly equipped insurgents to take the lead in overthrowing the regime.

As NATO continues to gain members and takes on a broader set of challenges, differences in opinion on 'out-of-area' operations will no doubt remain and most likely increase. But it is noteworthy that the Alliance did agree to take unprecedented collective action notwithstanding these differences, and remained unified despite media criticism. NATO's forte is its ability to act as a unit when stakes are high even when there is internal disagreement; NATO's Achilles Heel is its principle of consensus. In Libya we saw the potency of the Alliance in action. In hindsight, much was done right, both by design and good fortune. Operation Unified Protector merits praise and congratulations, but these must be followed by serious analyses of NATO's actions and those of others.

Such is the purpose of this book, and in the process it provides great insight into political, military, and legal aspects of NATO's intervention, including an examination of the inner dynamics of the Libya regime and the factors that led to its collapse, and of the Alliance's strategic communications and the handling of media. The strength of this work lies in its combination of depth, breadth and context, using earlier studies as points of departure and encouraging further work. Such undertakings must not be taken lightly, because history has taught us that removal of a dictator unleashes forces that have been held in check, and those forces affect thousands of human lives. Few mourn the loss of Colonel Gaddafi and most appreciate that the international intervention prevented a protracted civil war, but the methods used must be subject to debate.

The real successes and failures of the post-Gaddafi era will manifest themselves in the decades to come. Overthrowing a dictatorship that has ruled for more than four decades is one thing; building a state and society on the basis of democracy, individual liberty, and the rule of law is another. While the Libyan people must undertake comprehensive reforms, we must draw lessons about the NATO campaign that enabled regime change and do so without fear, bias or excuses.

The NATO Intervention in Libya provides a scholarly advance and should be of great interest to policy-makers, military professionals and researchers alike. I am honoured to have been invited to introduce it.

Acknowledgements

This volume began as an informal conversation between the three editors in early 2012, a few months after the war in Libya had ended. The idea to collaborate and bring in a wider set of contributors essentially stemmed from two circumstances, one being our common interest in the conflict and the sequence of events through which it evolved. The second circumstance is the curiosity that arose from all three of us approaching many of the issues in ways that revealed significant differences in academic and professional backgrounds: Kjell with an interest in the interplay between great power diplomacy and UN Security Council deliberations; Charlotte as engaged in security studies and NATO in particular; and Marcus with insights into the use of non-conventional assets, such as private and military security companies, in global politics and his professional outlook as a 'soldier scholar'.

The project received a faculty grant from the Swedish National Defence College, with additional money provided from the Department of Military Sciences, as well as the Department of Security, Strategy and Leadership. A little more than half of the participants in the project belong to the college staff, employed in research and teaching positions. But the project was further utilized to consolidate existing academic relationships as well as to make new ones, with contributors from the United Kingdom, the Netherlands, Denmark and the United States. We are extraordinarily satisfied with the level of quality of these external contributions, which in our view add much value to the finished product.

It has been our good fortune to find ourselves to be surrounded by so many friends and colleagues who have supported us throughout this work. Though frustrating at times (as careful scholarly work tends to be), our joint intellectual journey has for the most part been both fun and rewarding. We hope that the end result will be useful in more than one way, as our ambition from the outset was to produce something that could be valuable to policymakers as well as to scholars, to individuals and organizations who were engaged in the 2011 Libya intervention, as well as to observers and critics who followed it from afar. Since all of us are engaged in teaching at a defence college, moreover, a major objective has been to produce a high-quality volume that comprehensively analyses the Libya intervention as a military campaign in context, something we believe is largely missing in syllabi at institutions of higher learning associated with educating and training military officers and security policy advisers.

At a more personal level, the three of us would like to thank Professor Jan Hallenberg, Professor Maja Kirilova, Associate Professor Ola Engdahl, Dr Eva Haldén, Dr Caroline Holmqvist, Dr Jerker Widén, Major Stefan Wilson and Major Anders Wendel for their critical and constructive comments at various stages of the writing process. We are also indebted Dr. Arita Holmberg, who first came up with the idea of a book devoted to the Libya intervention, to Dr Maria Hellman and Viktoria Asp for invaluable editorial assistance, and to Colonel Jan Mörtberg and Lt Colonel Stefan Borén for encouragement and consistent administrative support. Finally we would also like to extend our gratitude to Annabelle Harris of Routledge for efficient and robust assistance throughout the publishing process.

Last but certainly not least, we would like to thank our respective families for their patience and unwavering support.

Kjell, Marcus and Charlotte

Introduction

Kjell Engelbrekt and Charlotte Wagnsson

> For many in Libya, NATO has literally made the difference between life and death. Operation Unified Protector has shown that when the cause is just – when the legal base is strong – and when the regional support is clear, NATO is the indispensable alliance.
>
> (Anders Fogh Rasmussen)[1]

This book addresses the overarching question of how we should regard the 2011 military/political campaign in Libya. Indeed, the operation has been much debated. Was the Libya campaign led by the North Atlantic Treaty Organization (NATO) a resounding success and therefore a model to be emulated in other military operations? Was it a failure of leadership and organization that, had not the US Air Force, the US Navy and auxiliary American units so effectively destroyed Libyan air defenses and blinded its ground troops, just as well might have ended in a protracted conflagration and major embarrassment to the Alliance? Or perhaps it should set no precedent at all, given the unique features of the country's political and humanitarian crisis? Finally, what can we infer from the Libyan experience about the present state, and future, of NATO?

This book sets out to question and nuance overly triumphant exclamations of the Libya campaign of 2011, yet it also challenges critics of the operation by suggesting that in some important ways, it can be seen as a success for the Western alliance. The basic assumption is that we still have work to do in examining the facts and issues associated with the campaign and that we need to take on this task by scrutinizing the operation from different angles, ranging from law and the media to various military perspectives. This exercise may generate new knowledge useful for anyone with an interest in the Libyan crisis – and in the potential of NATO – and perhaps in particular for those within the fields of war studies and security studies, for instance by providing new insights into contemporary military strategy and operations.

Evaluations of large-scale military operations often take the form of 'lessons learned' analyses, typically carried out mere months after the operation's end. Such exercises conducted by people who were actively engaged can help organizations sort bad practices from good, identify organizational deficiencies, and come up with detailed descriptions of how events unfolded that improve accountability and provide individual units with a better grasp of their own contribution toward the overall goals. Although such 'first impressions' are instructive for military organizations, it is important not to prematurely settle for conclusions drawn at an early stage of the learning cycle. Furthermore, conclusions from first-wave investigations may be distorted in that the analysis rarely is sufficiently comprehensive and conceptually consistent, and because the actors who contribute pieces of information to the overall picture are informed by narrower incentives and interests.[2]

In this volume the authors seek to go one step further and make a contribution to a *second wave* of evaluations of the 2011 Libya military campaign, building on but also re-examining early accounts produced by institutions and actors directly involved in planning and executing Operation Unified Protector and the national operations that preceded the NATO effort. The main problem is often simply that lessons drawn from first-wave analysis are not placed within the context of the precise objectives and values of those overall goals, as well as of other major organizational efforts (be they military campaigns or other types of crises) that precede and potentially succeed them. To be sure, it is when lessons learned from various branches of the armed forces, along with the impressions of diplomats, political decision makers, independent academics and civil society organizations, are added up and connected to each other that we acquire a systematic view of how events unfolded. It is ultimately from the vantage point of such a holistic foundation that some of the original lessons may have to be *re-learned*.

The stakes of the Libya war

There has indeed been considerable tension between different interpretations of the Libyan campaign. Whereas some commentators were quick to praise the pragmatic approach adopted in Operation Unified Protector toward integrating coalition partners, overcoming challenges of information-sharing, logistics and supply, others said the operational obstacles and material shortcomings – on the part of European allies in particular – constitute the overwhelming impression.[3] Some commentators, though not doubting that Libya is better off without the autocratic regime of Colonel Moammar Gadaffi, went as far as to question whether, at the end of the day, civilian lives were saved through the military intervention.[4] Others remarked that the intervention came about not to save civilians but out of concern for Western investments in Libyan oil.[5] By early 2013, many were also increasingly concerned with long-term repercussions resulting from the spread of Libyan weaponry and political extremism in Northern and West Africa.

The economic and energy resource dimensions to the 2011 Libya war are certainly not to be underestimated, but nor are the security and strategy dimensions. Starting with the former, it is a straightforward fact that Libya is estimated to have the fifth largest oil reserves on the planet, amounting to 76.7 billion barrels, and represented 2 per cent of world output before widespread hostilities interrupted production in early 2001.[6] When it comes to natural gas the proven reserves are more modest, at 1.5 trillion cubic metres, which makes up some 0.7 per cent of the world total.[7] As a result of production of both categories falling to historic lows during the course of the NATO-led military campaign, a number of other oil-producing countries stepped up their output to offset the economic consequences of the Libya outage and the ensuing spike in prices.

Eighty-five per cent of Libyan oil has in recent years been sold to European markets, which are located directly across the Mediterranean Sea. Other advantages associated with extraction of fossil fuels in Libya are that production costs are lower than in the case of alternative suppliers (Norway and Russia are the other two main suppliers), and that vast areas of the country remain to be properly explored. So far the oil fields selected for drilling and extraction have – for reasons of costs and accessibility to ports and labour – for the most part been located near the coastline in the north.

The 2003 shift in Colonel Gaddafi's diplomatic stance toward Western countries, and the United Kingdom and the United States in particular, allowed for business relations between Libya and a whole array of other countries to prosper. The decisive juncture was when the Libyan regime surrendered two suspects of the 1988 Lockerbie bombing (of Pan Am Flight 103) and announced that it was abandoning its weapons of mass destruction programme.[8] The Europeans were first to take advantage, with Italian ENI, Spanish Repsol and French Total to engage with the Libyan authorities and oil industry. Those investments, along with the EU's desire to reduce its dependence on Russian and Norwegian and North Sea assets, were suddenly at stake.[9]

With relatively speaking smaller stakes in the Libyan oil industry, Chinese companies had prior to 2011 also made significant inroads in this sector. Somewhere between 2 and 3 per cent of Chinese imports came from Libya and some 75 Chinese companies are reported to have been operating on Libyan soil at the outbreak of the war, mainly in the fields of telecommunications, irrigation and rail construction. But most importantly, China's National Petroleum Corporation had offered to assist Libyan counterparts in offshore exploration and the building of new pipeline systems.[10]

Even though the primary motivation for the civil unrest in Libyan cities may have been political in nature, leaders in the anti-Gaddafi movement quickly realized where the vulnerabilities of the regime lay and which prize armed rebels needed to secure. Taking control over oil reserves, oil fields, pipelines, ports and oil refineries would deprive the regime of a stable flow of fresh capital. From the outset, therefore, fighting between rebels and regime troops focused on the eastern cities. The majority of the oilfields are situated south of the Ras Lanuf/Brega/Ajdabiya area in the eastern half of the country and the main part of all pipelines terminate west of Ajdabiya city.[11] This explains the intense fighting that took place around the Ajdabiya/Benghazi area. Losing ground around Ajdabiya at an early stage would have been a substantial blow to the regime.

Refineries were also central to the unfolding of events. Anti-Gaddafi forces subsequently came to control the refineries in the Tobruk and Benghazi area, whereas the regime held on to the refinery in Tripoli and worked hard not to lose control over the remaining ones in the Ras Lanuf and Brega areas. Finally, of course, the storage and supply of refined oil was vital for keeping the vehicles of the armed forces on the road and for making sure that some level of economic activity was upheld.

The wider political context: the 'Arab Spring' reaches Libya

The Tunisian spark that ignited the first outburst of public discontent in mid-December 2010 was by all accounts a spontaneous, unexpected event. But street vendor Mohamed Bouazizi's self-immolation on 17 December prompted street protests in the city of Sidi Bouzid, where his attempted suicide had taken place, and later spread to several other towns and villages. It hereby turned into the largest social unrest seen in the country for three decades. By the time of Bouazizi's eventual passing in early January, the position of the government and president Ben Ali had been severely undermined through the inclusion of professional groups and wide segments of the Tunisian society in the protest movement. On 14 January Ben Ali fled the country.

Not unlike the communist revolutions in Central and Eastern Europe in the late 1980s, the Arab spring movement had a 'wildfire' quality of regional contagion, accelerated by the use of transnational and social media. Also reminiscent of the communist revolutions, precious few decision makers and observers – except for deeply committed area specialists – were able to discern the early signs of a mass uprising in the Arab world and predict what was coming. In Egypt the public protests latched onto the Tunisian criticism of autocratic Arab rule, though simultaneously fed into a deeper sense of discontent and lack of opportunities. Starting 25 January 2011 public demonstrations and protest marches could no longer be effectively quelled, which in part reflected a desire on the part of the regime to show restraint and in part the non-belligerent behaviour of the vast majority of the protesters. The sentiments of the Egyptian uprising soon converged around the demand for an immediate end to Hosni Mubarak's rule, a blatantly political objective that sent shockwaves throughout the Arab world. After a standoff that lasted for three weeks, occasionally interrupted by violent clashes between demonstrators and security forces, Mubarak announced his resignation on 11 February.

Geographically situated between Tunisia and Egypt, Libya did not stay unaffected by political developments in the neighbouring countries for long. In a society dominated by Colonel Moammar Gaddafi and his entourage for more than 40 years, large-scale demonstrations broke out in the eastern city of Benghazi less than one week after the demise of Mubarak. Minor incidents had previously occurred over local issues in other northern towns but the wider movement took off on 15 February when several hundred citizens of Benghazi gathered outside the police headquarters to demand the release of a human rights lawyer. Two days later protests had spread to at least half a dozen cities, prompting a heavy-handed crackdown by the Libyan security forces. Ten days later, on 27 February, the National Transitional Council was formed by opposition groups.

As the Libyan uprising progressed, protests were taking place in Yemen and Bahrain along the Arabian Gulf coast. These protests, however, were apparently much less important for developments in Libya than the preceding events in neighbouring Tunisia and Egypt, which had already succeeded in unseating autocratic rulers. One characteristic feature of the first phase of the Libya uprising was the immediate and unrelenting assault of the security forces, which forced opposition groups to arm themselves. Another characteristic feature was the rapid spread of support and sympathy for the anti-Gadaffi movement, based on the experience of ordinary people who had seen four decades of an arbitrary and brutal regime.

Between mid-February and mid-March the violence rapidly escalated in Libya, with an increasing number of army units becoming embroiled in the clashes with opposition forces. The latter, first composed by students, oil workers and other civilians, steadily received reinforcements through defections by regular Libyan army units and foreign fighters. Already in early March the use of heavy military equipment by the Libyan army against civilian-populated areas was common practice.[12]

The escalation of violence with the naked brutality of Gadaffi's forces, along with the crude and belligerent statements coming out of Tripoli, suggested that Libya's internal conflict could only worsen, and that the regime would not be inhibited by anyone in its use of massive and indiscriminate force in order to crush the uprising. Compounded with the economic concerns over the repercussions over a long-term civil war in an oil-rich country and the political fallout of an autocrat vehemently fighting to reverse the 'Arab spring' on his home turf, the crisis was perceived as multidimensional in several Western capitals. At the same time the scenario of a humanitarian disaster in case Gadaffi's military was left unchecked was rapidly shifting from possible to likely. Different from many other countries affected by the 'Arab spring' movement, several of these ingredients gave the international community reasons to reflect on whether to become directly engaged, or leave the Libyan and its citizens to their own devices and then be vulnerable to criticism.

Libya as a sui generis case

Particularly against this wider setting of Arab politics, the argument that NATO's 2011 Libya campaign in a variety of ways is a unique case, and therefore serves particularly badly as a model, appears to have considerable merit. The confluence of political, legal and strategic factors that came together in the spring of 2011 were – according to most observers – unusually conducive to an intervention. This was true for international law and diplomacy, to begin with. The notion that civilians deserve protection from autocratic leaders with the capability and stated intention to commit massive atrocities or acts of genocide had been established at the 2005 United Nations World Summit with the adoption of the 'responsibility to protect' formula. The rapidly deteriorating humanitarian situation in Libya in the first weeks of 2011, the regime's harsh crackdown on protesters and use of heavy guns, plus Colonel Gaddaffi's pledge 'to show no mercy' when rooting out the rebel stronghold in Benghazi 'alley by alley' combined to create powerful pressure on the Security Council to pass a robust resolution.[13] Resolution 1973, passed on 17 March 2011, for the first time authorized the use of military force primarily to protect civilian lives.

The uniqueness of circumstances also seemed true for most European and Arab countries that joined the coalition, prepared to put the resolution into practice. Some commentators argue that Libya in fact presented a 'best case' challenge to Europe by virtue of its geographic proximity, limited military resistance, and the small number of unintended casualties produced by Allied attacks.[14] The Europeans, in that they were in control of the latter parts of the campaign, could be more selective about targeting than American military units would have been. This, in turn, enabled British, French and other governments to politically sustain their efforts over several months.

Diplomatic support from the Arab League and coalition participation by Jordan, Qatar and the United Arab Emirates cannot be overestimated when it comes to providing much needed regional legitimation for the military intervention in Libya. Similarly to when Iraq was ejected from Kuwait in 1991, regional endorsement was significant for convincing Security Council member states to vote in favour of, or at least abstain from blocking, the 'all necessary measures' formula which in international law authorizes the use of military force. In addition, it was helpful in sustaining the coalition during the seven-month long military campaign. Even though their contribution to the military effort was marginal, the Arab coalition partners brought in a high level of area knowledge that was of value to the overall operation.

The proximity to the European continent certainly provided major advantages from the perspective of logistics, supply, regular maintenance, and use of existing equipment and munitions stockpiles. But despite those prerequisites for an effective deployment just outside the area of operation, several European NATO allies and partners were confronted with severe resupply and ammunition deficits, as well as other logistics bottlenecks. Had the supply lines been longer and access to alternative sources of critical equipment unavailable, reports indicate, the problems in this area would have been a lot more difficult to overcome.[15]

Fortunately, for the purpose of bringing Operation Unified Protector to a successful close, the United States could step in and compensate for European deficiencies and dwindling stockpiles. But the long-term repercussions of having to rely on American assets in an intervention driven by Europeans must be considered. Apart from a major embarrassment for European military and political leaders, it drove the costs of the American military contribution much higher than anticipated. 'Leading from behind' may have reduced the risk of US military casualties and of Washington yet again becoming the target of acrimonious criticism by radical Arab and/or Islamic leaders, but it still was not a burden to be carried lightly. At the end of the day, US military assets were engaged throughout the operation and were often indispensable for the success of individual missions.

The precise lessons that American political leaders and US armed forces will draw from the 2011 Libya experience remain to be determined. In some respects the comparison with Iraq and Afghanistan is quite favourable to the Libya campaign as a model. The total costs of US involvement in the 2011 Libya campaign constituted a small fraction of the two major wars that Washington has waged over the past 10 to 12 years. And, some would argue, the outcome is despite having added to the turmoil in northern Africa relatively promising for the future.

But it would seem to be equally plausible that the United States elicits other lessons from Operation Unified Protector, either by insisting that the Europeans take care of small-scale military operations in their own backyard or by deciding for itself that collaborative action is pointless as long as the United States eventually is expected to pick up the slack. As deep cuts in the American defence budget are underway and cannot but affect US capabilities in Europe and adjacent regions, this will presumably lead to a Europe that can no longer rely on assistance in similar situations.[16] As a result, the European allies and partners of the United States may very well be facing a critical decision point when it comes to levels of ambition and ability to engage with the world beyond the old continent, one that will not be affected by increases in defence spending alone.

Good or bad for NATO?

A few circumstances make the launching of the Libya campaign particularly intriguing. Notably, the decision to take action in Libya was taken at a point in time when the war in Afghanistan constituted NATO's major concern and commitment. Indeed, against the backdrop of the painful experiences of Iraq and Afghanistan, the prospect of NATO taking on another precarious mission that even risked destabilizing an entire region did not look very bright.

Moreover, and inextricably connected to the issue of addressing security challenges that European countries are facing, is the question of NATO cohesion and solidarity and the perception thereof. Arguably, looking back at the Libya operation, Secretary General Anders Fogh Rasmussen made the Alliance appear not only as an effective crisis manager but as a 'force for good'.[17] Yet are these roles actually well-established within NATO and can the alliance uphold them post-Libya?

The Libya campaign was preceded by NATO's Strategic Concept debate, during which the Alliance's tasks were widely contemplated. At the Lisbon summit of 2010 NATO finally decided to take on three core tasks; collective defence, crisis management and cooperative security, thus nominally shouldering responsibility for every type of contingency ranging from defence of territory to regional and global security.

This bold vision does not resonate well with economic realities and the main concern after the adoption of the Strategic Concept, which has been the generation of resources in an age of austerity. At a time when the United States is preparing to substantially cut its defence budget, doubts are similarly voiced over Europe's commitment to regional and global security. At one point former US Secretary of Defence Robert Gates argued that

> The demilitarization of Europe – where large swaths of the general public and political class are averse to military force and the risks that go with it – has gone from a blessing in the 20th century to an impediment to achieving real security and lasting peace in the 21st.[18]

Moreover, at the peak of the Libya operation, NATO's Secretary General Anders Fogh Rasmussen warned that 'the global order enjoys more stakeholders than ever before and yet it has very few guarantors. Europe is still one of them, but for how long?'[19] After the end of the operation, Rasmussen similarly praised Europe's contributions yet highlighted its insufficiencies and dependence on US capabilities,[20] suggesting that European states needed to solve their difficulties by adopting more of 'smart defence' (or 'pooling and sharing') measures in the future.[21]

In addition to financial problems, Europeans remain divided over the issue of NATO's main area of responsibility. While 'globalists' such as

Denmark and Great Britain are generally positive to future military operations out-of-area and foresee a global space of operation and a development of civilian capabilities, the Baltic countries, France and Germany lean more towards a focus on military capabilities and regional tasks.[22]

The communication among NATO officials during the Libya operation indeed displayed tensions between predominantly 'realist' regional and predominantly 'idealist' global motives. Officials highlighted NATO's capacity in situations of humanitarian crisis and framed the major aim of the operation as protecting civilians.[23] In discussing NATO's role in crisis management, Rasmussen described the operation as an example of how 'academic theories connect with the real world' in that he asserted, before the operation had been launched, that '[t]oday, we have a real crisis unfolding on our doorstep – in Libya. And NATO is not just sitting idly by.'[24] Nevertheless, crisis management could also be handily re-framed in the rhetoric of the Secretary General, from an allegedly humanitarian to a self-regarding practice. In this sense, NATO had 'increasingly understood that crisis prevention is a means of protecting our own security'. Rasmussen stated that NATO first of all remains a defence alliance, pointing to Libya as a potential breeding ground for terrorism and extremism and to the risk of regional spill-over of the crisis.[25]

Then again, despite the ongoing war in Afghanistan and diverging outlooks on the future of the Alliance, the member states did manage to get the Libya operation going within a matter of weeks. Various motives and rationales behind the decision to intervene that appear to have superseded such aggravating circumstances will be examined in the following two chapters.

Notably, even though populations were initially split over whether NATO should intervene or not, majorities in all states supported three objectives of a prospective intervention; the protection of civilians, the removing of Gadaffi, and the sending of military advisors to assist the rebels.[26] In retrospect, a plurality of populations in NATO member states (with the sole exception of the Turkish population) was supportive of the decision to intervene.[27] Notably, this included a slight majority of Germans, despite the fact that Germany had not taken part in the operation. Approval ran highest in non-NATO member Sweden (68 per cent), followed by the Netherlands and France (58 per cent respectively) (ibid).

This indicates that the Libya operation was predominantly beneficial to NATO; the Alliance acted in line with a stated intent that received broad popular support, which may serve to increase its internal legitimacy. Moreover, relatively widespread perceptions of operational success may have served to bolster the Alliance's image both internally and externally, at least in the short run. Yet, as will be suggested in some of the chapters below, the operation and its consequences for NATO could be interpreted a lot more critically. Also, it remains to be seen both whether the Alliance can sustain a coherent discourse about itself, given its diversified roles and internal divisions, and whether it can keep up with its ambitions given the harsh economic realities. Indeed, while discussing Europe's economic problems in 2011, Rasmussen stressed that NATO must be globally connected and confirmed its dependency on actors in other regions, using the phrase: 'delivering security must be a co-operative matter'.[28]

Organization of the book

If the rather disparate views of the lessons learned from Libya mentioned above were to form the foundation for future planning, the effects on NATO and on the contributing armed forces are unlikely to be beneficial. Some variation between the assessments conducted by different institutions and governments is to be expected, but candid reviews have in other instances promptly offered correction to unjustifiably positive or negative accounts. For instance, whereas NATO's heavily criticized campaign in Kosovo 1998–1999 was ultimately recognized as having thwarted large-scale ethnic cleansing in former Yugoslavia, the alliance's decade-long engagement in Afghanistan – under the International Security Assistance Force (ISAF) – is currently seen as not having produced a sustainable peace, nor is it likely to do so in its remaining two years. So how come the view is so fragmented when it comes to the NATO-led Libya campaign? Could it be a reflection of a growing divide in political and strategic reasoning on both sides of the Atlantic? Could it be due to the evolution of doctrine within branches of the military establishment in recent years? Or are there other reasons?

More time is indeed required before a truly mature state of knowledge regarding the 2011 Libyan campaign can be achieved. But we believe that the time is right to deepen and broaden our analysis of the military campaign in order to answer some of the questions above and to elicit mature insights and improve practices in the military profession, as well as among a wide range of decision makers and professionals who partook in planning and assessing developments during the campaign. Although ours cannot be an exhaustive treatment of the subject, we have tried to cover the most essential aspects of the NATO-led effort and thus to offer a comprehensive account of the key challenges that arose along the way. Many of the latter were provisionally solved for the purpose of bringing the campaign to a close, but are generic in character and will have to be considered in any analogous situation in the future.

The first part of the book is aimed at explaining the law and politics of the intervention. While Chapter 1 outlines the wider strategic context and analyses the problem of NATO cohesion once military actions commenced, Chapter 2 introduces the novelty of Responsibility to Protect (R2P) in international law and examines the political premises at the UN Security Council for arriving at resolution 1973, which in turn allowed for the use of military force to protect Libyan civilians via intervention. Chapter 3 goes on to explain in what ways resolution 1973 created the basis for a legal regime that regulated the military operation including rules of engagement, subsequently adopted by NATO and partner countries in the coalition that formed to carry out the Security Council mandate.

The second part of the book is devoted to the use of coercive force by NATO coalition's air force units, as well as the deployment of naval and other forces in support of the combat operations. At the core of the military intervention was consistently the surveillance, targeting and bombing missions carried out by NATO and coalition air forces and analysed in Chapter 4. But, for a number of important military objectives, naval forces (Chapter 5) and special land forces (Chapter 8) also played an important part, one that has gone virtually unnoticed in mass media. Chapter 6 examines why the regular Libyan army put up such limited resistance, given its impressive capacity on paper, tracing elements of an explanation in the patrimonialist, militarist and islamist political culture of Libya and the wider region.

The third part of the book deals with auxiliary measures and arrangements that governments and defence forces undertook in order to increasingly tilt the balance against the Gaddafi regime in order to bring about an end to the conflict and to the intervention as such. Chapter 7 is devoted to the ways in which an ambitious strategic communication policy was used as a crucial element of information warfare to oust Gaddafi, paying particular attention to the state-of-the-art approach adopted by Britain. Chapter 8 suggests that a small number of special forces, intelligence agents, trainers and liason officers were brought into the fray on the sidelines of the military effort, and appear to have played a substantial role by way of interacting directly with the Libyan political opposition and rebel forces. Although much of this story has yet to be clarified, a sufficient amount of information has been released to make a first analysis of its significance for the intervention effort at large.

In conclusion, the lessons from each chapter as to what can be learned from NATO's 2011 military intervention in Libya are summarized and discussed. In pulling together the lessons from military intervention in a wider context of events, an overall assessment of the broader experience made by NATO and coalition forces is formulated and contrasted to those made in Iraq and Afghanistan.

Notes

1 A.F. Rasmussen, 'Towards NATO's Chicago Summit'. Speech by NATO Secretary General Anders Fogh Rasmussen at the European Policy Centre, Brussels 30 September 2011. Online. Available: www.nato.int/cps/en/natolive/opinions_78600.htm. (accessed 13 February 2013).
2 The notion 'lessons learned' is often replaced by 'lessons identified', precisely because they are noted but not automatically assumed to be relevant for future operations.

3 I.H. Daalder and J.G. Stavridis, 'NATO's Success in Libya', *New York Times*, 30 October, 2011. Online. Available: www.nytimes.com/2011/10/31/opinion/31ihteddaalder31.html?_r=0C (accessed 13 February 2013); K. Volker, 'Don't Call It a Comeback: Four Reasons Why Libya Doesn't Equal Success for NATO'. *Foreign Policy*, 23 August. Online. Available: www.foreignpolicy.com/articles/2011/08/23/dont_call_it_a_comeback?page=0,1 (accessed 13 February 2013).
4 S. Milne, 'If the Libyan war was about saving lives, it was a catastrophic failure'. *The Guardian*, 26 October 2011. Online. Available: www.guardian.co.uk/commentisfree/2011/oct/26/libya-war-saving-lives-catastrophic-failure (accessed 13 February 2013).
5 A.C. Buckley, 'Learning from Libya, Acting in Syria.' *Journal of Strategic Security* 5, 2012, 87.
6 BP Statistical Review of World Energy 2011, 6, 9. Online. Available: www.bp.com/statisticalreview (accessed 13 February 2013).
7 Ibid., 20.
8 B. Jentleson, Bruce and C. Whytock, 'Who "Won" Libya? The Force-Diplomacy Debate and Its Implications for Theory and Policy', *International Security* 30, 2005/2006, 47.
9 A. Cala, 'Europe Rethinks Dependence on Libyan Oil', *Christian Science Monitor* 2011.
10 D. Pierson, 'Libyan Strife Exposes China's Risks in Global Quest for Oil', *Los Angeles Times*, 9 March 2011. Online. Available: http://articles.latimes.com/2011/mar/09/business/la-fi-china-oil-20110310 (accessed 13 February 2013).
11 Another important area is situated west of Sheeba. In the east, there is only one oil refinery (around the Tobruk area) with a pipeline from the oilfields south of Tobruk. There are pipelines from the different oilfields northwards to the coast but only a few terminate in Tripoli (Petro Views 10 March 2011 'Libyan Oil Field Maps'. Online. Available: http://petroviews.blogspot.se/2011/03/libyan-oil-fields-map.html (accessed 13 February 2013).
12 K. Fahim, 'Libyan Government Presses Rebel Assualt in East and West', *The New York Times*, 7 March 2011. Online. Available: www.nytimes.com/2011/03/08/world/africa/08libya.html?pagewanted=all&_r=0 (accessed 18 February 2013).
13 I. Tharoor, 'Gaddafi Warns Benghazi Rebels: We Are Coming, and There'll Be No Mercy', *TimeWorld*, 17 March 2011. Online. Available: http://world.time.com/2011/03/17/gaddafi-warns-benghazi-rebel-city-we-are-coming-and-therell-be-no-mercy/ (accessed 13 February 2013).
14 F. Heisbourg, 'All Alone? What US Retrenchment Means for Europe and NATO', Centre for European Reform, Brussels, February, 2012, 28–29.
15 E. Quintana, 'The War from the Air. In Short War, Long Shadow: The Political and Military Legacies of the 2011 Libya Campaign', in A. Johnson and S. Mueen, Royal United Services Institute for Defence and Security Studies, Whitehall Report 1–2, 2012. Online. Available: www.rusi.org/downloads/assets/WHR_1-12.pdf (accessed 13 February 2011).
16 Heisbourg, 'All alone', p. 32.
17 A.F. Rasmussen,' Towards NATO's Chicago Summit'. Speech by NATO Secretary General Anders Fogh Rasmussen at the European Policy Centre, Brussels 30 September 2011. Online. Available: www.nato.int/cps/en/natolive/opinions_78600.htm (accessed 13 February 2013).
18 B. Knowlton, 'Gates Calls European Mood a Danger to Peace.' *IHT*, 23 februari 2010.
19 A.F. Rasmussen, 'NATO After Libya: The Atlantic Alliance in Austere Times'. Online. Available: www.nato.int/cps/en/natolive/opinions_75836.htm (accessed 13 February 2013).

20 A.F. Rasmussen, 'Keynote speech by NATO Secretary General Anders Fogh Rasmussen at the NATO Parliamentary Assembly in Bucharest, Romania'. Online. Available: www.nato.int/cps/en/natolive/opinions_79064.htm (accessed 13 February 2013).
21 A.F. Rasmussen, 'Smart Defence'. Online. Available: www.nato.int/cps/en/natolive/78125.htm (accessed 13 February 2013).
22 B. Górka-Winter and M. Madej, *NATO Member States and the New Strategic Concept: An Overview*, The Polish Institue of International Affairs 2010.
23 C. Wagnsson, 'A security community in the making? Sweden and NATO post-Libya', *European Security* 20, 2011, 585–603.
24 A.F. Rasmussen, 'Hungry for Security: Can NATO help in a humanitarian crisis?' Online. Available: www.nato.int/cps/en/natolive/opinions_71864.htm (accessed 13 February 2013).
25 Ibid.
26 The German Marshall Fund of the United States. 'Transatlantic Trends 2011 – Topline Data july 2011. Transatlantic Trends'. 2011. Online. Available: www.gmfus.org/publications_/TT/TT2011_final_web.pdf (Accessed 8 October 2012).
27 The German Marshall Fund of the United States. 'Transatlantic Trends 2012 – Key findings 2012'. Transatlantic Trends. 2012. Available: http://trends.gmfus.org/files/2012/09/TT-2012-Key-Findings-Report.pdf. (Accessed 8 October 2012).
28 A.F. Rasmussen, 'Delivering security in the 21st century', In: Secretary General's video blog. Online. Available: http://andersfogh.info/2012/07/04/delivering-security-in-the-21st-century (accessed 13 February 2013).

Part I
The law and politics of intervention

1 Able but not willing

A critical assessment of NATO's Libya intervention

Jeffrey H. Michaels

Introduction

NATO's ostensibly 'successful' intervention in Libya was notable in many respects, not the least of which was that the mission occurred at all, and when it did, the majority of Alliance members had little enthusiasm to meaningfully participate. Yet when the 'defensive' mission that was originally envisaged to protect civilians soon became a 'regime change' operation, rather than withdraw their support, NATO members continued to ensure the primacy of Alliance solidarity, even though this did not translate into providing additional military assets. The result was a half-hearted air campaign that lasted for months with little change to the stalemate on the ground and with increasing political frustration at the lack of progress. Fortunately for NATO, a series of rebel military successes in mid-August that culminated in the capture of Tripoli transformed a potential 'quagmire' into a 'success'.

In the aftermath of Gaddafi's fall, the official narrative about the Libya campaign has, not surprisingly, tended to focus on those aspects that highlighted the Alliance's 'flexibility', 'openness', and 'strength'.[1] Where there have been 'lessons learned', or at least 'lessons identified', these have been limited to technical military matters. Overlooked in this 'critical' discourse are the political dynamics that shaped the military campaign. When examined through a political prism, rather than a strictly military one, the NATO campaign looks far less 'successful', and indeed, it will be argued that it is the political lessons that are likely to have more far reaching consequences for the future direction of the Alliance.

This chapter will examine the intra-Alliance politics of NATO's intervention, and to a lesser extent the Alliance's relations with partner nations and the rebel forces. As NATO's intervention was not a foregone conclusion, the chapter will begin by focusing on the debates within NATO that led to it taking the lead in Libya, to include the political compromises that were made to secure consensus, and the limits placed on the military mission. It will then analyse the varying levels of commitment made by NATO members and partners, with a focus on the limited participation of the United States. Related to this, the different national attitudes towards both the means to be employed and the ends to be achieved in Libya will also be assessed. For instance, some NATO members and partners chose to operate as a coalition within the Alliance, and also to conduct more sensitive operations outside the NATO framework altogether. The problem of transatlantic burden-sharing will be specifically addressed by examining NATO's failure to secure a handful of ground-attack aircraft shortly after it took over the mission from the US-led Operation Odyssey Dawn. Another key feature of the campaign to be examined were the limited, and often indirect contacts, NATO was obliged to maintain with the rebels, and the impediments this placed on achieving a more rapid downfall of Gaddafi's regime. The chapter will conclude with a discussion about how the political and diplomatic 'lessons' may influence future NATO interventions.

Deciding to intervene

Before proceeding to the specific circumstances surrounding the Alliance's decision to take on a military intervention in Libya, it is important to preface this with a few general remarks about the position in which NATO found itself at the start of 2011. The circumstances NATO was facing at this time were hardly ideal for the launching of a major military operation, since it was during this period in which the Alliance commitment to Afghanistan, in terms of attention and resources, was at its most significant point compared to any earlier period.[2] Nevertheless, the Alliance retained a plentiful supply of uncommitted air and naval assets, although a large-scale land campaign may have been beyond its capabilities.

However, it was not simply a matter of operational overstretch that constrained the Alliance. There were also important political and economic factors at play, most notably the decline in defence budgets brought about by the global financial crisis.[3] The combination of increasingly burdensome operational costs in Afghanistan and shrinking defence budgets at home meant that as of early 2011 most NATO member states wished to avoid any additional military expenditure, and to the extent these expenditures were necessary, it was essential to minimize them. Consequently, even with a significant number of air assets being technically uncommitted, there was little political willingness to employ them. As will be shown, the number of air assets committed to the Libya operation compared to other air campaigns, most notably the 1999 Kosovo campaign, was extremely limited.[4]

At the start of 2011, there was no notion that NATO would soon conduct a major military operation in North Africa. Similar to the 'Arab Spring' more generally, Western governments had little early warning of the political crisis that was to unfold, nor any coherent plans for how to deal with it. In the aftermath of large-scale protests in Tunisia, Egypt and elsewhere in the Middle East beginning in late 2010, the wave of demonstrations spread to Libya by mid-February. Initially, the protests in Libya gathered steam but were insufficient to overthrow Gaddafi's regime. In response, Gaddafi cracked down hard on the demonstrators. What had started as relatively peaceful protests soon developed into a full-fledged rebellion between those forces loyal to Gaddafi based in Tripoli, and the opposition based mainly in Benghazi. On 27 February, the rebel factions formed the National Transitional Council (NTC) in opposition to Gaddafi's government. Rebels also took over Libya's third-largest city, Misrata, while other outbreaks of rebellion occurred in the Nafusa mountains in northwestern Libya.[5] Although the rebels benefited from large-scale defections from the Libyan military, Gaddafi's forces had the advantage of heavier firepower at their disposal, including the country's air assets. There was also the fear, albeit somewhat exaggerated in the media, that Gaddafi might employ chemical weapons against the rebels.[6]

For Western policymakers, the situation in Libya presented three problems. First, there was the overriding priority to ensure the safety of their citizens who were in Libya. Second, due to the increasing turmoil, and the news coverage it generated, and with the prospect that the instability would worsen, Libya was high on the policy agenda. Therefore, some type of military action had at least to be contemplated, even if the prospect of actually conducting a military campaign was less certain. Third, it was initially unclear which side had the upper hand, and whether Gaddafi was likely to be able to survive for long anyway even without the necessity of an outside intervention. The converse was true of the rebels as well. At times it seemed as though they were winning, whereas at other times they appeared to be disorganized and on the verge of collapse. Had the rebels collapsed, the prospect of an outside intervention would have been very limited indeed.

On 25 February, an emergency meeting of the North Atlantic Council (NAC) was convened to discuss the Libya crisis and to consider preparations for evacuation operations and to provide humanitarian assistance.[7] By late February, both the British and French governments began planning for a no-fly zone, despite the scepticism expressed in both countries' militaries about detracting from the main effort in Afghanistan.[8] By early March, NATO members such as the US, UK and France began increasing their intelligence activities in Libya, to include dispatching personnel to rebel-held areas, as well as prioritizing intelligence collection by deploying more surveillance assets to monitor the situation.[9] During this period, a number of NATO countries also began contingency planning in the event a military deployment was necessary. On 3 March, the Danish military was ordered to initiate planning for possible land, air and sea contributions, and five days later the Danish Air Force was told to prepare a deployment of six F-16s.[10]

However, at this stage, apart from the preparations of individual NATO member states, there was still little prospect of Alliance involvement. In particular, the French government insisted that any military support for the rebels would need to be authorized by the United Nations Security Council (UNSC), but *not* carried out by NATO, since the Alliance was perceived to have an 'aggressive image in the Arab world'.[11]

While deliberations were ongoing in Brussels, the rebels scored some notable successes, capturing the coastal towns of Brega, Ras Lanouf and Bin Jawad, and moving closer to Tripoli. However, on 6 March, Gaddafi's forces launched a major counter-offensive against the rebels.[12] Operating with the advantage of air cover, Gaddafi's forces advanced towards Ajdabiya and Benghazi, though the rebels operating in Misrata continued to hold out.

As the rebels were placed on the defensive, the international community took an increasing interest, though there was considerable reluctance on the part of defence officials from NATO countries to take on another mission in Libya whilst preoccupied with Afghanistan. US Defense Secretary Robert Gates referred to 'loose talk' in reference to calls for setting up a no-fly zone, while Chairman of the Joint Chiefs of Staff Admiral Mike Mullen noted that it would be 'an extraordinarily complex operation to set up'.[13] At the 10 March NATO Defense Ministerial at which it was agreed to reposition warships in the region and plan for humanitarian aid, Gates said publicly that military planning for a no-fly zone would continue 'but that's the extent of it'.[14] Similarly, British defence officials were not enthusiastic about the prospect of another major military commitment either since they did not want a new mission to detract from Afghanistan.[15] Given the reluctance of the defence officials from these major military powers in NATO to become involved with Libya, there seemed little prospect that the Alliance would take on this mission.

That being said, whilst defence officials in most Western capitals played down the prospect of an intervention, it was the politicians who took a more hawkish stance, arguing in favour of a no-fly zone.[16] By some accounts, British Prime Minister David Cameron was concerned about a repeat of Srebrenica and pushed his defence officials for robust options.[17] On 10 March, the head of the NTC, Mustafa Abdel-Jalil, flew to Paris and met with French President Nicolas Sarkozy. Reportedly, it was as a result of this meeting that Sarkozy recognized the NTC as the legitimate government of Libya, and began taking the prospect of military action seriously. The next day, Sarkozy raised the prospect of air strikes at an EU summit in Brussels. At this meeting Sarkozy stated: 'The strikes would be solely of a defensive nature if Mr. Gaddafi makes use of chemical weapons or air strikes against non-violent protesters.'[18] Meanwhile, on 12 March, the Arab League formally requested the United Nations Security Council to impose a no-fly zone. On 14 March, rebel leader Mahmoud Jibril met with US Secretary of State Hillary Clinton in Paris.[19] Whereas previously Clinton had been lukewarm about the prospect of military intervention, it was after her Paris meetings with Jibril and other Arab diplomats that she altered her position and became an advocate of intervention.[20] It is noteworthy that the discussions of a no-fly zone that had occurred up to this point were extremely vague in terms of who would be responsible for setting it up, the likely duration and, most importantly, whether or not it would be sufficient to stop Gaddafi's forces from committing what was expected to be a massacre if they were to capture Benghazi.

Despite the mounting domestic and international pressure during the previous weeks to take some form of military action, the Obama administration played down this prospect. According to several accounts of US decision making during the Libya crisis, it was not until a 15 March National Security Council (NSC) meeting that Obama told his officials he was dissatisfied with the military option of a no-fly zone that was presented to him since it would not stop a massacre. He therefore pressed his officials for more aggressive military options. Interestingly, in the week preceding this meeting, the White House had been thinking more in terms of arming the rebels, as it was considered to be a cheaper alternative to policing a no-fly zone or launching air strikes. However, by the time of the NSC meeting, the number of advocates for a more forceful intervention, particularly among some middle-ranking administration officials, had been steadily growing. Although Obama insisted on more forceful military options at the NSC meeting, based on the belief that a no-fly zone in itself would be insufficient to stop Gaddafi's forces from crushing the rebels, he nevertheless insisted on keeping US action limited both in its size and in the time period in which the US would take the lead. The notion of handing off responsibility for this mission at the earliest possible date was considered essential, though it was far from certain at that point whether NATO would take on the mission.[21]

It was only following the 15 March NSC meeting that US officials began laying the groundwork for intervention, to include lobbying in favour of a NATO lead role. With US support for intervention now added to that of Britain and France, both of whom had been advocating more forceful options in the previous weeks, combined with the 'crisis' of Gaddafi's forces making a series of battlefield gains, the diplomatic efforts of these countries, as well as that of the Arab League, culminated on 17 March with the passing of UN Security Council Resolution (UNSCR) 1973. This resolution imposed a no-fly zone in Libyan airspace and allowed for 'all necessary measures' to protect civilians.[22] Among the countries that abstained from this resolution was NATO member Germany. Germany's Permanent Representative to the United Nations warned:

> Decisions regarding the use of military force were always extremely difficult to take … Germany saw great risks, and the likelihood of large-scale loss of life should not be underestimated … Those that

participated in its implementation [referring to UNSCR 1973] could be drawn into a protracted military conflict that could draw in the wider region ... it would be wrong to assume that any military intervention would be quickly and efficiently carried out.[23]

Though abstaining from the UN vote, German Chancellor Angela Merkel left open the prospect of political support to the military action of others:

> As everyone knows, Germany will not take part in military measures ... That is why we abstained in the vote. But we share the goals of the resolution unreservedly. Our abstention should not be confused with neutrality.[24]

Two days after the resolution was passed, a 'Coalition of the willing' would begin military strikes. On 19 March, French aircraft somewhat prematurely began attacking Gaddafi's forces, though a large-scale assault soon followed later that day which included US, British and French air attacks and sea-launched missiles that aimed to destroy Libya's air force and air defence system, as well as targeting Libyan military units that were attacking rebel positions. This Coalition was initially run under separate US, British and French commands, but would ultimately be coordinated under the auspices of the US Africa Command. During this period there was no centralized operational headquarters; instead both the British and French operated from their own headquarters, at Northwood and Mont Verdun respectively, but coordinated their actions with the American headquarters at Ramstein. The American name for the operation was Odyssey Dawn.[25]

In contrast to the more limited role the US would later play, from 19 March until the end of the month, the US was very much in the lead, particularly in suppressing enemy air defences and establishing command of the air. The amount of munitions expended was considerable, as can be discerned from the price tag that amounted to $340 million through 28 March. The total US operational expenditure during this period was $550 million. Yet from the start the Obama administration publicly stated that the US lead role would be transferred at the earliest possible time.[26]

Meanwhile, as air operations were underway, and despite the American pressure to hand over leadership of the operation, NATO members debated for more than a week whether or not Libya should become an Alliance mission. It is this critical week that deserves analysis, for even though NATO's assumption of the Libya mission may seem obvious in retrospect, it was not clear at the time that this would be a foregone conclusion.

NATO acquires a new mission

It is significant that as of 19 March, when military action began, it was not even clear what the mission NATO would be called on to carry out actually was. Initially, the only military actions being considered were evacuation operations and providing humanitarian assistance. Then came the prospect of using military force for an arms embargo, followed by the idea of creating and sustaining a no-fly zone. But to create an effective no-fly zone meant eliminating the Libyan capability to oppose it, which in practice meant destroying its air defence system.[27] By mid-March, the primary goal Western leaders had agreed on was limited to ensuring the rebel position did not collapse, and in this sense, military action was viewed in 'defensive' rather than 'offensive' terms. Beyond this, the prospect of using military force to assist the rebel forces in 'regime change' was not seriously considered.

The key point to note is that, given the short period that elapsed from the start of hostilities within Libya, with the battle lines moving back and forth, and with Western politicians unable to agree on what to do, this meant that in the days and weeks leading up to the start of military action, planners' assumptions were constantly changing.[28] Moreover, it was not clear whether or not NATO would have a role to play, or what the Alliance's role would amount to if it did become involved. It was quite possible, theoretically at least, to take action bilaterally, in the case of the UK and France, or as part of a wider 'Coalition of the willing', or even under the auspices of the European Union's Common Security and Defence Policy (CSDP).[29] Even if the EU had not taken over the air campaign, it was quite possible for them to have taken responsibility for the maritime campaign. According to one report, the French proposed this option but it had little support within the EU.[30]

As previously noted, while Odyssey Dawn was underway, intense negotiations took place at NATO HQ over the possibility of the Alliance taking over the various air and maritime operations. Among the key reasons why it was felt NATO should take over was that it would have greater legitimacy than a 'Coalition of the willing', and would be better able to bring in partners. Moreover, it had the established military command structure, regional facilities, and a transatlantic link that were not guaranteed under alternative schemes. This was the position advocated by the US and UK, among others. In particular, Cameron highlighted the idea that NATO had a 'tried and tested machinery' for running such an operation.[31]

However, getting NATO to take command of the Libya campaign was not universally supported within the Alliance. Initially, France did not want NATO participation on the grounds that this would undermine Arab support.[32] Additionally, German officials suggested non-military options such as targeted sanctions and other forms of diplomatic pressure.[33] Turkish leaders cast doubt on the motives behind Western intervention, suggesting that action was driven by oil and mineral wealth rather than a desire to protect the Libyan people.[34] The Turks also raised objections in relation to attacks on Libyan ground forces, and only later wanted NATO placed in charge on the grounds that this would allow Ankara to have a veto over the operation. Furthermore, a feud between the French and Turkish governments also had the effect of undermining any prospect of cooperation within the Alliance.[35]

Conversely, there were also problems with *not* having NATO in charge. For instance, the Norwegians were reluctant to participate in a non-NATO mission, and Italy issued a veiled threat to withdraw the use of its bases unless the Alliance was put in charge.[36] France eventually conceded to NATO's involvement in principle but proposed an alternative arrangement whereby NATO would take the operational lead, thus providing military command and control of both NATO and non-NATO forces, but overall command would fall to an ad hoc political committee consisting of the foreign ministers of countries involved in the operation.[37]

Among the key issues being disputed was the extent to which NATO would engage in offensive strikes against Libyan ground targets, rather than simply conducting an arms embargo and the no-fly zone. Tensions within NATO were high. At one NAC meeting, the French and German ambassadors walked out of the room after NATO Secretary General Anders Fogh Rasmussen criticized their countries' opposition to a NATO-run mission.[38] Nevertheless, on 23 March the Alliance agreed to enforce the arms embargo, and the following day agreed to enforce the no-fly zone. Though not all the Allies were keen to participate in the mission, they did not attempt to block it. Whilst supporting the NATO mission politically within the NAC, Germany took steps to distance itself militarily, going so far as to withdraw its ships from NATO command in the Mediterranean to avoid the prospect of their being requested to support the arms embargo. Berlin also withdrew German personnel attached to the NATO AWACS aircraft that would be operating near Libya.[39]

The agreement to go ahead with NATO taking control of the no-fly zone was reached after a four-way telephone conversation between the US Secretary of State and her British, French and Turkish equivalents.[40] Additionally, Obama had previously phoned Turkish Prime Minister Recep Tayyip Erdogan to obtain Ankara's support.[41] Among the key issues that needed to be sorted out prior to achieving a consensus on a NATO-led operation was the politically sensitive issue of who would command it. Whereas the US wished to maintain a low profile, both the UK and France had attempted to place one of their own officers in charge. Due to political objections, particularly from the Turks, a compromise candidate was found, namely the Canadian Air Force Lieutenant General Charles Bouchard, then serving as deputy head of Joint Force Command-Naples.[42]

Apart from NATO taking over the 'defensive' aspects of the Libya mission, there was still no consensus on whether the 'offensive' components should also be a NATO responsibility. However, after debating for several more days, both the French and Turks lifted their objections, with the result that all aspects of the mission, including offensive air operations, were turned over to NATO.⁴³ As such, on 27 March, Rasmussen announced that NATO would implement all aspects of the UNSCR 1973 in order to 'protect civilians and civilian-populated areas under attack or threat of attack from the Gaddafi regime'.⁴⁴ On 31 March, NATO formally assumed responsibility for the Libya campaign, which was named Operation Unified Protector. NATO authorized this military action for a 90-day period, though this deadline would be extended twice in the course of the conflict. This limited time period reflected the fact that initially senior officials were still thinking that the military campaign would be of a relatively short duration. For instance, the head of the French armed forces, Admiral Edouard Guillaud, predicted the campaign would last weeks rather than months.⁴⁵

A coalition inside the Alliance

Given the lacklustre levels of support provided by most NATO members, the mission in Libya could more appropriately be described as being conducted by a coalition within the Alliance. As of mid-April, the US, UK, France, Canada, Belgium, Denmark and Norway were the only countries conducting strike missions.⁴⁶ Julian Lindley-French mockingly referred to the mission as 'Operation Protecting Disunity'.⁴⁷ Notable absentees included the Netherlands, which had traditionally been quite active militarily within the Alliance and possessed aircraft that would be useful in a ground-attack role. The lack of meaningful NATO member participation was also quite evident among the central European states.⁴⁸ Despite his country officially supporting the mission, Polish Prime Minister Donald Tusk was particularly outspoken in his opposition to it. He stated:

> Although there exists a need to defend civilians from a regime's brutality, isn't the Libyan case yet another example of European hypocrisy in view of the way Europe has behaved toward Gaddafi in recent years or even months?... That is one of the reasons for our restraint ... If we want to defend people against dictators, reprisals, torture and prison, that principle must be universal and not invoked only when it is convenient, profitable or safe.⁴⁹

German Defense Minister Thomas De Maizière made a similar comment reflecting an ideological opposition to taking on the Libya mission:

> Could the fact that we are suddenly intervening now have something to do with oil? We can't get rid of all the dictators in the world with an international military mission.⁵⁰

Throughout the course of the conflict, the heads of government and other senior officials from NATO member states met regularly.⁵¹ In some respects, the frequency of meetings suggested a good deal of consultation among Alliance members. In actual fact, the NAC 'became only a secondary framework to where decisions were really discussed'. Instead, a common position would first be developed among those countries intent on pursuing more aggressive operations prior to it being presented to the Alliance as a whole.[52]

Thus, to the degree meaningful consultations occurred, these were limited to a coalition of nations operating within NATO, with the remaining member states choosing to remain uninvolved. Regardless of their private political objections to intervening in Libya, there was no desire on the part of reluctant countries such as Germany, Turkey or Poland to have a repeat of the debate leading up to the 2003 Iraq war that badly damaged Alliance solidarity.[53] Rather than oppose the intervention, they decided instead to officially support it, and remained on the sidelines politically so that the Alliance could at least appear united. There is little evidence to suggest they took an active part in making policy, except for the fact that their political support was purchased at a cost. Maintaining their political allegiance required taking extra precautions in the conduct of military operations. The political imperative that there should be 'no civilian casualties', or at least 'no excessive civilian casualties', which was a key concern of the reluctant allies, placed considerable restrictions on air strikes.[54] Nor could the mission officially be classed in terms of a 'regime change'. Instead, the NATO mission was always labelled a UN-mandated 'defensive' mission intended to protect civilians.

As highlighted earlier, Obama's decision to commit the United States to military action was made in a crisis atmosphere, and with little forethought beyond the short-term.[55] The two key guiding themes driving American policy at that point were that the US would need to act quickly with its unique military capabilities to ensure the safety of Benghazi, and that to avoid any lengthy commitments the US would gradually pull back and let someone else take the lead. Beyond this, there is no evidence to suggest the Obama administration had formulated a policy that was aimed at regime change, nor had they determined precisely for how long the US would remain in the military lead before handing over lead responsibility.

Interestingly, despite the experience of Afghanistan and Iraq, there also seems to have been no meaningful consideration of the post-conflict period. Several problems with this initial approach would quickly impact on the NATO operation. The first problem was that having encouraged NATO to take on the mission, and given its recent history in waging military operations, Alliance members assumed the US would maintain a substantial military commitment for the duration of the operation. While it was recognized that the US would wish to reduce its military commitment, there was no precedent, and therefore no conception, of the degree to which the US would pull back from the lead.

At a NATO summit in Berlin in mid-April, US officials played down rifts among the allies, yet also rebuffed calls for more involvement. For instance, French Foreign Minister Alain Juppé specifically asked Clinton for more fighter planes but did not get an encouraging response.[56] Instead, the US insisted on the necessity for the European allies to commit more of their own forces to this mission, and only agreed to remain militarily active in a *supporting* role. As one Washington Post editorial put it:

> If his real aim were to plunge NATO into a political crisis, or to exhaust the air forces and military budgets of France and Britain ... this would be a brilliant strategy ... Mr. Obama appears less intent on ousting Mr. Gaddafi or ensuring NATO's success than in proving an ideological point – that the United States will not take the lead in a military operation that does not involve vital US interests.[57]

For the next several months, despite repeated requests by European allies to step up their support, the US refused to budge.[58] Furthermore, the Americans also complained not just about European countries that were not participating in the mission, but also about those which were. The complaint was mainly to do with the insufficient military means that NATO allies had available to employ in Libya, especially the limited stocks of precision guided munitions. Gates privately castigated NATO allies, including the British, for requiring the US to make up for shortfalls in munitions.[59]

Internal tensions were also observable with regards to the lack of clarity and consensus about the nature of the mission being conducted. Rasmussen would refer to it as one of protecting civilians, rather than helping the rebels win the war, and this remained the official NATO line.[60] On the other hand, in mid-April, Obama, Cameron and Sarkozy issued a joint statement that 'Gaddafi must go, and go for good'.[61] Other NATO leaders made similar statements. For example, in early May, Turkish Prime Minister Erdogan stated that Gaddafi must 'immediately step down'.[62] Yet this view was not shared by all NATO members. Dutch Defence Minister Hans Hillen insisted publicly that NATO should stick to protecting civilians and not try to oust Gaddafi.[63] He also implied that if 'regime change' really was the actual mission, then it should be discussed within NATO so that it could be officially classed as such.[64]

Regardless of the tensions that were present at the start of the military campaign, the failure to achieve any major breakthroughs early on and the prospect of a stalemate led some NATO nations to break ranks and suggest that a negotiated settlement with the Gaddafi regime was possible. Comments by senior Italian and French officials hinted at the possibility that a ceasefire could be negotiated with Gaddafi, though still insisting he step down from power. Most notably, in early July, French Defense Minister Gerard Longuet said the rebels should negotiate with Gaddafi's forces.[65] These statements were strongly resented by other members of the Alliance.[66]

Meanwhile, some NATO countries that had been at the forefront of operations began to reduce their military contributions. Among these countries, Italy withdrew its aircraft carrier in early July as a matter of cost-savings. At the end of June, Norway pulled out its six planes.[67] Other members complained about the sustainability of their declining munitions inventories, the rising costs of the mission, and the apparent inability to break the battlefield stalemate. As Dutch Defense Minister Hillen observed in early July: 'People who thought that merely throwing some bombs would not only help the people but also convince Gaddafi that he could step down or alter his policy were a little bit naive.'[68]

The ground attack aircraft crisis

Of all the political crises impacting NATO over the course of the conflict, probably the most important had to do with burden-sharing. Shortly after the transition from the US-led mission to a NATO-led mission, of the Alliance's 28 member states, only seven were employing their aircraft for ground attack missions.[69] As the US pulled back from conducting strike missions in early April, an important crisis developed as the number of ground attack aircraft committed to the offensive part of the campaign was deemed to be insufficient, particularly given the distances involved and the strain on pilots. For instance, NATO ambassadors held an unscheduled meeting following complaints from French Foreign Minister Juppé that the Libya campaign risked getting bogged down unless the pace of air support was picked up.[70] Juppé even hinted that opting for a NATO operation, as opposed to a 'Coalition of the willing', might have been a mistake. He stated that 'NATO must play its role fully. It wanted to take the lead in operations, we accepted that.' British Foreign Secretary William Hague also requested that NATO step up its attacks on Gaddafi's forces.[71]

In terms of the actual military requirements that were deemed essential, Rasmussen stated: 'To avoid civilian casualties we need very sophisticated equipment, so we need a few more precision fighter ground attack aircraft for air-to-ground missions.'[72] Moreover, senior NATO officials publicly noted that the Alliance was short of eight to ten additional ground attack aircraft to conduct strike missions, a number which highlighted how difficult it was to gain access to just a handful of additional planes.[73] Although there were more than enough aircraft already patrolling the no-fly zone, to say nothing of the uncommitted aircraft that NATO's European members had available in their arsenals, most of these countries refused to give permission for their planes to be used in a ground attack role. For example, the Dutch, Spanish, Italians and Turks limited their participation to patrolling the no-fly zone and enforcing the arms embargo, whilst other NATO members with ground attack capability, such as Germany and Poland, did not participate at all in the air campaign. Although Poland was already heavily committed to Afghanistan, it still had the capacity to provide 'a small number of F-16 fighters' to signal its support, but chose not to on the grounds that Libya did not represent a significant security interest for Warsaw.[74] Even with the UK adding more Tornado jets in early April, the NATO numbers remained too low.[75]

This shortage of planes had several important consequences. From an operational perspective, insufficient aircraft meant more limited coverage of the battle-space, as well as fewer sorties. In order to make up for the shortage, US, British and French officials tried to persuade other NATO nations to contribute aircraft, while both the UK and France sought to persuade President Obama to commit more US assets.[76] However, Obama was adamant that no additional US support would be forthcoming, despite the fact that the US retained an ample number of strike aircraft based in the region on 12-hour standby.[77] The American argument was that US ground attack air assets were unnecessary since the European members of NATO had enough capability of their own. According to US Vice President Joe Biden:

> If the Lord Almighty extricated the US out of NATO and dropped it on the planet of Mars so we were no longer participating, it is bizarre to suggest NATO and the rest of the world lacks the capacity to deal with Libya – it does not ... Occasionally other countries lack the will, but this is not about capacity.[78]

By late April, following weeks of diplomatic efforts by the US, UK and France, as well as a phone call between Obama and Italian Prime Minister Silvio Berlusconi, Italy was finally persuaded to contribute most of its 12 aircraft that had been supporting the no-fly zone to be allocated to strike missions.[79] For the remainder of the air campaign though, no additional NATO member states would contribute ground attack aircraft for strike missions, even if they participated in other ways, typically by sending ships for the arms embargo.[80]

While the US was quite pleased with those NATO allies that were disproportionately contributing to the air campaign, such as the Danes and Norwegians, they were increasingly frustrated with those allies who refused to participate. During his early June visit to Brussels for a NATO defence ministerial, Gates chided a number of allies for this reason. At one meeting of the NATO defence ministers, Gates singled out the Netherlands, Spain, Turkey, Germany and Poland for refusing to take part in ground attacks. Gates reportedly chose these countries, rather than any number of other NATO allies who were not participating, because he wanted to target those countries with an 'actual military capacity'. Despite the strong criticism by Gates, these NATO allies continued to refuse further assistance.[81]

While it is unclear whether the US would have continued to avoid taking a more active role if the battlefield stalemate had continued longer than it did, there was definitely no indication they were ready to reverse their position by bringing more forces to bear. Rather, the preferred US strategy was to continue diplomatic pressure on its allies. Meanwhile, Rasmussen continued to press NATO allies for more ground attack aircraft but to little avail. During a visit to the Netherlands in mid-July, he stated:

> We can't protect civilians in Libya effectively if we are not prepared to take out critical military units on the ground that can be used to attack civilians. This is the reason why we do air-to-ground strikes ... I encourage all allies that have aircraft at their disposal to take part in that operation as well.[82]

However, neither the Dutch nor other reluctant NATO countries decided to send more planes. It remains unclear precisely why they were reluctant to do so, but this was most probably due to a combination of domestic political and financial concerns, and perhaps some degree of ideological opposition as well.

The controversy over the ground attack aircraft was arguably the key issue instigating the wider debates over burden-sharing. On the one hand, European states were frustrated with the lack of US commitment, for the US maintained plenty of capability at hand to rapidly escalate the pace and scale of air attacks on Gaddafi's forces. That the Obama administration chose not only to withhold these assets, but to simultaneously complain about the lack of European support, caused a great deal of resentment.

Beyond the short-term negative effects on the robustness of the air campaign, there were also important long-term implications for the future of the Atlantic Alliance. Libya represented the first time when NATO's most important military member state had chosen to commit to an operation, but then revert to a *supporting* role, whereas traditionally it had always been the *supported* power. As a harbinger for future missions, this meant that the US might not fully commit its resources, with the consequence that NATO's European members would be obliged to 'pick up the slack'.

Yet this argument does not relate simply to the problem of resources. Instead, it also relates to a strong deterrent image NATO wishes to project to would-be adversaries. In other words, the Alliance's credibility was intimately tied to the perception that NATO power equated to American power. This issue was not purely hypothetical, but was a concern of NATO officials at the time of the Libya crisis when it was believed that the withdrawal of US air assets would likely invigorate Gaddafi's will to resist. For the US, on the other hand, Libya represented a glaring example of the lack of political willpower on the part of many of its European allies to match words with deeds, epitomized by their failure to commit more ground attack aircraft for a mission that they officially supported. In fact, Libya could have presented an ideal opportunity for the Alliance's European members to reverse the negative images of uneven burden-sharing that have plagued NATO since 1949. Instead, the failure to commit the ground attack aircraft further entrenched these negative images.

Partners and unofficial allies

Apart from Alliance member states, the contribution of NATO partners was vital, as they provided an external source of legitimacy for the mission. Their participation also represented a 'return on investment' demonstrating the value of NATO's partnership programmes. Partners contributing to the military campaign included Sweden, the United Arab Emirates and Qatar, and to a much lesser extent Morocco and Jordan. These partners were granted the same status in the NAC as other NATO members when it was discussing Libya-related topics. But whereas partner contributions to the air campaign were important, especially for political reasons, their overall military impact was marginal at best, given that they were limited to patrolling the no-fly zone rather than engaging in ground attack missions.[83]

By contrast, the key contribution made by a NATO partner was not its support in the air, but on the ground, and this was conducted outside the NATO framework. This contribution was the unilateral deployment of Qatari Special Forces to train and equip the rebel forces based in both Benghazi and the Nafusa mountains. Not only did the Qataris provide basic training in Libya, but they also brought groups of Libyans to Qatar for small-unit leadership training. These Libyans were returned home prior to the rebel advance on Tripoli in August. By conducting this 'deniable' operation to support the rebels on the ground, Qatar almost certainly made the most important military contribution by a NATO partner, despite the fact that this clandestine operation was run independently of NATO.[84] Nevertheless, had Qatar not been integrated with the NATO operation in the first place, it would have been difficult for them to contribute effectively on the ground.

Since NATO was not officially taking sides, coordination with the rebels was limited. This not only raised the problem of 'friendly fire' incidents, but also reduced the actionable intelligence available. As the conflict wore on, means would be found to work more closely with the rebels, but at the start of the conflict, these relations were kept to a minimum. Actions taken on the ground in Libya in support of the rebels were conducted by individual states and kept separate from the NATO command structure to avoid compromising it. These actions included provision of logistical support, advisers, forward air controllers, as well as intelligence operatives, damage assessment analysts and other experts.[85] Apart from providing advice and equipment, intelligence was collected and then passed through national intelligence channels, then to be fed into the NATO intelligence system. As NATO Military Chairman Admiral Giampaolo Di Paolo observed:

> any nation, not the Alliance, any nation has the right to take the decision which pertain to sovereign government. We are collecting intelligence by allies. And the allies, they are providing to the Alliance the intelligence.... It's up to that nation to provide us what kind of intelligence they want to provide, and we are not questioning which sources is coming from.[86]

Providing this intelligence was crucial to ensure that the risk of friendly fire incidents was minimized and to improve coordination of air and ground manoeuvres (see Mohlin, Chapter 8 of this volume). Given that NATO was not officially providing air support to the rebels, it was problematic to be receiving targeting information from them directly. Hence, the indirect route through national intelligence chains allowed the Alliance to claim a 'plausible deniability'. As General Bouchard noted:

> Our actions were not coordinated with the NTC. It was not in my mandate, and our mandate remained the protection of civilians.... But in many ways, parallel to whatever NATO will be doing, nations have got their own rights to do certain actions that may not necessarily be shared with the Alliance itself. And various nations will decide that; it's their sovereign right to take certain decisions as they go in.[87]

While the details of activities on the ground in Libya are explored elsewhere in this volume (see Mohlin, Chapter 8 and Sorensen, Chapter 6), the important point is the broader political significance of these activities. For those countries actively seeking the ouster of Gaddafi, the NATO mechanism was viewed as insufficient, due to the political objections of some of its members to being seen conducting a 'regime change'. Consequently, more sensitive operations were conducted at the national level *alongside* the Alliance operation. However, Libya was not the first time that both national and multinational operations have been conducted in the same battle space. The same approach was also taken in both Kosovo and Afghanistan, with the Libya case merely representing a continuation of this trend.[88]

Implications for the future

By mid-August 2011, the combination of air attacks and the increasing competence of the rebel forces finally broke the battlefield stalemate, and on 20 August the rebels pushed into Tripoli. Although Gaddafi escaped, and forces loyal to him continued to fight on, the fall of Tripoli foreshadowed Gaddafi's eventual defeat. Though his forces continued fighting for an additional two months, on 20 October, Gaddafi was killed. On 31 October, Operation Unified Protector was concluded.

Officially, NATO portrayed the operation as a 'success', and even as a 'model'. Yet the legacy of the Libya campaign suggests that in many respects NATO members were less than satisfied. At the same time NATO was militarily engaged in Libya, a similar crisis was ongoing in Syria, and would continue long after the end of Operation Unified Protector. Was NATO's lack of involvement in Syria related in any way to the political problems that arose in Libya? Given the limited information available, the short answer to this question is that the political problems that arose in the Libya campaign probably did have a restraining influence on advocates for intervention in Syria, although there were many other factors distinguishing the two conflicts, such as the lack of a UN mandate, Syria's possession of a more sophisticated air defence system, lack of confidence in the rebel forces, and so forth. Moreover, having just undertaken the Libya operation, there was also the problem of fatigue to consider. Additionally, it was generally recognized among Western politicians that the initial hubristic belief that the Libya conflict would not be a lengthy one, which probably contributed to NATO's relatively quick decision to respond to this international crisis in March 2011, was clearly misinformed, and that when considering future interventions more cautious assessments of the likely conflict duration should serve as the starting assumption.

While it is difficult to speculate on the extent to which the 'Libya analogy' will inform future NATO decision-making, it is much easier to derive at least several key political issues that are likely to constitute the analogy. One issue that has stood out quite prominently as a result of Libya, but also in conjunction with the Obama administration's announcement of an increasing strategic emphasis on Asia, is the questionable degree to which American military support will be forthcoming in future contingencies, particularly those that occur in Europe and around Europe's periphery.[89] Again, it must be stressed that any action the US takes in support of NATO will be based on the circumstances that apply to the specific case. Even so, for many European member states, Libya has firmly implanted the idea that the US could choose to play a *supporting* rather than *supported* military role.

A second issue relates to both the good and bad aspects of the limited nature of the NATO mission. In many respects, the NATO mission was influenced by Afghanistan, especially the reluctance of both NATO governments and their populations to place large military forces in Muslim countries for the purpose of 'stabilization'. The lack of stability that has emerged in the 'post-conflict' period in Libya has also raised questions about the desirability of 'regime change' more generally.

Third, the political and military support provided by some NATO states but not others highlighted the unpredictable nature of Alliance decision making. This was amply demonstrated by the reluctance of militarily important allies such as Turkey, Germany, Holland, Poland and Spain to fully support the mission, whereas other countries such as Belgium, Denmark and Norway provided a disproportionately high level of support. The Libya case also contributed additional evidence of how reluctant NATO members could use the Alliance mechanism to shape the contours of a mission in exchange for providing their political support while not having to make actual military commitments.

A fourth lesson Libya highlights, though the same could also be said of other missions such as Afghanistan, is that partnerships matter, not only for what they can do as part of an official mission, but what they can achieve unofficially in support of that mission. Finally, the conflict in Libya underscored the gap between official and unofficial political goals and military activities. Curiously, Operation Unified Protector was never evaluated purely on its own merits, officially at least. In other words, NATO's 'success' is usually attributed to the 'regime change' that occurred in Libya rather than the more limited 'defensive' mission for which it received an official mandate. NATO members and partners that essentially worked as a Coalition under the auspices of the Alliance were able to transform the mission from a 'defensive' to an 'offensive' one, albeit with the 'silent' approval of reluctant members.

Conclusion

In the wake of Gaddafi's fall from power, the narrative of NATO's 'success' gradually became dominant. Quickly marginalized was any notion either that prior to Tripoli's fall, support for the mission within NATO had been increasingly fading, or that through the whole course of the operation the Alliance had to deal with numerous internal political crises. In fact, NATO members were split on many fundamental issues, including the very purpose of the mission. At best, Libya provided a demonstration of a divided Alliance consisting of at least three distinct elements. The first element consisted of those members who were fully committed to waging an offensive war against Gaddafi's regime. The second element included members who were partially committed, preferring instead to limit themselves to defensive actions only. Finally, there were those members who chose not to participate at all militarily but provided political support. The key point to note is that regardless of the military support provided, each NATO member provided a minimum level of political support to allow the mission to go ahead, and to sustain this support even as the nature of the original 'defensive' mission quickly morphed into an 'offensive' mission.

Of course, there are other means of classifying the support of NATO members. For instance, there were those who gave their full support militarily within the Alliance, but also chose to initiate actions on their own that would run parallel to the NATO mission, notably France, Britain and the US. The reason for this unilateral action was that some NATO member states felt constrained by the political limitations placed on the Alliance mission, the most important of which was the relationship with the rebel forces. Officially, NATO was not taking sides in favour of the rebels and therefore went to great lengths to keep its distance. Instead, individual NATO members built up their relationships with the rebel forces, thereby technically bypassing the political limitations, yet at the same time were able to use these links to enable a rebel victory, which in turn meant a 'success' for the Alliance. Had the rebels not received close air support, made possible in large measure by the presence of allied personnel on the ground, it is difficult to imagine the rebels being able to take Tripoli when they did. Indeed, had a battlefield stalemate continued indefinitely, NATO would likely have been forced either to escalate militarily or seek a negotiated settlement. Therefore, when discussing NATO's 'success' it is crucial to give due credit to the actions taken by individual Alliance members who sought to escape from the NATO political 'straitjacket' that limited their ties to the rebels.

Arguably the most divisive issue affecting the Alliance was the politics of burden-sharing, particularly with regards to employing ground attack aircraft for strike sorties. It was this issue that exposed important Transatlantic tensions, with the European powers seeking greater American involvement, whereas the Obama administration tried to obtain more commitment from its European allies. Curiously, it was this political conflict within NATO that at times may very well have superseded the actual military operations. Put another way, during the height of the fighting, and with Gaddafi's forces still posing a major threat to the rebels, the Allies chose to prioritize their own differences over burden-sharing, and therefore did not provide the ground attack aircraft that could have allowed for more aggressive air operations. As this and many other examples that occurred during the Libya campaign highlight, it was the lack of political will, and not the lack of military means, that nearly plunged the Alliance into a 'quagmire'. Despite the official narrative of 'success', the leaders of NATO member states are unlikely to want to repeat this 'success' anytime soon.

Notes

1 A.F. Rasmussen, *NATO's Monthly Press Briefing*, 5 September 2011. Online. Available: www.nato.int/cps/en/natolive/opinions_77640.htm (accessed 14 February 2013).
2 For troop levels in Afghanistan at this time, see: The Guardian Datablog (2009) *Afghanistan Troop Numbers Data: How many does each country send to the Nato mission there?* Online. Available: www.guardian.co.uk/news/datablog/2009/sep/21/afghanistan-troop-numbers-nato-data (accessed 14 February 2013).
3 For more details on the impact of austerity measures on NATO defence budgets, particularly among those Alliance members with the 'highest proportion of deployable and sustainable forces', see: J. Gordon, S. Johnson, F.S. Larrabee and P.A. Wilson, 'NATO and the Challenge of Austerity', *Survival* 54, 2012, 121–42.

4 For Kosovo figures, see: Department of Defense (2000) *Kosovo/Operation Allied Force After-Action Report*. Online. Available: www.au.af.mil/au/awc/awcgate/kosovoaa/kaar02072000.pdf (accessed 14 February 2013); S.L. Myers and E. Schmitt, 'Pace of Attacks in Libya Conflict is Dividing NATO', *The New York Times*, 13 April 2011.
5 For background information on the first weeks of the conflict within Libya, see: C.M. Blanchard, 'Libya: Unrest and US Policy', *CRS Reports for Congress*, 18 March 2011; 'Libya Revolt Timeline', *Agence France Presse*, 28 February 2011.
6 R.J. Smith, 'Gaddafi Could Turn to Libya's Mustard Gas Stockpile, Some Officials Fear', *The Washington Post*, 19 March 2011.
7 NATO (2011) *NATO Secretary General Convenes Emergency Meeting of the North Atlantic Council*. Online. Available: www.nato.int/cps/en/natolive/news_70800.htm (accessed 14 February 2013).
8 P. Wintour and N. Watt, 'Cameron's War: Why the PM Felt Gaddafi had to be Stopped', *The Guardian*, 3 October 2011; Private information.
9 Y.J. Dreazen and M.Ambinder, 'CIA Deploys to Libya as White House Authorized Direct Assistance to Rebels', *The National Journal*, 30 March 2011; C. Hughes, 'Britain's Secret War in Libya: British Special Forces Uncovered on the Ground', *The Mirror*, 1 June 2011.
10 P.V. Jakobsen and K.J. Moller, 'Good News: Libya and the Danish Way of War', in N. Hvidt and H. Mouritzen, *Foreign Policy Yearbook*, Copenhagen: Danish Institute for International Studies, 2012, 106–28.
11 A. Cowell and S. Erlanger, 'France Become First Country to Recognize Libyan Rebels', *The New York Times*, 10 March 2011.
12 M. Chulov, P. Beaumont and J. Doward, 'How the Revolt Against Libya's Dictator Stalled', *The Observer*, 6 March 2011.
13 E. Bumiller, 'Gates Plays Down Idea of US Force in Libya', *The New York Times*, 1 March 2011.
14 E. Bumiller, 'NATO Steps Back from Military Intervention in Libya', *The New York Times*, 10 March 2011.
15 M. Clarke, 'The Making of Britain's Libya Strategy', in A. Johnson and S. Mueen (eds) *Short War, Long Shadow: The Political and Military Legacies of the 2011 Libya Campaign*, London: RUSI, 2012, 7–8; Wintour and Watt, 'Cameron's War'; Private information.
16 For an overview of the various motives for British and French intervention, see: M. Elliott, 'Viewpoint: How Libya Became a French and British War', *Time*, 19 March 2011.
17 Wintour and Watt, 'Cameron's War'.
18 Sarkozy, cited in N. Watt, 'Nicholas Sarkozy Calls for Air Strikes on Libya if Gaddafi Attacks Civilians', *The Guardian*, 11 March 2011.
19 B. Wallace-Wells, 'European Superhero Quashes Libyan Dictator', *New York Magazine*, 26 December 2011; S. Erlanger, 'By His Own Reckoning, One Man Made Libya a French Cause', *The New York Times*, 1 April 2011.
20 J. Warrick, 'Clinton Credited with Key Role in Success of NATO Airstrikes, Libyan Rebels', *The Washington Post*, 30 October 2011.
21 For a discussion of US decision-making, see: M. Hastings, 'Inside Obama's War Room', *Rolling Stone*, 13 October 2011; D.E. Sanger, *Confront and Conceal: Obama's Secret Wars and Surprising Use of American Power*, New York: Crown Publishers, 2012, 338–56; J. Mann, *The Obamians: The Struggle Inside the White House to Redefine American Power*, London: Viking, 2012, 281–301; M. Lewis, 'Obama's Way', *Vanity Fair*, October 2012.
22 Notably, China, Russia, Germany, India and Brazil abstained. The African Union came out publicly against any military intervention.

23 Statement by P. Wittig in Department of Public Information, Security Council 6498th Meeting, 'Security Council Approves No Fly Zone over Libya, Authorizing All Necessary Measures to Protect Civilians, by Vote of 10 in Favour with 5 Abstentions', *United Nations*, 17 March 2011.
24 Merkel, cited in Q. Peel, 'Merkel Explains German Abstention', *The Financial Times*, 18 March 2011.
25 C.P. Cavas, 'Coalition against Gadhafi Growing', *Defense News*, 20 March 2011. The British referred to their participation as Operation Ellamy, whereas the French named it Operation Harmattan.
26 For details on Odyssey Dawn, see: J. Quartararo Sr., M. Rovenolt and R. White, 'Libya's Operation Odyssey Dawn: Command and Control', *PRISM* 3, 2012, 137–50; J. Gertler, 'Operation Odyssey Dawn (Libya): Background and Issues for Congress', *Congressional Research Service Report for Congress*, 30 March 2011; G.K. James, L. Holcomb and C.T. Manske, 'Joint Task Force Odyssey Dawn: A Model for Joint Experience, Training, and Education', *Joint Forces Quarterly* 64, 2012, 24–9; J.A. Tirpak, 'Lessons from Libya', *Air Force Magazine*, December 2011, 34–8.
27 At least this was the American view of what it would take to create a no-fly zone. See: D.E. Sanger and T. Shanker, 'Gates Warns of Risks of a No-Flight Zone', *The New York Times*, 2 March 2011.
28 James *et al.*, 'Joint Task Force Odyssey Dawn'; Lieutenant General C. Bouchard, 'Coalition Building and the Future of NATO Operations', Transcript of Speech Delivered at the Atlantic Council, Washington, DC, 14 February 2012.
29 For a critical account of the CSDP during the Libya crisis, see: A. Menon, 'European Defence Policy from Lisbon to Libya', *Survival* 53, 2011, 75–90.
30 P. Tan, 'UK, France Vault to Center of Euro Defense', *Defense News*, 11 April 2011.
31 Cited on official site of the British Prime Minister's Office, (2011) *Cameron and Obama Discuss Key Role of NATO in Libya*. Online. Available: www.number10.gov.uk/news/cameron-and-obama-discusses-key-role-of-nato-in-libya (accessed 14 February 2013).
32 S. Erlanger, 'Confusion Over Who Leads Libya Strikes, and for How Long', *The New York Times*, 21 March 2011.
33 L. Harding, 'Germany Won't Send Forces to Libya, Foreign Minister Declares', *The Guardian*, 17 March 2011.
34 D. Brunnstrom and P. Taylor, 'Turkey Sees NATO Deal On Libya but Talks Go On', *Reuters*, 24 March 2011.
35 G. Le Roux, 'Libya Operations Expose France–Turkey Diplomatic Rift', *France-24*, 29 March 2011.
36 K. Willsher, 'Sarkozy Opposes NATO Taking Control of Libya Operation', *Guardian Unlimited*, 22 March 2011; D. Melvin, 'Tension Growing in NATO over Libya Military Operation', *Associated Press*, 22 March 2011; I. Traynor, 'Warships Enforce Arms Embargo as Squabbles Continue', *The Guardian*, 24 March 2011; A. Davis and A. Migliaccio, 'Berlusconi Hedges Bets on Libya War Outcome by Pushing for NATO Takeover', *Bloomberg*, 23 March 2011.
37 M. Landler and S. Erlanger, 'US Seeks to Unify Allies as Airstrikes Rock Tripoli', *The New York Times*, 23 March 2011; G. Viscusi, 'France's Juppé Proposes Political Committee for Libya Mission', *Bloomberg*, 22 March 2011.
38 S. Wilson and K. DeYoung, 'Coalition Nears Agreement on Transition for Operations in Libya', *The Washington Post*, 23 March 2011.
39 J. Dempsey, 'Germany Would Join Aid Mission to Libya', *The New York Times*, 8 April 2011; 'Merkel Government Approves AWACS for Afghanistan', *Der Spiegel*, 23 March 2011.
40 Brunnstrom and Taylor, 'Turkey Sees NATO deal on Libya but Talks go on'.
41 Landler and Erlanger, 'US Seeks to Unify Allies'.

42 O. Ward, 'Canadian General to Lead Coalition of the Wobbling in Libya', *The Star*, 25 March 2011.
43 I. Traynor, 'NATO to Oversee Libya Campaign after France and Turkey Strike Deal', *The Guardian Unlimited*, 24 March 2011.
44 Rasmussen, cited in I. Pannell, 'Libya: NATO Assumes Control of Military Operation', *BBC*, 27 March 2011.
45 M. Abbas 'West Strikes Libya Forces, NATO Sees 90-day Campaign', *Reuters*, 25 March 2011.
46 During this period, the US officially admitted to limiting its attacks to air defence sites.
47 J. Lindley-French, 'Welcome to NATO Operation Protecting Disunity', *Atlantic Council*, 15 April 2011.
48 J.P. Bell and R.C. Hendrickson, 'NATO's Višegrad Allies and the Bombing of Qaddafi: The Consequence of Alliance Free-Riders', *The Journal of Slavic Military Studies* 25, 2012, 149–61.
49 Tusk, cited in Reuters, 'Polish PM Chides Europe over Libya "hypocrisy"', *Reuters*, 9 April 2011.
50 Comment cited in R. Beste and D. Kurbjuweit, 'Spiegel Interview with Defense Minister De Maizière', *Spiegel Online*, 20 June 2011.
51 British Prime Minister's Office, *Libya Crisis: National Security Adviser's Review of Central Coordination and Lessons Learned*. Online. Available: www.number10.gov.uk/wp-content/uploads/2011/12/Lessons-Learned-30-Nov.pdf (accessed 14 February 2013).
52 A. Cameron, 'The Channel Axis: France, the UK and NATO', in A. Johnson and S. Mueen (eds) *Short War, Long Shadow: The Political and Military Legacies of the 2011 Libya Campaign*, London: RUSI, 2012, 18.
53 For an elaboration of this point, see: S. Kreps, 'Elite Consensus as a Determinant of Alliance Cohesion: Why Public Opinion Hardly Matters in Afghanistan', *Foreign Policy Analysis* 6, 2010, 191–215.
54 R. Laird, 'French Libya Lessons Learned: Better Targeting, Flexible ROEs, Limits to Armed UAVs', *AOL Defense*, 23 September 2011; C. Coughlin, 'Inside the Art Deco War Room for NATO on Libya', *The Telegraph*, 14 May 2011.
55 See note 20.
56 W. Wan and L. Fadel, 'US Rebuffs Appeals for More Forces for Libya Mission', *The Washington Post*, 15 April 2011.
57 The Washington Post Editorial, 'The Libya Stalemate', *The Washington Post*, 16 April 2011.
58 D. Dobey and K. Stacey, 'Britain Urges US to Step Up Libya Support', *The Financial Times*, 17 July 2011.
59 Private information.
60 E. Cody, 'French, British Leaders Meet about West's Role in Libyan Uprising', *The Washington Post*, 14 April 2011.
61 The text of this letter is available at: BBC (2011) *Libya letter by Obama, Cameron and Sarkozy: Full text*. Online. Available: www.bbc.co.uk/news/world-africa-13090646 (accessed 14 February 2013).
62 S. Arsu and K. Fahim, 'Turkish Prime Minister Says Qaddafi Must Leave Now', *The New York Times*, 4 May 2011.
63 M. Birnbaum, 'NATO Rifts Strain Libya Campaign', *The Washington Post*, 5 July 2011.
64 D. Brunnstrom, 'Dutch Warn of Heated NATO Debate as Libya Drags On', *Reuters*, 29 June 2011.
65 L. Chikhi, 'France Tells Libya Rebels to Seek Peace with Gaddafi', *Reuters*, 10 July 2011; M. Robinson, 'Italy Ceasefire Call Exposes NATO Split on Libya', *Reuters*, 22 June 2011.

66 J. Lichfield, 'France Confirms Negotiations with Gaddafi Regime', *The Independent*, 12 July 2011; S. Erlanger, 'France Says Qaddafi Can Stay in Libya if He Relinquishes Power', *The New York Times*, 20 July 2011.
67 M. Birnbaum, 'NATO Rifts Strain Libya Campaign'; W. Moskwa, 'Norway Set to Curb Libya Air Strike Role', *Reuters*, 9 May 2011.
68 P. Richter, 'NATO Feels the Pressure from Libya Campaign', *Los Angeles Times*, 5 July 2011.
69 These seven countries were the US, UK, France, Canada, Belgium, Denmark and Norway.
70 L. Fadel and S. Denyer, 'NATO's Credibility Takes a Hit in Libya', *The Washington Post*, 8 April 2011.
71 'France and Britain Criticise NATO over Libya', *France 24*, 12 April 2011.
72 G. Moulson and M. Lee, 'NATO Struggles to Resolve Dispute Over Libya Fight', *Associated Press*, 14 April 2011.
73 S. Fidler, A. Entous and S. Dagher, 'US, Allies Raise Ante on Ouster of Gadhafi', *The Wall Street Journal*, 15 April 2011; M. Spetalnick and D. Brunnstrom, 'NATO States Buck French, British Call over Libya', *Reuters*, 14 April 2011.
74 D. Dylla, 'Poland, Libya, and NATO', *Atlantic Council*, 3 June 2011; J. Puhl, 'I'm Incapable of Getting Angry with Angela Merkel: Interview with Polish Prime Minister Donald Tusk', *Der Spiegel*, 8 April 2011.
75 I. Traynor, 'NATO Lacking Strike Aircraft for Libya Campaign', *The Guardian*, 5 April 2011.
76 BBC, 'Libya Conflict: NATO Summit Fails to Secure New Planes', *BBC News*, 15 April 2011; E. Cody, 'French, British Leaders Meet about West's Role in Libyan Uprising', *The Washington Post*, 14 April 2011.
77 K. DeYoung and G. Jaffe, 'NATO Runs Short on some Munitions in Libya', *The Washington Post*, 16 April 2011.
78 Biden, cited in D. Dombey, 'Nato can Fulfil Libya mission, says Biden', *The Financial Times*, 19 April 2011.
79 D. Kennedy, 'Libya: Berlusconi Backs NATO Strikes by Italy Jets', *BBC News*, 25 April 2011; D.D. Kirkpatrick, 'NATO Strikes Qaddafi Compound; Italy Joins the Fight', *The New York Times*, 26 April 2011.
80 Spetalnick and Brunnstrom, 'NATO States Buck French, British Call over Libya'.
81 I. Traynor, 'Libya Campaign will Falter without More Help, NATO Bystanders Warned', *The Guardian*, 9 June 2011; D.S. Cloud, 'Gates Hits NATO Allies Hard', *The Baltimore Sun*, 11 June 2011; T. Shanker and S. Castle, 'Gates Urges Allies to Do More in Libya; Secretary Puts Pressure on Germany, Turkey and 3 Other NATO Members', *The International Herald Tribune*, 9 June 2011.
82 Rasmussen, cited in A. Gray-Block, 'NATO Chief Calls for More Planes to Bomb Libyan Targets', *Reuters*, 14 July 2011.
83 In addition to patrolling the no-fly zone, similar to the UAE and Qatar, Swedish planes also collected intelligence which it delivered to the Combined Air Operations Center for exploitation. See: R. Pengelley, 'Swedish Gripens over Libya', *Jane's International Defence Review*, January 2012, 35.
84 S. Ackerman, 'Tiny Qatar Flexed Big Muscles in Libya', *Wired.com*, 25 August 2011; A. Loyd, 'Rebels Armed with Blast from the Past', *Weekend Australian*, 2 July 2011; H. Eakin, 'The Strange Power of Qatar', *The New York Review of Books*, 27 October 2011.
85 L.C. Baldor and S. Lekic, 'NATO Covert Guidance Steered Libyan Rebel Gains', *Army Times*, 23 August 2011.
86 These comments by Admiral Di Paolo were made during a NATO Press Briefing on 31 March 2011. NATO (2011) *Press briefing*. Online. Available: www.nato.int/cps/en/natolive/opinions_71897.htm (accessed 14 February 2013).

87 Bouchard, 'Coalition Building'.
88 For examples of numerous instances in which unilateral planning and operations were undertaken alongside the Alliance during the Kosovo war, see: D. Priest, 'United NATO Front was Divided within', *The Washington Post*, 21 September 1999; D. Priest, 'France Played Skeptic on Kosovo Attacks', *The Washington Post*, 20 September 1999; D. Priest, 'Kosovo Land Threat may have Won War', *The Washington Post*, 19 September 1999. As for Afghanistan, the US operation 'Enduring Freedom' was conducted alongside NATO/ISAF operations for many years.
89 The increasing emphasis on Asia is highlighted in the US military's strategic guidance document: US Department of Defense (2012) *Sustaining US Global Leadership: Priorities for 21st Century Defense*. Online. Available: www.defense.gov/news/defense_strategic_guidance.pdf (accessed 14 February 2013).

2 Why Libya?
Security Council Resolution 1973 and the politics of justification

Kjell Engelbrekt

The *raison d'être* of the United Nations Security Council lies, one might argue, in trying to prevent its own demise, which effectively would abolish the world's most authoritative forum for great power deliberations on matters of peace and security. As noted by an author of a recent introduction to the history of the Security Council, there has in over 60 years of its existence 'never been a sustained clash between permanent council members'.[1] In order to uphold this rather impressive record and the primary collective good – global order – associated with it, the council does not have to adopt any single binding resolution, let alone facilitate political or military intervention so as to thwart a particular scenario or redress a situation that has already come about.

The legal standing of the Security Council is of course chiefly derived from the UN Charter agreed between the major great powers after the Second World War, an arrangement which paved the way for 'council jurisprudence' that consists of what today amount to more than 2,000 resolutions with binding effect for all UN member states. That jurisprudence, Ian Hurd explains in a book devoted to legitimacy and power in the Security Council, has over time induced states to

> behave as if they acknowledge the sovereignty of the Council, and their behavior is changed by their efforts to accommodate and exploit it in the pursuit of their interests. The Council's presence changes the incentives in ways that states have not consented to and from which they cannot simply choose to free themselves.[2]

More broadly the legitimacy of the Security Council depends on a wider system of written and unwritten rules, including international law and the practices of diplomacy, many of which existed prior to the UN. As the UN Charter implicitly directed the council toward creating new international law, it also made it the chief custodian of a broad set of transnationally accepted rules that have evolved over several centuries, even though the precise scope of those powers remains a point of contestation.[3] As one might expect, concern with its primary objective and with *procedural* legitimacy induces the Security Council to handle both council jurisprudence and the wider institutional legacy prudently, an aspect which along with the veto mechanism generates caution and conservatism.

Yet although many rules associated with peace and security are stable and deeply entrenched, for the sake of *substantive* legitimacy they cannot be immutable. In recent years a partial reinterpretation of the said rules and the Security Council's obligations in relation to them has taken place by way of an enhanced focus on civilians in conflict situations, on the particular vulnerability of women and children in such contexts, associated with a conceptual recalibration from state to human security as well as a tendency to place greater emphasis on the responsibility of governments. A significant development in this partial reinterpretation was the adoption of the Responsibility to Protect (R2P) concept by the UN General Assembly in 2005, declaring that the international community carries a responsibility to prevent and halt mass atrocity crimes perpetrated against civilians.

And so, in early 2011, over the threat of widely anticipated massacres in northeastern Libya by the regime of Colonel Muammar Gaddafi, an opportunity to bring this partial reinterpretation in line with Security Council practice suddenly presented itself. In merely a matter of weeks the political principles associated with the R2P doctrine were conjoined with an anti-authoritarian wave of demonstrations sweeping across the Middle East, the foreign policy priorities of a new constellation of non-permanent members of the Security Council and a specific set of operational circumstances, to form what has been referred to as a 'perfect storm'.[4] For the first time since the Gulf War of 1991, a near-consensus on the need to intervene was formed and a coalition of willing member states committed to a military effort that would implement the resolution.

In this chapter the critical components that made up this alleged 'perfect storm' will be examined, in an attempt to provide a plausible response to the simple question posed in the first part of the title of this chapter. The analytical emphasis is on what can be referred to as 'the politics of justification', both in the sense of explicit and precise formulations used by Security Council members, and in terms of implicit motives that reasonably can be ascribed to the relevant actors who participated in the process. A full-fledged rationalistic explanation would say that the council in this case, like in many others, engaged in bargaining until it produced an agreement (a 'focal solution') with the status of a temporary 'elite pact'.[5] Below it will be argued that, besides the motives of individual council member states and constellations of interest among them, a heightened concern about the legitimacy of the Security Council and integrity of the process by which it takes decisions constituted a powerful additional influence on the narrative of justification.

But if a 'perfect storm' descended on Libya, are there any lessons to be drawn with regard to the Security Council and the wider international community? Well, if many of the contributing factors that shaped the decision making are indicative of future trends the case of Libya might in fact be more forward-looking than other instances. This chapter ends by suggesting that the Libya intervention debate of 2011 could prove significant for the long-term sustainability of Security Council legitimacy, even though it temporarily may have set things back due to the partly unanticipated (on the part of some council members), and partly unintended, consequences of adopting resolution 1973 which authorized the use of 'all necessary measures'.[6]

That being said, the overall assessment of any intervention is typically also influenced by the eventual fallout from the application of military force and its long-term repercussions. With Nicholas Wheeler, there is a case to be made for ultimately assessing interventions against the outcome that they produce.[7] That is, if Libyan society does not revert into turmoil and civil war but prospers and establishes a reasonably well-functioning political system over the next few years, the likelihood that predominantly positive lessons are drawn from the military action taken on the basis of resolution 1973 is bound to increase.

The emerging norm of R2P

The speed at which the protection of civilians from mass atrocities took centre stage in the case of Libya in February 2011 seems to have surprised scholars and decision makers alike. United States Ambassador Susan Rice, at the centre of the early 2011 deliberations at the Security Council, at one point expressed what sounded like genuine surprise at the 'swift, decisive and unanimous action on Libya'.[8] The term 'unanimity' may or may not be a deliberate oversimplification on the ambassador's part, given that five countries eventually abstained in the vote on 17 March. But although resolution 1973 contains no explicit mention of the Responsibility to Protect, hardly anybody disputes that the R2P norm constitutes the key doctrine behind the outcome.[9] For the first time, the R2P norm was applied in practice, over a decade after its emergence in the political arena.

In December 2001 the International Commission on Intervention and State Sovereignty (ICISS) released *Responsibility to Protect*, a report that sought to forge a sustainable compromise between countries that find humanitarian intervention an acceptable means to prevent or halt genocide or mass atrocities on the one hand, and governments that strongly support state sovereignty and non-interference into domestic affairs on the other. Three years later, in December 2004, a High-Level Panel on new global security threats appointed by Secretary-General Annan expressly endorsed

> the emerging norm that there is a collective international responsibility to protect, exercisable by the Security Council authorising military

intervention as a last resort, in the event of genocide and other large-scale killing, ethnic cleansing or serious violations of international humanitarian law which sovereign Governments have proved powerless or unwilling to prevent.[10]

In slightly revised form the R2P norm was the centre-piece of a 2005 UN Summit Outcome Document, adopted in September 2005. This document, which lends support to R2P as an emerging norm, can be said to include a moral and a political component. The moral component outlines the responsibility of the international community at large, through the UN, to help protect civilian populations to escape genocide, ethnic cleansing and crimes against humanity. The political component stresses that there is a responsibility to protect that may entail humanitarian intervention by military means, inherent to the norm, although the latter does not amount to a duty. In turn, the option to use military means in order to realize this responsibility is connected to criteria that underscore the centrality of the Security Council and Chapter VII of the UN Charter.[11]

Whether the R2P norm should be regarded as one primarily originating with the UN-induced conceptual development in the past few years, or as an extension of the customary practice of humanitarian international law over several centuries is, justifiably, the subject of an intriguing academic debate.[12] It takes its point of departure in the conventional understanding of international law as originating from two sources, namely international treaties, ratified by signatory states, and customary law that arises through widespread state practice (recognized as such by prominent legal experts), including *jus cogens* (compelling legal norms that override lesser ones).

When it comes to the protection of civilians in situations of military combat, it would appear that the entire spectrum of international law applies in some measure. Codification of the protection of civilians through international treaties occurred with the adoption of the Geneva Conventions of 1949 (building on the treaties of 1864, 1906, 1929) and enforcement has been bolstered by the International Court of Justice (ICJ) in The Hague and – more recently – the International Criminal Court (ICC). Meanwhile, a general prohibition on mass atrocities perpetrated against non-combatants constitutes a well-entrenched principle in customary international law, associated with military practice in most societies and, in turn, reinforced by modern-day codification.[13] Finally, the non-targeting of civilians and vulnerable groups (such as children and women) in situations of military combat has arguably at least some properties of a *jus cogens* principle.[14]

But in the past ten to fifteen years a narrower notion has been elaborated within the context of the UN, more loosely associated with conventional sources of law. A couple of reports adopted by the Security Council in the late 1990s emphasized the importance of safeguarding the lives of civilians in the context of violent conflicts.[15] In late 2000 then UN Secretary-General Kofi Annan helped initiate the conceptual basis for a more ambitious development through the establishment of an ad hoc ICISS. Significant are also the renewed activities of regional organizations, most notably the European Union and, more recently, the African Union. Elements of the overall approach to protecting civilians have undoubtedly been influenced by the evolution of state practice and international law with regard to the conflicts in northern Iraq, Bosnia and Herzegovina, Rwanda, Kosovo, Liberia and Darfur. In his 2007 report on the protection of civilians in armed conflict Annan's successor as Secretary-General, Ban Ki-Moon, referred to agreements on R2P as a 'cardinal achievement'.[16]

As could be expected, a number of legal difficulties arose from actually protecting civilians while implementing the resolution 1973 in relation to the military campaign in Libya. For instance, the question arose whether the heavy military action in which NATO countries became engaged was proportionate to the objective of protecting 'civilians or civilian populated areas', as outlined in the resolution.[17] Considering this particular objective and the circumstance that the intervention was justified against the backdrop of a longstanding debate on R2P, there is widespread agreement that an unusually high standard with regard to international humanitarian law ought to apply to the implementation of the resolution.[18] Furthermore, as the number and intensity of attacks on civilians and civilian inhabited areas fell toward the end of NATO's engagement in Libya, was it justifiable to sustain an evenly high level of military action?[19]

Other important legal problems were related to what type of assistance rebel forces could be offered, given that a comprehensive arms embargo had been imposed through a preceding resolution (1970) and that the dispatching of 'a foreign occupying force' was expressly precluded in resolution 1973.[20] Could Colonel Gaddafi be considered a legitimate target, in his capacity as the top military commander, implying that regime change had emerged as a direct objective although never mentioned by the Security Council? Finally, how do we assess the fact that resolution 1973, once adopted, became virtually irrevocable as a result of the fact that several council member states took an active part in the military campaign?

At this point it has been established that the R2P norm served an important purpose in framing a narrative on the part of influential actors that favoured Security Council activism and, by extension, international intervention. In the remainder of this chapter, the focus is on the politics of justification of intervention itself and the shape that it took, leaving aside legal matters that did not impinge on the (sufficiently) complex process that led up to the adoption of resolution 1973.[21]

The Libyan crisis and council agenda-setting

As in most organizations the framing of problems and solutions is critical to the outcome of decision making at the UN Security Council. Yet only few issues make it beyond the initial hurdle – getting onto the formal agenda. The agenda of the Security Council is filled up with a great number of issues that an influential constellation of political forces at some point have identified and raised in this high forum. Once an issue has entered the council agenda and become subject of one of the council's numerous sub-organs and procedures, the burden of proof is virtually reversed. From then on the Security Council will, as the technical phrase goes, be 'seized of the matter'. As a result, a sufficiently influential political constellation has to be formed around a justification to deliberately jettison the item.

Not even the powerful permanent five member states can suppress formal consultations once an agenda item has been listed. A good illustration of this agenda-setting inertia are the recurring sessions devoted to Israel's settlement policy, which in 2011 took place on 18 February, merely four days before the first meeting called to discuss the deteriorating situation in Libya. The United States, which then faced a draft resolution signed by seventy-nine sponsor countries and fourteen votes condemning Israel, had to resort to its veto power in order to save Tel Aviv from an embarrassing defeat. As it happens, the draft resolution condemning the settlement expansion of the Israeli state strongly leaned on the applicability of the Geneva Convention relative to the Protection of Civilian Persons in Time of War (of 12 August 1949), with a quintessential human rights perspective pitted against state sovereignty, for its legal justification.

But at the same time as criticism of Israel was being voiced in the council chamber dramatic events were unfolding in Libya with potentially more immediate and grave consequences for civilians at the mercy of a ruthless government. In fact, on the afternoon of the day that 79 UN member states introduced the anti-Israeli draft resolution that Washington decided to veto, the Security Council turned from item 'Protection of Civilians' to 'The Middle East' in February's programme of work, as prepared by Brazil as that month's chair of the council. Since the format was that of 'consultations' no protocol or press conference exists to reflect what was said; but the escalating situation in Libya will undoubtedly have featured in the deliberations.

As usual in council diplomacy, a regional euphemism heralded the newfound preoccupation with Libya. For 22 February 2011 a seemingly inconspicuous item (not anticipated in the forecast schedule) was subsequently inserted on the updated programme of work, entitled 'Peace and Security in Africa'. At the end of two full sessions Brazil's Ambassador Viotti, acting as Security Council president for February, issued a press statement condemning the use of violence against civilians and, on behalf of Security Council members, calling on the Libyan government 'to meet its responsibility to protect its population'.[22] This was the very first time the phrase 'responsibility to protect' was used in the context of the Libyan crisis, no doubt reflecting the proximity of the notion to ongoing council deliberations. Although the text was not a formalized Presidential Statement

(PRST) with potential legal implications, it will only have been released after consultations and so represents a good indication of the council majority view.

Three days later a second so-called 'private meeting' of the Security Council was devoted to 'Peace and Security in Africa', followed by formal consultations at which Secretary-General Ban Ki-Moon took the floor, along with the Permanent Representative of Libya. At this meeting Libya's Ambassador Shalgham, in an unprecedented move, broke ranks with the Tripoli government and sharply criticized Colonel Gaddafi's 22 February speech at which he had issued sweeping threats to kill all opponents to the regime. At the Security Council, Ambassador Shalgham ended his impassionate address by referring to his earlier service as ambassador on the Security Council and by directly appealing for UN-mandated intervention on the behalf of the Libyan population:

> Libya was established by the United Nations. Please, United Nations, save Libya. No to bloodshed. No to the killing of innocents. We want a swift, decisive and courageous resolution.[23]

As of 25 February, there is no doubt that the Libya uprising was on the agenda of the Security Council. It had in fact, in pushing aside a number of routine matters, within a few days climbed to the very top of that agenda. The following discussion will demonstrate the various interests at play; but it will also show that legitimacy concerns affected most actors within, and in close proximity to, the Security Council. Below I briefly deal with the interests and options of key constituencies, that is, constellations of political actors that in part competed, and in part collaborated, in framing the problem as well as the way forward. Although I do find the metaphor of a 'perfect storm' a fruitful one to describe the multitude of components that needed to be wedded together in order for resolution 1973 to be take shape, I take issue with the image of a serendipitous decision making process that might be construed to follow from it.

Linking justification to constituency

Among the permanent five Security Council member states it was the United Kingdom and France which spearheaded the coalition of the willing, hinting that they were ready to authorize the use of military means and assume the daunting task of implementing resolutions. Already by the last week of February their position can be described as one of *assertive interventionism*. As the smallest member states among the ranking permanent five in the Security Council, the UK and France tend to be quite active on humanitarian issues and relatively relaxed about protecting the principle of sovereignty. But a decision to take on a challenge of this magnitude is unusual, and should probably be interpreted against the backdrop of domestic, intra-EU as well as intra-NATO political relations. In fact, not since the disastrous Suez crisis debacle in 1956 had Britain and France been prepared to accept a leading role in a military mission in the Middle East.

Clearly, the leaders of France and the United Kingdom had important domestic reasons to demonstrate their skills in the field of foreign and security policy. French President Sarkozy was approaching the 2012 election with slipping ratings, whereas British Prime Minister David Cameron was new to his office, each leader untested when it comes to presiding over a cabinet engaged in a military campaign. At the EU level actors had incentives to demonstrate the significance of the entry into force of the Lisbon Treaty, theoretically paving the way for an expanded role in world affairs, though by early 2011 with no major achievements in practice. Finally, there were the usual concerns about the vitality of the transatlantic relationship, which Washington in recent years has been trying to rebalance toward Europe in matters where the United States has no immediate stakes.

Outside the Security Council assertive interventionism was promoted by a wide range of countries and influential non-government organizations and networks, namely the humanitarian, pro-R2P constituency. This constituency was in a position to act in a variety of political arenas during the unfolding of the Libya crisis. The wider UN arena, with the General Assembly and the UN Human Rights Council as key institutions, constituted one battleground of ideas. On 25 February the UN's Human Rights Council in Geneva held its first special, non-regular session ever, exclusively devoted to the crisis in Libya. Almost fifty countries, some but not all members of the Human Rights Council, had called for the extraordinary session. The meeting ended in a recommendation that the UN General Assembly should promptly suspend Libya's membership in the council. The General Assembly also did so, unanimously, on 1 March, and further adopted a strong statement sponsored by Lebanon.

Within the humanitarian, pro-R2P constituency others lobbied diplomatic networks in the traditional, bilateral manner. Among the original supporters of the R2P doctrine, Australian Prime Minister Kevin Rudd is reported to have acted behind the scenes throughout February–March 2011, writing letters and meeting with like-minded European leaders in order to promote the R2P agenda at this crucial turn of events.[24] Rudd was well aware that Australia's diplomats, albeit not on the Security Council at the time, had an advantage in terms of accumulated expertise and policymaking networks through which it could promote the notion of protecting civilians in conflict situations. In 1999–2001 Australia's former foreign minister, Gareth Evans, had in fact co-chaired the ICISS and later helped maintain the country's advocacy role on R2P in the non-government community.[25]

With regard to the worsening situation in Libya at the end of February the stance of the United States can be described as that of *moderate interventionism*. Whereas the original reaction of many Washington decision makers was to resist calls for direct US engagement, the rapidly deteriorating human rights situation and the potential geopolitical fallout prompted a gradual shift in their positions. By early March the White House was closely following developments on the ground and in the second week of March specific policy options were being prepared by the State Department, the Pentagon, the National Security Council and President Obama's own staff.

What pressure the United States may have brought to bear on other governments during the course of the Libya crisis is difficult to precisely ascertain. The diplomatic interaction with other EU states, beyond Britain and France as part of the informal Western 'G3' core at the Security Council, was apparently extensive, and soon extended into departments of defence. As mentioned above, the 10–11 March NATO meeting helped forge an understanding beyond these three main protagonists, with basic acceptance for the criteria-based approach advocated by Britain. That agreement among the transatlantic powers may in turn have helped tip the balance in favour of symbolically significant G8 endorsement adopted at the foreign ministers' meeting in Paris on 15 March. Here Secretary of State Hillary Clinton managed to sway her seven colleagues to sign onto a somewhat bland statement in favour of the rights of Libyans to strive for democracy and prosperity.[26]

Militarily, of course, France, the UK and the wider coalition that assembled to implement resolution 1973 all along knew that they had no choice but to rely on American resources, especially in launching a massive air campaign that would destroy the air defence system of the Libyan regime. But politically the United States came very close to 'leading from behind', a notion that experts close to the Obama administration had promoted in order not to bolster anti-American sentiments in places like the Middle East. The US Ambassador to the UN, Susan Rice, was uncharacteristically measured in most of her statements with regard to the deteriorating situation in Libya, leaving other countries to drive public debate. In the region proper, US officials were even more restrained, supporting the democratic impetus of the Arab Spring movement but avoiding the perception that they actively sponsored it. If Washington was able to exert a calming effect on the Egyptian military during the turmoil in that country, it had of course no such leverage in Libya.

The third critical constituency in this context was therefore made up of regional actors, and their representatives on the Security Council and in organizations such as the Arab League, the Gulf Cooperation Council and NATO proper. For the most part these countries represented *ambivalent interventionism*. The importance of the perception that a powerful impetus toward council activism came from regional political leaders whose views and arguments were channelled through the Gulf Cooperation Council, the Organization of Islamic States and the League of Arab States cannot be overstated. This was, as already indicated, a *sine qua non* condition for several Western powers. The dire need for strong regional support was inextricably related to the issue of legitimacy, in that actions mandated by Security Council need to be perceived as procedurally and substantively fair, and that this especially applies to regions where international institutions are frequently regarded as instruments of Western great powers.

It may also have been significant that the idea of establishing a no-fly zone was first mentioned publicly by Libya's own Deputy Permanent representative to the UN, Ibrahim Dabbashi, at a news conference at the UN Headquarters in New York on 1 March.[27] Less than a week later, the Gulf Cooperation Council echoed this proposal. More broadly, the Organization of Islamic States – gathering 57 countries – was unanimous in its appeal to the regime of Gaddafi to cease all violent acts directed at the Libyan population.

The underlying ambivalence of many regional governments, however, did not always shine through the news reports. Out of the 21 attending member states at the 12 March meeting of the League of Arab States at least three had serious reservations against a statement directly urging the Security Council to set up a no-fly zone over Libya in order to protect its citizens. While reports are partially conflicting on details of that meeting, it appears that Syria, Mauretania and Algeria eventually dropped their open opposition against the statement. Once the air attacks were launched a week later, mutual recriminations among Arab League states came to the fore. Although wary of the consequences of not helping to thwart a mass massacre against fellow Arabs, most members of the league presumably opposed providing Western powers with a mandate to oust Gaddafi by military means.

Meanwhile, at a corresponding meeting at the EU level, foreign ministers decided not to enlist in the British and French diplomatic effort to pursue a resolution authorizing a no-fly zone.[28] Obviously, not even NATO endorsement was universal. As would transpire in the weeks to come, Germany was deeply uncomfortable about supporting renewed Western intervention in North Africa and the Middle East, though not as vehemently as under the Social Democratic government that opposed the invasion of Iraq in 2003. So Berlin eventually decided it would not block its NATO partners from trying to avert what everyone agreed was a major humanitarian disaster in the making, primarily caused by the brutality of the Libyan regime.

Brazil and India, serving on the Security Council for two-year mandates, were facing a similar dilemma vis-à-vis domestic opinion and the international community at large. They were keen to demonstrate a steadfast and principled foreign policy toward people at home, which included avoiding the impression of subservience to Western powers. They also needed to consider the views of the wider humanitarian community while not alienating any of the permanent Security Council members, especially as both Brazil and India have long been vying for permanent seats if, and when, the council is expanded to major emerging powers.

More surprisingly, China should be counted to the group of ambivalent interventionists. As a permanent member of the Security Council, China has ever since joining the body defended sovereignty and non-interventionism as core principles of universally applicable international law, and especially vigorously in its own vicinity. At the same time Beijing has at times demonstrated flexibility and an acceptance of the notion that the handling of challenges to peace and security may be 'delegated' to authoritative transnational bodies in the regions concerned, when there is widespread agreement on a course of action.[29] For that reason the appeals of the Arab League, the Gulf Cooperation Council and the Islamic Conference Organization could not be easily ignored by Chinese policymakers.

Finally, there were a few actors whose interests and policy options led them to the stance *of reluctant interventionism*. First and foremost there was the Russian Federation, with the potential to block a resolution from within the five permanent members' group (P5). Judging from official statements by Russian diplomats and government officials, until mid-March Russia never seriously contemplated lending support for a no-fly zone, let alone a resolution that would authorize a more extensive type of military intervention. Indeed, Russia is a straightforward player in the sense that it quite consistently upholds state sovereignty and non-intervention. But ever since the end of the Cold War Moscow has manifested discomfort at the prospect of standing alone on a major dispute in the council.

Also in the reluctant interventionist category, though just having left the council as a non-permanent member, Turkey found itself caught in a dilemma between solidarity with leading military allies and anti-Western sentiments at home and in the region overall. Given that Ankara had a formal opportunity to veto NATO action at the political level, the prospects of Turkey wreaking havoc in an operation already underway was a concern to the French political leadership as soon as the NATO option surfaced in the G3 constellation. Not unlike Russia, Turkey was temporarily persuaded by the US and others to hold back its criticism and avoid interfering in the political process.

Resolution 1970: the Security Council imposes sanctions

It is easy to see how the two latter constituencies (the ambivalent and the reluctant categories) were unable to agree to an approach that would fully satisfy the two former (the assertive and the moderate). But at the early, intense stages of the crisis a compromise formula emerged that consisted of several elements. On 26 February the Security Council was able to unanimously pass resolution 1970. The resolution text began by demanding 'an immediate end to the violence and calls for steps to fulfill the legitimate demands of the population', followed by an appeal to the Libyan authorities to act with the utmost restraint, ensure the safety of foreign nationals and their assets, extend safe passage of humanitarian and medical supplies, and lift restrictions on all forms of media.

The second part of resolution 1970 enacted four concrete measures. The first measure was a general referral of the matter to the International Criminal Court, whose prosecutor is authorized to monitor the situation in Libya with a view of launching investigations or prosecutions. The second concrete measure was a comprehensive arms embargo which beyond sale and delivery of weapons also precluded 'technical assistance, training, financial or other assistance, related to military activities'. In order to monitor the embargo, the resolution provided for inspection of all cargo destined for or originating in Libyan sea- or airports 'if the State concerned has information that provides reasonable grounds to believe the cargo contains items the supply, sale, transfer, or export of which is prohibited by paragraphs 9 or 10 of this resolution' (and thus elaborated the details of the travel ban).

The third and fourth concrete measures consisted of a travel ban and an asset freeze for Gadaffi, his closest family members and associates, and a wider category of top government officials. Given the already accumulated expertise and experience among Security Council staff in applying targeted sanctions against high-value terrorism suspects, such measures are expected to go some way toward limiting the freedom for maneuver of high-value target individuals. At the same time, in this case the G3 country intelligence services probably volunteered to provide details in order for a particularly sharp sanctions regime to be put in place.

Except for the mere speed at which resolution 1970 had been passed, the concrete measures had other noteworthy features that helped satisfy assertive, moderate, as well as ambivalent and reluctant interventionists. Many in the pro-human rights and pro-R2P communities especially appreciated the referral to the International Criminal Court (ICC), endorsed by the P5 great powers including the previously aloof United States, as a positive move that over time may strengthen international humanitarian law. With regard to the arms embargo, moreover, the sanctions committee was authorized to monitor the situation and to decide on exemptions from the rather comprehensive regime. The latter helped convince some governments that fairness and due process would be respected by the sponsor states, and that the economic interests of (and potential damages to) third-party countries were minimized.

Mid-March: the tipping point

As the French and the British governments had anticipated, the adoption of a unanimous resolution by the Security Council had no demonstrable effect on the escalating conflict and humanitarian situation in Libya in the week that followed. But by now public awareness of the increasingly dire situation spread via international media, and decision makers throughout the Middle East and the world at large were highly sensitized. As noted above, on 1 March the UN General Assembly voted to suspend Libya's membership in the Human Rights Council (HRC), based on the rapidly worsening human rights situation in the country.

North American and European governments were already deliberating in various political arenas, starting up wider consultations with political partners in the next couple of days. Crucially, a meeting of NATO defence ministers on 10 and 11 March paved the way for NATO involvement. At the meeting the British government outlined three conditions for NATO engagement, namely a demonstrable need for military action, a sound legal basis and strong regional support for outside intervention. In summarizing the results of the meeting, NATO Secretary-General Anders Fogh Rasmussen more succinctly told a news conference that the alliance was prepared to assume an operational role provided that 'a clear political and legal mandate' was forthcoming from the international community.

Between the adoption of resolutions 1970 and 1973 on 26 February and 17 March, respectively, convergence grew around a specific solution to the most acute threat to Libya's civilian population, namely a broadly mandated no-fly zone. As noted above, the idea of a no-fly zone was first floated by a top-level official appointed by the Libyan regime, Deputy Permanent Representative Dabasshi, at a UN news conference in late February. It was subsequently picked up by British Prime Minster David Cameron and the Gulf Cooperation Council. In a statement released on 3 March the Gulf Cooperation Council expressly urged the UN Security Council to set up a no-fly zone over Libya. While still not won over by the assertive European duo, the White House could now witness how two of the three conditions listed at the NATO meeting were close to being fulfilled.

Due to the authority of the institution in the regional setting, the 12 March endorsement of a no-fly zone by the League of Arab States was particularly consequential.[30] Whatever sentiments were voiced at the meeting, a signal of unity was sent that significantly helped tip the scales toward council activism. Three days later the G8 foreign ministers held a meeting in Paris and ended up calling on the Libyan leader to 'respect the legitimate claim of the Libyan people to fundamental rights, freedom of expression, and a representative form of government'. In making all eight great powers sign a statement that endorsed the political aspirations of the Libyan people, London, Paris and Washington had now accomplished that Beijing and Moscow appeared to be siding with the protesters against Gadaffi's regime.

On the eve of the Security Council meeting on 17 March a considerable number of essential prerequisites for a pro-active decision were thus in place. The Libya crisis was at the top of the council agenda, and the previous resolution (1970) had proved ineffective in halting the regime's assault on the citizens of Libya. The G8 foreign ministers had according to news reports been weighing the options only a few days in advance, narrowing them down to a framework that would involve a no-fly zone. It was now a matter of providing the military with a mandate that would ensure effective action. For the Security Council meeting, the French foreign minister Alain Juppé had arrived in New York to make the case of the G3, in fact representing the only official of his rank in the room and thereby re-emphasizing French political leadership.

At this point the objective of the French and the British was probably not to get each Security Council member state to sign off on the no-fly zone, but to blunt the opposition against such a move. The G3 powers needed to convince the rest of the council to accept their framing of the problem at hand, including the necessity to act promptly or face a humanitarian disaster that might for many years tarnish the legitimacy of the council. Juppé and the G3 diplomats further needed to persuade council members that military intervention would not exacerbate the problem or create more resentment in the region, that is, that it might undo the legitimacy gained by decisive action. Ultimately, London and Paris also had to show that they were prepared to take the lead in implementing the resolution, with the United States backing up the effort.

The major ingredients for an agreement were now at hand, but a draft resolution still required careful wording in order to be acceptable to all four constituencies. And then there was the broader issue of action that conformed to the spirit and the letter of international law, and humanitarian purposes that the former should ultimately serve. The R2P doctrine, which was universally accepted in 2005, therefore came to form the core first element of the draft resolution in order for all sides to either get onboard, or at least consider 'constructive abstention'. The second key element was the express ban on a 'foreign occupying force' that, for the very first time, was inserted into the central passage. A third critical element was the fifth paragraph, emphasizing the role of the League of Arab States and requesting it to cooperate with other council members in implementing the resolution.

If the first element successfully catered to the sensibilities of the humanitarian law and R2P constituency, the second addressed the worst fears of regional actors and countries that consistently protect the principles of state sovereignty and non-intervention. With a formalized prohibition against the dispatching of ground troops, the 'neo-colonialist' route would appear to have been blocked. The third element similarly helped persuade regional actors that they could have a say in how the resolution was put into practice, but had an additional purpose, namely to gain a sympathetic hearing from China, in its capacity as sponsor of regional security organizations.

The latter was important not only because China is a permanent veto member of the council and could block the decision, but because Beijing held the presidency of the council for March. So Chinese diplomats and senior government officials organized and, when necessary, updated the council agenda as well as possessed a trump card – its veto – that could easily undo all efforts by the G3 powers. Over the years, however, an informal practice has evolved that says that the country in charge of the council presidency should do its utmost to avoid using its chairmanship to influence the proceedings to its own advantage. The circumstance that the government of a country holding the presidency will want to be perceived as doing so in a fair and nonpartisan way, may marginally have favoured the pro-interventionists in this case.

With China sympathetic to some aspects of the proposed resolution and prominent Muslim and Arab states favouring council activism, 'constructive abstention' also looked like the least non-attractive option for the three attending frontrunners for permanent membership in the Security Council. Brazil and Germany were unwilling to directly oppose measures that might halt mass atrocities of civilians in eastern Libya, as much news reporting and intelligence suggested were in the cards over the next few weeks. As also India came to the same conclusion, Russia found itself virtually isolated in its opposition against the creation of a no-fly zone. While comfortable in a minority view, Moscow did not enjoy the prospect of becoming the sole outlier in the council. Were a major massacre to occur in the city of Benghazi, as many anticipated, the Russian leadership would have to take the brunt of what would have been universal criticism from governments and international civil society alike. Grudgingly, it appears, Moscow eventually bowed to the considerable pressure.

Resolution 1973 and its interpretations

Resolution 1973 was adopted on 17 March 2011. It mandated the use of force through the phrase 'all necessary measures' in order to achieve the objective of protecting civilians in Libya, although it explicitly prohibited the use of ground forces in doing so. Acting under Chapter VII of the UN Charter, the Security Council for the first time since its inception in the mid-1940s expressly endorsed the use of force for the primary purpose of protecting the civilian population of an individual country, an objective grounded in the Geneva Conventions as well as in the R2P doctrine aiming to thwart mass atrocities.

> Authorizes Member States that have notified the Secretary-General, acting nationally or through regional organizations or arrangements, and acting in cooperation with the Secretary-General, to take all necessary measures, notwithstanding paragraph 9 of resolution 1970

(2011), to protect civilians and civilian populated areas under threat of attack in the Libyan Arab Jamahiriya, including Benghazi, while excluding a foreign occupation force of any form on any part of Libyan territory.[31]

The following paragraph, highlighting the importance of consultations with the Arab League on regional issues related to peace and security, was seemingly critical to allow for the passing of the resolution, for reasons explained above. A source of subsequent disappointment, however, was that the Arab League and other regional organizations played virtually no role once the resolution had been adopted and military operations set in motion.

Recognizes the important role of the League of Arab States in matters relating to the maintenance of international peace and security in the region, and bearing in mind Chapter VIII of the Charter of the United Nations, requests the Member States of the League of Arab States to cooperate with other Member States in the implementation of paragraph 4.[32]

The portions of the resolution which authorize the setting up of a no-fly zone were directly linked to the purpose of protecting civilians, a feature appreciated by the R2P constituency that is as keen on the means being used to achieve this being effective as it is on insisting that they are proportionate to the humanitarian objective. In reiterating the overarching purpose when outlining the conditions for establishing and enforcing the no-fly zone, the risk of overreach would appear to have been restricted:

Decides to establish a ban on all flights in the airspace of the Libyan Arab Jamahiriya in order to help protect civilians.[33]

A second paragraph regulating the flight ban at a superficial reading appeared to say, as was just mentioned, that the Arab League would have a continued role in the implementation of the no-fly zone. On closer scrutiny, however, the more consequential aspect turned out to be that UN member states were authorized to act 'nationally or through regional organizations or arrangements'. The latter clearly opened the door either for a coalition of the willing, or for the transatlantic alliance, to assume responsibility for implementing the no-fly zone.

Authorizes Member States that have notified the Secretary-General and the Secretary-General of the League of Arab States, acting nationally or through regional organizations or arrangements, to take all necessary measures to enforce compliance with the ban on flights imposed by paragraph 6 above.[34]

Even after specifying the use of force in several such respects, many governments and diplomats at the UN no doubt realized the potential for alternative interpretations that lay in the text. As demonstrated in the reservations expressed after taking the vote on 17 March, the permanent representatives of China and Russia were far from naïve. After listing several reservations regarding a draft that extended beyond the Arab League appeal and left questions about the situation in Libya and the use of force unanswered, Ambassador Churkin declared that Russia abstained from the vote due to a commitment to the protection of Libya's civilian population and with reference to 'common humanitarian values that we share with both the sponsors [of the resolution] and other Council members'. For its part, China stated that it had 'serious difficulty with parts of the resolution' yet 'attaches great importance to the relevant position by the 22-member Arab League on the establishment of a no-fly zone over Libya', and therefore similarly abstained from voting.

India, Brazil and Germany voiced lesser concerns, largely linked to unanticipated and unintended consequences of military action. It was nonetheless clear that all three struggled with weighing those concerns against thwarting what might have become a major humanitarian disaster in North Africa. At the same time, other council members appeared to take comfort in the fact that this was the first ever resolution that authorized the use of 'all necessary measures' for the purpose of protecting civilians and civilian inhabited areas.[35] And the broad, robust mandate signified to some that the UN was less likely to be ineffective in, or made hostage to, an escalating military situation. In Bosnia and Herzegovina in the early 1990s, many could recall, no-fly zones had been established with a much weaker mandate, allowing military and paramilitary forces to carry out massacres despite the presence of UN troops.

At the point of its adoption, however, a number of legal difficulties were still unknown. For instance, controversy later arose over the 'necessity' requirement in the core passages of the resolution ('all necessary measures') from the way in which the resolution was applied. A narrow interpretation would place strict constraints on military action with regard to the concept of necessity, especially since the stated objective of the council resolution was one of protecting civilians along the lines of international humanitarian law. A wide interpretation could produce the reverse conclusion, citing the escalating violence that originated within the regime itself as justification for unleashing a broad range of measures designed to suppress further violence against civilians and civilian populated areas, as well as to prevent future violence by downgrading the means by which the regime would be in a position to launch attacks with such consequences.[36]

Hardly surprisingly, the politics of justification proceeded far beyond council deliberations and even the duration of the NATO-led military operation. By 2012–2013 the views on how the status of the R2P norm had been affected by the adoption of resolution 1973 and its application in Libya differed across a wide range, reflecting the contested nature of the original debate and the struggle over the legacy of Security Council action in February and March 2011. Ramesh Thakur, a key author of the ICISS report in his capacity as UN Assistant Secretary-General and professor of international relations at the Australian National University, favourably cited resolution 1973 as 'a triumph' for Libya's citizen soldiers as well as for R2P.[37] Others, by contrast, appear convinced that the Libya intervention demonstrated that R2P is an inherently flawed notion,[38] whereas a third category of commentators maintain that it can only prove viable over time and if it overcomes various challenges associated with implementation.[39]

Conclusion

The pivotal role of the permanent five member states in the Security Council is probably the most widely known conventional wisdom regarding that institution, and reasons for awarding veto power to those particular great powers have been explored at length by policymakers and scholars. As was mentioned at the outset, few doubt that the *raison d'être* of the UN Security Council continues to reside in its *être*, that is, its mere existence as the most authoritative forum for great power deliberations on peace and security. Indeed, since its inception in the UN Charter in the aftermath of the Second World War the UN Security Council has faced most challenges to world peace and security by either passing a resolution that urges the parties to a conflict to show restraint but without taking concrete action itself, or by failing to add it to the Security Council agenda in the first place.

Yet it is clear that the potency of an institution such as the UN Security Council, which in one sense therefore mainly 'exists to exist', becomes more difficult to sustain when its significance rarely is put to the test, even when the discrepancy between words and deeds is glaring. The council's overall legitimacy comes from respecting procedures and living up to its primary objective but also from producing tangible results, at least when the immediate interests of the permanent five are not directly jeopardized. Also member states that have little interest in supporting a majority view regarding a particular course of action are therefore under pressure to contribute – at least from time to time – to the pursuit of secondary, more specific, collective goods so as to keep the institution relevant. While the Security Council first of all seeks to live up to its primary role pertaining to matters of peace and security, it cannot ignore values such as justice, equity and representativeness.

The 'perfect storm' that brought together a wide set of circumstances conducive to an intervention designed to protect civilians in early 2011 projected a slightly more activist future trajectory for the Security Council, but politically it appears to have got ahead of itself. In a period when the council has become increasingly questioned for its limited representativeness, efficacy and implementation weaknesses, as well as for its selective approach to dealing with specific issues related to peace and security, the permanent five member states are acutely aware that they need to be receptive to the arguments and sentiments of other countries, including the pro-humanitarian constituency that forms a large portion of the broader UN community. The council relies heavily on this constituency to help provide critical resources to UN operations as well as on countries that take seriously their contributions as non-permanent member states, and as such partake directly in the council's deliberations.

Meanwhile, the outcome of the Security Council's decision to act decisively during the 2011 Libya crisis is a mixed one on several levels, when assessed in the aftermath of a military intervention that lasted for five months. Mass atrocities in the city of Bengazi were prevented, as well as in other cities where rebel fighters resisted the crackdown of the regime. But some 30,000 Libyans perished in the military struggle that accompanied the intervention and in the harsh humanitarian situation that ensued.

In some preliminary evaluations, furthermore, the 'regional collateral damage' was not at all taken into consideration. Many today agree that the situation in neighboring Mali, for instance, would probably not have become so precarious in 2012–2013, had not the Libyan regime collapsed and a variety of weapons gone astray, together with the returning mercenary soldiers that Gaddafi previously had employed.

Then, of course, once outright military combat between the Gaddafi regime and rebel forces had been unleashed, a protracted civil war was quite likely to have caused an even higher level of casualties in Libya proper. The Libyan state within its present borders might have been dismembered, given the renewed tensions between the eastern and western parts of the country, plus those between the north and the south. In fact, Libya might have been facing a very prolonged civil war also if NATO's Unified Protector operation had been put under too restrictive rules of engagement. In many ways, proponents of the Libya intervention insist, the situation might have been akin to that disastrous stalemate which 2011–2013 evolved in Syria.

But then, what about the Security Council and its primary mandate to ensure peace and security in the world? Has the humanitarian legal agenda been advanced or reversed as a result? It is clear that one-third of the Security Council decided not to endorse resolution 1973. Moreover, not a single one of the so-called four BRIC (Brazil, Russia, India and China) countries – two of which are permanent members of the Security Council and the other two acknowledged front-runners for a permanent seat there – voted in its favour. On the other hand, one might suspect that the political leaders of Brazil, India as well as Germany, which held rotating seats in 2011–2012, were wary of antagonizing either of the permanent five member states on one of the most consequential decisions taken in recent years, so as not to create resentment on either side of the dispute. At least two or three of the non-permanent council member states, in other words, may have abstained in part so as to create more political space for others to join that 'ambivalent/reluctant yet constructive' position which made the resolution possible.

In that respect it could be pointed out that China and Russia, in not opposing the resolution, acted precisely in the spirit of the ICISS which gave rise to the R2P norm in its original shape. The ICISS had namely urged the Security Council, and its permanent member states in particular, to practice 'constructive abstention' more frequently. In allowing for the resolution to go ahead despite various reservations, the two great powers most closely affiliated with the pro-sovereignty, non-interventionist view on the Security Council indicated an unusual degree of flexibility when it comes to dealing with a specific humanitarian contingency. If the right lessons are drawn from the experience of implementing resolution 1973, that readiness to assess a set of unique features of a given situation combined with an evolving set of generic criteria for unleashing 'all necessary measures' just might, over the long term, help bolster the humanitarian dimension of international law and at the same time enhance the legitimacy of the Security Council and the global security regime of which it remains the linchpin.

Notes

1 D.L. Bosco, *Five to Rule Them All: The UN Security Council and the Making of the Modern World*, Oxford: Oxford University Press, 2009, 6.
2 I. Hurd, *After Anarchy: Legitimacy and Power in the United Nations Security Council*, Princeton: Princeton University Press, 2007, 187.
3 C. Gray, *International Law and the Use of Force*, Oxford: Oxford University Press, 2008, 3rd edition, 13–14.
4 T. Dunne and J. Gifkins. (2011) *Libya and R2P: Norm Consolidation or a Perfect Storm?* Online. Available: www.opendemocracy.net/tim-dunne-jess-gifkins/libya-and-r2p-norm-consolidation-or-perfect-storm (accessed 14 February 2013). A roughly analogous phrase, referring to a 'singularly unique moment where the international stars [...] had aligned', is used in A. Johnson and S. Mueen (eds) *Short War, Long Shadow: The Political and Military Legacies of the 2011 Libya Campaign*, London: Royal United Services Institute, 2012, 4.
5 E. Voeten, 'The Political Origins of the UN Security Council's Ability to Legitimize the Use of Force', *International Organization* 59, 2005, 227–57, at 259.
6 'All necessary measures' is Security Council terminology for the legal use of military force, as mandated by Chapter VII of the UN Charter.
7 N. Wheeler, *Saving Strangers: Humanitarian Intervention in International Society*, New York: Oxford University Press, 2000, 295.
8 Ambassador Susan E. Rice, cited in Dunne and Gifkins, *Libya and R2P*, 522.
9 C. Henderson, 'International Measures for the Protection of Civilians in Libya and Côte d'Ivoire', *International and Comparative Law Quarterly* 60, 2012, 767–78, at 267.

10 United Nations (2004) *A More Secure World: Our Shared Responsibility. Report of the Secretary-General's High-Level Panel on Threats, Challenges and Change*, New York: United Nations, 66 (paragraph 203). Online. Available: www.un.org/secureworld/report2.pdf (accessed 14 February 2013).
11 D. Amnéus, *Responsibility to Protect by Military Means: Emerging Norms on Humanitarian Intervention*, Stockholm: Department of Law, 2008, 201–2.
12 A. Orford, *International Authority and the Responsibility to Protect*, Cambridge: Cambridge University Press, 2011.
13 T. Meron, 'Geneva Conventions as Customary Law', *American Journal of International Law* 81, 1987, 348–70.
14 K. Parker and L.B. Neylon, 'Jus Cogens: Compelling the Law of Human Rights', *Hastings International and Comparative Law* 12, 1988–89, 427–43, at 441ff; D. Fleck, 'The Law of Non-International Armed Conflict', in D. Fleck (ed.) *The Handbook of International Humanitarian Law*, New York: Oxford University Press, 2008, paragraph 135.
15 J.M. Lehmann, 'All Necessary Means to Protect Civilians: What the Intervention in Libya Says about the Relationship between the Jus in Bello and the Jus ad Bellum', *Journal of Conflict and Security Law* 17, 2012, 117–46, at 122.
16 United Nations, *A More Secure World*, 4.
17 Henderson, 'International Measures for the Protection of Civilians', 767–8.
18 Lehmann, 'All Necessary Means to Protect Civilians', 122–7, 138.
19 S. Adams (2012) *Libya and the Responsibility to Protect*. Online. Available: www.globalr2p.org/media/files/libyaandr2poccasionalpaper-1.pdf (accessed 14 February 2013); Lehmann, 'All Necessary Means to Protect Civilians', 140–1.
20 Henderson, 'International Measures for the Protection of Civilians', 771–2.
21 See Chapter 3 in this volume by Holst and Fink.
22 UN Department of Public Information (2011) *Security Council Press Statement on Libya*. Online. Available: www.un.org/News/Press/docs//2011/sc10180.doc.htm (accessed 14 February 2013).
23 Ambassador Abdurrahman Mohamed Shalgham, cited in United Nations Security Council, S/PV/6490, Security Council meeting on 'Peace and Security in Africa', 25 February 2011. UN Department of Public Information (2011) *Peace and Security in Africa*. Online. Available: www.un.org/en/sc/meetings/records/2011.shtml (accessed 14 February 2013).
24 Dunne and Gifkins, *Libya and R2P*, 519–21.
25 Dunne and Gifkins, *Libya and R2P*, 518–19.
26 BBC News (2011) *Libya: G8 fails to Agree on No-Fly Zone*. Online. Available: www.bbc.co.uk/news/world-africa-12747875 (accessed 14 February 2013).
27 B. Plett (2011) 'How Libya's UN Diplomats Split in Two over Gaddafi', *BBC News*. Online. Available: http://news.bbc.co.uk/2/hi/programmes/from_our_own_correspondent/9407530.stm (accessed 14 February 2013).
28 I. Traynor and N. Watt (2011) 'Libya No-Fly Zone Plan Rejected by EU Leaders', *The Guardian*. Online. Available: www.guardian.co.uk/world/2011/mar/11/libya-no-fly-zone-plan-rejected (accessed 14 February 2013).
29 S. Xiao Yang, *China in UN Security Council Decision-Making on Iraq*, London: Routledge, 2013, 185–92.
30 Adams, *Libya and the Responsibility to Protect*, 15.
31 United Nations Security Council (2011) *Resolution 1973 (2011)*, United Nations. Online. Available: www.un.org/en/sc/documents/resolutions/2011.shtml (accessed 14 February 2013).
32 Ibid.
33 Ibid.
34 Ibid.
35 Dunne and Gifkins, *Libya and R2P*, 522.

36 Lehmann, 'All Necessary Means to Protect Civilians', 130–1. See also Chapter 8 by Mohlin in this volume.
37 R. Thakur (2012) *Libya and the Responsibility to Protect: Between Opportunistic Humanitarianism and Value-Free Pragmatism*, International Coalition for the Responsibility to Protect. Online. Available: www.responsibilitytoprotect.org/index.php/crises/190-crisis-in-libya/4066-ramesh-thakur-institute-for-security-studies-libya-and-the-responsibility-to-protect-between-opportunistic-humanitarianism-and-value-free-pragmatism (accessed 14 February 2013).
38 A. Hehir (2011) 'The Illusion of Progress: Libya and the Future of R2P', in *The Responsibility to Protect: Challenges and Opportunities in Light of the Libyan Intervention*, e-International Relations, 18–19. Online. Available: www.e-ir.info/wp-content/uploads/R2P.pdf (accessed 14 February 2013).
39 A.J. Bellamy and P.D. Williams, 'The New Politics of Protection? Côte d'Ivoire, Libya and the Responsibility to Protect', *International Affairs* 87, 2011, 825–50; Dunne and Gifkins, *Libya and R2P*.

3 A legal view on NATO's campaign in Libya

Fredrik A. Holst and Martin D. Fink[1]

Introduction

Late at night, on 17 March 2011, a statement was released from the United Nations (UN) in New York that ran as follows:

> Demanding an immediate ceasefire in Libya, including an end to the current attacks against civilians, which it said might constitute 'crimes against humanity', the Security Council this evening imposed a ban on all flights in the country's airspace – a no-fly zone – and tightened sanctions on the Qadhafi [sic] regime and its supporters.
>
> Adopting resolution 1973 (2011) by a vote of 10 in favour to none against, with 5 abstentions (Brazil, China, Germany, India, Russian Federation), the Council authorized Member States, acting nationally or through regional organizations or arrangements, to take all necessary measures to protect civilians under threat of attack in the country, including Benghazi, while excluding a foreign occupation force of any form on any part of Libyan territory – requesting them to immediately inform the Secretary-General of such measures.[2]

The statement accompanied the adoption of UN Security Council Resolution (SC Res.) 1973 that authorized the use of armed force in Libya. The Security Council's (UNSC) decision resulted in two multinational military operations. The first generally became known as *Operation Odyssey Dawn* (OOD) and was launched by a coalition of states only a day after Resolution 1973 was adopted. About a week later, a second multinational operation was launched that superseded OOD; the NATO-led force *Operation Unified Protector* (OUP).[3]

This chapter aims at highlighting some legal aspects of NATO's military engagement in Libya. The legal aspects can be considered from several different strands of which three, indeed intertwined, have caught particular interest of the authors. One concerns the questions that have arisen on the scope of the authority of the UNSC. The Council's actions with regard to Libya spurred the debate among scholars on the notion of the responsibility to protect (R2P) as a legal ground to deploy an armed force to stop human rights violations.[4] This strand will only be briefly touched upon in this chapter. The second strand considers the interpretation of the mandate in the resolution itself. Did for instance the SC Res. 1973 ultimately authorize regime change in Libya or did it not? As a third strand, one can mention the legal aspects from a more operational perspective. This strand focuses on the translation of the mandate into military activities. How was the language of the resolution used to conduct the military campaign?

Two aspects or core questions must be addressed when analysing the Libya campaign from these last two strands. First, what was the legal basis for the use of force in Libya and what are the general questions that could be raised regarding resorting to use of force by the military (*ius ad bellum*)? We take on this aspect by analysing how SC Res. 1973 – with the UN mandate – was interpreted, in light of the notions humanitarian intervention and responsibility to protect. Second, what laws were referred to and how were they implemented? This emanates from what general questions could be raised about the laws of armed conflict (*ius in bello*) as applicable to military operations. For OUP this is done by analysing how the resolutions and the international humanitarian law were interpreted at the operational level.

The next section will briefly introduce the framework of the international law applicable to military operations. Section 3 will deal with this chapter's main focus – the third strand – and consider how NATO interpreted the legal framework and conducted its military campaign, including the less known operations at sea. The chapter will end with conclusions and some thoughts for the future (section 4). An overview of the legal aspects is given in Figure 3.1.

The legal framework

Traditionally, international law is divided into two major areas of law: the law of peace and the law of war – both of which have relevance to our understanding of the legal dilemmas that NATO faced during the Libya campaign.

The law of peace is rather extensive and comprises, for instance, of the law of diplomatic relations, the law of the sea and international human rights law (IHRL), which also continues to apply during armed conflict (although derogations could be made in reference to IHRL). Within the area of law of peace the 'sub-area' of the law of conflict prevention can be found. Governmental organizations that have a purpose to mitigate tensions between states have their origin in this legal realm. The most obvious is the United Nations with its Charter. Within its overall aim of maintaining, and preventing breaches of, international peace and security,[5] the UN Charter for instance regulates an important part of the conditions on the

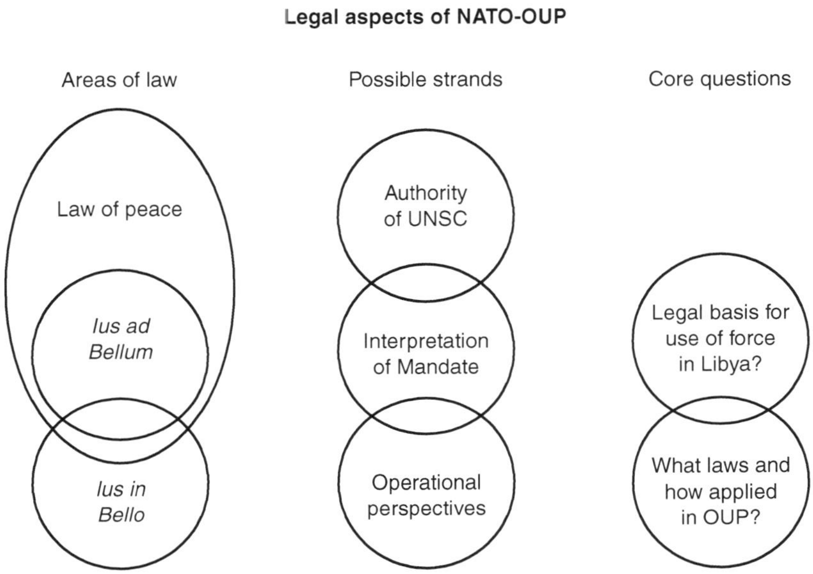

Legal aspects of NATO-OUP

Figure 3.1 Overview of the legal aspects.

use of force in international relations. In public international law this is known as constituting an essential part of the *ius ad bellum*.

The laws of war (*ius in bello*), often called Laws of Armed Conflict (LOAC) or International Humanitarian Law (IHL, which also used henceforth),[6] are one of the most important legal regimes during armed conflict and occupation. In order to ensure protection of civilians and to regulate the warfare during armed conflict, the application of IHL should not be influenced by *ius ad bellum*, in the sense that the rules in armed conflict apply without taking into account the reasons behind the conflict and whether those reasons were, or were not, legitimate. A conflict that possibly was started on illegal grounds does not therefore exclude the application of IHL, by any party. However, a mandate that embodies the notion of R2P, in fact, may influence the manner in which the principles of IHL, such as proportionality and military necessity, are interpreted.[7]

In short, IHL covers the conduct of operations (means and methods), and what protection combatants and non-combatants enjoy under certain circumstances. In addition to IHL and rules on belligerent occupation *ius in bello* also includes rules on neutrality. Other areas of international law may remain applicable throughout the conflict. Most notably, and for the purposes of this chapter, the law of the sea and international human rights law (IHRL) remains applicable during conflict and must be taken into account whilst conducting military operations.[8]

IHRL, generally no longer to be seen as peace-time area of law only, plays an important role particularly where an intervening state conducting military operations outside its own territory assumes what is known as 'effective control' over an area. The European Court of Human Rights (ECtHR) has not addressed the situation in Libya. By analogy the current views of the court on the issue however suggest that NATO did not have sufficient effective control over Libya to bring it within the jurisdiction of OUP states thus triggering the extra-territorial application of IHRL, *because* NATO did not have any actual presence on the ground.[9] Notwithstanding its relevance in the overall sense this is the primary reason why IHRL will stay outside the scope of this chapter.

Ius ad bellum

In international law the prohibition on the use of force is well grounded in both treaty law and international customary law, and even considered a peremptory norm (so-called *ius cogens*).[10] After the Second World War, a prohibition on the use of force was adopted in article 2(4) of the UN Charter. This article must be read in conjunction with the other fundamental rules in article 2 of the Charter, such as the responsibility for states to settle their international disputes peacefully, and the obligation for the UN not to intervene in domestic matters. Article 2(4) reads:

> All Members shall refrain in their international relations from the threat or use of force against the territorial integrity or political independence of any state, or in any other manner inconsistent with the Purposes of the United Nations.

The Charter also includes two exceptions to the prohibition on the use of force. First, according to article 51 of the UN Charter, nothing limits the inherent right of a member state to use force in self-defence if it is subject to an armed attack.[11] The second exception to the prohibition on the use of force is when the UNSC exercises its right to adopt collective security measures. These measures can be found in Chapter VII of the UN Charter. In the initial article of Chapter VII (Art. 39), it is stated that the UNSC has to:

> determine the existence of any threat to the peace, breach of the peace, or act of aggression and shall make recommendations, or decide what measures shall be taken in accordance with Articles 41 and 42, to maintain or restore international peace and security.

In other words, the UNSC has a broad mandate to determine collective actions against for instance a state that is acting against the prohibition on the use of force.[12] Article 41 of the Charter allows for taking economic and other measures against a state, short of the use of armed force, for example the interruption of economic relations and severance of diplomatic relations. Article 42 includes actions with the use of armed force, in situations where the UNSC considers that the article 41 measures would be, or have proven to be, inadequate.[13]

Humanitarian intervention

Apart from the exceptions on the prohibition on the use of force within the framework of the UN Charter, there are also a number of possible exceptions that are not mentioned within the Charter's framework. The most obvious example that has no explicit base in the Charter is the controversial humanitarian intervention.[14] As Andrew Clapham notes there has been a:

> developing recognition of the need to repress and prevent international crimes, such as genocide and crimes against humanity, [which] has been linked to the developing possibility of a right for a state to intervene militarily in another state on humanitarian grounds (so-called 'humanitarian intervention').[15]

Also Christine Gray sees a change in attitude: states that earlier were reluctant about or in opposition to a wide interpretation of article 2(4) have over time become more open.[16] She sees the 'current debate [as] ... a reincarnation of earlier disagreements on the interpretation' and refers to discussions among scholars where:

> the controversy centred on the second part of Article 2(4): should the words 'against territorial integrity or political independence of any state, or in other manner inconsistent with the purposes of the United Nations' be construed as a strict prohibition on all use of force against another state, or did they allow the use of force provided that the aim was not to overthrow the government or seize the territory of the state and provided that the action was consistent with the purposes of the UN?[17]

Various criteria have been presented to justify a 'humanitarian intervention'.[18] In a public statement on humanitarian intervention, the UK Foreign Affairs Committee at the turn of this century (further) outlined the conditions that should apply. It should be a response to an overwhelming humanitarian catastrophe, without any realistic domestic solutions in sight and with the UNSC in a state of inactiveness; the response must be 'collective, proportionate, likely to achieve its objective and carried out in accordance with international law'.[19] Another frequently mentioned criterion is that the intervention should be carried out without ulterior motives, such as expansive national policy objectives, solely aimed at stopping the humanitarian crisis. The force must neither be directed towards the territorial integrity, nor against the political independence of the state that will be intervened.

A responsibility to protect

The invocation of humanitarian concerns to legitimize military operations has been much criticised after NATO's intervention in Kosovo in 1999, but did not disappear from the options. On the contrary, the political and legal currents of humanitarian intervention that spun off around 2000 evolved into a closely related doctrine called 'Responsibility to protect' (henceforth R2P).[20] R2P was formally endorsed at the UN World Summit in 2005, when representatives agreed that:

> 138. Each individual State has the responsibility to protect its populations from genocide, war crimes, ethnic cleansing and crimes against humanity. This responsibility entails the prevention of such crimes, including their incitement, through appropriate and necessary means. We accept that responsibility and will act in accordance with it. The international community should, as appropriate, encourage and help States to exercise this responsibility and support the United Nations in establishing an early warning capability.[21]

Bruno Pommier gives a background and states:

> Specifically, R2P rests on three pillars: first the responsibility of each state; second, the responsibility of the international community to support a particular state in exercising its responsibility to protect its people; and finally, in cases where a state fails in its duty, the responsibility of the international community to take diplomatic, humanitarian action or other means to stop these violations. While initially non-violent, these additional measures may be extended to armed or unarmed coercive means, as authorized under Chapter VII of the UN Charter. According to those who developed R2P, responsibility for the use of force should be guided by strict criteria: seriousness of the harm done to the population; a just cause for intervention; intervention as a last resort; proportionality of the means used and an assessment of its consequences. While these criteria ... as such are not formally attached to the concept [it] does not detract from their relevance.[22]

Although quite similar to the conditions for humanitarian intervention as developed over time one can assume that with this concept states might find it easier to justify the use of armed force against another state if it fails to protect its people. Given a development in this direction a strict interpretation of the UN World Summit text still would assume a UNSC approval before resorting to military force. Ideally such approval is provided, but what if not – would states or organisations 'give-a-go' because they are more comfortable with R2P? That question remains open.[23]

Clapham states that 'We can say that in light of recent failure ... there is a greater expectation that effective protection will be offered in the face of ongoing genocide or crimes against humanity.'[24] This expectation seems not to hinder Clapham, as it appears, from being sceptical. With reference to the situation in Darfur he concludes that '[t]he grand principle of the responsibility to protect looks rather hollow from the perspective of today's victims of armed conflict.'[25] The debate is ongoing whether or not R2P is the development or even replacement – a natural heir – of humanitarian intervention, or if it constitutes a recognized principle under international law at all.[26] Even if considered a remake or political concept or doctrine rather than a new norm of international law, the notion of responsibility to protect has lifted a sensitive issue back on the agenda. Uniquely, in the Libya conflict, the UNSC put the notion of R2P into action.

Ius ad bellum and Libya

In the Libya case the UNSC took steps that followed the collective security system of the UN Charter to authorize the use of force against Libya. At the emergence of the conflict and during the ongoing military operations, the UNSC adopted four resolutions (1970 (2011), 1973 (2011), 2009 (2011) and 2016 (2011)) that are accounted for below.

The deteriorating situation in Libya in February 2011 first led to the adoption of SC Res. 1970. The resolution condemned 'the violence and use of force against civilians' and recalled 'the Libyan authorities' responsibilities to protect its population', indeed a specific reference to the first of the three pillars of R2P. SC Res. 1970 adopted mandatory economic sanctions, explicitly taken under article 41 of the UN Charter. It imposed a travel ban, an asset freeze on certain named individuals close to the regime and an arms embargo. It also created a Sanctions Committee that would oversee the implementation of the sanctions. Furthermore, and uniquely, the resolution referred the matter in Libya to the International Criminal Court (ICC). This paved the way for the Chief Prosecutor to seek arrest warrants and in June to issue three arrest warrants by the Court, for Qaddafi himself, for his son Saif Al-Islam and for his intelligence chief, Al-Senussi. The arrest and subsequent detention of Saif Al-Islam in November 2011 by the Libyan interim authorities ultimately led to a jurisdictional dispute over his trial between the Libyan authorities and the ICC.[27] Al-Senussi was captured in Mauritania and ultimately handed over to Libya. In November 2012 the ICC indicated that the trials probably could be held in Libya given its Office of the Prosecutor deems the country's legal system able of providing due process and a fair trial.[28]

Despite the UNSC adoption of SC Res. 1970 the Libyan leadership seemed to do little or nothing to comply with the demands for 'an immediate end to the violence'. In early March Qaddafi started to use military aircrafts for attacks on his own population, which prompted the call for a no-fly zone to (NFZ) be established.[29] When the UNSC adopted SC Res. 1973, it authorized member states ('acting nationally or through regional organizations') to use 'all necessary measures' to fulfil the mandates on the protection of civilians and establish a no-fly zone. The phrase 'all necessary measures' is widely accepted as authorizing the use of armed force within the limitations of the mandate.[30] Although not stated explicitly, it is clear that the UNSC adopted this resolution under article 42 of the UN Charter.[31] A third mandate with regard to the arms embargo that was adopted in SC Res. 1970 was issued, with the less enforcing phrase to use 'all measures commensurate to the specific circumstances'.

In September, the UNSC adopted SC Res. 2009. This resolution made some adjustments to the arms embargo. The Libyan authorities – no longer considered the Qaddafi regime – were permitted to receive arms if intended solely for security or disarmament assistance.[32] SC Res. 2009 also created the *United Nations Support Mission in Libya* (UNSMIL), which was the first step in the direction of post-conflict thinking. Ultimately, in October 2011 the UNSC adopted SC Res. 2016 which ended its provided authority to use force to protect civilians. The UNSC however kept the economic sanctions in place.

In one of the opening paragraphs of UN Res. 1973 the UNSC, on 17 March 2011, states that it is: '*Reiterating* the responsibility of the Libyan authorities to protect the Libyan population..'. It emphasizes the concept of R2P and frames the mandate to use armed force within the realm of this notion. R2P also appeared to be the justification for states and international organizations, both to support the UNSC in the above-mentioned resolutions, and for the subsequent military contribution and engagement in NATO's OUP. For instance, already by 10 March 2011, the European Union Parliament stressed that 'the EU and its Member States must honour their Responsibility to Protect, in order to save Libyan civilians from large-scale armed attacks; [and] points out that no option provided for in the UN Charter can therefore be ruled out.'[33] At the UNSC itself, upon the SC Res. 1973 decision, the French minister of foreign affairs, the Lebanese representative, whose country along with France and the UK was one of the initiators of the resolution, and the Colombian representative highlighted the human rights violations and therefore the need to protect the civilian population.[34] Furthermore, as another example, along with the UNSC Res. mandate itself, the *particular* basis for the Swedish government motion on OUP participation, presented late March 2011, was the protection of civilians, although the R2P principle was not spelled out explicitly.[35]

The authorization of the use of force and the R2P mandate did not explicitly authorize regime change. The measures taken based on the mandate of 1973 may not have had the *purpose* of regime change in Libya and may have genuinely been based on the concerns of violations of human rights, but it is certainly arguable that the mandate did open a door to regime change as a *result* of intervening military operations, which eventually in fact happened. Although article 2(7) of the UN Charter[36] states a principle that it is prohibited to intervene in domestic matters of member states, it also states that this principle does not prejudice the application of enforcement measures that the UNSC takes under Chapter VII. The unfortunate effect of the Libya military campaign for the notion of R2P is that the same notion now could be politically linked to regime change, at least in situations where a government is the main actor against its own population. Although it is arguable that in other cases regime change may not be the outcome of a military intervention, the results of the Libya campaign may have resulted in a more reluctant use of R2P.

Ius in Bello

The laws of war with IHL is the body of law that aims to protect civilians during armed conflict and sets rules for the application of force in armed conflict. The number of treaties and customary rules that are part of the IHL framework is vast and detailed. The essence is generally captured in a number of intertwined, but separate principles, such as humanity, distinction and necessity. It applies during situations of armed conflict. IHL furthermore distinguishes between international armed conflicts (IAC) and non-international armed conflict (NIAC), to which specific parts of IHL apply. In other words, once the threshold of armed conflict is passed, another question relates to the nature of the conflict; if it should be characterized as an international or internal (non-international) armed conflict.

Common Article 2 to all of the four Geneva Conventions (1949) states:

> the present Convention shall apply to all cases of declared war or of any other armed conflict which may arise between two or more of the High Contracting Parties, even if the state of war is not recognized by one of them...[37]

Whether an armed conflict exists is judged by the factual circumstances.[38] Because there is no clear-cut definition of armed conflict, the question whether or not an armed conflict exists has developed also through case law, such as the *Haradinaj*,[39] *Boškoski*[40] and *Tadic*-cases, all from the International Criminal Tribunal for Former Yugoslavia (ICTY). In the latter case, the ICTY considers when a situation of armed conflict exists. In one of the most quoted passages, the Court found that:

> An armed conflict exists whenever there is a resort to armed force between States or protracted armed violence between governmental authorities and organized armed groups or between such groups.[41]

In an international context this *normally* means that, for instance, single skirmishes in a border area or a short change of fire at sea does not reach the level of armed conflict. In a non-international – domestic – context it has been accepted that insurrection or riots with less violence and no or very limited military coordination *normally* does not reach the level of armed conflict. In fact, the writing in the Second Additional Protocol to the Geneva Conventions (AP II), Art 1(2) could be deemed as representing customary international law:

> This protocol shall not apply to situations of internal disturbances and tensions, such as riots, isolated and sporadic acts of violence and other acts of a similar nature, as not being armed conflicts.[42]

In the same Article, 1(1) the scope, or material application, of the Protocol also is presented positively. It applies:

> to all armed conflicts which are not covered by Article 1 ... [of AP I] ... and which take place in the territory of a High Contracting Party between its armed forces and dissident armed forces or other organized armed groups which, under responsible command, exercise such control over a part of its territory as to enable them to carry out sustained and concerted military operations...[43]

It could be concluded that the traditional distinction between the different types of conflicts remains in the two 1977 Additional Protocols to the Geneva Conventions of 1949 (AP I and II). The first supplements the four from 1949 on international armed conflicts (IAC) and the second 'specifically states that it develops and supplements Article 3 common to the four Geneva Conventions', on non-international armed conflicts.[44]

From this it could be understood that the mentioned article, Common Article 3, was the one and single regulation which aimed at 'armed conflicts not of an international character' until the adoption of the two Additional Protocols (and in particular AP II).[45] It extends 'the most rudimentary principles of humanitarian protection to those persons taking no active part in hostilities and placed *hors de combat*'.[46]

Assuming being on the verge of a NIAC, indeed the most common kind of conflicts today, how do we know whether there really is a conflict and, if so, which of the above-mentioned rules that applies: Common Article 3 only, or also AP II? James G. Stewart, who '[i]n the context of internationalized armed conflicts, which by definition contain both international and internal elements, [finds that] determining which set of rules applies and to what aspect of the conflict is critically important.'⁴⁷ He also states 'while providing greater clarity to the broad principles identified in common Article 3, Additional Protocol II set[s] a significantly higher threshold for its own application, limiting its scope.'⁴⁸ However, and no matter the 'bystanders' view', Elizabeth Wilmshurst claims that there is normally a 'reluctance of States to acknowledge that internal violence has reached the level of armed conflict and that the opposition must be regarded as an "equal" party to a conflict rather than a group of common criminals'.⁴⁹

Clearly, the determination of armed conflict, in particular of non-international character, provides challenges. In conjunction with this, the various triggers or thresholds, such as the application of AP II, need to be determined. Indeed a great responsibility normally lies with the state party, which from its own – political – perspective will be reluctant to acknowledge the existence of a conflict at all. Notably, Libya was one of the first contracting parties to AP II, ratifying it already in 1978.⁵⁰

As mentioned the IHL framework is vast and detailed and could therefore in no way be covered in a chapter like this. For our purposes of discussing the legal aspects of the Libya Campaign we will come back to some essential IHL rules and principles and how they were applied in OUP in section 3.⁵¹ Before doing so we believe it is important to elaborate on the determination of the conflict or conflicts in Libya. Although the ICRC, in its IHL Customary Law Study, has endeavoured to dismiss the distinction between IACs and NIACs where it concerns IHL that is considered customary law,⁵² it is not fully clear if the tendency goes towards a single standard. At least this was not a generally accepted standpoint during the Libya Campaign and arguably still is not why *both* the determination that armed conflicts exist *and* what area of law that is applicable in the conflict or conflicts remains to be of relevance.⁵³

Determination of the conflict in Libya

With regard to the conflict in Libya, two challenges arose and arise with regard to the determination of the applicable legal framework.⁵⁴ It first depends on what moment during the conflict this question is asked. And second, there is the issue in relation to *which parties* to the conflict this question is asked. As indicated the determination is important to decide what area of law, and which rules were applicable and to whom, for our purposes mainly to NATO and partner countries in the OUP mission.

The Libya uprising grew steadily from the turn of the year 2010/2011. Although no clear definition exists on when such a situation is reached, it is clear that the situation in early 2011 rose beyond the situation of internal disturbances to a situation that can be called a civil war, or NIAC. This factual and thus legal situation was concluded by the Human Rights

Council Commission to exist, at least from 24 February onwards based on its (then) preliminary findings.[55] The UNSC stated on 26 February in the preamble of SC Res. 1970 that:

> *Welcoming* the condemnation by the Arab League, the African Union, and the Secretary General of the Organization of the Islamic Conference of the serious violations of human rights and *international humanitarian law* [emphasis added] that are being committed in the Libyan Arab Jamahiriya.

With this factual situation, legally the threshold was passed to apply IHL applicable to NIACs, although peace time law such as IHRL also remained relevant.

The question then becomes whether AP II or only Common Article 3 of the Geneva Conventions was applicable? It appears that at the moment before the multinational military operations started, organized armed groups and dissident armed forces fought together and were carrying out operations against the Qaddafi-government. They appear also to have held territory east of Ajdabiyah, or at least the city and surroundings of Benghazi. It however remains open to debate whether the opposition at that stage actually acted under responsible command.

Accepting that AP II has a high threshold for application, this is the typical situation for which it was planned to be applied from the outset. Interestingly, in an undated Press Statement, the Libyan National Transitional Council (NTC) concluded that: 'We are bound by Common Article 3 to the four Geneva Conventions and to the provisions of Additional Protocol II Relating to the Protection of Victims of Non-International Armed Conflicts, as are the Qadhafi [sic] regime's forces.'[56] Remembering that Libya was one of the first contracting parties to AP II – thus indicating the acceptance by the Libyan forces under Qaddafi – nothing seemed to hinder the application also of that treaty.

After the initiation of the military operations of the Coalition (OOD) and NATO (OUP) started in March 2011, other actors stepped into the Libyan theatre, which changed the situation. Although NATO had never taken a stand on the character of the conflict (see below, section 3), it follows from the factual situation that NATO's military activities to protect the civilian population meaning that OUP *repeatedly* carried out military operations against pro-Qaddafi forces in Libya were to be seen within the context of an international armed conflict.

This has also been the view of the ICRC. An ICRC position paper on the Libya conflict concluded that:

> It is ... the ICRC's view that, irrespective of any *jus ad bellum* issue, the hostilities opposing the military forces deployed under the NATO-led Operation Unified Protector and the Libyan Armed Forces constitute

an armed conflict to which international humanitarian law applicable in international armed conflict fully applies *de jure*.[57]

In reality this meant that both parties in the IAC, the OOD followed by OUP on one side and the Libyan Forces under Qaddafi on the other assumed responsibilities that follows from IHL, such as the above mentioned principles (see further section 3). Also the (first) Human Right Council Commission report states that: 'The airstrikes to enforce the no-fly zone imposed by the Security Council through Resolution 1973, which began on 19 March brought into being an international armed conflict…'[58] As such, an IAC existed between NATO and the Qaddafi forces, and a NIAC between Qaddafi forces and the opposition. Once the military operations started, based on UN Res. 1973, both types co-existed at the same time. Although the UN appeared to have accepted the opposition as the new effective government in Libya in UN Res. 2009, and more and more states also 'recognized' the National Transitional Council (NTC) as the new government, the mandate of military operations (as based on SC Res. 1973) did not change.[59] Accordingly, OUP operated as before until the cessation of hostilities and until the mandate ended at the end of October with the adoption of UN Res. 2016.

From mid-September onwards, there could be different ways to view the status of the conflict. It could for instance be argued that the conflict by then once again became a NIAC between NATO and the NTC on the one hand and the former regime forces on the other, indicating that NATO now was invited by the new de facto rulers and thus was supporting NTC against the pro-Qaddafi forces.[60] Another non-UN Charter based – but from international law accepted – ground for intervening militarily is thus an unforced and sincere invitation of another, receiving, state.[61]

However, neither earlier nor during this latter part of the Libya campaign was such a shift in mandate, or formal agreement between NATO and the NTC reached. Given the unclear and still fragile situation – also in reference to governance – the stance of NATO did not change as long as civilians were still under threat from the pro-Qaddafi forces. From a practical perspective it would therefore be too simplistic to say the conflict again became a NIAC only. Although UN Res. 2009 spoke of 'the Libyan authorities', which was no more under the Qaddafi regime, no change to the mandate was thus made indicating that the authorized international armed force was in support of the [new] Libyan authorities.

Operation Unified Protector: NATO's interpretation and execution of the mandate

End goals

NATO's political end goals for its Libya campaign were determined during the Berlin Ministerial Meeting on 14 April 2011: all attacks on civilians and civilian populated areas were to end, Qaddafi was to withdraw his forces, and access to humanitarian aid was to be unhindered.[62] After slightly more than two months of NATO involvement the International Crisis Group concluded that: 'The expectations that NATO operations ... would be the final nail in Khaddafi's [sic] coffin has proved to be mistaken, and the resilience of the regime has been underestimated.'[63] Ultimately, the operations ended another five months later, on 31 October, shortly after Qaddafi's death, when the UNSC ended the authorization to use force, with the adoption of SC Res. 2016.

NATO organized its military campaign along the lines of the three sub-mandates stated in the operative paragraphs of SC Res. 1973. Under the overall military campaign two operations with three distinctive (but not separate) elements were ongoing: one operation enforcing the arms embargo; and one operation enforcing the no-fly zone, and executing the air targeting campaign to protect civilians and civilian populated areas. The fact that the UNSC did not authorize the occupation by land forces was widely discussed by scholars whether it meant that no land forces were allowed on the ground at all.[64] NATO took the political decision that OUP would not put forces on the ground in Libya.[65] Arguably, it made military operations from an air targeting perspective more challenging in urban areas, such as in Misratah or Sirte, which were under constant threat from Qaddafi's forces (see Nygren's Chapter 4 in this volume). According to media reports, the fact that NATO did not put forces on the ground did not stop individual states putting operators into Libya, albeit outside the scope of the NATO-mission and command structure (see Chapter 8 by Mohlin and Chapter 1 by Michaels in this volume).[66] NATO did however allow warships from OUP-participating countries to enter Libyan territorial waters (but for the purpose of protecting civilians only, see below 'Operations at sea').

NATO's press release on 31 October 2011, the day that the operation ended, states that a total of 26530 sorties, of which 9710 strike sorties were flown; a total of 3175 vessels were hailed, 296 vessels were boarded and 11 vessels were denied passage by the NATO fleet to Libyan ports.[67] For instance, 7642 air-to-surface weapons were dropped by the air assets, approximately 470 naval rounds were fired[68] and also illumination rounds were fired from warships over coastal areas.[69] The air operation initially involved only fixed wing air assets and unmanned aerial vehicles (UAVs), but from the beginning of June also included rotary wing assets (helicopters), provided by France and the UK, that were able to move closer onto targets, enabling better accuracy in built-up areas.[70]

Application of IHL in OUP

NATO did not issue a formal statement that legally characterized the conflict and NATO's position in it. As concluded above, the military operations did pass the threshold of an international armed conflict. Although NATO may have considered itself impartial in the (non-international) conflict, we would argue that in terms of legal application of IHL and by the application of force, it became a party to an international armed conflict.[71] Throughout its campaign, NATO carried out military operations observing IHL, which was reflected also in the targeting process and the rules of engagement (ROE, see below). Hence, IHL was applicable to NATO military operations and for its purposes OUP used AP I as basis.

Distinction, necessity – aspects of military objectives

One of the most fundamental principles when engaging in hostilities is to distinguish between civilians and combatants. Art. 48 AP I states the basic rule:

> In order to ensure respect for and protection of the civilian population and civilian objects, the Parties to the conflict shall at all times distinguish between the civilian population and combatants and between civilian objects and military objectives and accordingly shall direct their operations only against military objectives.[72]

The aim of attack must not only be objects that 'by their nature, location, purpose or use, make an effective contribution to military action', but also objects whose 'total or partial destruction, capture or neutralization, in the circumstances ruling at the time' offers a definite military advantage.[73] The latter sentence from article 52(2) AP I underlines the principle of military necessity.

The main part of the military campaign was the protection of civilians and civilian populated areas by means of a targeting campaign, mostly conducted through air operations. The operational focus of NATO's targeting in OUP was expressed during several press conferences. In one press briefing the Director of Operations, [then] Brigadier Robert Weighill, stated that NATO forces are 'successfully degrading the pro-Qaddafi forces' ability to coordinate their attacks by hitting their command and control centres, and … to attack ammunition storage sites in depth'.[74] Clearly, in its targeting policy NATO had not stopped short of only reactive operations in which civilians were physically in danger, but took a broader and more active approach in the interpretation of 'all necessary measures'. On this approach, Mehrdad Payandeh, discussing necessity in both *ad bellum* and *in bello*, seems to suggest a lenient interpretation in that: 'It is not required that each single act is strictly necessary to avoid violations of human rights in the sense that no alternative, less intrusive means is available.'[75] Clearly, the context must be taken into consideration. From a strict legal perspective, however, it could be argued that one cannot lessen the own requirements for single acts, or accept own forces' negligence even once. This goes both for the planning and the execution of operations.

Without addressing particular individual attacks others, such as the Russian Minister of Foreign Affairs Lavrov,[76] have suggested that the broad and active approach of the military campaign, at least at a certain stage, went beyond the given mandate. Pommier wrote that:

> Indeed, it appeared that the military operations, at least in part, were aimed at supporting the forces assembled by the National Transition Council (NTC) – the representative body of the Libyan opposition – in its efforts to rout the elements loyal to the regime. Once the threat of a massacre in Benghazi had been ruled out, but with actions by Gaddafi's [sic] troops against other cities continuing, the operations entrusted to the ... [NATO] continued, with an increasingly blurred line between the prevention of massacres on the one hand and, on the other, a systematic air campaign that aimed to dismantle the military apparatus and whose ultimate goal was regime change.[77]

In contrast to NATO's Kosovo campaign *Allied Force* in 1999, in which NATO targeted and damaged Serbia's oil infrastructure,[78] NATO's targeting policy in Libya generally appeared to exclude 'economic objects' such as oil refineries. Only in rare and exceptional cases did NATO consider these types of targets.[79] For instance, allegations of attacking oil infrastructures, such as the oil fields in the Sarir region were false allegations made by Qaddafi.[80]

Dual use objects

Many objects that were hit were targets that were clearly military by nature, such as tanks, air defence sites or ammunition dumps. NATO tried to separate the military command from the forces in the field by targeting, for instance, command-and-control nodes. In addition, weapons depots directly connected with servicing field forces were targeted to degrade the logistic support of Qaddafi's operations. From both operational and legal perspectives the least controversial targets were the air defence sites as they represented a threat to enforcing the no-fly zone (NFZ) and to the protection of the mission.

But also civilian objects that by their use could become legitimate military targets were attacked, such as residence buildings that according to NATO were used as command-and-control nodes. Although not a 'legal' term these are called dual use objects. On 30 July NATO air assets struck the transmission dishes of a television station, allegedly killing several persons although the NATO contention is that no-one was killed. Attacking television stations, such as NATO's raid on the television station in Belgrade in

1999, or the coalition attack on the television stations in Baghdad and Basra during the 2003 invasion of Iraq, have not been without criticism in the past.[81] The NATO press officer stated that the Libyan television station was 'being used as an integral component of the regime apparatus designed to systematically oppress and threaten civilians and to incite attacks against them'.[82] The strike was intended to degrade Qaddafi's use of the television station 'as a means to intimidate the Libyan people and incite acts of violence against them'.[83] Interestingly, the use of the state-owned television network and various other communication networks in threatening the civilian population appeared to have played an important part in the decision of the pre-trial chamber of the ICC to issue arrest warrants.[84]

In addition to the 'classic' TV-station example other objects were *discussed* from the military targeting perspective. These included for example bridge-like constructions in the vicinity of military installations and targets in the vicinity of the man-made water canals ('The Great Man Made River'). However, targets were refused due to the proximity of the canals. The provision of water to the population was considered as essential as was post-conflict restoration of services: this although it was suspected that even the system itself was being used as hide-outs by pro-Qaddafi forces.

Additionally, the difficulty in differentiating between Qaddafi forces and opposition forces was problematic for NATO forces. In two separate incidents, in April and June respectively, NATO aircraft bombed tanks that later appeared to be opposition forces operating in tanks. A NATO press release of the latter incident argues that the mistake took place because of the 'complex and fluid battle scenario'.[85] The Deputy Commander of OUP, Rear Admiral Russel Harding, used the same argument about the first incident.[86]

Qaddafi's forces did not just use solely military means, but also modes of operations, like the typical white pick-up truck that made them hard to distinguish from opposition forces.[87] Also the *Economist* reported that Qaddafi's forces were 'deploying civilian vehicles on the front line in the hope of confusing NATO's pilots'.[88] The deputy commander OUP said in an interview: 'We've seen them use private cars, trucks, technicals [flatbeds pick-up trucks with guns mounted on the back] sometimes hundreds at the time.'[89]

Qaddafi

Philippe Sands wrote in *The Guardian*:

> The authorization of 'all necessary measures' is broad and appears to allow the targeting of Qaddafi and others who act to put civilians 'under threat of attack', words that go beyond the need to establish a connection with actual attacks.[90]

However, another exclusion of targets was made from the outset of the operation: NATO kept underlining that Qaddafi was not a target. Clearly, it would have been extremely difficult to uphold the view that targeting Qaddafi specifically would not also directly result in another regime taking up the vacancy. NATO did strike at *Bab-al-Aziziyah* in Tripoli, a military compound containing a military headquarters, and which also held Qaddafi's residence.[91] On 14 April 2011, Presidents Obama and Sarkozy and Prime Minister Cameron wrote an open letter to the public, which stated that:

> Our duty and our mandate under U.N. Security Council Resolution 1973 is to protect civilians, and we are doing that. It is not to remove Qaddafi by force. But it is impossible to imagine a future for Libya with Qaddafi in power.[92]

The interpretation of the mandate by the United States, France and the United Kingdom seemed to be linked therefore to the political fate of Qaddafi that some would have seen as regime change.[93] Although not speaking for NATO, it may also be argued that politically the letter implicitly linked the success of the NATO-led operation to the permanent resignation of Qaddafi. In a press-conference Italian Brigadier General Claudio Gabellini, who participated in the targeting process of OUP at the operational HQ level in Naples, answered the question whether NATO considers Qaddafi as a target:

> our mandate is clear, to protect the population from the attacks ... NATO is not targeting individuals. No individuals are a target for NATO. We only look after command-and-control centre because we want the targets we're after ... to stop Mr. Qadhafi [sic] to give orders to his troops to keep slaughtering the civilians and to prevent humanitarian aid to enter the country. So, again,... we're not really interested in individuals, not in Mr. Qadhafi's [sic] life. We're after command-and-control centres.[94]

This view was repeated in a more general sense by NATO's Legal Advisor, Peter Olson, in a letter to the Human Rights Council Commission, in which he states that: 'As explicitly directed by the Operation plan for OUP as approved by the North Atlantic Council, no civilians, and no specific individual, civilian or military, were ever intentionally targeted in that operation.'[95] The commander of OUP, Canadian General Lieutenant Charles Bouchard, also repeatedly stated that 'I'm not doing regime change.'[96] The Chief of the British Armed Forces, General Sir David Richards in a mid-May 2011 interview expressed his own and slightly different approach on targeting Qaddafi: 'We are not targeting Gaddafi [sic] directly, but if it happened that he was in a command-and-control centre that was hit by NATO and he was killed, then that is within the rules.'[97]

The situation deteriorated and NATO assumed responsibility for the multinational military efforts justified by the mandate in SC Res. 1973. In this context it must be remembered that in an operation with 19 countries of which 14 were NATO countries there is a wide range of opinions, although to most of them it must have appeared obvious that the ousting of Qaddafi would have shortened the conflict(s) in Libya. To be able to work coherently under one unified command common documents and policies are drafted and put in place, such as operational plans, orders and guidelines. From this it must be understood that the high-level political rhetoric by leaders from some troop contributing nations will not automatically be transformed into military action and is also not very easily carried out in multinational military operations.[98]

Proportionality

Proportionality in the *ius in bello* context centralizes around the loss of civilian life. Even if an attack is limited to military objectives, planners and operators must take into account the risk of incidental harm to the civilian population. IHL however does not say that all civilian casualties are prohibited and a breach of IHL, but rather that incidental loss of civilian life, injury to civilians, or harm to civilian property must not be 'excessive in relation to the concrete and direct military advantage anticipated'.[99] So-called collateral damage that is not excessive is thus not prohibited.

Although high-tech and precision means (weaponry)[100] was used during the campaign, civilian casualties were not totally excluded. In its second report that also investigated a number of alleged casualties by NATO bombing, the Human Rights Council Commission concluded that: 'NATO conducted a highly precise campaign with a demonstrable determination to avoid civilian casualties. On some limited occasions the Commission confirmed civilian casualties and found targets that showed no evidence of military utility.'[101] Many of the air attacks were initially executed during the night to minimize the likelihood of civilian casualties, but at a later stage attacks during the day also occurred.[102] The Commission mentions 60 civilians killed during the NATO air attacks,[103] however it becomes evident from the exchange of letters between NATO and the Commission, that the Commission is satisfied that NATO did not deliberately target civilians.[104]

As said, IHL does not require a zero casualty rate with regard to civilians; however in situations such as the one in Libya, in which the mandate is specifically the protection of civilians, civilian casualties are extremely sensitive for the internal coherency, legitimacy and international acceptance of the mission. In other words one could argue that on the one hand in IHL a certain degree of civilian loss may be accepted in terms of implementing a task (or mandate). On the other hand civilian loss during OUP was not in line with the nature of the mandate and thus less acceptable, if at all. To execute a mandate that is based on R2P – explicitly stated or not – would therefore put extra constraints on the use of force and may affect proportionality considerations. A R2P-mandate accordingly has a tendency to blur the lines between *ius ad bellum* and *ius in bello*.

Precautionary measures

The general meaning of the principle of precautionary measures is contained in Rule 15 of the ICRC study on customary international humanitarian law and reads:

> In the conduct of military operations, constant care must be taken to spare the civilian population, civilians and civilian objects. All feasible precautions must be taken to avoid, and in any event to minimise, incidental loss of civilian life, injury loss of civilian life, injury to civilians and damage to civilian objects.[105]

In addition to the generally accepted principle of precaution under IHL, there are also specific rules in IHL on precautionary measures.[106] During the Libya campaign, general and specific warnings were issued by the NATO-led force. In particular, since no forces were on the ground, warnings as part of information operations became an important tool. For instance warnings were issued to the population with the purpose to have them stay away from military units and compounds.[107] Also throughout its campaign NATO engaged in extensive operations by means of psychological elements (or operations, so-called PsyOps). These operations were, among other things, meant to pressure Qaddafi forces into putting down their arms. This was done through a variety of means, such as radio messages and leaflet drops. An example of a leaflet is presented in Figure 3.2.[108]

Targeting process[109]

As said, NATO tried to separate the military command from the forces in the field by targeting, for instance, command-and-control nodes, weapons depots and air defence sites.

The operational level targeting process cycle at the Combined Joint Task Force (CJTF) HQ was run through daily *targeting working-groups* and *targeting boards* that validated the planned, so-called deliberate, targets. All the required specialists, from weapon specialists and intelligence personnel to political, legal and media advisors were part of these boards. The targets were ultimately presented to the commander of OUP, who could put forward his considerations and validation of the targets. In the evenings the *Air Tasking Order* was presented to the commander of OUP who on this occasion could get a condensed overview and put forward final considerations. If there were (additional) doubts the target was not engaged pending, for instance, further intelligence.

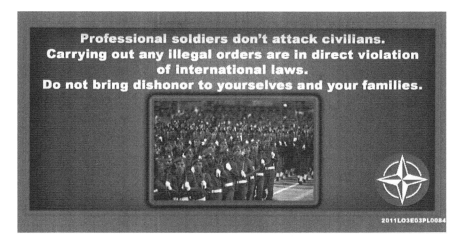

Figure 3.2 Example of leaflet distributed in Libya.[108]

Journalist Eric Schmitt describes the follow-on process after validation by the operational HQ:

> From Naples, the authorized target list is sent to an air operations center near Bologna, Italy, where a U.S. Air Force officer, Lt. Gen. Ralph J. Jodice 2nd, oversees the pivotal process of matching specified allied aircraft, armed with specific weapons, to specific targets to achieve the best effects on the ground with the least risk to civilians.[110]

In addition senior representatives from nations whose units would carry out the task could still 'pull red card' if in any way they disapproved of the use of their units to engage the target. Normally this was done if the specific targets or mission planned fell outside the limits of the national mandate. Like in other operations one of the most challenging aspects during OUP was at times where targets, not on a particular list or yet fully validated, were upcoming and deemed time-sensitive by air crews. Although carried out in a 'fast-track' this so-called dynamic targeting must also be subject to legal advice.

NATO Rules of Engagement

An essential instrument to regulate force in military operations are the rules of engagement (ROE). 'Effective targeting, in accordance with Rules of Engagement, is essential to achieve mission success and to maintain international support' is a paraphrased quote of the OUP commander's intent, given the authors' best recollection. The manner in which ROEs are created and the documents used in their creation are unclassified.[111] NATO's ROE for a specific mission are however confidential. In general, ROE consist not only of rules that have a legal character, such as IHL, but also include political and military/operational aspects.[112] The application of ROE does not stand on its own, but must be understood in conjunction with the mandate, the legal regimes applicable and other internal guidelines, such as targeting guidelines or guidelines for avoidance of collateral damage. Generally speaking, before force can be used, at least a four stepconsideration must be made: IHL and other considerations such as IHRL; UN and NATO-mandate considerations; ROE; and finally other internal guidelines that shape NATO's execution of the operation.[113] In addition, national mandates could influence the choice of assets including the possibility to use force.

The legal advisor plays an advisory role, for instance in the drafting process of the ROE, which is done by operators.[114] Specific mission ROE for OUP were first drafted at NATO's Joint Force Command level headquarters. In conformity with standard NATO ROE planning, the draft ROE were requested up the chain of command, and were ultimately authorized by the North Atlantic Council (NAC), NATO's highest political body. After authorization, the ROE were implemented by SACEUR[115] into its subordinate command levels. This comprehensive way of handling ROE which includes many different levels, the changing or revision of ROE during a campaign is not a quick and easy thing to do. As in OUP it implies reinterpretation of existing ROE in the light of new situations that occur, rather than change or addition of ROE. Of course there is a limit to the amount of leeway that can be given to interpreting the existing rules. Had that been the case in OUP the authors believe that the perceived reluctance to request additional ROE would have been overcome.

Because of the phased manner in which NATO ultimately started OUP and took on the different sub-mandates from the resolution, rather unusually, the operation had two operational plans (OPLANS) with two different ROE-profiles or catalogues (one for embargo operations, one for protection of civilians including no-fly zone), to be applied in one overall campaign.[116] One of the challenges, in particular at sea (see below), therefore was to understand under what circumstances which ROE-set would be applicable.

As NATO in essence consists of a group of individual member states, in which none have a say over the other, they can restrict (via so-called caveats) their own national forces from certain authorities or activities that are allowed under NATO ROE. The same right exists for partnership countries and other states that take part in NATO-led operations.[117] Because states participating in OUP took a piece-meal approach to involvement with its military means, it is not surprising that caveats existed on the use of military means during OUP. The governments of the Netherlands and Sweden for example restricted their F-16s and Gripen fighter jets respectively not to be engaged in air-to-ground attacks. At sea, OUP contributor discussions included initial geographical restrictions, for instance not to sail in the territorial sea of Libya. Having caveats caused and causes additional challenges for military planners and commanders, since they might not be able to use forces to the extent desired. At the appropriate levels in the NATO command, several states deployed additional national legal and political advisors and other representatives to ensure that their forces were deployed within their national political, operational and legal limits.

Operations at sea

The maritime operations in OUP basically consisted of two parts that supported two elements of the mandate: first, the UN-mandated maritime arms embargo operation and, second, the maritime operations that supported the protection of civilians and civilian populated areas. As mentioned above, SC Res. 1970 put the arms embargo regime in place. The UNSC specifically stated that the measure was taken under article 41 of the UN Charter, which does not allow for the use of armed force to enforce the adopted sanctions. SC Res. 1973 expanded the authority for actual enforcement of the arms embargo on the high seas. SC Res. 2009 made some changes in the manner in which way the arms embargo was to be implemented (see further below).[118] Finally, with the adoption of SC Res. 2016 the UNSC ended the authorization for military operations.

At a first glance, the embargo seemed a rather standard type of arms embargo and appeared to be executed as such. But because of the wording the UNSC used to authorize the arms embargo regime, it featured several aspects that made this one unique compared to other maritime arms embargo operations that have been enforced, for instance in relation to the crisis in Iraq, Former Yugoslavia, Haiti, Sierra Leone, or off the coast of Lebanon. To name just one example here, the Libya embargo included the wording that '[r]easonable grounds to believe' were needed in order to carry out inspections by boarding a vessel. In other words patrolling ships were not allowed to approach or halt ships arbitrarily. This constituted a higher threshold than the more traditional wording of: 'to halt *all* inward and outward shipping' (emphasis by authors), which has been the usual phrase coined by the UNSC in relation to enforcing embargoes at sea.[119]

The operational area

NATO's maritime operational area for the purpose of the arms embargo was situated outside the territorial waters of Libya. The text of the UN-resolution appeared only to authorize sanctions to be enforced on the high seas (which normally means that an interpretation including the

Economic Exclusive Zone (EEZ) is acceptable). Therefore, NATO established a maritime surveillance area (MSA) that did not include the territorial sea of Libya, or any other territorial seas.[120] This construction allowed in practice physical manoeuvre room for both sides in the conflict to move vessels within the territorial sea and internal waters from one port to another. For instance, weapons and ammunition allegedly kept moving into Misratah, the city under siege.[121] It also kept open the door to the adjacent territorial seas of Tunisia and Egypt. Interestingly, when one considers NATO's area of operation to protect civilians and civilian populated areas this was clearly situated within the Libyan territory which includes the Libyan sea territory. As mentioned earlier, the mandate only prohibited occupational forces. Arguably, sailing warships in the territorial sea could not have been considered an occupational force. Consequently, OUP naval assets that were mandated by their nations were able to move closer to the coast and enabled them to take on *other* measures than enforcing economic sanctions or stopping arms or mercenaries; measures that would minimize the harm against civilians, such as mine clearing operations, or naval gunfire support (land-attacks from the sea, see also below).

Enforcement of arms embargo or interception to protect civilians; stopping mercenaries, arms, arms related materiel, and other items

Unique for a maritime embargo operation, but not surprising in light of the fact that Qaddafi appears to have used *armed mercenary personnel* to suppress the Libyan people, the resolutions authorized the stopping of mercenaries. Thus, the issue was not so much the authority to detain persons but rather what to do next with persons if captured in the maritime domain. The issue of mercenaries however proved to have little application at sea. Rather the main issue became the *arms embargo*. This also included *arms related materiel*. As such, this broadened the scope of items that could be stopped (again outside the Libyan territorial waters).

From an early stage of the conflict the Libyan regime forces not only resorted to military items, but also to civilian ones that could be used to sustain the war effort. What was then defined as *arms related materiel*? For example, did it include flatbed trucks, on which guns (as mentioned above) could easily be mounted? Could a load of imported lorries be halted, which although not arms related as such, could on reasonable grounds be remade and used for military purposes? One view that arguably broadened the scope of items that could be stopped was that it was permissible to stop such items under the (other) mandate that allowed all necessary means to protect civilians and civilian populated areas. The issue was highlighted in relation to refined oil products such as petroleum, which to a large extent is imported to Libya.[122] *The Economist* grasped the essence of the situation and noted that:

NATO is also stopping seaborne fuel from reaching the regime. On May 19th it prevented a tanker, the *Jupiter*, from delivering its load. Worried by this precedent, the Indian crew of a bigger vessel, the *Cartagena*, has since refused to let its 37,500-tonne cargo of fuel be delivered to Tripoli. On June 13th one of the colonel's sons, Hannibal, who controls the state-owned General National Transport Maritime Company (GNMTC), sent a tugboat full of Libyan sailors to take control of the *Cartagena* and bring it home. The plan failed.... NATO justified its interdiction of the *Jupiter* on the ground that its fuel would have been used by the army to attack civilians.[123]

From this example it appears that the mandate of *protection of civilians* also justified the stopping of items that would have been used to ultimately harm civilians. In other words, OUP occasionally did expand the enforcement of the arms embargo under the *protection of civilians* mandate to justify its actions, and it was not necessarily contrary to the UNSCR mandate. At the same time, NATO – conscious of the risk of a 'slippery slope' – did not want to be accused of mission-creep towards a full trade embargo or blockade, which in turn could be seen as a support for regime change.

On the one hand, NATO wanted to enforce the mandates. On the other hand, it also wanted to minimize the impact on merchant shipping. To underline this, the commander of OUP Maritime Component Command, Vice Admiral Rinaldo Veri, announced early on that:

> This mission is not only about enforcement. There are ships out there trying to carry out legitimate business with Libya. The country needs supplies ... My headquarters and the crews of the NATO maritime group carry out an essential coordination role to allow these legitimate movements to take place. We tell these ships exactly what they must do, and if they follow all our instructions they can proceed with minimum disturbance.[124]

However, as a matter of prediction in particular for merchant shipping, the NATO information proved to be a challenge in what specific items could be transported to and from Libya.[125]

Naturally, the practical aspects of dealing with possible non-compliant ships were discussed within NATO. Although the situation never arose, one potential solution included the establishment of so-called diversion ports. Authorized personnel in these ports were supposed to take over the inspection once there was a suspicion that a vessel had breached the resolutions. If activated and required this would have allowed for thorough inspections and further judicial actions under national law.

Protection of civilians from the sea

Occasionally, there were also hostile activities at sea and from the shore against naval vessels[126] which forced NATO-led forces to react. Following mine-laying in late April 2011, in the vicinity of Misratah and the use of inflatable boats rigged with dummies and explosive devices,[127] preparedness to support civilians with humanitarian aid into Libya was taken to engage the Libyan forces as their activities posed a serious threat to the traffic to Misratah. Under the mandate of protection of civilians, naval gunfire support (NG(F)S) was launched on a number of occasions against targets on land. This followed thorough planning to avoid possible collateral damage. In fact, one experience the UK Royal Navy has drawn from OUP, with both legal and operational elements, is that the existing weapon systems on naval vessels are not adapted for directing naval gunfire support with desired precision.[128]

Persons in distress at sea

Another issue encountered by NATO naval assets was the large stream of refugees that tried to reach the European mainland via the sea. The Italian island of Lampedusa has at times been flooded with people fleeing from North Africa, something which increased from the beginning of the so-called Arab Spring. The Libyan crises exacerbated the situation. With more people going into vessels with poor buoyancy during bad weather conditions it also resulted in a greater number of fatalities at sea. Debate arose on who was responsible for the rescue operations, which led to different discussions, such as on the responsibilities of individual warships that were also in the command-chain of OUP.[129] For instance the Council of Europe took a strong interest in one of the incidents that happened at the beginning of the operation and investigated who was responsible for the lives lost at sea.[130] In a reaction to the Council of Europe investigation, NATO mentioned that it *aided* the rescue of over 600 migrants in distress at sea and that commanders of warships are fully aware of their responsibility under the international law of the sea.[131] From this, the NATO position was drawn that rendering assistance at sea remains a national responsibility. The Netherlands government also underlined with regard to rendering assistance that NATO as an organization does not have a formal responsibility or role in rescue operations.[132] After several incidents, the Italian Minister of Foreign Affairs Frattini, argued that NATO, based on the UN mandate, should seek a broader interpretation of the mandate to include responsibility for refugees at sea.[133]

Conclusions

OUP commenced at the end of March 2011 and ended seven months later, on 31 October 2011, shortly after Qaddafi's capture and death. After the operation Admiral James G. Stavridis, NATO's Supreme Allied Commander, and the US-representative to NATO, Ivo Daalder, concluded: 'By any measure, NATO succeeded in Libya.'[134] The main aim of this chapter was to consider the legal aspects, in particular at operational level, of NATO's military operations in Libya. By way of conclusion and possibly a future outlook, three concluding remarks can be made.

First, it is clear that the interpretation of a mandate based on responsibility to protect has a very high potential of blurring the dividing lines between protecting civilians and activities that go beyond that, such as regime change. In particular this will be the case if it is the regime that is attacking the civilians in the first place. In theory, terms such as protecting civilians and regime change may not appear to be very close to each other, or at least we are able to see the difference – again in theory. The reality, with the politics involved, however appears to be much more blurred and harder to separate. It is a fact that as a result of NATO airstrikes the equation between the opposition forces and Qaddafi's forces changed. It is also a fact that ultimately Qaddafi was removed from power, which opened the door to a new regime to settle in Libya. When the opposition forces reached the outskirts of Tripoli, the commander of OUP was asked about his role in the opposition advancement. He answered:

> [...] and let me make myself perfectly clear, the only people that are causing violence against the population are pro-Qadhafi [sic] forces. These are the forces that we will bring to an end. *Ours is not to support any anti-Qadhafi [sic] advance, but rather to bring an end to the violence against the population.* [Emphasis by authors] And that is what we are doing. Thank you very much. I have to go back. So have a good day.[135]

The UN spokesman stated in a press-conference in August that: 'the Secretary-General believes that resolution 1973 has been used properly in order to protect civilians in Libya and he has continually emphasized the need, as this proceeds, to make sure that civilians in Libya will be protected.'[136] Therewith, the UN had seemed to give its approval to the overall manner in which NATO was conducting its operations and that the mission objectives were carried out within the mandate.

Second, military operations based on the responsibility to protect, R2P, or protection of civilians mandate, are likely to be viewed with even more scrutiny with regard to civilian casualties than current military operations already are. Such a mandate and the use of high level precision weaponry, combined with increased media pressure and inquiry committees that are charged with investigating incidents, increasingly seems to push military operations towards zero civilian casualty wars as the only publicly and politically accepted level. From a legal perspective, this level is stricter than the established legal parameters within which hostilities may be conducted. The acceptance of fewer and fewer civilian casualties creates an impression that the law of armed conflict has been breached in situations, when in fact, it was not. This may diminish the [moral] legitimacy of the overall military operation. Interestingly, responsibility to protect as a basis for military operations also appears to have effect on the *ius in bello* aspects of conducting hostilities, as it may have effect on the questions of proportionality and necessity, at least in the sense of moral (normative) legitimacy but possibly also of legal (practical) legitimacy. There may be both a higher threshold of military necessity and a different, stricter, interpretation of what is deemed excessive, seen against the purpose of the mandate. If not legally, then at least morally the acceptance of civilian casualties becomes a politically sensitive issue when executing a R2P-mandate. The operational realism of this must however be taken into account.

Third, and last, the Libya operation has shown from a maritime perspective that naval forces must be prepared to operate in a 'multi-role' capacity. The Libya campaign put some naval forces in both an enforcement role in reference to economic sanctions and arms embargo, as well as supporting an 'all necessary measures' mandate that involved kinetic targeting. As such, naval forces were an integral part of the overall mandate (including the protection of civilians), and not just there to prevent certain items reaching land from the sea. In addition, the Libya campaign showed that the maritime dimension must take into consideration that refugee streams may be an issue not only on land, but similar challenges which could affect the mission occur also at sea.

Notes

1 The views expressed in this chapter are those of the authors alone and do not necessarily coincide with their governments, or with the NATO view.
2 Excerpt from the UN Security Council 6498th Meeting (Night). UN Department of Public Information. (17 March 2011) *Security Council approves 'no-fly zone' over Libya, authorizing 'all necessary measures' to protect civilians, by vote of 10 in favour with 5 abstentions.* Online. Available: www.un.org/News/Press/docs/2011/sc10200.doc.htm (accessed 15 February 2013).
3 A number of military initiatives by individual states were also undertaken during the Libya campaign that did not fall under the command of the NATO-led force. See for instance Mohlin's Chapter 8 in this volume.
4 On this topic, see for instance: A.J. Bellamy and P.D. Williams, 'The new politics of protection? Côte d'Ivoire, Libya and the responsibility to protect', *International Affairs* 87: 4, 2011, 825–50. Online. Available: http://.doi/10.1111/j.1468–2346.2011.01006.x/pdf (accessed 17 January 2013); and C. Pippan, 'The 2011 Libyan uprising, foreign military intervention, and international law', *Juridikum: Zeitschrift für Kritik–Recht–Gesellschaft* 2, 2011, 159–69. Online. Available: http://ssrn.com/abstract=1878444 (accessed 15 February 2013).
5 See article 1 of the Charter of the United Nations.
6 On the differences between LOAC and IHL, see: R. Kolb and R. Hyde, *An Introduction to the International Law of Armed Conflicts*, Oxford: Hart, 2008, Chapters 3 and 4.

7 Notwithstanding this, it must be emphasized that far from all military operations (with or without a UN Mandate) will reach a conflict level where *ius in bello*-principles or rules (IHL) become applicable.
8 See, for instance, M. Milanovic, 'Al-Skeini and Al-Jedda in Strasbourg', *European Journal of International Law* 1, 2012, 121–39. About the overlap between IHL and HRL this is for instance discussed in a condensed form in J.M. Henckaerts and L. Doswald-Beck, *Customary International Humanitarian Law. Introduction to ICRC Study*, Cambridge: Cambridge University Press, 2005, Vol. 1, p. xxxi. See also Kolb and Hyde, *An Introduction*, Chapter 33.
9 The precise definition of 'effective control' for the purposes of the application of IHRL is a matter of substantial judicial and academic debate. It is beyond the scope of this chapter. See generally Milanovic, 'Al-Skeini', 122.
10 This principle evolved to its current form via the Covenant of the League of Nations after the First World War and in the 1928 Kellog-Briand Pact that prohibited aggressive war. About use of force see, for instance, Y. Dinstein, *War, Aggression and Self-Defence*, Cambridge: Cambridge University Press, 2001, 3rd edn, 78–98.
11 Self-defence may be exercised by the member state itself (individually), or upon its request by several states, collectively. Article 51 states that actions based on self-defence must immediately be reported to the UNSC, and that actions based on self-defence will only continue until the Council has taken 'such action as it deems necessary in order to maintain international peace and security'. Apart from the Charter requirement of being subject to an armed attack, other substantive requirements also exist for states to exercise the right of self-defence, which include that the reaction must be immediate (proximity in time), necessary (the wrongful invader or its agents remains an imminent threat) and proportionate (the applied use of force aims at repelling the invader and restoring order).
12 In reality the UNSC over time has determined on collective actions in order to limit the effect of matters other than traditional use of force which possibly could pose a threat to peace and security. See, for instance, C. Gray, *International Law and the Use of Force*, Oxford: Oxford University Press, 2008, 3rd edn, 55–9 and 193–253.
13 See for instance O. Bring, *FN-stadgan och världspolitiken – om folkrättens roll i en föränderlig värld*, Stockholm: Nordstedts juridik, 2002, 4 uppl. [edn], 277–9.
14 P.A. L. Ducheine and T.D. Gill, 'De legitimering van statelijk geweldgebruik', *Netherlands Annual Review of Military Studies*, 2011, 216–34, at 229.
15 A. Clapham, *Human Rights – A Very Short Introduction*, Oxford: Oxford University Press, 2007, 61.
16 Gray, *International Law*, 36 (example of the UK in early 1990s).
17 Ibid., 31.
18 See, for example, T.D. Gill, 'Humanitarian intervention', in T.D. Gill and D. Fleck (eds) *The Handbook of the International Law of Military Operations*, Oxford: Oxford University Press, 2010, Chapter 13.
19 Foreign Affairs Committee (7 June 2000) *Select Committee on Foreign Affairs Fourth Report*, UK House of Commons, para. 141. Online. Available: www.publications.parliament.uk/pa/cm199900/cmselect/cmfaff/28/2813.htm (accessed 15 February 2013).
20 The evolution of R2P is briefly recounted in Engelbrekt's Chapter 2 in this volume. See further D. Amnéus, *Responsibility to Protect by Military Means – Emerging Norms on Humanitarian Intervention*, Stockholm: Department of Law Stockholm University, 2008 and D. Amnéus, *A Right to Humanitarian Intervention?* Stockholm: The Living History Forum, 2008, 13. Online. Available:

www.levandehistoria.se/files/A%20right%20to%20humanitarian_final.pdf (accessed 15 February 2013).
21 World Summit Outcome, GA Res. 60/1, 15 September 2005, UN Doc A/RES/60/1, para 138, 2005.
22 B. Pommier, 'The use of force to protect civilians and humanitarian action: the case of Libya and beyond', *International Review of the Red Cross* 884, 2011, 1063–83, 1066.
23 Following a speech before the Swedish National Defence College Association (Föreningen FHS), 21 February 2011 (just before the UNSC action on Libya), the [then] chairman of EU's Military Committee, General Håkan Syrén, responded to a question from the audience (one of the authors) in relation to the situation in Northern Africa: 'Would EU engage in armed operations without a prior UNSC mandate?' It was ruled out by a laconic 'No'.
24 Clapham, *Human Rights*, 2007, 62 (reference for instance to Bosnia-Herzegovina and Rwanda).
25 Ibid.
26 See, for example, the statement in Pommier, 'The use of force to protect civilians', 1066.
27 D.D. Kirkpatrick and M. Simons, 'Jurisdiction feud over Qaddafis heats up', *International Herald Tribune*, 23 March 2012, 5. Online. Available: www.highbeam.com/doc/1P1-204036394.html (accessed 15 February 2013).
28 Office of the Prosecutor (7 November 2012) *ICC Prosecutor Statement to the United Nations Security Council on the situation in Libya, pursuant to UNSCR 1970 (2011)*, ICC. Online. Available: www.icc-cpi.int/en_menus/icc/press%20and%20media/press%20releases/news%20and%20highlights/Pages/ICC-Prosecutor-Statement-to-the-United-Nations-Security-Council-on-the-situation-in-Libya,-pursuant-to-UNSCR-1970-(2011).aspx (accessed 15 February 2013).
29 De NOS (6 March 2011) *Libië zet oorlogsvliegtuigen in tegen rebellen*, De NOS. Online. Available: http://nos.nl/artikel/223560-libie-zet-oorlogsvliegtuigen-in-tegen-rebellen.html (accessed 1 December 2012).
30 See, for instance, R. McLaughlin, 'The legal regime applicable to use of lethal force when operating under a United Nations Security Council chapter VII mandate authorizing "all necessary means"', *Journal of Conflict and Security Law* 3, 2007, 389–417.
31 In Article 42 of the UN Charter the SC 'may take such action by air, sea, or land forces as may be necessary to maintain or restore international peace and security' if 'measures provided for in Article 41 would be inadequate or have proved to be inadequate'.
32 SC Res. 2009, para.13.
33 European Parliament, Resolution of 10 March 2011, on the Southern Neighbourhood, and Libya in particular, P7_TA(2011)0095, para. 10. Online. Available: www.europarl.europa.eu/sides/getDoc.do?pubRef=-//EP//TEXT+TA+P7-TA-2011-0095+0+DOC+XML+V0//EN (accessed 15 February 2013).
34 On the arguments and commentaries, as well as legal aspects, surrounding the adoption of UNSCR 1973, see UN Security Council, Press Release on the Security Council's 6498th Meeting (Night), UN Doc. SC/10200, 17 March 2011, or the meeting notes, UN Doc S/PV.6498, 17 March 2011, and M. Payandeh, 'The United Nations, military intervention, and regime change in Libya', *Virginia Journal of International Law* 2, 2012, 383ff. Online. Available: www.vjil.org/assets/pdfs/vol. 52/issue2/Payandeh_Post_Production.pdf (accessed 15 February 2013).
35 Regeringens proposition 2010/11:111, *Svenskt deltagande i den internationella militära insatsen i Libyen*, Regeringen, 2011. Online. Available: www.regeringen.se/content/1/c6/16/49/75/8b46bcd2.pdf (accessed 15 February 2013).

36 Article 2(7) UN Charter reads as follows:

> Nothing contained in the present Charter shall authorize the United Nations to intervene in matters which are essentially within the domestic jurisdiction of any state or shall require the Members to submit such matters to settlement under the present Charter; but this principle shall not prejudice the application of enforcement measures under Chapter VII.

37 Common Article 2 to the four Geneva Conventions of 1949.
38 A publication dedicated in full to the issue of determination of conflicts is E. Wilmshurst (ed.), *International Law and the Classification of Conflicts*, Oxford: Oxford University Press, 2012. In part the issue was also dealt with during the 31st International Conference of ICRC in late 2011, see the report *International Humanitarian Law and the Challenges of Contemporary Armed Conflicts* 31IC/11/5.1.2, Geneva: ICRC, 2011. Online. Available: www.icrc.org/eng/resources/documents/report/31-international-conference-ihl-challenges-report-2011-10-31.htm (accessed 15 February 2013).
39 Prosecutor v. Ramush Haradinai e.a., ICTY, 3 April 2008, IT-04-84-T.
40 Prosecutor v. Boškoski and Tarčulovski, ICTY, 10 July 2008, IT-04-82-T.
41 Prosecutor v. Tadic, ICTY (Appeals Chamber), Decision on ... Jurisdiction, 2 October 1995, IT-94–1-AR72, para. 70. (Here the issue was discussed with reference to a non-international armed conflict and both Common Article 3 of the Geneva Conventions and Additional Protocol II.) A similar formulation was adopted in the Rome Statute (Article 8(2)(f)).
42 Protocol Additional to the Geneva Conventions of 12 August 1949, and Relating to the Protection of Victims of Non-International Armed Conflict (1977 Additional Protocol II), Art. 1(2).
43 Ibid., Art. 1(1).
44 A. Roberts and R. Guelff, *Documents on the Laws on War*, Oxford: Oxford University Press, 2000, 3rd edn, 196.
45 Common Article 3 to the four Geneva Conventions of 1949 stipulates in para. 2: 'that [t]he wounded and sick shall be collected and cared for' and the principles (in 3(1)) include prohibition of

> (a) violence to life and person, in particular murder of all kinds, mutilation, cruel treatment and torture; (b) taking of hostages; (c) outrages upon personal dignity, in particular humiliating and degrading treatment; (d) the passing of sentences and the carrying out of executions without previous judgment pronounced by a regularly constituted court, affording all the judicial guarantees which are recognized as indispensable by civilized peoples.

46 J.G. Stewart, 'Towards a single definition of armed conflict in international humanitarian law: A critique of internationalized armed conflict', *International Review of the Red Cross* 850, 2003, 317. Online. Available: www.icrc.org/eng/assets/files/other/irrc_850_stewart.pdf (accessed 15 February 2013). *Hors de combat* means '[left] outside the fight'.
47 Stewart, 'Towards a single definition', 319. While elaborating on Common Article 3 on page 318 Stewart concludes that it [only] 'defines certain principles and stipulates certain imperative rules' but 'does not contain specific provisions'.
48 Ibid. ('[H]igher threshold' aims at the above quoted passage in Additional Protocol II, Art 1(2) meaning a minimum in the degree of organization of the armed groups, including a responsible command, and capability of carrying out lasting and collected operations along with controlling parts of territory, something which was not an explicit demand in Common Article 3.)

49 Wilmshurst, *International Law*, 479 (referring to UK's position on Northern Ireland crisis).
50 See ICRC. Protocol Additional to the Geneva Conventions of 12 August 1949, and relating to the Protection of Victims of Non-International Armed Conflicts (Protocol II), 8 June 1977. Online. Available: www.icrc.org/ihl.nsf/WebSign?ReadForm&id=475&ps=P (accessed 13 July 2012).
51 Thus, there is no subsection here called, for instance, *Ius in bello and Libya*.
52 Henckaerts and Doswald-Beck, *Customary International Humanitarian Law*, Foreword by Jakob Kellenberger, p. x: 'State practice goes beyond what those same States have accepted at diplomatic conferences, since most of them agree that the essence of customary rules on the conduct of hostilities applies to *all* armed conflicts, both international and non-international.'
53 A challenge in this respect, in particular to multilateral military operations, is that states not only have different views on the application and interpretation of international law; they may not have ratified the same treaties or accept certain customary principles.
54 'Arose' mainly to NATO and others involved at the time and 'arise' to analysts, scholars, possible investigators and others after the conflict(s).
55 Human Rights Council 17th Session, *Report of the International Commission of Inquiry to investigate all alleged violations of international human rights law in the Libyan Arab Jamahiriya*, UN, 1 June 2011, A/HRC/17/44, Advance unedited version, 4 and 30. Online. Available: http://www2.ohchr.org/english/bodies/hrcouncil/docs/17session/A.HRC.17.44_AUV.pdf (accessed 19 July 2012). (Hereinafter UN HRC, First Libya Inquiry) Interestingly, the ICRC however states that the unrest was 'reaching the level of conflict by March', see ICRC's 2011 report, 136.
56 See: National Transitional Council (2011) *Press statement*. Online. Available: http://ntclibyaus.files.wordpress.com/2011/08/ntc-ps-laws2.pdf (accessed 15 February 2013).
57 ICRC position paper, working document handed out during the 2011 NATO Legal Conference in Lisbon, 24–27 October 2011, on file with the authors.
58 UN HRC, First Libya Inquiry, para. 66.
59 Other states do not normally recognize governments as it [indirectly] could be seen as involvement in internal matters. This term anyway appears to be frequently used in situations when totalitarian regimes are ousted.
60 Compare, for instance, to the situation in Afghanistan where ISAF is supporting the government against the (ousted) Taleban and other anti-government forces.
61 Ducheine and Gill, 'De legitimering', 229 and Gray, *International Law*, 80–8.
62 Details from NATO Ministerial Meeting in Berlin 2011. NATO Press Release (14 April 2011) *Statement on Libya*. Online. Available: www.nato.int/cps/en/SID-E4A23ED5-3CFA2421/natolive/official_texts_72544.htm?mode=pressrelease (accessed 15 February 2013). This did not necessarily equate to the military end-state determined by the North Atlantic Council (NAC) and reinforced through the OUP Operational plans. It could be suggested that the Ministerial moved the goalposts, and had an impact upon (but did not change) the mission, as it made the likelihood of Qaddafi standing down a virtual impossibility.
63 Middle East/North Africa Report 107. *Popular protest in North Africa and the Middle East (V): Making sense of Libya*, International Crisis Group, 2011. Online. Available: www.crisisgroup.org/~/media/Files/Middle%20East%20North%20Africa/North%20Africa/107%20-%20Popular%20Protest%20in%20North%20Africa%20and%20the%20Middle%20East%20V%20-%20Making%20Sense%20of%20Libya.pdf (accessed 15 February 2013).

64 For instance N. Ronzitti (20 March 2011) *Intervento in Libia, cosa è permesso a cosa no*, Affar Internationali. Online. Available: www.affarinternazionali.it/articolo.asp?ID=1699 (accessed 15 February 2013); M. Shaw, 'Our Panel of legal experts discuss UK's basis for military action in Libya', *The Guardian*, 21 March 2011. Online. Available: www.guardian.co.uk/law/2011/mar/21/international-law-panel-libya-military (accessed 15 February 2013); and Payandeh, 'The United Nations, Military Intervention', 386.
65 The NATO website on Libya mentions that: 'No troops under NATO command were on the ground in Libya at any point during OUP'. *NATO and Libya*, Online. Available: www.nato.int/cps/en/natolive/topics_71652.htm (accessed 15 February 2013).
66 M. Mazetti, E. Schmitt and R. Somaiya, 'C.I.A. operatives present in Libya; Although West says no troops active, Britain and U.S. send agents', *International Herald Tribune*, 31 March 2011. Online. Available: www.iiss.org/whats-new/iiss-in-the-press/press-coverage-2011/march-2011/cia-operatives-present-in-libya-although-west-says-no-troops-active-britain-and-us-send-agents (accessed 15 February 2013).
67 Operational Media Update (31 October 2011) *NATO and Libya*, NATO, Online. Available: www.jfcnaples.nato.int/Unified_Protector/page191573217.aspx (accessed 15 February 2013).
68 Human Rights Council, 19th Session, 'Report of the International Commission of Inquiry on Libya', *UN Human Rights Council*, 2 March 2012, A/HRC/19/68, Advance unedited version, para 605. Online. Available: www.ohchr.org/Documents/HRBodies/HRCouncil/RegularSession/Session19/A_HRC_19_68_en.doc (accessed 15 February 2013) (hereinafter UN HRC, Second Libya Inquiry).
69 Letter by P. Olson on 23 January 2012, attached to the UN HRC, Second Libya Inquiry, Annex II, 5.
70 Unified Protector Press Release (4 June 2011) *NATO attack helicopters increase pressure on Qadhafi regime*, NATO. Online. Available: www.jfcnaples.nato.int/Unified_Protector/page19090381.aspx (accessed 15 February 2013).
71 This was also concluded by the First Libya inquiry; 'co-existing' and 'legally separate to the continuing non-international armed conflict' (para. 66). The question of who is the respective party in a multilateral military (peace) operation is a matter of some debate. There is not sufficient room to address the matter fully. However, NATO is an international organization with responsibilities and has therefore legal capacity.
72 Art. 48 AP I. See also articles 44(3) and 51 AP I, and art. 13 AP II.
73 Art. 52 (2) AP I.
74 Unified Protector Press briefing OUP Director of Operations (29 April 2011) *NATO having 'clear impact' relieving Libya violence*, NATO. Online. Available: www.jfcnaples.nato.int/Unified_Protector/page19090310.aspx (accessed 15 February 2013) and www.youtube.com/watch?v=Eny_HA01RCM (accessed 15 February 2013); Bellamy and Williams, The new politics of protection', 845.
75 Payandeh, 'The United Nations, military intervention', 385ff.
76 Y. Shestakov, 'Play by the rules, says Lavrov', *The Daily Telegraph*, 20 April 2011. Online. Available: http://rbth.ru/articles/2011/04/20/play_by_the_rules_says_lavrov_12782.html (accessed 15 February 2013).
77 Pommier, 'The use of force to protect civilians', 1068.
78 W.J. Fenrick, 'Targeting and proportionality during the NATO bombing campaign against Yugoslavia', *European Journal of International Law* 3, 2001, 489–502. Online. Available: http://ejil.oxfordjournals.org/content/12/3/489.full.pdf+html (accessed 21 January 2013).
79 E. Schmitt and D.E. Sanger, 'Tensions persist over Libya Goals', *International Herald Tribune*, 27 May 2011. See also C. Coughlin, 'Nato must target Gaddafi

regime, says Armed Forces chief Gen Sir David Richards', *The Telegraph*, 14 May 2011. Online. Available: www.telegraph.co.uk/news/worldnews/africaandindianocean/libya/8514034/Nato-must-target-Gaddafi-regime-says-Armed-Forces-chief-Gen-Sir-David-Richards.html (accessed 15 February 2013).

80 See Statement by NATO Joint Force Command Naples (7 April 2011) *Gaddafi attacks Libyan oil field*, NATO. Online. Available: www.nato.int/cps/en/natolive/news_72118.htm (accessed 15 February 2013).

81 A.P. V. Rogers, *Law on the Battlefield*, Manchester: Manchester University Press, 2004, 2nd edn, 82–3.

82 Statement by the Spokesperson for NATO Operation Unified Protector, Colonel Roland Lavoie, regarding air strike in Tripoli. NATO statement (30 July 2011) *NATO strikes Libyan state TV satellite facility*, NATO. Online. Available: www.nato.int/cps/en/natolive/news_76776.htm (accessed 15 February 2013).

83 Ibid. It could be argued that the activity that was being incited was a war crime – or Genocide as in the case of Rwandan radio misuse – in which case it is a crime of international jurisdiction and states can therefore take action to prevent its continuance.

84 See, for example, para. 77. ICC-01/11, Pre-trial Chamber I, *Decision on the 'Prosecutor's application Pursuant to article 58 as to Muammar Mohammed Abu Minyar Gaddafi, Saif Al-Islam Gaddafi and Abdullah Al Senussi'*, ICC, 27 June 2011.

85 Unified Protector Press release (19 June 2011) *Incident involving opposition forces on 16 June 2011*, NATO. Online. Available: www.jfcnaples.nato.int/Unified_Protector/page190902044.aspx (accessed 15 February 2013).

86 C.J. Chivers and K. Fahim, 'NATO acknowledges error in deadly airstrike', *International Herald Tribune*, 9–10 April 2011, 8. Note that it was challenging to judge if, for instance, a tank heading in the direction of civilian populated areas actually was driven by pro-Qaddafi forces, or rather had been seized and used by the rebels.

87 S. Erlanger, 'NATO says its hands are tied in air war', *International Herald Tribune*, 7 April 2011, 6.

88 The Economist, 'The colonel is running on empty', *The Economist*, 18 June 2011, 45.

89 K. Sengupta, 'Nato strikes at Libya's oil in bid to oust Gaddafi', *The Independent*, 8 July 2011. Online. Available: www.independent.co.uk/news/world/africa/nato-strikes-atlibyas-oil-in-bid-to-oust-gaddafi-2308962.html (accessed 18 February 2013).

90 P. Sands, 'UN's Libya resolution 1973 is better late than never', *The Guardian*, 18 March 2011. Online. Available: www.guardian.co.uk/law/2011/mar/18/libya-un-resolution-1973 (accessed 18 February 2013) See also The Economist leader, 'Crunch time in Libya', *The Economist*, 23 April 2011. Online. Available: www.economist.com/node/18586995 (accessed 18 February 2013):

> [T]he UN resolution endorses 'all necessary measures', barring an occupying force, to protect civilians. That helpful elasticity plainly gives the intervening coalition the right to bomb military assets, such as tanks and artillery, that the colonel is using to fire indiscriminately at civilians.

91 UN HRC, Second Libya Inquiry, 2 March 2012, para. 609. The same compound was also struck in 1986 by the United States.

92 B. Obama, D. Cameron and N. Sarkozy, 'Libya's pathway to peace', *New York Times*, 14 April 2011. Online. Available: www.nytimes.com/2011/04/15/opinion/15iht-edlibya15.html (accessed 18 February 2013).

93 See, for example, P. Dryer (22 April 2011) 'NATO pushes "regime change" in Libya', *Consortiumnews.com*. Online. Available: www.consortiumnews.com/2011/042211a.html (accessed 18 February 2013).
94 NATO (10 May 2011) *Press briefing on Libya*. Online. Available: www.nato.int/cps/en/SID-0C7DFC68-B867B13B/natolive/opinions_73660.htm (accessed 18 February 2013).
95 Letter by P. Olson on 23 January 2012, attached to the UN HRC, Second Libya Inquiry, Annex II, 3.
96 In briefings and meetings attended by the authors (April to July 2011).
97 C. Coughlin, 'Nato must target Gaddafi [sic] regime, says Armed Forces chief Gen Sir David Richards', *The Telegraph*, 14 May 2011. Online, Available: www.telegraph.co.uk/news/worldnews/africaandindianocean/libya/8514034/Nato-must-target-Gaddafi-regime-says-Armed-Forces-chief-Gen-Sir-David-Richards.html (accessed 18 February 2013).
98 Nevertheless, as indicated above, statements can have impact on missions; pressure may be put on commanding officers etc. Formal revision of operational orders and plans including their annexes remains however to be decided by NATO's highest political body, the NAC.
99 Art. 51 (5 b) AP I.
100 So-called precision-guided munitions (PGMs) together with Tomahawk land attack missiles (TLAMs).
101 UN HRC, Second Libya Inquiry, for instance in the Summary, 2.
102 Associated Press, 'As bombings rise, Qaddafi says NATO will pull out', *International Herald Tribune*, 18–19 June 2011, 8.
103 In comparison, Rogers mentions that during operation Allied Force the numbers were around 500 civilian deaths to around 10,000 strike sorties. Rogers, *Law*, 107.
104 UN HRC, Second Libya Inquiry, para. 611.
105 Henckaerts and Doswald-Beck, *Customary International Humanitarian Law*, 51–67.
106 See, for instance, arts. 57 and 58 AP I.
107 UN HRC, Second Libya Inquiry, para. 605.
108 PsyOps leaflets are not meant to give an account of the law, but rather to encourage the target audience to a certain (non-)action. As long as they remain stratagems and not perfidy, they are legally acceptable. In addition, texts are subject to translation, so the provided example may not read exactly the same in Arabic. Leaflet, original in four-colour printing, presented with approval from NATO (SHAPE and JFC Naples).
109 For a relatively detailed presentation of various targeting aspects in OUP, see Letter by Peter Olson on 23 January 2012, attached to the UN HRC, Second Libya Inquiry, Annex II.
110 E. Schmitt, 'A high-tech effort to battle Qaddafi', *International Herald Tribune*, 25 May 2011, 1 and 7.
111 See MC 362/1, NATO *Rules of Engagement*.
112 See more elaborately on this, for example: G.S. Corn and G.P. Corn, 'The law of operational targeting: Viewing the LOAC through an operational lens', *Texas International Law Journal* 2, 2012, 337–80.
113 Internal guidelines could, for example, include checking application of a certain rule against the NAC approved target sets, which include definitions and explanations of what constitutes a certain phenomenon. Would, for instance, conventional police or other security forces be included in 'Libyan [armed] forces'?
114 In a round table with New York Times journalist Eric Schmitt, 20 May 2011, OUP's Chief Legal Adviser, Wing Commander Mark Phelps stated: 'LEGAD neither has a veto, nor takes part in a vote. It's all about giving advice, nothing

more, and nothing less.' Notwithstanding this modest approach and that the support from, for example, legal and political advisers occasionally could be seen as show-stoppers, their support was repeatedly highlighted as being of utmost importance, and remains so, in particular in military operations with UNSC mandate and strong international attention. In OUP headquarters, except from different decision briefs etc., the Commander of OUP daily had informal meetings with his LEGADs.

115 SACEUR stands for Supreme Allied Commander over armed forces in Europe and is the highest-ranking military officer in Allied Command Operations (ACO), which is one of the two NATO Commands (the other being Allied Command Transformation).
116 Letter of the Netherlands Government to the Parliament (Kamerstukken II, 2010–2011, 32623, nr. 15), 30 March 2011.
117 Five non-NATO nations (Sweden, Qatar, Jordan, UAE and Morocco) along with 14 NATO Countries took an active part in OUP.
118 SC Res. 2009 (2011), para. 13.
119 See, for instance, UN Res. 665 (1990) and 787 (1992). For more detail on the legal aspects of the arms embargo in OUP, see: M.D. Fink, 'UN-mandated Maritime Arms Embargo Operations in Operation Unified Protector', *Military Law and the Laws of War* 1–2, 2011, 237–60. Online. Available: http://dare.uva.nl/document/456665 (accessed 18 February 2013).
120 NATO Unified Protector (undated) *Arms embargo update*. Online. Available: www.jfcnaples.nato.int/unified_Protector/arms_embargo.aspx (accessed 18 February 2013). The MSA, however, included Libya's exclusive economic zone (EEZ). See further Fink, 'Maritime Arms Embargo', 247.
121 C.J. Chivers, 'Stealthy fleet lets rebels in Libya carry on resistance', *International Herald Tribune*, 24 May 2011, 1 and 6.
122 Although a major oil exporting nation Libya does not refine enough petroleum for its domestic needs.
123 *The Economist*, 'The colonel is running on empty', 45.
124 NATO Unified Protector (spring 2011) 'VADM Veri holds Press Conference aboard *ITS Etna*'. Online. Available: www.jfcnaples.nato.int/page167503642.aspx (accessed 18 February 2013).
125 Generally NATO warnings and information, however, for instance about routing through the Maritime Surveillance Area, proved to be helpful. See for instance World Maritime News (23 June 2011) *NATO to minimize impact of Libyan Operation on Merchant Shipping*, World Maritime News. Online. Available: http://worldmaritimenews.com/archives/21278 (accessed 18 February 2013).
126 T. Harding, 'Libya: Royal Navy warship *HMS Liverpool* comes under heavy fire', *The Telegraph*, 4 August 2011. Online. Available: www.telegraph.co.uk/news/worldnews/africaandindianocean/libya/8682572/Libya-Royal-Navy-warship-HMS-Liverpool-comes-under-heavy-fire.html (accessed 16 January 2013).
127 NATO press release (12 May 2011) *NATO ships thwart attack on Misrata harbour*. Online. Available: www.nato.int/cps/en/natolive/news_74389.htm (accessed 18 February 2013).
128 T. Ripley, 'RN Libya Report calls for new land-attack options', *IHS Jane's Defence Weekly* 49/03, 4–5. As far as is known, no mishaps occurred; however, the authors recall discussion about the risk of ammunition with a low trajectory level bouncing in the sand and continuing in an unwanted direction. NG(F)S was also discussed as to whether, from a legal point of view, areas of land could be seen as objectives. On this topic, see for instance Henckaerts and Doswald-Beck, *Customary*, 32 (Rule 8).

129 See, for instance, R. Donadio, 'Migrants pour ashore and some see a plot', *International Herald Tribune*, 14–15 May 2011, 1 and 3.
130 See report: Council of Europe: Parliamentary Assembly, *Lives lost in the Mediterranean Sea: who is responsible*, Council of Europe, 5 April 2012, doc. 12895. Online. Available: www.unhcr.org/refworld/docid/4f7be86b2.html (accessed 18 February 2013).
131 Letter from NATO, dated 27 March 2012, attached to the Council of Europe report.
132 Letter from the Netherlands Ministers of Foreign Affairs and Defence to Parliament (Kamerstukken II, 2011-2012, 28 676, nr. 151), 7 May 2012. Available: https://zoek.officielebekendmakingen.nl/kst-28676-151.html (accessed 27 June 2013).
133 C. Felice, 'Nuova strage di migranti "La Nato non li ha aiutati"', *Corriere della Sera*, 5 August 2011, 20–21. Online. Available: http://archiviostorico.corriere.it/2011/agosto/05/Nuova_strage_migranti_Nato_non_co_9_110805017.shtml (accessed 22 January 2013).
134 I.H. Daalder and J.G. Stavridis, 'NATO's Victory in Libya: The Right Way to Run an Intervention', *Foreign Affairs* 2, 2012, 2–7. Online. Available: www.foreignaffairs.com/articles/137073/ivo-h-daalder-and-james-g-stavridis/natos-victory-in-libya (accessed 18 February 2013).
135 NATO Unified Protector (28 June 2011) *Operation UNIFIED PROTECTOR Press conference 28 June*. Online. Available: www.jfcnaples.nato.int/Unified_Protector/page19090159.aspx (accessed 18 February 2013).
136 UN Department of Public Information (9 August 2011) *Daily press briefing by the office of the spokesperson for the Secretary-General*. Online. Available: www.un.org/News/briefings/docs/2011/db110809.doc.htm (accessed 18 February 2013).

Part II
The military campaign

4 Executing strategy from the air

Anders Nygren

Introduction

Air power played a decisive role from start to end in the 2011 military campaign mounted by NATO and coalition forces in Libya. Less than 48 hours following the adoption of resolution 1973 on 17 March, French warplanes and American and British Tomahawk cruise missiles were heading for Libya in an effort to eliminate a significant portion of Colonel Muammar Gaddafi's air defence. Within a week NATO declared that it would assume leadership over the implementation of the UN-mandated no-fly zone, along with the arms embargo.[1] When Operation Unified Protector ended seven months later, NATO and the broader coalition of national forces had carried out an estimated 26,000 sorties over Libya, more than half of which were strike sorties, with most targets in major cities or ports such as Tripoli, Brega, Misrata and Sirte.[2] All in all almost 6000 targets were reportedly hit, among which roughly 300 ammunition dumps, 600 battle tanks and armoured personnel carriers and 400 rocket launchers.

In the 2011 Libya campaign airpower thus played the lead role, a development that students of war science have just begun to examine more seriously. The experiences from Libya will no doubt feed into the intense debate over the utility of airpower in contemporary military conflict that has been going on for at least two decades. Arguably, it was the massive use of airpower in the first Gulf War against Iraq in 1991, inspired by the ideas of US Air Force Colonel John Warden, which first provoked this debate. The discussion widened and deepened following NATO's bombing campaign against Serbian forces in Kosovo and parts of Serbia in 1999, as a result of the specific challenges in the European theatre of operations. While the Libya campaign resembled the first Gulf War in several respects, there is no denying that the complex political management of the operation had similarities with the 1999 Kosovo operation.

The reasons for relying heavily on airpower in the Libya campaign was the UN Security Council resolution 1973, which prohibited the deployment of ground troops.[3] There were simply few realistic alternatives to launching a massive air assault. But can and should airpower have a leading role in executing strategy as well? For example, would it be possible to degrade the Libyan air defences to such an extent that the enemy's capability to challenge the no-fly zone as well as to attack the civilian population was virtually eliminated?

This chapter begins by posing some generic questions concerning the use of airpower while paying attention to the experience of using airpower since the end of the Cold War. After a brief description of the particular legal requirements put in place by Security Council resolution 1973, the chapter turns to the Libyan setting. The evolution of and tensions within the mission are outlined and analysed, from the overlapping national operations launched in late March by the United States, the United Kingdom, France and Canada, to the NATO-led Unified Protector framework replacing the former.[4] The chapter concludes by arguing that depending on the setting, airpower can indeed be a vital instrument in regaining the peace.

Airpower as a strategic tool

There is not one set air warfare theory but several ones based upon different types of war or conflict. For example, Colonel (retd) John Warden, United States Air Force believes that airpower is an offensive and strategic tool by nature, while Robert Pape and Martin van Creveld believe that air force should be subordinated to the army and primarily support the ground commanders, as the strategic effect of air power is overrated.[5] In the aftermath of the first Gulf War, Warden nevertheless created a model that was supposedly applicable to any given situation. This so-called '5 ring model' aims at furthering a general understanding of what factors impact on airpower performances.[6] However useful, Warden's 5 ring model overlooks the fact that modern conflicts tend to be very complicated. The fight against insurgents and pirates requires new approaches. Moreover, acting against regimes suppressing its citizens requires cautious campaigns. Use of power in modern wars also involves delicate legal issues (see Chapter 3 in this volume) and acceptance of collateral damage is low. The acceptance of collateral damage might depend on the level of conflict, but aerial warfare has never been as restricted as in the current era.

Still, recent technological developments impacting on *reach*, *range* and *speed* have changed both the usage of and understanding of airpower and provide reasons for strengthened belief in Warden's general view of airpower as a strategic tool. Whereas in the past fighters barely made it to the battlefield and back, today they are able to perform undetected deep strikes with precision.

The altered significance of *reach* has changed the settings for aerial warfare. The range of modern fighters is steadily increasing, as is the ability to conduct air-to-air refuelling (AAR). In the Libyan conflict almost every aircraft was able to conduct AAR. British and US warplanes left from their regular bases in the UK and the US, flew to the Mediterranean, performed their missions and returned home.[7] For the B-2s, the missions were 25 hours long and demanded several refuellings, both on the way to Libya and back.[8] This demonstrates that it is possible to do out-of-area missions without having to re-deploy the air units to forward bases. The strike may also be delivered without warning the opponent in advance.

Next to reach, *speed* makes air power unique. No other military division service can provide a credible worldwide power projection in less than hours. However, most of the tanker fleet belongs to the US. Aircraft carriers can compensate for the lack of AAR, but the hull is limited to a certain number of aircraft. The development of platforms and different weapon systems has changed the settings during the past 30 years. Instead of carpet bombing delivered from huge bombers, there are precision guided munitions in every aspect. Precision guided munitions existed before, but in recent conflicts the need to avoid collateral damage has increased their usage. A typical example is the American Tomahawk cruise missile, which was constructed in the 1970s but whose real breakthrough came with increased demands on precision bombing in the first Gulf War. In the Libyan campaign, both old and new versions of the Tomahawk Land Attack Missile (TLAM) came into frequent use. The demand for precision was extraordinary as noncombatant losses caused by the coalition forces would affect the overall mission decisively.

The accuracy of the cruise missiles in general must be considered very good, since their navigation is controlled by multiple systems. Alongside the Royal and Italian Air Force, the French Air Force used an air-launched cruise missile based on the same platform, named Storm Shadow (British version) or Scalp (French version).[9] This is a lethal stand-off weapon as it enables strikes at long distance, while keeping the platform and aircrew at a safer distance from the opponents' surface-to-air missiles (SAM) and anti-aircraft artillery (AAA). The cruise missiles are used primarily for striking at fixed targets, although the latest development may include both moving targets and multiple mode targets.[10] Another stand-off weapon is the British Brimstone missile.[11] Its dual-mode seeker and long range makes it a lethal weapon for every mechanized unit. The French Air Force also uses several stand-off missiles, which showed an extraordinary degree of precision despite operating far away from the targets. They took out a Libyan battle tank at over 55 km using the Armament Air-Sol Modulaire (AASM), as well as an aircraft that violated the no-fly zone, after it landed.[12] Striking targets such as tanks or mechanized units are not unique, but what is noticeable here is the large distance from which they operated. Stealth is not a new technology, but reduces the ability of detection in view of an old air defence system. During the early stages of operation, the US used the B-2 Spirit bomber to reduce the Libyan possibility to gain and maintain air superiority. Stealth aircraft, combined with active jamming of both radar and communications, served to avoid detection.

Unmanned aerial systems are another area that has a big impact on operations. The possibility to launch an unmanned mission reduces the risks in operations. Moreover, the ability of unmanned aerial vehicles (UAV) to stay in an area for a long time, performing surveillance and even limited close air support missions, might prove decisive in a ground war, especially if the opponent is unable to respond and claims any form of air superiority. Continuous surveillance makes it hard for the opponent's ground and surface forces to remain hidden. Both the US Global Hawk and the Predator were used during the conflict, especially after the Libyan SAM-sites were taken out. When it comes to exploiting the latest technology, the US stands out as the main contributor in Operation Unified Protector. Despite its low profile, the US commitment was the key to unlock the Libya air defence.

Another absolutely vital asset was the P-3 Orion, but not in its ordinary role as a maritime patrol asset; rather, it provided the commanders with intelligence and surveyed specially designated areas. The P-3 Orion is not new, but its cameras and sensors provided the coalition with unique capabilities. One of the tools that is often overlooked and not counted as an extremely valuable contributor are the different link systems. To achieve situational awareness, information is shared and passed on between different platforms, to maximize the efficiency and minimize the risk for each mission.

Is then airpower able to deliver strategic effect in lack of ground forces? It is easy to be seduced by all the airpower possibilities listed above. Yet, airpower certainly has its limitations – including with regards to weather conditions during take-offs and landings – and especially when it comes to peace building operations. It is hard to 'gain hearts and minds' from 10,000 feet. In Afghanistan, the use of airpower mainly consisted of supporting the ground units. The strategic effect was also limited as most of the strategic targets were located outside of Afghanistan. Nonetheless, with regards to Libya, airpower delivered the strategic lever so badly needed. When airborne, the fighters and the air defense can provide force protection for both Army and Navy units. It can use a variety of weapons, including precision guided munitions and, if necessary, carpet bomb an area to prohibit a massive force build-up by the opponent. Without force protection from above, all surface and ground operations are subject to considerable risks. The second battle of Benghazi demonstrates that a fairly straightforward regime ground operation was brought to nothing when the threat from the coalition airpower was neglected. The air campaign is analysed in greater detail below.

Resolution 1973 from the viewpoint of air operations

With the UN Security Council Resolution 1973, it was clear that the situation in Libya required a quick and strong response. Some military officers and politicians had argued that airpower was unsuitable to do the job, yet the Arab League had called for an operation that would secure lives of the civilians and prevent Libyan government forces from using airpower. The statement by the Arab League was essential to provide a military intervention with legitimacy.[13] There was in the end no alternative for the coalition but to rely on airpower and a naval contribution (see Chapter 5 of this volume). The situation in Libya had to be stabilized before any humanitarian aid and assistance could be provided and before any peace talks could take place.

A no-fly zone cannot prevent an actor from flying, but ensures that any activity will be dealt with according to the pre-set conditions decided for the zone. The no-fly zone in Libya included preventing any unauthorized flight from taking place, regardless of origin. From a strictly military point of view several problems arose when establishing the no-fly zone.

First, the no-fly zone had to be enforced while protecting civilians on the ground.[14] Second, the large area required large assets to enforce the no-fly zone. The size of the zone made it hard for the coalition forces to reach all over the area.[15] AAR was mandatory to reach the southern part of the no-fly zone, as was the case for targets in and around the Sheeba region. Third, there was the avoidance of possible threats from SAM. The Libyan Armed Forces were considered as a force to be reckoned with. At the start of the conflict, Libya was one of the largest Air Forces in northern Africa and while it might not have been a major problem for the coalition forces, it would certainly be out of reach of the rebels. The SAM-systems were old and the majority of the missiles were not operational.[16] According to several sources, parts were taken from many different systems to ensure a few operational SAM-sites along the coastline. Even if numbers were exaggerated, the SAM-threat was imminent in northern Libya. Fourth, enforcing the UNSCR 1973 was problematic as it would be hard to separate the rebels from the Libyan army – who used practically the same equipment and tactics – when airborne, especially in close quarter combat. The coalition soon recognized that rather than carpet bombing, there was a need for intelligence and taking out small and specific targets.

Fifth, the Libyan Navy was a concern, as it was equipped with the surface-to-air missile SA-N-4 and posed a limited threat to all air operations below 15,000 feet.[17] The ability to support Libyan ground forces with naval gunfire and the capability to enforce a blockade outside important seaports would make the rebel situation difficult. The Libyan Navy might also pose a threat to coalition air operations if they were allowed to leave port, not only with its SAM-systems, but also potentially affecting other ships that supported the air operations. The French aircraft carrier *Charles de Gaulle* would be a major target for the Libyan Navy. Despite the fact that they were outnumbered, they still possessed the surface-to-surface missile OTOMAT onboard the frigates.[18] In addition, there were other systems onboard the corvettes.[19] Other ships in the region, for example the USS *Kearsarge*, contributed to the air operation, providing combat search and rescue (CSAR), to name a few.[20] They would be vulnerable to an attack, even though a quick view of the coalition order of battle makes this less realistic. The threat to the coalition's maritime operations should still not be overrated, as the coalition forces were massive. The vital question, then, remains; would the Libyan forces be able to pose substantial problems for the air campaign?

The air arena capabilities of the Libyan Defense Forces

A closer look indicates several weaknesses of the Libyan Armed Forces (see Chapter 6 for further detail of the Libyan Army). The Libyan Army had been used in Chad quite recently, yet there were no indications that it had been able to implement current experiences in the training of units.[21] Furthermore, the units were poorly trained and badly equipped. Most of the equipment and armament had been purchased from the Soviet Union in the early 1980s. Some of the stock had been upgraded, but most of it was more or less outdated by Western standards. The exception might have been a few brigades, including the 'Khamis' Brigade (see below). Yet, the rebels had problems dealing with armoured units, attack helicopters and the airpower belonging to the regime. Moreover, shelling from the artillery units made rebel movements more or less impossible. It needs to be pointed out that the rebels' main weapons were assault rifles and at best a few old Russian-built battle tanks.

The Libyan Air Force was established in 1951 and was normally used to fly trainers and transport. The first fighters were bought in the late 1960s and early 1970s, as the Gadaffi regime's Air Force was established. The majority of the equipment was purchased from the Soviet Union, but Libya also bought 36 Mirage F1 from France, to be used as air superiority fighters. At the time, Libya could demonstrate impressive numbers with regards to the total number of airframes.

At the start of the Libyan Civil War; Libya had one of the largest air forces in North Africa, although many of the aircraft had never been upgraded or modernized. For instance, only 12 out of the 36 F1s were modernized. Much of the air fleet was old and outdated. The Mirage F1 could serve as an example: originally 36 were bought from France, as a multirole fighter; only four were actually upgraded; two of these fled to Malta, after having received an order to bomb Libyan civilians, and another one was shot down by anti-Gadaffi forces. The Libyan MiG-21s are another example; these did not fly at all, due to reported serviceability issues.[22] Out of 170 MiG-23s delivered, only 20 per cent are believed to have been flyable aircraft.

Moreover, since the majority of aircraft were manufactured in the former Soviet Union, the doctrinal perspective and adopted philosophy were inspired by the Soviet Union, which meant that pilots were more or less controlled from the ground, leaving many of the decisions to the fighter controller. The same applied to the SAM-systems. The strong hierarchy made improvising and adapting difficult at unit level, especially as the system relied on orders and information coming from the higher command. With orders and information missing, the whole air defence system was crippled. This might have been one of the reasons for the passive reactions to the no-fly zone on the part of the Libyans.

Furthermore, a fair share of contracted Libyan officers were involved, pilots as well as maintenance personnel and technical crews, from a variety of countries such as Syria, former Yugoslavia, Russia, South Africa, North Korea and Pakistan.[23] Libya also purchased a substantial number of trainers and light attack aircraft from former Yugoslavia. When purchasing the Mirage F1, Libyans frequently visited and were trained in the Dassault factory. Interestingly enough, this was a time when French and Libyan forces went head to head south of Libya.[24] Russian pilots have confirmed that the Libyan pilots had several problems. They were not accustomed to high G-force manoeuvres and seemed to have had problems with detecting air targets and making lock-ons. Night operations were avoided completely, probably due to old navigation and radar systems, and the training was almost exclusively done in daylight as the pilots were unwilling to conduct night operations as they cannot locate their airbases going home.[25] The Libyan Air Force was indeed involved in the Chad conflict, yet did not play a significant part; many of the operations were conducted at high altitude with a meagre result as a consequence.

These shortcomings might be traced to insufficient training and to the fact that the Libyan airframes were downgraded by second-class Russian technology purchased in the 1980s. Three decades later it was outdated and its ineffectiveness affected the overall performance.

In sum, the Libyan Air Force did not pose a threat for the coalition Air Forces (other than the SAM-systems), but it could be used to overrun the rebels, who faced difficulties even against old and outdated aircraft. Especially, the attack helicopters, such as the Mi-24 and Mi-35, and the light attack aircraft must be considered as a serious threat to the rebels. According to Marine Corps Commandant General James F. Amos, the helicopter force was the biggest threat to anti-Gadaffi forces.[26]

Finally, as concerns the Libyan surface-to-air systems, it should be pointed out that the Air Defense Command seems to have merged with the Air Force from the late 1980s or early 1990s. The Air Defense Command had a variety of Soviet Union built surface-to-air missiles (SAM) and anti-aircraft artillery (AAA). Libya operated the SA-2 GAINFUL, SA-3 GOA, SA-5 GAMMON and SA-6 GAINFUL. These different kinds of systems were used to protect the northern coastline with major SAM-systems around Tripoli, Misrata, Sirt, Benghazi and Tobruk. In addition, there were the SA-8 GECKO and several handheld systems. The setup for the air defense can be compared to the situation around Baghdad in the first Gulf War.[27]

The SA-2 system is perhaps most well-known for the shooting down of U-2 pilot Gary Powers over Soviet Union in 1960. It was used by North Vietnam to defend Hanoi and the main seaport of Haiphong during the Vietnam War. The SA-2 (or S-75) was designed for non-manoeuvring, high-altitude targets, such as the B-52 bomber. As the accuracy is not impressive multiple missiles are fired at each target. Each SAM-site has its own radar attached. The SA-2 must be considered a threat to non-manoeuvring, high-altitude targets. It is sensitive to jamming and counter-measures and its effectiveness against low-flying targets is questionable. Nevertheless, it has actually downed F-4C and a SU-27, the latter in the vicinity of Gudauta in the Abkhazian wars in 1993.

The SA-3 GOA medium-altitude surface-to-air missile system must be considered as a complement to the SA-2. It has overall a shorter range than the SA-2 but better manoeuvrability at low to medium levels and can make up for the low-level deficiencies of the SA-2. It must still be acknowledged as outdated and obsolete for modern fighters. SA-5 GAMMON is a limited theatre air defence system. Its long range and high altitude capability needs to be considered even for a modern fighter. The SA-5 system has limitations when it comes to low-level targets. The SA-5 system might be dealt with using low-level tactics, but it can still pose problems for air-to-air refueling and AWACS flying in orbits at high altitudes. The SA-6 is the most up-to-date of the larger SAM-systems existing in Libya.

The SA-6 might have a shorter range compared to the other surface-to-air missiles, but it has a better accuracy. Possibly, the biggest advantage is the ability to follow the ground units, providing cover up to 30,000 feet. In a comparison between the different systems, the SA-6 would be harder to locate and hit since it is not limited by fixed positions like the SA-2, SA-3 and SA-5. In addition the Libyan Army possessed the SA-8 and the Crotale systems. These systems would still be a concern but could be avoided with manoeuvre, speed and altitude; the same goes for the multiple hand-held systems used by the Libyans.

Most of the old outdated systems were hampered by their single target capability and were vulnerable to countermeasures, especially when it comes to the older SAM-systems as the SA-2, SA-3 and SA-5. Regardless of the date of the equipment, the systems existed in fairly large numbers, which caused some challenges. Some of the missiles were certainly not operational, but even if just 10 per cent worked, this would be enough to expose some of the air-crews to danger.

In conclusion, it can be argued that the Libyan surface-to-air missiles posed a real threat to air operations and that the threat level was particularly high for the big, slow movers at high altitude. In spite of the fact that the majority of the SAM-systems were outdated, it was risky to enter the airspace without taking proper precautions. The Libyan SAM-systems were one of the main concerns when enforcing the no-fly zone. When the threat was reduced by the absence of Libyan fighters, the no-fly zone could still be challenged by mobile surface-to-air missiles such as the SA-6. Yet, even though the Libyan Armed forces had large forces at the government's disposal, equipment was largely outdated and maintenance neglected. Moreover, although Libya had participated in several conflicts, the Armed Forces seemed not to have implemented their experiences from this training. The experiences of officers and crews from the many countries involved in the Libyan Air Force did not seem to have been passed on. One of the reasons might be that many of the advanced systems were controlled by mercenaries. It seems as though the loyalist forces lacked the strategic, operational and tactical acuity to counter the coalition, and the outcome was almost a given.

From Odyssey Dawn to Unified Protector

During the spring of 2011, it became obvious that Colonel Gadaffi would respond to the uprising using Security Forces and harsh measures against civilians. Colonel Gaddafi ordered the Army, Navy and Air Force into operations against the Libyan people. Opposition forces were badly armed at the start of the conflict, having no more than handguns and AK-47s at their disposal. The threat from the regular Army was massive, yet controllable, but the threat from the Navy and the Air Force was out of reach of the anti-Gaddafi forces.

When the situation in Libya took a turn for the worse, there were four ongoing air operations:

- US Operation Odyssey Dawn[28]
- UK Operation Ellamy[29]
- French Operation Harmattan[30]
- Canadian Operation Mobile.[31]

These four operations may not have been completely integrated. The Odyssey Dawn operation was supposed to take the lead. The command and control were partly performed from USS *Mount Whitney* and liaison officers from France and UK were present.[32] Despite having French liaisons onboard, the British and the Americans were taken off-guard when the French decided to strike against ground forces outside Benghazi. When NATO took over, the command and control were performed from ACC Izmir and the CAOC in Poggio Renatico.

The risk for blue-on-blue was present in the early stages of the conflict, since there were four separate chains of command and national interests involved. While the American operation started with a conventional approach by degrading the Libyan air defence and targeting SAM-sites, command and control and communication nodes before tasking air operations over Libya, the French launched an attack on the Gaddafi field forces outside Benghazi. Either the French intelligence concerning SAM-threats was updated, or they took a risk sending in fighters in the vicinity of Gaddafi ground forces. Simultaneously, there was another ongoing operation – Unified Protector – which at the time had a naval focus, using maritime assets to form a blockade outside Libya (see Chapter 5 in this volume.).

Merging the efforts into a united action would require solving numerous issues. The United States was engaged at an early stage and provided the most kinetic effect of all countries included, but was reluctant to take over the command and control. The French were more positive, but the question was whether they had the abilities. Turkish Prime Minister Recep Tayyip Erdoğan argued that the French president was starting his re-election campaign rather than supporting the civilians in Libya.[33] The UK would have the ability, but was reluctant.

The command and control finally ended up inside NATO, yet many of the NATO nations could not agree upon the level of commitment (see Chapter 1 in this volume). The command and control was certainly the main issue but there were others. Only a few of the key players in NATO actually contributed to the operation as a whole. One contributing factor might have been the involvement in Afghanistan and Iraq. The Netherlands used to be one of the driving nations in air operations, but seems to have adopted a lower profile recently. Despite the limited size of their air forces, it seems as if the Scandinavian countries could provide a valuable contribution in different roles. Noticeably, Norway and Denmark contributed to the same degree as other nations. Even if Norway pulled out early, its contribution was acknowledged. The Danes almost ran out of bombs and had to make sudden mid-operations replenishment.[34]

Contributing nations from outside NATO experienced some obstacles. The participation of Qatar, Jordan and the United Arab Emirates was important in providing the operation with legitimacy in the Arab world. Sweden also joined the operation, based at the Sigonella Airbase. Although the participating countries were well received, there were issues when it came to IFF (Identification, friend or foe), crypto and modem.[35] Receiving an air tasking order (ATO) and airspace control order (ACO) required knowledge of the NATO setup. Coalition members outside of NATO needed to hook up with a mentor inside the Alliance community in order to get all the information needed.[36] The Swedish Air Force provided tactical reconnaissance for the operation, yet despite being one of the providers of tactical reconnaissance alongside the Italians, they had difficulties in accessing reports.

The initial phase: the battle of Benghazi

The battle of Benghazi, taken to be the start of the Libyan Civil war, started on 17 February and ended three days later, when the rebels took control of the city. Benghazi was a crucial city in the civil war. It was vital for the rebels and the coalition to keep Benghazi under rebel control. For the government forces, taking Benghazi would have been a big step in crushing the rebellions, although the rest of eastern Libya needed to be controlled as well.

During March, government forces gathered south of Benghazi to prepare for a big push. Around 7.30 a.m. on 19 March loyalist artillery started to fire and one hour later mechanized units entered the city limits through the west gate. Opposition armoured units started to engage the 12 T-72 that were first to enter the city. The leading T-72 tank was hit and the initial attack by the loyalist troops was repulsed.[37] In the afternoon, the rebels even launched a MiG-23 that crashed in the Benghazi surroundings. Whether the cause of the accident was an engine failure or friendly fire remains unclear. In the afternoon, it became obvious that another push by the loyalists was being prepared.

Simultaneously, president Nicolas Sarkozy held a private session concerning the Libyan crisis in Paris, informing British prime minister David Cameron and secretary of state Hillary Clinton that French aircraft from Armée de la Air was about to strike targets inside Libya, if they had no objections.[38] About 48 hours after the resolution was implemented, the French Air Force tasked fighters to the northeastern coastline of Libya. At 4.00 p.m. on 19 March, French Mirage and Rafale fighters entered Libyan airspace. The fighters patrolled the skies over Benghazi to prevent any attempt by the Gaddafi forces to enter the city of Benghazi. The Rafales engaged multiple tanks and four tanks were destroyed.[39]

The loyalist unit stopped outside Benghazi and the attempt to take the city was temporarily abandoned. The units withdrew to regroup southwest of the city. From an operational point of view, the strike might not have changed the outcome but the psychological impact on both sides cannot be underestimated. The Libyan government forces seem to have underestimated the determination and fighting will of the rebels. Moreover, according to several sources, many of the soldiers in the regular Army committed mutiny and helped the anti-Gaddafi forces to re-equip.[40] After a few days of intense fighting, the rebels gained control over an Army base and the Katiba compound. Much of the better equipment was however stored closer to Tripoli. Some mercenaries were executed during the process and according to unofficial sources about 500 rebels and 200 soldiers from the Libyan Army were killed.[41] Benghazi ended up being the rebel stronghold. In the former Army bases, the rebels found weapons, military vehicles and older tanks.

This was the start for the massive air campaign of the coalition forces directed against the Libyan Armed Forces under Gaddafi's control. Shortly after the French attack on Benghazi, US and UK ships fired more than 110 Tomahawk cruise missiles at multiple targets.[42] The 20-plus targets were mainly connected to the integrated air defence system, such as

C2-nodes, SAM-sites and other command and control centres.[43] AV-8 Harriers from USMC assault ship USS *Kearsarge* continued to attack Libyan army convoys heading for Benghazi. At the end of the day (19 March) the government forces eventually came to a stop outside of Benghazi. After the first days of fighting it became clear to the coalition forces that one of the objectives of the campaign must be to prevent Libyan forces from entering the rebel stronghold.

The battle for Benghazi was on hold, but the US and UK forces continued to pound the air defence and air bases. British Tornados starting from the UK air-to-air refuelled three times, dropped Storm Shadow cruise missiles against air bases and fixed SAM-sites and returned.[44] Italian, US and UK aircraft provided a cover, jamming radars and communication. Libyan government forces could barely get a grip over the situation, let alone act to gain some freedom of movement. In the first day, almost every radar site was blacked out or hit by precision guided munitions. Some of the cruise missiles targeted Tripoli and the Gaddafi compound. Rumours said that Gaddafi himself was targeted, even though missiles were allegedly aimed at the command centre inside the vast presidential compound and not at Gaddafi himself.[45] The intelligence reports stated that the command post was connected to the objectives of the operation. Confidence in US ability was high and a statement by the Joint Chiefs of Staff indicated target areas and even specific targets on the following days.[46]

After the first day of air operations, the outcome seemed successful, although battle damage assessment not had reached the Pentagon.[47] More than 110 missiles had been launched from ships, submarines and airplanes and over 20 strategic targets had been taken out. Areas around Tripoli, Misrata, Sirte, Ajdabiya and Benghazi were prioritized. Later, in a press conference held in Washington, the Director of Joint Chiefs of Staff acknowledged that 126 Tomahawk cruise missiles were initially fired at more than 20 targets. The cruise missiles were fired from both US ships and one UK ship. At the time, the units involved were not revealed, but one of the ships was the UK submarine HMS Triumph that later participated in several ways to end the conflict.[48]

The locations of the targets, primarily Tripoli, Misrata and Sirte, were shown at a press conference and Vice Admiral William Gortney admitted that the targets were mainly connected to the Libyan integrated air defence. The US and UK fired another 12 missiles at several targets and seemed to be targeting the area south of Benghazi as well. It is not farfetched to assume that those targets were connected to the loyalist mechanized units on their way to Benghazi.

The first days seem to have been shattering for the Libyan air defence. After 23 March there were no indications of Libyan radar emissions. Before the SA-5s were taken out, the use of the coalition forces' UAV system Global Hawk – used to gather intelligence – was limited. Even though modern fighters have electronic countermeasures available, the systems would still pose a threat to supporting air operations such as air-to-air refuelling, airborne command and control and maritime surveillance. For the same reasons, the U-2s were used, but only after the SAM-threat was reduced.

Other targets did not end up on the target list. According to US officials, Muammar Gaddafi was not on the target list.[49] The anti-aircraft artillery and the mobile SAM-systems were also left out initially, partly because of the difficulty of taking out mobile targets and partly because the threat could be handled with manoeuvres, speed, altitude and countermeasures. Only targets violating the no-fly zone or units that might pose a threat to Libyan civilians ended up on the target list. The problems with separating civilians from Gaddafi troops were thoroughly examined, but it was also stressed that all air crews were thoroughly briefed and rather would abort than attack a target not identified as loyalist troops engaging or preparing to engage civilians.[50]

Gaining and maintaining air superiority

It is remarkable how fast the US, UK and France achieved air superiority. Equally interesting is that the Libyan Armed Forces did very little to counter the situation. There were almost no radar emissions after the first few days of fighting, which indicates that the Libyan Air Force had almost given up the war in the air. The Libyan inability to challenge the no-fly zone might have depended on several factors. If the Libyan Air Force partly consisted of pilots from other nations being paid to undertake low-risk missions against neighbours, what is the likelihood of them engaging in an aerial combat with a low chance of success? There is also a good chance that the Libyan Air Force did not wanted to engage civilian targets and even supported the uprising. Shortly before the coalition entered the arena two Libyan pilots fled to Malta after being ordered to bomb civilians.[51] There are unconfirmed rumours that the whole Air Force academy outside Misrata defected.[52]

Early in the morning of 20 March three B-2 Spirits penetrated Libyan airspace and targeted the Ghardabiya airfield outside of Sirte.[53] The B-2s were stationed at Whiteman AFB in Missouri, US, and had to make a fairly long flight before entering Libyan airspace. The B-2s were used in order to avoid detection by Libyan radar. Stealth in combination with electronic countermeasures and massive jamming from EA-18 Growlers made them practically invisible to the Libyan radar system.[54] The B-2s took out 45 hardened shelters during their raid and cruise missiles took out another 15 shelters. The targeting of the Ghardabiya airbase might have served several purposes. The Libyan Air Force was, for example, prevented from using the shelters for hiding and protecting aircraft, and lost some of the few remaining operational fighters. Whatever the damage, the hardened shelters would no longer protect any Libyan asset.

Later during the campaign, the B-2s were replaced by the B-1B Lancer.[55] Even if the crucial parts of the Libyan air defence had been taken out at this point, the remaining air defence was a concern to the coalition forces. In particular, the mobile SA-6 systems could cause problems if they appeared in key areas. Leaving other missions in Iraq, US F/A–18 Growlers were retasked to join the operation, their main objectives being to jam radars, making a coalition aircraft lock-on impossible for the Libyans. Jamming radars and hitting aircraft shelters were part of the tactics to gain air superiority, which was a fundamental to the enforcement of the no-fly zone. At the same time, British Tornados and US F-15s were pounding targets inside Libya. It soon became evident that the Libyan Air Force was incapable of countering these initial actions by the coalition forces.

Shortly after the air operations started, a psyops version of the C-130 (EC-130J)[56] would patrol the waters outside Libya, transmitting radio messages in Arabic, English and French (see Chapter 5 for further detail on the naval dimensions of the campaign). The message was simple: if a vessel leaves port it becomes a legal target and will be destroyed.[57] There were several reasons for keeping the Libyan Navy in port: the rebels would not have any chance to counter naval gunfire support, the freedom of movement using the sea for the rebels, refugees and wounded would be limited and, finally, the Libyan navy could be a threat to the coalition's Navy operations. USMC assault ship USS *Kearsarge* and the aircraft carrier *Charles De Gaulle* could be targeted by the Libyan Navy. Keeping all Libyan vessels in port would certainly remove some of the risks, and in addition would limit the Libyan attempt to effect low-level air operations.

Benghazi was still not taken by the government forces and after a build-up the loyalist forces advanced again towards the city. French fighters took action and stopped the convoy just south of Benghazi. The attack was devastating for the government troops. In just an hour 70 battle tanks, APCs and trucks were destroyed.[58] A rocket launcher and a mobile SAM-battery were also taken out. The brigade-sized unit came to a stop in the Benghazi suburbs.

From a strictly military standpoint the outcome of the situation was important. Benghazi remained intact as a rebel stronghold and again, the morale of the rebels was significantly boosted. For the government side the outcome was fearsome. It became clear that any further advance on the ground was subject to high risks and the current positions were exposed, with the lack of reinforcement from ground-based air defence. The personnel and equipment lost in the fight was more or less irreplaceable. Even if reinforcements arrived, the air superiority held by the French speeded up reinforcements for the opposing force. The morale in the government troops decreased and the situation was uncontrollable.

On 22 March, the US lost an F-15, due to technical failure. It went down close to the city of Benghazi, after a mission against Gaddafi 'missile capabilities'.⁵⁹ Both the pilot and the navigator ejected. The pilot was shortly afterwards picked up by a USMC unit and the navigator was taken care of by the 'Libya Free Forces' and was soon back in US hands. The wreck of the F-15 was later bombed, to avoid parts and information ending up in other countries. The no-fly zone was protected by the Eurofighter Typhoon and tactical reconnaissance was carried out by a Tornado. Remaining SAM-sites showing hostile intent were taken out. Simultaneously there was fighting in the vicinity of some cities that coalition forces managed to end only momentarily. This was the case in Misrata, where the distance was short between fighting units with similar equipment and uniforms. The risks of hitting the wrong targets were high.⁶⁰

During the early phases of the operation the missions were carried out by the US, UK and France. Gradually other nations joined the operation, such as Canada, Belgium, the Netherlands and Denmark. Between 17 and 23 March the air operations focused on:

- maintaining air superiority;
- protecting Benghazi;
- targeting command and control installations;
- taking out ground-based air defence (GBAD) systems showing hostile intent.

On 23 March, Vice Air Marshal Gregory Bagwell (RAF) stated that the Libyan Air Force no longer existed as a fighting force and that the integrated air defence systems were so degraded that it was possible to operate in Libyan airspace without any severe risk.⁶¹ Despite the loyalist defeat in Benghazi, hostilities continued. The opposing forces had held the western part of Misrata for some time and the loyalist forces began training gunfire on several targets, among them the hospital in western Misrata.⁶² In the first 13 days of the conflict the coalition forces had focused mainly on preventing the Libyan army or government forces from entering Benghazi but also on significantly reducing the risk for air operations over Libya. Although the threat from the SAM-systems remained constant into April, the Libyan Air Force was no longer a fighting force that caused any concern.

Operation Unified Protector started early as a result of the arms embargo. In the initial stage the main focus was to prevent the passage of any weapons into or out of the area and primarily it was a naval operation. Nevertheless, when the 1973 resolution was implemented and the disagreements over command and control issues between US, UK and France emerged, NATO and Unified Protector worked as the key to unlock the chain of command. Turkey had previously raised doubts about French leadership of the air operations.⁶³ The French decided to step down and shortly after, the chain of command was declared, Operation Unified Protector begun and the former operations merged into one.

Taking a different perspective, the battle for air superiority was over. However, there was still a need to mop up all ground units fighting against civilians and potentially committing war crimes. The projection of air power was no easier, the objectives had simply changed. The threat level for the aircrews reduced, but there was still much to do. The chase was on to neutralize all units on the surface.[64] The coming months the coalition were targeting the remaining parts of SAM-systems, tanks, trucks, ammunition facilities, command and control centres and artillery.

Civilian casualties and sinking of Navy vessels

The enforcement of the no-fly zone was mainly to prevent the Libyan Air Force using air assets against civilians. Despite the strict rules of engagement and the self-imposed limitations mistakes did occur. On 1 April a convoy fired at an A-10 Thunderbolt, which returned the fire in self-defence. Several rebels were killed and a few trucks were taken out.[65] The same day, civilians were killed and wounded when an ammunition truck was taken. The explosion damaged several buildings in the surroundings.[66] On 9 April the coalition detected and engaged a rebel MiG-23 that took off from a base east of Benghazi. The MiG-23 later returned to the base. The ground campaign was the focus of the operation throughout May. Some of the Libyan government vessels caused problems for the coalition, offsetting the rebels and continuing to support harassment of civilians.

When fighting occurred along the coastline, the Libyan Navy avoided using their frigates and corvettes, most likely because they were easy to spot and consequently would be targeted (see Chapter 5 for further detail on the naval dimensions of the campaign). Libyan Special Forces were using smaller boats to avoid detection, managing to mine the ports of Misrata and disembark troops in the rebels' rear area. The Libyan Navy and the Libyan Special Forces also prevented any movements around the coast, including that of wounded and displaced persons. The Libyan loyalists relied heavily on the Army, but the Navy was used for various supporting operations. It became necessary to make a statement and on 20 May several Navy vessels were targeted. British Tornados and French Mirages were tasked to an anti-surface mission in order to reduce or neutralize Libyan possibilities of using the Navy. Almost every one of the remaining Libyan Navy vessels was targeted. A few missions were aborted, due to the risk of collateral damage, but most of the vessels were either sunk or damaged. A factory constructing small patrol boats and, according to some sources, the location of some of the Special Forces were also hit. The decision to take out the Libyan Navy was questioned, but it led to the isolation of the Army and rendering it vulnerable to attacks from the air.

The chase of the Khamis Brigade

From May to August the coalition forces flew about 140 missions per day, of which roughly one-third were strike missions. By mid-June it became hard to find targets to engage. One of the reasons was that the loyalist troops were using civilian vehicles and infrastructure. Due to the strict rules of engagement and self-imposed limitations, the smaller number of targets affected the missions. In September and October air activities reduced as remaining targets were few.

Yet when the Air Force, SAM-sites and the Navy were neutralized, the operation picked up pace and moved on to push the Gaddafi loyalist ground units, especially those considered a threat to the Libyan population. After the first strikes it was apparent that government troops in exposed positions could be taken out from a distance. Loyalists then started to blend among civilians or act dispersed in the cities. During convoys on public roads they purposely tried to move along with the civilians, who became human shields.

The UN pressure for no collateral damage made surgical strikes a prerequisite for engaging targets. A fighter could do the job, but there were other air assets better suited with a lower speed. The British and French brought in their attack helicopter units in early June and took part in the operations shortly after.[67] Attack helicopters would be a valuable asset as they could move in closer to the targets than the regular aircraft, apart from the A-10.

The regime forces and the rebels carried the same weapons, which made it necessary to make adjustments to avoid collateral damage. For the same reasons the Americans provided the operation with some special assets such as AC-130 gunships and A-10 Warthogs. In a situation with existing SAM-systems those assets would be vulnerable and the threat to a big slow mover like the AC-130 would be crucial. Its deployment is built around the freedom of action in the air. The same goes for the A-10. The vast benefit of bringing in the AC-130 and A-10 is the capacity to identify objects and precision in taking out ground targets.

In early May the loyalist forces were pushed from Benghazi around the coast to Ajdabiya and Sirte. Rebels were still controlling the western parts of Misrata while the security brigades were making life difficult for citizens in the rest of the city. It was hard to move around, in particular to the western part where the hospital was located. Getting in and out of Misrata was also difficult since loyalist forces controlled the ports at the time. It became apparent that something needed to be done.

The dissolution of the Khamis Brigade was one major key to ending the conflict. Khamis Gaddafi, the youngest son of Muammar Gaddafi, was the commander of the 32nd Reinforced Brigade. If the abilities of other parts of the Libyan Army could be doubted, the Khamis Brigade was an exception. The Brigade was manned by a substantial number of mercenaries, where other brigades were manned by conscripts.[68] The Brigade seemed to be a melting pot of mercenaries from several countries, including for instance Chad and Niger.[69] The rate of desertion was lower and the troops were regarded as the loyal protector of the Gaddafi regime. The Brigade itself was referred to as the security brigade of the armed forces.[70]

Khamis had received his military education in Russia and the Frunze military academy. The standard of armaments and training must be considered as much higher than the regular Army, and it is confirmed by Belgian authorities that armament was sold and shipped to Libya.[71] The coalition monitored the Brigade closely, since neutralizing the Khamis Brigade might be a crucial factor. During Operation Unified Protector the coalition attacked the headquarters of the Khamis Brigade several times.

When the anti-Gaddafi protest started in mid-February the call went to the Khamis Brigade. Smaller units of the 10,000 men Brigade were sent to Benghazi, Bauda and other cities to stop the riots. As the fighting started on 19 February and soon got out of hand the Khamis Brigade withdrew. The loss outside Benghazi was a blow to morale but, as a whole, the main part of the Brigade was intact. Other army units were left behind to sort the situation out and on 24 February, Khamis and his headquarters tried to get the rebels out of the western parts of Misrata.[72] Snipers were posted on rooftops, making life difficult for anyone in the streets of Benghazi, including transports to the main hospital. A month later, the Khamis Brigade was back, killing several rebels and civilians.[73] After several battles along the coast at Misrata, Ajdabiya, Benghazi and Bauda, the unit was called back to Tripoli. Members of the Brigade committed several atrocities on the way, including the burning of a supermarket, killing of prisoners and harassing and killing civilians along the way.[74] On 21 August the Brigade was stationed west of Tripoli to safeguard the city when its headquarters was overrun by rebels. The Brigade was reduced to a few hundred men. On 29 August Brigade Commander Khamis Ghadaffi was shot dead by an AH-64 Apache attack helicopter while heading south in a jeep with the remainder of the Brigade.[75]

Conclusions

Some military strategists have argued that the role of air power belongs to the Cold War era and will be obsolete in the near future, as it has no role in a low-intensity conflict and should be used merely to support ground forces. The Libya campaign might prove that statement wrong, especially since the absence of coalition ground forces made the situation as complicated as it could be, leaving the strategy in and over Libya to the air component.

Arguably, the air power delivered according to the resolution, despite the absence of coalition ground troops. One might argue that the role of coalition ground forces was taken over by the rebels. The rebels had their own agenda and their own objectives and were definitely not under the command of the coalition, but they forced the loyalist troops to expose their assets and positions. However, it would be unfair to compare the Libyan rebels to a coalition ground unit of any kind. Understanding the overall campaign objectives was not in the interest of the rebels, as it would have been for a coalition force. One might also argue that the Libyan Army had so many flaws that it could not be counted as a worthy opponent. On the other hand, no one can tell exactly what the coalition air power in Libya would have been capable of if it had been unleashed.

As a whole then, the use of air power could be considered to have followed Warden's model. Colonel Warden might have taken the air operations a few steps further, but the limitations imposed by the resolution restricted the planners. The Libya campaign shows that air power alone can play a decisive role when it comes to affecting the outcome of a conflict. The campaign was designed to uphold UNSCR 1973, yet it employed a top-down approach in choosing targets and achieving desired effect. It was not in the coalition mandate to hunt down Muammar Gaddafi, but instead it decapitated the leadership and isolated the commanders. Command centres were taken out and early warning radars were either taken out or jammed. The Libyan regime was more or less blindfolded and became reactive. Instead of focusing on pounding ground units, efforts were made to reduce command and control, wasting the energy of every ground unit short of the Khamis Brigade.

Several approaches have been demonstrated. A traditional method included taking air defence, radar sites, command and control and air bases and effectively prohibiting the opponent of using airspace and air assets, thus ensuring that the overall risk for the air-crews was fairly low. Another more direct approach was employed by the French Air Force in the early stages in the battle of Benghazi, when flying in a package and more or less orbiting over the area, preventing the Gaddafi forces from entering the Benghazi area.

The latter approach is interesting, since it would either require a bold commander and pilots, or good intelligence about the SAM-situation in the area. Most likely it was a combination. Even with good intelligence and a good situation overview there is still a risk entering an area. Libyan loyalists could have deployed several SAM-units unknown to the French, or to the rest of the coalition forces, which makes it an interesting case. Whether this is a new approach in aerial warfare remains to be seen. Such an approach would be more in line with Pape and perhaps van Creveld, despite the lack of ground troops. In a conflict or a civil war, the obvious infrastructural targets identified in a regular war, such as power plants, roads, communication, ports and airfields, must be carefully evaluated since the country or area has to function after the end of the conflict. The direct approach of the French Air Force might serve as an example of the direct use of air power projection in limited conflicts when a higher level of risk is accepted.

Several additional observations need to be made. First, the situation in Libya demonstrates the importance of air superiority. Had the Libyan armed forces been able to challenge the coalition, dominating the skies, the result might have been different. Control of the air to some degree is imperative. Control of the air is even more important if the terrain is flat, lacking vegetation: there are simply no places to hide for the ground troops. Neglecting control of the air leaves a fairly strong ground or surface unit exposed and vulnerable. In Libya, loyalist T-72 tanks were struck from over 35 kilometres on several occasions. According to some French pilots the distance might have been even greater. If you cannot control the air, the ground forces and surface forces will be sitting ducks; airspace must be controlled in order to get relief in and casualties out.

Second, air-to-air refueling was a must for upholding the no-fly zone. Fuel was an issue for any kind of operations in the southern part of Libya. Although the range of modern fighters is impressive, they still needed air-to-air refueling. Even with AAR, it would have been hard to reach the entire no-fly zone with a competitive Libyan Air Force based in the south making the coalition fighters manoeuvre. Third, although the air operation was an overall success, with the Libyans unable to affect the coalition, there was one F-15 lost due to technical problems. This highlights that personnel recovery/combat search and rescue is vital. Highly trained and skilled personnel are not easy to replace. Moreover, besides raising moral, ensuring that flight crews will be retrieved, it is also vital to get the crew back for evaluation of the situation.

Fourth, the threat from the Libyan Air Force and the SAM-systems was never neglected. The ability to jam radar stations and communications was a vital part of the strategy. The outcome of the operation might have been the same without it, but at a higher risk. This demonstrates that there is still a place for SEAD (suppression of enemy air defenses), including electronic jamming. Fifth and finally, when it comes to intelligence and information, the Libyan campaign shows that the value of tactical reconaissance is absolutely vital. Regardless of whether the intelligence or the live video feed comes from an UAV or a reconaissance aircraft, it will allow penetration of the opponent's decision cycle. Live video feed is extremely valuable, but so are evaluated reconaissance photos, they simply serve different purposes. The major difficulty was known prior to the conflict. The ability to engage targets inside cities with low collateral damage is limited, since there are simply too many obstacles and low visibility after a target has been struck. This additionally explains why the coalition forces were determined not to let the regime forces into Benghazi.

Regardless of the problems along the way, the final conclusion must be that the coalition launched a successful air operation. The main questions will remain until the next conflict, because change will not take place overnight. The command and control issue clearly indicates that there are only a few countries capable of staging a multi-country air campaign. This is even clearer with participants from outside the NATO community. NATO will still be around as the command and control agency, yet it needs to work towards further integration of future partners – even unexpected ones – without giving the alliance's intelligence away.

In conclusion, then, the Libya conflict has proved that air power can be a decisive tool in regaining the peace. As long as the objective is clear and the politicians understand the possibilities and limitations of air power, there is no reason to hesitate. Every conflict and war is unique with regards to scenario, order of battle, tactics, technical development and the very reason for conflict. Hence, the lessons from Libya might not be applicable in the future. In practice, despite different views, the usage of air power is left to the on-scene commander to decide upon. Air power can surely bring a swift, yet powerful response. Despite its inability to hold ground over time, air power has – in the right circumstances – the possibility of achieving an effect that is beyond the capacity of other services in the armed forces. It can both isolate, and if necessary decapitate, leadership. In the Libyan conflict, the inability to hold ground can indeed be considered strength, since it made air power the only credible solution.

Notes

1 NATO. *No-fly zones explained*. Online. Available: www.nato.int/cps/en/natolive/news_71959.htm (accessed 18 February 2013).
2 NATO. *NATO and Libya*. Online. Available: www.nato.int/cps/en/natolive/topics_71652.htm (accessed 18 February 2013).
3 Excerpt from the UN Security Council 6498th Meeting (Night). UN Department of Public Information. (17 March 2011) *Security Council approves 'no-fly zone' over Libya, authorizing 'all necessary measures' to protect civilians, by vote of 10 in favour with 5 abstentions*. Online. Available: www.un.org/News/Press/docs/2011/sc10200.doc.htm (accessed 18 February 2013).
4 This chapter relies on official data and on the author's interviews with servicemen and commanders who took part in various stages of the operations. The latter spoke to the author in confidentiality and their names will not be listed unless they have provided their explicit consent.
5 The main difference between Warden and Pape is that the former applies a strategic top-down or inside-out approach while the latter is oriented towards the battlefield. R. Pape, *Bombing to win: Air power and coercion in war*, Ithaca: Cornell University Press, 1999, p. 314; M. van Creveld, *Air power and Maneuver Warfare*, Honolulu: University Press of the Pacific, 2002, p. 219; J.A. Olsen, *John Warden and the renaissance of American air power*, 2007, Dulles: Potomac books, p. 2.
6 J.A. Warden III, 'The enemy as a system', *Air Power Journal*, Spring 1995. Online. Available: www.airpower.maxwell.af.mil/airchronicles/apj/apj95/spr95_files/warden.htm (accessed 18 February 2013).
7 BBC News. *Libya: RAF 'comfortable' with outcome of airstrikes*, 20 March 2011. Online. Available: www.bbc.co.uk/news/uk-12799493 (accessed 18 February 2013).

8 US Air Force, 'Air force global strike command supports operation Oddesey Dawn', *Warrior*, 2, 2012. Online. Available: www.whiteman.af.mil/shared/media/document/AFD-110324–151.pdf (accessed 18 February 2013).
9 MBDA. *Storm Shadow/Scalp* (2012). Online. Available: www.mbda-systems.com/products/air-dominance/storm-shadow-scalp/30 (accessed 18 February 2013).
10 In the early stages of the campaign, the main targets were fixed, i.e. command and control bunkers, C2 nodes, radar sites and SAM-sites, especially the SA-2, SA-3 and SA-5.
11 MBDA. *Air Dominance Brimstone* (2012). Online. Available: www.mbda-systems.com/products/air-dominance/dual-mode-brimstone/23 (accessed 18 February 2013).
12 Safran. *AASM: la nouvelle génération d'armements air-sol de précision* (2012). Online. Available: www.sagem-ds.com/spip.php?rubrique80&lang=fr; Mail Online. *Libya in flames: French fighter jets shoot down Gaddafi warplane in battle for Misratah*, 24 March 2011. Online. Available: www.dailymail.co.uk/news/article-1369452/Libya-Fighter-jets-shoot-Gaddafi-warplane-regimes-troops-parade-charred-bodies.html (accessed 18 February 2013).
13 CBS News. *Boots on the ground on Libya*, 7 June 2011. Online. Available: www.cbsnews.com/video/watch/?id=7368713n (accessed 18 February 2013); Associated Press. *Arab League urges U.N. to impose no-fly zone over Libya* (2011). Online. Available: www.nbcnews.com/id/42045460/ns/world_news-mideast_n_africa/t/arab-league-asks-un-impose-no-fly-zone-over-libya/ (accessed 18 February 2013).
14 NATO. 'NATO No-Fly zone over Libya. Operation Unified Protector', *NATO fact sheet*. Online. Available: www.nato.int/nato_static/assets/pdf/pdf_2011_03/20110325_110325-unified-protector-no-fly-zone.pdf (accessed 18 February 2013).
15 US Department of Defense. *Coalition first strikes* (2011). Online. Available: www.defense.gov/news/PAO_DJS_Slides_19Mar11_v3.pdf (accessed 18 February 2013).
16 Global Research. *The Libyan air defense system. Libya's surface to air missile (SAM) network* (2011). Online. Available: www.globalresearch.ca/the-libyan-air-defense-system-libya-s-surface-to-air-missile-sam-network (accessed 18 February 2013).
17 Federation of American Scientists. *SA-8 GECKO*. Online. Available: www.fas.org/man/dod-101/sys/missile/row/sa-8.htm (accessed 4 February 2000).
18 MBDA. *MBDA missile systems*. Online. Available: www.mbda-systems.com/products/maritime-superiority/otomat-teseo/49 (accessed 18 February 2013); Federation of American Scientists. *Project 1159 Koni Class*. Online. Available: www.fas.org/man/dod-101/sys/ship/row/rus/1159.htm (accessed 18 February 2013).
19 Federation of American Scientists. *Project 1234 Nanuchka Class*. Online. Available: www.fas.org/man/dod-101/sys/ship/row/rus/1234.htm (accessed 18 February 2013).
20 United States Navy. *USS Kearsarge*. Online. Available: www.kearsarge.navy.mil (accessed 18 February 2013).
21 Global Security. *Libyan Air Force*. Online. Available: www.globalsecurity.org/military/world/libya/af.htm (accessed 18 February 2013).
22 Ibid.
23 The influence from former Yugoslavia was particularly strong. Yugoslavs mainly staffed the Air Force Academy when it was established 1975. Ibid.
24 Ibid.
25 Ibid.
26 J. Gertler, 'Operation Odyssey Dawn (Libya): Background and issues for the Congress', *Congressional Research Service*, 28 March 2011. Online. Available: http://fpc.state.gov/documents/organization/159790.pdf (accessed 18 February 2013).

27 W. Gortney, 'Vice Adm. Bill Gortney announces the start of Operation Odyssey Dawn', 19 March 2011. Online. Available: www.youtube.com/watch?v=DFMh0QISV64 (accessed 18 February 2013).
28 US Air Force. *Operation Oddessey Dawn.* Online. Available: www.af.mil/operationodysseydawn.asp (accessed 18 February 2013).
29 Royal Air Force. *Libya Operation Ellamy.* Online. Available: www.raf.mod.uk/news/Libya-OpELLAMY.cfm (accessed 18 February 2013).
30 Ministère de la Défense. *Opération Harmattan Libye.* Online. Available: www.defense.gouv.fr/operations/autres-operations/operation-harmattan-libye (accessed 18 February 2013).
31 National Defence and the Canadian Forces. *Operation Mobile.* Online. Available: www.forces.gc.ca/site/feature-vedette/2011/02/libya-libye-eng.asp (accessed 18 February 2013).
32 Gortney, 'Vice Adm. Bill Gortney announces the start of Operation Odyssey Dawn'.
33 I. Traynor, 'Turkey and France clash over Libya air campaign', *The Guardian*, 24 March 2011. Online. Available: http://m.guardian.co.uk/world/2011/mar/24/turkey-france-clash-libya-campaign?cat=world&type=article (accessed 18 February 2013).
34 Defense News. *Danish Planes in Libya running out of bombs: Report* (2011). Online. Available: www.defensenews.com/article/20110609/DEFSECT01/106090302/Danish-Planes-Libya-Running-Out-Bombs-Report (accessed 18 February 2013).
35 R. Pengelley, 'Gripens over Libya', *Janes International Defence Review*, January 2012.
36 LTC Stefan Wilson, CO Swedish Air Force Unit, FL01.
37 The Washington Post, 26 June 2011.
38 Gertler, 'Operation Odyssey Dawn (Libya)'.
39 S. Aroor, 'Gaddafi's forces in crosshairs, Rafaels crank up op experience', *Livefist*, 20 March 2011. Online. Available: http://livefist.blogspot.se/2011/03/gaddafis-forces-in-crosshairs-rafales.html (accessed 18 February 2013).
40 Many of the defectors were reportedly executed for refusing to open fire on pro-democracy protestors. PressTV. *130 Libyan Soldiers Executed For Mutiny*, 24 February 2011. Online. Available: http://edition.presstv.ir/detail/166757.html (accessed 18 February 2013).
41 Live Leak. *African mercenary harshly executed by Libyans in Benghazi*, 30 March 2011. Online. Available: www.liveleak.com/view?i=02a_1301531604 (accessed 18 February 2013).
42 W. Gortney, 'Pentagon Press Briefing on Day 2 of Operation Oddysey Dawn', 20 March 2011. Online. Available: www.youtube.com/watch?v=LRMJKFA7hq4 (accessed 18 February 2013).
43 Ibid.
44 I. Drury, 'Tornado Top Guns' 3000-mile mission to hammer tyrant's military machine', *Daily Mail*, 21 March 2011. Online. Available: www.dailymail.co.uk/news/article-1368259/Libya-Tornado-Top-Guns-3-000-mile-mission-hammer-Gaddafis-military-machine.html (accessed 18 February 2013).
45 C.F. Ham, 'USA General Carter Ham Operation Odyssey Dawn in Libya', 21 March 2011. Online. Available: www.youtube.com/watch?v=PZLkwbeROa0&playnext=1&list=PLEBA5F477AA666409&feature=results_main (accessed 18 February 2013).
46 Gortney, 'Vice Adm. Bill Gortney announces the start of Operation Odyssey Dawn'.
47 Ibid.
48 Ministry of Defence. *HMS Triumph return from Libya Operations*, 4 April 2011. Online. Available: www.mod.uk/DefenceInternet/DefenceNews/Military

Operations/HmsTriumphReturnsFromLibyaOperations.htm (accessed 18 February 2013).
49 C.F. Ham, 'Gen. Ham: Air strikes in Libya continue, no-fly zone may expand', 21 March 2011. Online. Available: www.youtube.com/watch?v=cl8ec3x-1qE&feature=related (accessed 18 February 2013); Gortney, 'Pentagon Press Briefing'.
50 Ibid.
51 J. Hooper and I. Black, 'Libya defectors: Pilots told to bomb protesters flee to Malta', *The Guardian*, 21 February 2011. Online. Available: www.guardian.co.uk/world/2011/feb/21/libya-pilots-flee-to-malta (accessed 18 February 2013).
52 Wikipedia. *Timeline of the Libyan civil war*. Online. Available: http://en.wikipedia.org/wiki/Timeline_of_the_Libyan_civil_war (accessed 18 February 2013).
53 R.H. Parkinson, 'Touchdown B-2 Stealth jets return after epic 11,500 mile journey to bomb Libyan aircraft shelters', *Daily Mail*, 21 March 2011. Online. Available: www.dailymail.co.uk/news/article-1368337/Libya-crisis-B2-stealth-bombers-25-hour-flight-Missouri-Tripoli.html (accessed 18 February 2013).
54 M.A. Tichenor, 'Bombers over Libya', *Air Force Magazine*, July 2011.
55 F.L. Carpenter, 'Bombers over Libya', *Air Force Magazine*, July 2011.
56 US Air Force. *EC-130J commando solo*, 9 September 2011. Online. Available: www.af.mil/information/factsheets/factsheet.asp?id=182 (accessed 18 February 2013).
57 S. Fontaine, 'EC-130J transmissions over Libya posted online', *Air Force Times*, 22 March 2011. Online. Available: www.airforcetimes.com/news/2011/03/airforce-ec-130j-transmissions-psyops-libya-032111w (accessed 18 February 2013).
58 CNN Wire Staff, 'US Official: Gadhafi's momentum stopped', *CNN*, 21 March 2011. Online. Available: http://edition.cnn.com/2011/WORLD/africa/03/21/libya.civil.war/index.html?hpt=T1&iref=BN1 (accessed 18 February 2013).
59 US Africa Command. *TRANSCRIPT: Update by Admiral Locklear, III, on Operation Odyssey Dawn*, 22 March 2011. Online. Available: www.africom.mil/getArticle.asp?art=6259 (accessed 18 February 2013).
60 Unnamed pilot involved in Air Operations over Misrata.
61 BBC News Africa. *Libya Air force 'no longer exists as a fighting force'*, 23 March 2011. Online. Available: www.bbc.co.uk./news/world-afric-12837330 (accessed 19 February 2013).
62 Ibid.
63 Traynor, 'Turkey and France clash over Libya air campaign'.
64 Channel News Asia. *NATO forces Libyan Rebel's fighter jet to land*, 10 April 2011. Online. Available: www.channelnewsasia.com/stories/afp_world/view/1121823/1/.html (accessed 18 February 2013).
65 N. Springgate, 'Libya: Coalition air strike near Brega kills rebels', *BBC News*, 2 April 2011. Online. Available: www.webcitation.org/5xeJjpyOg (accessed 18 February 2013).
66 BBC News. *Libya air raid 'killed civilians'*, 1 April 2011. Online. Available: www.webcitation.org/5xeJuYiUd (accessed 18 February 2013).
67 BBC News. *Libya: UK Apache helicopters used in Nato attacks*, 4 June 2011. Online. Available: www.bbc.co.uk/news/uk-13651736 (accessed 18 February 2013).
68 BBC News. *Profile: Khamis Gaddafi*, 4 September 2011. Online. Available: www.bbc.co.uk/news/world-africa-14723041 (accessed 18 February 2013).
69 H. Li, 'Khamis Gaddafi recruits mercenaries to shoot protestors', *International Business Times*, 21 February 2011. Online. Available: www.ibtimes.com/khamis-gaddafi-recruits-mercenaries-shoot-protestors-269249 (accessed 18 February 2013).
70 BBC News. *Profile: Khamis Gaddafi*.

71 D. Spleeters, 'Tracking Belgian weapons in Libya', *New York Times*, 28 December 2011. Online. Available: http://atwar.blogs.nytimes.com/2011/12/28/tracking-belgian-weapons-in-libya (accessed 18 February 2013).
72 BBC News. *Profile: Khamis Gaddafi*.
73 D. McElroy, 'Libya: Gaddafi stages show of force in Misurata', *The Telegraph*, 29 March 2011. Online. Available: www.telegraph.co.uk/news/worldnews/africaand-indianocean/libya/8412427/Libya-Gaddafi-stages-show-of-force-in-Misurata.html (accessed 18 February 2013).
74 Ibid.
75 Sky News. *Rebels: Gaddafi's son 'killed in air strike'*, 30 August 2011. Online. Available: http://news.sky.com/story/876826/rebels-gaddafis-son-killed-in-air-strike (accessed 18 February 2013).

5 Naval assets – not just a tool for war

Christian Wollert

Introduction

Over the past decades, the utilization of naval forces in peace operations has become more prominent and has been given more political and diplomatic weight.[1] Rather than primarily being designated to fight naval battles, naval forces are also used during peace, in crises as well as in conflicts other than war, as a strategic tool. The objective in such scenarios is to uphold international law and agreements or perhaps to influence, persuade or coerce other actors. Developments after the end of the Cold War have also led to a desire to build warships optimized for support of globalized trade routes and order at sea. The increased production of Offshore/Ocean Patrol Vessels (OPVs), such as the Italian Commander-class and the Spanish Serviola-class, or ships for both coastguard duties and military tasks, like the Danish Absalon-class and the Norwegian Fritjof Nansen-class, are examples of this development.

Paradoxically, and at the same time, there is still a need for naval units that are capable of supporting the achievement of political and military objectives throughout the whole spectrum of conflict from influencing an opponent, via naval presence, through power projection on shore over to sea battle. The competition between different naval functions thus affects military procurement in terms of ship size, numbers built, capabilities, and the level of versatility expected from most new vessels (and their crews).[2]

This dual requirement is not entirely new. Naval forces have always been an instrument for the political leadership in their efforts to secure and exercise control of the sea, either in protecting sea lines of communications or affecting events on shore.[3] In this regard, the characteristics and prerequisites of naval forces, to exploit the oceans, make them a suitable diplomatic tool. Moreover, the freedom of navigation on the high seas enables naval forces to use their mobility and adaptability.[4] A warship moving at 25 knots speed reaches a distance of 600 nautical miles (1,100 km) per day (the distance between Rome and Tripoli). If the unit is large enough to store supplies or is reinforced by support vessels, it can increase its sustainability and spend an even longer time at sea without further replenishment. After arriving at a potential area of operations the forces may be deployed undetected well off the coastline to gather intelligence about events onshore, and, depending on the development of the situation, then withdraw undetected or switch to an active and visible posture.

Today's British maritime doctrine, widely regarded as state-of-art with regard to the use of naval assets, outlines the following capability attributes for naval forces; access (around the world); mobility (exploiting the access); great lift capacity (ammunitions, troops, supplies, etc); sustained reach (integral logistic and repair capability); versatility (change of military posture); poise (perception effect); resilience (self damage restore); and leverage (effect against the opponent).[5] These capability attributes, inherent in all naval forces, provide decision makers with considerable freedom of action regarding choices; they can be used to underwrite a political message, or to exert political pressure on a specific actor. The latter type of option is particularly attractive when a government wants to protect its interests at sea or suppress a situation, so that it does not escalate into an uncontrollable conflict or war.

Several theories or concepts with this latter focus were developed during the Cold War, several of which can be summarized under the term 'Naval Diplomacy'. These were later, after the end of the Cold War, reinforced with additional conceptualizations bordering that notion. The latter dealt with, for instance, geopolitical changes that occurred after the end of the Cold War and as a result of the globalization of trade.[6] There is, however, some confusion with regards to the different concepts that describe the use of naval forces in peace. For instance, they sometime overlap and the boundaries between different concepts are diffuse and unclear. Since concepts such as that of Naval Diplomacy inevitably will have different legal and political implications, and further repercussions on military doctrine and defence procurement, it is important to describe the boundaries and interrelationships between concepts. Nor must the significance of the general public's views and interpretations of the different concepts be underestimated. A related problem is that there is no general theory of 'Sea Power during Peace' that corresponds to thoughts on 'Sea Power during War'.[7]

So which of all theoretical concepts is actually used in current international operations? One way to analyse this is to review larger multinational campaigns that involve naval forces and investigate which concepts best describe the execution of the naval operations. A campaign that is suitable for this kind assessment is NATO's 2011 military engagement in Libya.

From a legal perspective the military campaign in Libya cannot be characterized as a war. It was not an act under the laws of war. It was, however, a military campaign, and as such executed under a UN mandate for the purpose of stabilizing the situation and to protect the civilian population in Libya. Several political statements gave a clear message that the Libyan campaign was not a military intervention with a political mandate other than to protect civilians and civilian areas in Libya.[8] It was not a war; the objective was not to defeat Libyan forces or to change the political leadership (at least not officially or during the initial part of the campaign). Instead it used a UN Security Council mandate for political coercion through, inter alia, maritime power projection with naval forces to achieve political objectives. The situation prevailing during the Libyan conflict and the conditions for the military action have by some experts been described as unique, and that it is impossible to draw valid lessons from it. There is, of course, an important point to this claim: all military operations take place in their own context; the geopolitical situation will always differ, as will the nature of the various actors; the mission area will change; the environmental impacts will look different; and the technological capabilities will shift. To draw long-term conclusions about the use of naval forces in future conflicts on the basis of experiences from the Libyan conflict may therefore be hazardous. Yet, there are some lessons that could and probably should be drawn, as from any recent military conflict.[9]

The chapter consists of three separate sections. The first tries to identify which concepts can be used to describe the application of naval forces in peace and how the boundaries/relationships between these concepts ought to be delineated. In particular, do concepts cover all use of naval forces in peace, or are there gaps, and are several concepts relevant to one and the same area?

The next section deals with the use of naval forces during the Libyan campaign, its estimated contribution to the larger campaign and how it can be linked to the previously described concepts. The most important naval actions during the Libya operation are presented in detail, then linked to the chosen concepts for the purpose of a discussion on whether, and (if so) how, the naval operations had an impact on the development of the conflict and its outcomes. In order to secure critical distance from the sequence of events and military measures adopted, the account relies heavily on news sources, and especially the timeline constructed by the BBC, instead of on official information provided by NATO or national defence forces of the countries involved.

The final part discusses the applicability of the chosen concepts beyond the case of Libya. Are the operations in the Libya conflict characteristic of the use of naval forces in peace? What conclusions can be drawn from the Libya conflict with a bearing on the use of naval forces in future conflicts? Is there a need to further define or clarify the concepts for the use of naval forces in peace?

The roles of naval forces during peacetime

It is a paradox of sorts, that even if a man-of-war is constructed for war, it has mostly performed duties during peacetime.[10] This statement seems even more relevant today, with a wide international focus on crisis management and peace support operations. The use of naval forces in peace operations can conceptually be divided in different ways, one being offered by Geoffrey Till, an authoritative writer on naval theory. Till outlines four separate though inter-related concepts; humanitarian operations, naval diplomacy, expeditionary operations and maritime security operations.[11]

Before moving on to individual concepts, it may be useful to elaborate how different concepts regarding peace operations relate to each other. The conceptual overview will start with a description of Naval Diplomacy, then move into Humanitarian Operations, Expeditionary Operations and then finally over to Maritime Security Operations. The overview will focus on how the concept in question relates to the political level, and the aim of the specific operation, in order to create an analytical tool that can be used to examine naval operations during a military campaign.

So how can Naval Diplomacy, overall, be described?[12] First of all, the concept implies that naval forces, in combination with other policy instruments, are used by the political leadership as an instrument in the diplomatic dialogue between the political leadership of states, as an instrument of communication somewhat akin to 'body language'. The generic aim of diplomacy is to support negotiations, in a broad sense, between sovereign states.[13] A Naval Diplomacy operation thus consists of a political message containing an element of negotiation, a choice which the adversary must consider. The actions of a designated naval force used in such a scenario is closely dependent on how the adversary makes his choice. For instance, by following the desires of the sender the receiver may avoid punishment or severe repercussions.

Sometimes Naval Diplomacy is primarily a show of force, a demonstration of power and presence. US aircraft carriers sailing around the globe may be characterized as instruments of Naval Diplomacy in that sense. In other instances the deployment of naval force concerns a political negotiation where both parties supposedly give and take. In the case of the Libya operation the political message was clearly expressed in UN resolutions 1970 and 1973; Gaddafi's violence against civilians should cease and if it did not, the assigned naval force, together with other military assets except occupation troops on Libyan soil, was mandated to enforce them. This seems to be a fairly clear example of the concept of Naval Diplomacy. The primary purpose of the military deployment in such an operation is to support the achievement of a positive advantage and, secondarily, to inflict physical damage on an adversary. Actions are therefore focused towards the opponent's will and not against his military or physical strengths. The opening and closing of force actions are driven by whether the strategic objective (the positive advantage) is achieved or not.

Humanitarian operations are carried out after natural disasters, civil wars or other situations when people are suffering from existential needs. Humanitarian assistance and disaster relief are best handled by civilian governmental and non-governmental organizations. But normally it takes some time for them to have an effect. Naval forces may then be appropriate to use, at least initially, due to their flexibility and ability to quickly provide emergency assistance such as fresh water, food, medical assistance and other needs. When other organizations have established an infrastructure for humanitarian support, naval forces can continue to support with logistics, coordination and protection.[14] Notably, Geoffrey Till claims that humanitarian operations and naval diplomacy are closely connected, as are expeditionary operations. In fact, he argues, the three can be said to constitute a spectrum, with Naval Diplomacy in the middle and blurry boundaries between the three.[15] Humanitarian operations are, according to Till, not only used in the aftermath of natural disasters or civil wars, but also to counter threats to good order at sea. This could include attacks on actors trying to exploit disasters or threatening good order at sea or evacuations of non-combatants.

Humanitarian operations may have political ambitions but, more importantly, they virtually always produce political effects. For instance, a successful Humanitarian (Support) Operation, like the one during the Tsunami in the Indian Ocean in 2004, can generate goodwill and thus an incentive for coalition building. At the time, British and US naval units, together with several other nations, coordinated and assisted the different national authorities, as well as international organizations, with intelligence, surveillance and reconnaissance to estimate the range of the catastrophe. It was also naval units that delivered most supplies to civilians stranded in chaos. The overlap between Humanitarian Operations and Naval Diplomacy should therefore primarily be seen as related to the purpose of the operation, and not the operational design.[16]

In Libya, naval forces were used to conduct non-combatant evacuations, according to NATO bringing more than 2,500 civilians to safety. The main part of the evacuations was in fact conducted by national efforts before the military campaign started, and not by NATO. The aim of the military operation was, according to resolution 1973, primarily to protect civilians, including the protection of humanitarian organizations' transporting of supplies to Libya.

If Humanitarian Operations could be seen as compatible with the non-coercive side of Naval Diplomacy, it is reasonable to argue that Expeditionary Operations can be found on the opposite side. Till explains that Expeditionary Operations typically grow out of the coercive, or compellence-oriented, dimension of Naval Diplomacy.[17] In fact, when the British task force was sent to the Falklands in 1982 it started as a Naval Diplomacy action to compel the Argentineans to leave the islands. When it was clear that this would not happen, the operation was changed to (limited) war. The boundary between Expeditionary Operations and Naval Diplomacy operations seems to be inescapably fluid and the former overlaps with the latter in one end and (limited) war in the other. The Libyan conflict could, from a purely conceptual point of view, be described as both an Expeditionary and a Naval Diplomacy operation. This indicates that there is great affinity between the two in that Expeditionary Operations are aimed at physical kinetic effects rather than subtle cognitive ones. The coercive part of Naval Diplomacy has many similarities with Expeditionary Operations though, as Till emphasizes, it is the purpose of the operation that finally defines which type of operation it is.

Finally, Maritime Security Operations are about securing the peaceful activities that benefit global trade and national welfare development around the world. The basis for such operations are international agreements and international laws, often combined with a specific mandate for their execution (or rule enforcement) which in turn depends on the fact that they are regulated and accepted by all states. Such mandates may be derived from UN Security Council resolutions, but also be executed under existing and customary international law. It is thus a question of maintaining an international regime already in place (what Booth refers to as a policing role).[18] The boundary between Maritime Security Operations and Naval Diplomacy is, as in the previous types of operations, in the physical and cognitive domain. Maritime Security Operations are not primarily used to influence political actors, but to maintain internationally accepted regimes and norms.

In the 2011 Libya campaign formed the bulk of activities performed by allied naval forces after the adoption, by the UN Security Council, of resolution 1970. That resolution authorized sanctions with the purpose of upholding the arms embargo. Resolution 1973, which soon followed suit, expanded the mandate to encompass intrusive inspections onboard ships that were either in- or outbound vis-à-vis Libya.

If we now return to Till's concepts they offer us tools that can be used to analyse the naval operations during the Libya campaign (which will be carried out in the next section).[19] He explains that Humanitarian Operations could include providing assistance in case of disasters, non-combat evacuations, proactive humanitarian missions or sea-based attacks on forces of disorder at sea.[20] Naval Diplomacy could have the political purpose of collecting intelligence in an interesting area, which is what Till calls 'picture building', or just support 'coalition building'. The third political purpose could be to coerce an actor either to act as you want against his will (compellence) or to prevent him from doing something you do not want him to do (deterrence).[21] Expeditionary Operations constitute, according to Till, an intervention conducted at some distance with self-sustaining forces in an operation limited in aim and of short duration and highly politicized.[22] Maritime Security Operations, finally, are focused on soft security or good order at sea, such as secure transportations and trade at sea, extractions of resources at sea and preventing international crimes or terrorism.[23]

Naval actions during the Libyan conflict 2011

This section of the chapter analyses the naval operations and their effects during the Libyan conflict, in accordance with the chronological evolution of events. This will be accomplished by linking them to the concepts described above. What most people know about the Libya conflict is that it entailed a NATO-led air campaign, but what is not widely known is that there was also extensive naval presence throughout the campaign. The deployment of naval forces during the conflict can chronologically be subdivided into four phases.

The first phase began at the start of the revolt in Libya on 17 February 2011 and lasted ten days.[24] In this phase naval units conducted non-combatant evacuation operations from Libya and neighbouring states, and assisted refugees trying to escape by ships and boats from Libya. The second phase took place between the two United Nation Security Council (UNSC) resolutions 1970 (26 February) and 1973 (17 March). Under the mandate of UN resolution 1970 an arms embargo was imposed against Libya,[25] and several nations, such the United States and Canada, repositioned naval forces towards the coast off Libya.[26] When the UNSC passed resolution 1973, indicating the start of the third phase, the conditions for naval operations against Libya changed dramatically. From being national operations conducted mostly off Libyan territory, they now transitioned into military kinetic actions performed by a coalition of states aimed at targets on Libyan territory. The fourth and final phase started when NATO took full control over the campaign and termed it Operation Unified Protector (OUP). This final phase ended when NATOs operation was concluded on 30 October 2011.

Since this period was preceded by unrest in the wider Arab world, including the toppling of dictators in Tunisia and Egypt, there were already a significant number of warships in the vicinity of Libya. A lot of diplomatic work by individual nations and organizations was already being conducted in order to mitigate the various (indirectly interrelated) crises. The naval forces in the area were used on a national basis and primarily engaged in what Till calls 'picture building' or what James Cable refers to as 'Expressive Force', a symbolic naval presence not associated with a specific political goal.[27]

Phase 1 (17–26 February)

When the rebellion in Libya began in mid-February 2011, several different international and national naval operations and exercises were ongoing in the Mediterranean Sea and its vicinity. NATO was also present in the area and conducted two major operations, Operation Active Endeavour and Operation Ocean Shield. The former was focused on terrorist activities while the latter was focused on piracy. A rapid reaction force from the

Royal Navy, the *Response Force Task Group (RFTG)*, was conducting exercise COUGAR 11 together with vessels from the French *Charles de Gaulle Task Group*. The limited distance between Libya and European states such as (NATO members) Spain, France, Italy, Greece and Turkey, allowed naval forces to cross the distance in less than a few days. Consequently, several naval units were readily available for operations off the coast of Libya, should it be necessary.

The turmoil and often disorganized fighting between civilians and security forces in Libya created a high-risk situation for foreign labourers and large parts of the domestic population. The situation led to a stream of internally displaced persons (IDP) and refugees into Tunisia and Egypt, and further to migrants fleeing by boat to the islands and ports outside areas controlled by the Libyan government. Several states were therefore engaged in non-combatant evacuation operations for the purpose of bringing nationals back to safety. These operations were conducted both by air and ship. For instance, on 24 February the British frigate HMS *Cumberland* arrived in Malta carrying 207 people, 69 British nationals and 138 passengers from other nations, all successfully evacuated from Benghazi. The HMS *Cumberland* conducted two more emergency visits to Benghazi and evacuated a total of 454 people, including 129 British citizens.[28] The HMS *Cumberland* had just ten days previously been part of an entirely unrelated Maritime Security Operation, fighting pirates off the coast of Somalia. This illustrates the ability to move quickly from one operational area to another and the flexibility to change from one type of operation to another, two characteristics of naval force deployment.

Phase 2 (26 February–17 March)

When the UN Security Council adopted resolution 1970 the pressure on the Libyan authorities to end the violence and to respect the international rights increased abruptly. The resolution introduced targeted UN sanctions against the Libyan government.[29] The resolution further urged each state to interrupt and prevent any arms trade with Libya, directly or indirectly. Each state was obligated to inspect ships if it had information that it was transporting unauthorized cargo to or from Libya. However, the mandate did not authorize actions against shipments outside a country's own territory or actions within Libyan territory.[30]

According to the mandate inherent in resolution 1970, naval forces could not be used for interdiction operations. National naval forces deployed in the region therefore continued conducting evacuation operations of stranded non-combatants or reinforced their presence of warships off the coast of Libya. On 1 March for instance, the US repositioned both naval and air forces towards the vicinity of Libya.[31] The amphibious assault ship, USS *Kearsarge*, which usually carries around 2,000 marines,[32] and the amphibious transport dock USS *Ponce* entered the Mediterranean through the Suez Canal. The United States declared that it was moving military assets closer to Libya as preparation for a humanitarian emergency.[33]

Similarly, the Canadian frigate HMCS *Charlottetown* left Halifax on 2 February to take part in the ongoing evacuation operations in Libya.[34] Meanwhile, Egyptian state media announced that navy ship *Halayib* had set sail for Tunisia in order to pick up stranded Egyptians.[35] France also sent naval forces, including its second-largest warship, the helicopter carrier *Mistral*, to the waters off Libya in order to help evacuate refugees.[36] Likewise, on 4 February, Germany announced the dispatch of three ships to evacuate 4,000 Egyptians.[37] The large number of refugees necessitated a maritime contribution that could both transport and supply them. Due to the spread of armed struggle there was also a growing need to protect the transports, a task for which naval forces were well suited.

Sea traffic in the waters off Libya was extensive during this period. The Mediterranean Sea is normally one of the most trafficked areas in the world, but the conflict in Libya resulted in additional activities in the area. Many refugees fled by boat to the Italian island of Lampedusa, where the humanitarian situation soon became troublesome. On 3 February, 57 barges arrived in Lampedusa, one of them carrying as many as 370 people. A week later, during the night of 8 February, 11 boats carrying around 1,000 people reached the island.[38] These transports were sometimes conducted on small, less seaworthy and overloaded boats. The risk of any of them ending up in distress was considerable. The flow of refugees also created, albeit temporarily, a surge in 'black market sea transports'.

Meanwhile, humanitarian organizations tried to provide aid to the Libyan people. The fighting and the unwillingness of the authorities to accept or support humanitarian help made it difficult for the organizations, which were occasionally attacked by pro-Gaddaffi forces, to reach the suffering people in key areas. For instance, the World Food Programme stated that a ship carrying 1,000 tonnes of flour to Benghazi had turned back without unloading its cargo due to aerial bombardments.[39] Normal sea traffic to and from the Libyan ports dropped off as fighting intensified around and in the harbours. On 8 February the major Libyan oil ports of Ras Lanuf and Brega were closed. Both towns had seen major clashes between pro- and anti-government forces.[40] There were several successful evacuations but some failed, in some cases after disruption by Libyan authorities.

UN resolution 1970 may have amounted to a politically strong signal to the Libyan leadership, but it did not give governments participating in naval activities much room for the use of naval forces. While it failed to provide a clear mandate to effectively maintain the arms embargo on Libyan territorial waters, it created some legal opportunities for an increase in naval presence. The outcome was an understanding among several states to try and exploit Naval Diplomacy operations by increasing naval presence. At the same time, most operations were at this point manly focused on the evacuation of nationals and the protection of humanitarian aid and relief operations. Only a handful of countries used their forward positions to move personnel ashore in conjunction with evacuations or with the purpose ot establishing diplomatic relations with rebel groups.[41] The former can be described as a Humanitarian Operation and the latter as a diplomacy operation or as a limited/subtle form of Expeditionary Operation.

Phase 3 (17–31 March)

On 17 March the United Nations Security Council adopted Resolution 1973.[42] The core of the resolution was similar to its predecessor devoted to the protection of civilians and civilian areas in Libya. But the mandate to accomplish this expanded to include 'all necessary measures', thus allowing for military action, to protect civilians and civilian populated areas under attack. Since foreign occupation force of any form on any part of the Libyan land territory was precluded, the objective had to be achieved principally through the establishment of a No-Fly Zone (NFZ) in the airspace over Libya. The expanded arms embargo against Libya this time provided for inspections of ships and aircrafts bound for, or leaving, Libya. The resolution thereby offered naval forces a reinforced mandate to act in Libyan territorial waters and outside Libyan ports. The positioning of naval forces very close to the Libyan mainland helped enhance 'picture-building' regarding the situation ashore and to underpin the establishment of the NFZ. It also meant that cruise missiles, naval air strikes and naval gun support could be used against targets ashore in order to protect civilians and support the NFZ.

At 7 p.m. on 19 March, a multi-national coalition thus launched an outright military campaign, Operation Odyssey Dawn, against Libya so as to implement resolution 1973. The operation was under operational command of General Carter Ham, commander of the US Africa Command. The commander of the Joint Task Force Odyssey Dawn was Admiral Sam Locklear, embarked with his staff onboard USS *Mount Whitney*.[43] The coalition consisted of nine states: Belgium, Canada, Denmark, France, Norway, Italy, Spain, UK and the United States. Some nations partook in the operation on a national basis rather than as part of the US-led operation. For instance, France launched Operation Harmattan, while UK had their Operation Ellamy and Canada executed Operation Mobile.

The naval forces involved in Operation Odyssey Dawn were the US Command ship USS *Mount Whitney*, the guided missile destroyers USS *Barry* and USS *Stout*, the nuclear attack submarines USS *Providence* and USS *Scranton*, the cruise missile submarine USS *Florida*, the amphibious assault ship USS *Kearsarge* and the amphibious transport dock USS *Ponce*. In addition to American vessels there was the Canadian frigate HMCS

Charlottentown, the Spanish Aegis defence frigate *F-104 Mendez Núñez* and attack submarine *S-74 Tramontana*, the British frigates HMS *Cumberland*, HMS *Sutherland* and HMS *Iron Duke*, along with the destroyer HMS *Liverpool*, submarines HMS *Triumph* and HMS *Turbulent*, minehunter HMS *Bangor*, the MCMV HMS *Brocklesby* and the helicopter carrier HMS *Ocean*, the latter equipped with five helicopters. The force was supported at sea by oiler USNS *Kanawha* and dry cargo ships USNS *Robert E. Peary* and USNS *Lewis and Clark*. In all, the allied effort amounted to a strong and self-sustained sea-based force of total number of 23 ships, with the ability to project power ashore, execute sea control and sea surveillance, and uphold the arms embargo against Libya.

Naval actions were initiated by US and British surface and submarine units firing over 110 Tomahawk land attack cruise missiles (TLAM) against targets on the Libyan mainland.[44] Able to fire TLAMs were HMS *Barry* and USS *Stout*, each carrying 56 Tomahawks, HMS *Triumph*, HMS *Turbulent*, USS *Providence*, USS *Scranton* and USS *Florida*, the latter alone capable of carrying 154 cruise missiles.[45] The British forces launched six TLAMs from a Trafalgar Class submarine, HMS *Triumph*. The rest of the missiles were fired from US units. The purpose of these strikes was to set the conditions for the international coalition to establish a NFZ over Libya and to take measures to prevent attacks on the Libyan people, in accordance with resolution 1973. The targets were military sites and surface-to-air defence systems along the Libyan coast and mainland. By knocking these out, the road was paved for the coalition's air sorties over the Libyan mainland. In this early stage of the coalition campaign, targeting was focused on command, control, communications and intelligence (C3I) infrastructures, in an effort to disrupt the ability of Libyan air defence and to continue offensive operations against the rebels and civilians in the east, especially in the area around Benghazi.[46] After the intense initial effort, the naval force turned its focus to the arms embargo and to upholding the NFZ.

Further efforts to protect civilians ensued. AV-8B aircraft operating from USS *Kearsarge* conducted, on 20 March, attacks on Libyan troops in the area around Ajdabiyah, south of Benghazi. On 21 March an F-15 aircraft crashed, officially due to technical problems, on Libyan territory, creating a flurry of search and rescue activities. Both crew members ejected, but landed without major injuries. A search and rescue task force (CSAR), consisting of two AV-8B Harriers, two MV-22A Osprey and two CH-53E Super Stallion helicopters from USS *Kearsarge*, was quickly sent in to bring the crew back to safety. One of the crew was immediately recovered by the rescue force while the second was temporarily detained by rebels. He was also allowed to return to the force after a few days.

The French Navy's flagship, the aircraft carrier *Charles de Gaulle* with its battle group, set off from the southern port of Toulon towards Libya on 20 March.[47] *Charles de Gaulle* carried 18 aircraft (ten Rafael M fighters, six

Super Étendard strike aircraft, two E-2C airborne early warning aircraft and seven helicopters). On 22 March *Charles de Gaulle* and its escort (anti-submarine destroyer *D 641 Dupleix*, Frigate *F 713 Aconit*, nuclear attack submarine *S 605 Améthyste* and replenishment tanker *A 607 Meuse*) joined the operation. The two anti-air destroyers *D 620 Forbin* and *D 615 Jean Bart*, which normally form part of that battle group and had been in the area since the operations began, also joined the group, now called Task Force 473. On the same day aircraft from *Charles de Gaulle* commenced air sorties over the Libyan mainland.

The Joint Task Force Odyssey Dawn could now participate in air strikes with both SLAMs and air assets (partly provided by US Marine Corps). The task force also participated in the enforcement of the NFZ and the wider protection of civilians in Libya. The ability to deploy naval units near the Libyan coast meant that aircraft now had a shorter distance to their potential targets and no need to utilize air refuelling, though at the same time they were asked to respond faster to intelligence reports and spent less time deprived of operating in the air. When *Charles de Gaulle* joined the force its Rafael F3 and Super Étendard started to conduct both surveillance operations and attacks against targets ashore. On 23 March, 162 SLAMs were fired on targets in Libya, after which US military sources declared that the Libyan air defence no longer existed as a force to be reckoned with.[48]

The initial problem that the humanitarian organizations had faced during the fighting between pro-Gaddafi forces and the rebels slowly decreased. The first aid ship under military protection, *Medeor*, arrived in Misrata on 24 March, at the time of a severe humanitarian crisis. The port was reportedly occupied by pro-Gaddafi troops and witnesses said the Libyan regime was dispatching two warships and several boats to the harbour, yet no attacks were ever reported against the *Medeor* or the escorting warships.[49] The threat against civilians and the humanitarian assistance nevertheless increased, especially in the area of Misrata. In the night between the 28 and 29 March, coalition forces experienced their first naval engagement as the frigate USS *Barry* coordinated an action, with a US Navy *P-3C* patrol aircraft and a US Air Force *A-10 Thunderbolt* attack aircraft, against the Libyan Coast Guard vessel *Vittoria* and two smaller craft which were firing indiscriminately at merchant vessels in the port of Misrata. A BBC contact in Misrata reported of 'strong bombing' in the direction of the port, explaining that Libyan warships were shelling the port 'because this is the only remaining portal for international aid'.[50] USS *Barry* coordinated the action in which the *P-3C* fired a missile (ACM-65F Maverick) that disabled *Vittoria*, which was then forced to beach before the crew abandoned ship. The *A-10* fired its 30mm gun against the two smaller boats, sinking one and forcing the crew of the other to abandon ship.[51]

The Libyan navy was a weak opponent with a very long coastline to secure, in all 956 nautical miles. Naval bases were located at Al Khums

(100 kilometres east of Tripoli) and Tobruq in the eastern part of the country, a submarine base at Ras Hilal, a navy air station at Al Girdabiyah and a naval infantry battalion at Sidi Bilal. The Naval HQ was located at Al Khums. In terms of naval assets, the Libyan navy was also weak; it had two Russian built Foxtrot-class submarines, none of them operational when the operation started. The surface warfare capability was restricted to two frigates of Koni-class, one corvette of Nanuchka-class and four OSA II-class, all ex-Soviet units purchased and transferred during the 1970s and 1980s. All units could carry four SS-N-2C, an active radar/IR homing surface-to-surface missile from the 1960s. The Libyan navy also possessed seven French-built Fast Attack Craft Missile (FAC) boats from the 1980s, each armed with four OTO Melara/Matra Otomat surface-to-surface missiles. Only one frigate, one corvette and ten FACs could be described as operational, though most of them were in limited operational status.

In terms of smaller vessels Libya had four minesweepers of Natya-class and a dozen auxiliary ships (transport ships, salvation ship, tugs). For transportation of amphibious forces the country possessed no more than two ships and two hovercraft.[52] Libya lacked a special coastal defence system, although army artillery units on the coast could fire on ships passing near the coast. In short, Libya's naval capability was very limited. Ships and weapon systems were old and the crews poorly trained. As such, they represented a very limited threat against the coalition force. They could, however, muster smaller operations against the civilian traffic sailing along the coast, or into and out from the ports. There was also a limited capability to support fighting on land. The biggest threat, it seems reasonable to conclude, was that most units could lay sea mines which would impede or halt sea traffic in the area.

With the mandate embedded in the resolution 1973 the political message to the Libyan political leadership could legitimately be accompanied by the threat of, or actual use of, military force. Gaddafi could agree to the demands of the international community if he wished to avoid international intervention in Libya's internal affairs, but otherwise the demands could be enforced with 'all necessary means'. Implicit in the communication on the part of the UN Security Council to the Libyan leadership was a diplomatic gamble.

Yet from the moment at which the international sea-based task force was authorized to launch an attack against targets in Libya onwards, one could argue that the Naval Diplomacy operation shaded into an Expeditionary Operation. More curiously, perhaps, in parallel with these operations a Humanitarian Operation was also carried out by way of escorting humanitarian aid transports through ports that were still open for business. The skirmishes that had occurred between coalition forces and Libyan naval units outside Misrata might also be defined as parts of the Humanitarian Operation. In this case the purpose was to meet a threat against good order at sea, that is, Libyan attacks on civilian sea traffic.

Finally, the sea embargo operation can be regarded as Naval Diplomacy and a Maritime Security Operation at the same time. Either it was aimed at enhancing the impact on the Libyan political leadership to agree to the stipulated political demands, or it should be regarded as a police operation intended to prevent the import and export of prohibited goods to or from Libya.

Phase 4 (31 March–31 October)

After the first intense days the Pentagon declared that it would transfer command of Operation Odyssey Dawn to NATO. In Brussels NATO ambassadors agreed on using NATO warships to enforce the UN arms embargo against Libya.[53] On 23 March NATO assumed responsibility for upholding the arms embargo and two days later the maintenance of the NFZ, both to be included in Operation Unified Protector. CJTF (Combined Joint Task Force) Odyssey Dawn narrowed its activities to the protection of civilians and support to NATO with logistics and intelligence operations. On 27 March NATO decided that it would take control over all military operations over Libya under resolutions 1970 and 1973. Thus the explicit aim of Operation Unified Protector was to protect civilians and civilian-populated areas under attack or threat of attack, in a mission consisting of three elements: an arms embargo, a NFZ, and actions to protect civilians from attack or the threat of attack. On 31 March NATO then assumed full control over all operations against Libya.[54]

The command was transferred from the US African Command to NATO JFC (Joint Force Command) Naples. The new Operational commander was to be LtGen Charles Bouchard of the Canadian Air Force. Responsible for all naval operations was Vice Admiral Rinaldo Veri, the Italian navy, and Task Force commander at sea was Italian Rear Admiral Filippo Maria Foffi aboard his flagship ITS *San Giusto*. Nine nations participated with ten naval surface units and one submarine at the start of the operation. They were Belgium (with the minehunter BNS *Lobelia*), Canada (with the frigate HMCS *Vancouver*), France (with the frigate FS *Commodant Birot*), Greece (with the support ship HS *Aliakamon*), Italy (with the flagship LPD ITS *San Giusto*), Netherlands (with the mine hunter HMNLS *Vlaardingen*), Spain (with the frigate ESPS *Alvaro de Bazán*), Turkey (with the submarine TCG *Doganay* and the frigates TCG *Gelibolu* and TCG *Salihreis*) and United Kingdom (with the destroyer HMS *Liverpool* and the minehunter HMS *Bangor*). In addition, the naval force was assisted by maritime patrol aircraft (NATO AWACS E3A, Spanish Casa CN 235, Canadian Lockheed CP 140 X2 and US P3C Orion).[55]

During the course of the operation different ships were attached to, left, or returned to, the task force. From the start of the Operation Unified Protector until 30 April a total of 18 to 21 ships under NATO command actively patrolled the Central Mediterranean and contributed to the establishment of an arms embargo against Libya. The total number of units was almost identical throughout the campaign though the individual units changed. When the operation ended 12 nations and – at its peak – 21 individual naval units had been assigned to NATO in support of the operation.[56]

At the operational level sea traffic control was executed by NATO through communication with all inbound shipping. An exchange of information to keep approaching vessels fully informed of the maritime situation in the operation area was continually published as a so-called Notice to Mariners.[57] Coordination between NATO forces and civilian shipping was conducted by a special organization, the Naval Cooperation and Guidance for Shipping (NCAGS). In charge was Admiral Veri, who in late April declared that: "NATO urges civilian shipping companies to continue to coordinate with the NATO [NCAGS] organization to provide for the safe transit of shipping in the Region."[58]

Individual acts of violence did occur, but rarely with serious ramifications. During patrols outside Misrata on 29 April, NATO naval forces detected a number of small vessels near the Libyan port. Further investigating indicated a mine-laying operation conducted by pro-Gaddafi forces. Sea-mines seemed to be laid out in the approaches to Misrata by sinking inflatable boats that carried mines, and NATO's assessment was that this was designed to stem the flow of humanitarian aid into Libya. The Misrata port authorities were quickly warned by NATO forces whereby the port was temporarily closed. The immediate result was that two humanitarian shipments were cancelled. Italian Navy Vice Admiral Rinaldo Veri, Commander of the Maritime Headquarters in Naples, insisted that 'The mining of a civilian port by pro-Gaddafi forces is clearly designed to disrupt the lawful flow of humanitarian aid to the innocent civilian people of Libya and [represents] another deliberate violation of United Nations Security Council Resolution 1973'. NATO regarded this as an attempt to prevent sea traffic from passing in and out of the harbour, most of which constituted aid to Libyan citizens.[59]

A few days later NATO mine-countermeasure ships swept the approaches to Misrata harbour to provide protection for sea traffic entering the harbour. NATO had information that three mines had been laid by pro-Gadaffi forces. As the mines were small and difficult to detect, yet able to cause serious damage to shipping, two were found and destroyed, whereas a third drifted away before specialized ships could arrive on the scene. The Misrata port authority then temporarily closed the harbour and let mariners decide whether to risk approach or not. During the weekend at least two vessels left the harbour and one humanitarian vessel safely unloaded its cargo and left.[60] Admiral Veri stated that NATO forces were now 'actively engaged in countering the mine threat to ensure the flow of aid continues'.[61]

Another incident took place in the early hours of 12 May. While maintaining the arms embargo and conducting surveillance patrols in the waters off the coast of Libya, NATO warships were ordered to intercept a small boat attack threatening the port city of Misrata. At approximately 2 a.m. the Canadian Frigate HMCS *Charlottetown* together with the British Destroyer HMS *Liverpool* and a French warship outside NATO Command detected small, high-speed inflatable crafts moving towards the port of Misrata. The boats were forced to cease their operation and leave the area. Pro-Gaddafi forces ashore, apparently operating alongside the former, covered their retreat with artillery and rockets fired directly towards the allied warships. NATO vessels responded with artillery and small arms and the battery was effectively silenced. No damage or injury was inflicted on the allied vessels during the engagement and they could resume their regular tasks. This was the second action in less than two weeks in which pro-Gaddafi forces at sea used small boats in actions against Misrata. One can assume that they were manned by Special Forces since no regular units from the Libyan navy took part in the action.[62]

Just four days after the episode outside Misrata another minor clash between pro-Gaddafi sea units and NATO naval forces occurred. In the early hours of 16 May NATO naval forces detected two rigid-hull inflatable boats (RHIBs) headed towards Misrata. Their performance resembled previous actions from pro-Gadaffi forces at sea in the area of Misrata, and NATO forces were quickly assigned to investigate and identify the target. As NATO warships and helicopters made their approach, one of the boats was abandoned while the second escaped westward at high speed towards Zlintan. Afterwards a disposal team inspected the abandoned boat and found a large quantity of explosives (approximately one ton) and two human mannequins onboard. With regard to safety and the risk of an unplanned explosion the boat was destroyed by small arms fire from one of the warships. This third incident bore certain similarities with another incident near Misrata, but the use of an improvised explosive device and decoy human mannequins lacked precedent. All three incidents displayed an ability to alter and improve tactical behaviour.[63]

Repeated pro-Gaddafi action against the port of Misrata eventually prompted NATO to destroy parts of the Libyan navy. The nearest concentration of regime warships was the naval base at Al Khums. On the night of 20 May aircraft from Royal Air Force (RAF) participated in a major NATO air strike against the Libyan navy, resulting in the destruction of two corvettes. A facility in the dockyard, constructing fast inflatable boats, was also successfully targeted. It seems as if the facility was the origin of the attacks on Misrata and that its elimination, alongside a significant stockpile of small boats, limited the regime's ability to conduct further naval action. The elimination of assets at Al Khums effectively ended the naval engagement between NATO forces and pro-Gaddafi forces at sea.[64]

Operation Unified Protector ended on 31 October 2011, after a stunning display of naval activity. During the operation the naval forces covered around 61,000 nautical square miles during surveillance operations, hailed 3,100 vessels of which 300 vessels were boarded and 11 diverted. The naval forces aided in the rescue of at least 600 refugees in distress at sea.[65] In most respects the missions and actions carried out under Operation Unified Protector were identical with those under Operation Odyssey Dawn, suggesting that naval missions could be equally appropriately described in terms of Naval Diplomacy, Humanitarian Operation, Expeditionary Operation and Maritime Security Operation also during the initial stages of the NATO-led Libya campaign.

Both of the latter operations were mandated by resolutions 1970 and 1973 and conveyed the same message to the Libya political leadership. The choice for Gaddafi was to go along with the requirements of the resolutions so as to avoid actions of military violence against Libyan targets. The Task Force, which during the whole operation was deployed off the coast of Libya, conducted frequent attacks against targets ashore in support of the NFZ and the protection of civilians. As the campaign continued the possibility that Gaddafi would accept the political demands decreased, and military actions were sustained for the purpose of protecting civilians and civilian populated areas. The campaign can thus be described as having shifted toward an Expeditionary Operation, and by the same token having distanced itself from Naval Diplomacy. The scope of the sea embargo, the protection of humanitarian shipments and the confrontations around Misrata and aid to refugees in distress at sea also indicate that Humanitarian Operations and Maritime Security Operations are more apt as labels here.

How can the naval operations in the course of the Libyan conflict, from the first spark of unrest to the closure of Operation Unified Protector, be linked to the concepts described in the first section? The attempts by pro-Gadaffi forces to disrupt the humanitarian transports in the Misrata area, and the actions NATO forces took to protect these transports and also refugees at sea, showed that naval operations within the framework of the concept of Humanitarian Operations was applicable over time. As mentioned earlier, a Maritime Security Operation is performed in order secure transports at sea and to maintain already politically agreed rules and agreements. The mandated arms embargo in the UN Security Council resolution 1973 could be seen as a Maritime Security Operation, at least in the sense that the import of prohibited goods was a crime against the resolution. The same goes for the protection of civilian sea traffic in the area. The use of naval forces as a tool of Naval Diplomacy varied over time. Prior to resolution 1973 naval forces were primarily used within a national framework, and only with a gradual increase of naval presence. With the increased requirements of the resolution, the Naval Diplomacy part of the operation became a consistent feature of the Libyan campaign.

It can be discussed whether Naval Diplomacy remained an accurate label for the final phase of the larger campaign, especially since military operations expanded and encompassed so many military targets.

Expeditionary Operations, in the sense of a forward deployed self-sustaining naval force influencing events ashore, are on the other hand not always distinguishable from Naval Diplomacy when the latter entail components of coercion and/or compellence. One line of argumentation is that, when the aim shifts from the physical realm to the cognitive realm, we move into Expeditionary Operations. Conversely, an operation designed to attack the perceptions of an antagonist only, and not his physical assets, may be labelled Naval Diplomacy. The nationally organized actions during the first phases and the creation of the naval task forces and associated coercive actions with kinetic effects in the last two phases can therefore be attributed to the concept of Expeditionary Operations.

It has been noted that there are indeed a large number of concepts that describe naval forces activities in peacetime, and only a few have been used here. The reason is, as was stated at the outset, that the selected concepts cover the activities naval forces conduct in peace. It has also been affirmed that it is often virtually impossible to differentiate between different concepts, as Till himself predicted. As he emphasized in unambiguous terms: 'Naval diplomacy is a spectrum, a continuum, in which the boundaries between the functions are inherently fuzzy. The activities they lead to may differ not in type, but merely in degree.'[66]

Conclusions and naval lessons from Libya

The purpose of this chapter has been to discuss and apply concepts describing the use and roles of naval forces in peace, and further to examine whether the naval operations during the Libyan campaign can be linked to these concepts. The first section was devoted to a description of the selected concepts and the boundaries between them. The second section attempted to apply them to the NATO-led military campaign in Libya 2011 (including the national predecessors to Operation Unified Protector), whereas the results reaffirmed Till's own view that we cannot expect to fully differentiate the tasks of the naval forces in any specific campaign. The purpose of this concluding section is to discuss the significance of this recurrent overlap, the advantages and disadvantages of using Till's concepts, and how they might be developed further. This part will also touch upon whether the naval operations during the Libyan campaign could serve as a model for future naval campaigns.

One conclusion is that, analytically speaking, it is neither fruitful nor feasible to unambiguously distinguish one naval operation from another in Till's conceptual universe. Operationally, however, this analytical flexibility means that there is little danger that an operation ever falls between the concepts. The latter may actually be an advantage when we examine events and need to make adjustments during a campaign. In fairness, there seems to be less risk for such overlap during a more limited naval operation, while the problem is likely to surface especially when we analyse major naval operations or campaigns. For instance, the narrower operations against piracy off the coast of Somalia, or in the Straits of Malacca, are easily described as Maritime Security Operations. The Libyan campaign, on the other hand, demonstrably contains aspects of all four concepts. Another advantage following from that analytical flexibility is that political statements can be aligned with the use of a specific concept and, conversely, that there is some 'wiggle room' when it comes to operations that are deemed to precipitate a strongly positive or negative response in public opinion (at home or where the action is taken).

If the selected concepts cover the entire spectrum of conflict other than war, the Libyan campaign illustrates an important practical lesson derived from the conclusion about conceptual overlap. A warship can obviously, at least during a military campaign such as that in Libya, be involved in actions under each of the concepts. This, in turn, implies that the potential use of capabilities of various platforms (such as vessels, aircraft) is typically quite wide. If this is also true in other cases, then nations are required to choose either platforms that can be used in roles covered by all four concepts, or to develop ships and platforms tailored only to specific roles. One general difference could possibly be that military missions at the lower end of the capabilities spectrum, towards Humanitarian Operations, necessitate more in the form of endurance and less technologically advanced systems. This would also imply smaller and less specialized crews. On the other hand, the other end of the spectrum would require ships with very sophisticated and advanced technology, such as highly qualified and expensive sensors and weapon systems. This is a major challenge not only for politicians, but also for military strategists and planners of the next generation of naval platforms. How should they prioritize between these requirements, especially when the current tendency is declining defence budgets and an increase in the cost of platforms?

The concepts used above are unfortunately not a sufficient answer; instead what is needed is a general theory which lays down the aims and methods for the use of naval forces in peace. Such a theory should ideally correspond to traditional sea power theories on the use of naval force in wartime. Only then would it provide ample support for the development of new men-of-war.

The tension between the need for clarity of purpose and the demand for versatility and platforms and crew performance can probably never be eliminated. Since naval operations in peace are closely linked to a nation's foreign policy it is on the one hand only appropriate that concepts are linked to the political purpose of the naval activities per se. But at the same time, from a military perspective, strategy and procurement planning specialists must specify what capabilities the individual warship must possess and under what conditions it will be used. To achieve the latter while maintaining a strong connection to the possible range of political objectives, different operation-oriented concepts are usefully clustered within an overall strategic concept, albeit one with sharper boundaries than hitherto. The latest British Maritime Doctrine, using War-fighting, Maritime Security and International Engagement as a basic vocabulary, may be a step in that direction.[67] Precisely how classical Naval Diplomacy fits into this categorization and to what extent it squares with a political purpose and legal mandate will nevertheless need to be studied further.

Another set of naval lessons is related to what we should conclude from the 'Libya model' of military campaign. To be sure, each conflict has its unique features and they cannot easily be compared. Naval forces, with their strategic mobility, can move into areas of interest and intervene at a time, place and extent of their choosing. In the case of Libya, there were naval forces in the vicinity and the distance to several NATO states was short. Several units nevertheless needed to be repositioned from other areas to participate in operations in the Mediterranean. When the conflict escalated there were similarly a large number of naval units in or near the area of operations.

If there is a major crisis related to international peace and security like that preceding the Libyan intervention but in an area farther away, where airfields or ports cannot be used as launching pads, the necessity of acting with a sea-based task force is obvious. Such a sea-based task force deployed off the coast of an operational area could carry out both intelligence gathering as well as it could execute attacks against targets on land, as was clearly illustrated by the Libya campaign. Both coalition and NATO naval task forces showed a capability to project power on the Libyan main land with a combination of airstrikes, cruise missiles and naval gun support. Although there were indications that the intensity of the operation nearly (or entirely) emptied certain ammunition stocks in some European states and so re-emphasized their operational dependence on US military infrastructure and logistics, the campaign indicated that an aggregate European capacity exists.

Perhaps more importantly, the Libyan resistance at sea presented no problem for the allied naval forces, which was superior in terms of equipment as well as training. Even if the Libyan fleet had had a higher capacity, the allied force was so superior that it would not have been significantly affected by the resistance. In the future, other states in the proximity of Europe or further afield could end up in a situation that results in a UN resolution and a military campaign to implement it; but most of these countries also typically possess limited naval resources. Despite the coordination problems that inevitably arise when a multinational force is created for a specific purpose, the naval operations in the Libya campaign demonstrated that even a rapidly cobbled together constellation of American, European and Middle East navies may very well be in a position to substantively assist other military efforts in the enforcement of a robust UN Security Council resolution.

Notes

1 During the period 1993–2012, the UN Security Council passed 1,278 resolutions. The majority concerned actions against threats to international peace and security; many including mandated military interventions, also supported by naval forces. UN Security Council. *Security Council Resolutions*. Online. Available: www.un.org/en/sc/documents/resolutions/index.shtml (accessed 19 February 2013).
2 For a deeper discussion, see N. Young. (30 November 2012) *The Contemporary Warship Challenge*, Defence IQ. Online. Available: www.defenceiq.com/naval-and-maritime-defence/articles/the-contemporary-warship-challenge/&mac=DFIQ_OI_Featured_2011&utm_source=defenceiq.com&utm_medium=email&utm_campaign=DFIQOptIn&utm_content=12/6/12 (accessed 19 February 2013).
3 J.S. Corbett, *Some Principles of Maritime Strategy*, Annapolis, MD: Naval Institute Press, 1988; originally published 1911. Corbett discusses the constitution of a fleet in Part II, Chapter II.
4 *The Law of the Sea – UNCLOS*, New York: United Nations, 1997, p. 53.
5 Ministry of Defence (MoD), *British Maritime Doctrine*, Shrivenham: DCDC, 2011, p. 2–1.
6 S.J. Tangredi, *Globalisation and Maritime Power*, Washington: National Defence University Press, 2002, p. 18.
7 See, for example, Alfred Mahan's and Julian Corbett's theories of Seapower: A. Mahan, *The Influence of Sea Power upon History 1660–1783*, Boston: Little, Brown and Co, 1890 and J. Corbett, *Some Principles of Maritime Strategy*.
8 J. Gertler, *Operation Odyssey Dawn (Libya): Background and Issues for Congress*, US Congressional Research Service, R41725, p. 19. Online. Available: www.fas.org/sgp/crs/natsec/R41725.pdf (accessed 19 February 2013).
9 One simple reason is that military professionals around the world always observe and assess ongoing and recent military conflicts and try to elicit lessons that are relevant for their own strategic and operational environment.
10 K. Booth, *Navies and Foreign Policy*, New York: Holmes & Meier, 1979, p. 4.
11 In his book *Seapower* Till introduces, besides traditional sea power theory, concepts that describe the use of marine forces in peace. G. Till, *Seapower: A Guide for the Twenty-First Century*, London: Frank Cass, 2004.
12 A less subtle term is 'gunboat diplomacy', used by authors such as J. Cable; see J. Cable, *Gunboat Diplomacy: Limited Applications of Naval Force*, 3rd edition, New York: Palgrave Macmillan, 1994.
13 G.R. Berridge, Maurice Keens-Soper and T.G. Otte, *Diplomatic Theory from Machiavelli to Kissinger*, Basingstoke: Palgrave, 2001, p. 1.
14 MoD, *British Maritime Doctrine*, pp. 2–19.
15 Till, *Seapower*, p. 258.
16 Till, *Seapower*, p. 257.
17 Till, *Seapower*, p. 267.
18 Booth, *Navies and Foreign Policy*, p. 17.
19 There are of course competing concepts which also describe the use of naval forces in peace, developed by other authors. But the selected concepts (Humanitarian Operations, Naval Diplomacy, Expeditionary Operations and Maritime Security Operations) appear to cover the full spectrum of military operations other than war, which is why they are deemed sufficient to achieve the purpose of this chapter.
20 Till, *Seapower*, p. 251.
21 Till, *Seapower*, p. 257.
22 Till, *Seapower*, p. 223.

23 Till, *Seapower*, p. 286.
24 A. Johnson and S. Mueen (eds), *Short War, Long Shadow: The Political and Military Legacies of the 2011 Libya Campaign*, London: RUSI, 2012, pp. 1–12, vi.
25 Ibid., p. vi.
26 BBC News. (1 March 2011) *Libya Revolt as it happened: Tuesday*. Online. Available: http://news.bbc.co.uk/2/hi/africa/9410847.stm (accessed 19 February 2013).
27 Cable, *Gunboat Diplomacy 1919–1991*, p. 62.
28 UK Ministry of Defence Announcement. (18 April 2011) *HMS Cumberland welcomed home from Libya operations*. Online. Available: www.mod.uk/DefenceInternet/DefenceNews/MilitaryOperations/HmsCumberlandWelcomedHomeFromLibyaOperations.htm (accessed 19 February 2014).
29 See Engelbrekt's Chapter 2 in this volume.
30 UN Security Council. (26 February 2011) *Resolution 1970 (2011)*. Online. Available: www.un.org/ga/search/view_doc.asp?symbol=S/RES/1970(2011) (accessed 19 February 2013).
31 BBC News, *Libya revolt as it happened: Tuesday*.
32 BBC News. (2 March 2011) *Libya revolt as it happened: Wednesday*. Online. Available: http://news.bbc.co.uk/2/hi/africa/9412340.stm (accessed 19 February 2013).
33 BBC News, *Libya revolt as it happened: Tuesday*.
34 BBC News, *Libya revolt as it happened: Tuesday*.
35 BBC News, *Libya revolt as it happened: Wednesday*.
36 BBC News Africa. (2 March 2011) *Libya: UK and France to fly Egyptians from Tunisia*. Online. Available: www.bbc.co.uk/news/world-africa-12625084 (accessed 15 February 2013).
37 BBC News. (3 March 2011) *Libya revolt as it happened: Thursday*. Online. Available: http://news.bbc.co.uk/2/hi/africa/9413822.stm (accessed 19 February 2013).
38 BBC News. (8 March 2011) *Libya revolt as it happened: Monday*. Online. Available: http://news.bbc.co.uk/2/hi/africa/9417359.stm (accessed 15 February 2013).
39 BBC News, *Libya revolt as it happened: Thursday*.
40 BBC News, *Libya revolt as it happened: Monday*.
41 BBC News, *Libya revolt as it happened: Monday*. See also Mohlin's Chapter 8 in this volume.
42 Johnson and Mueen, *Short War, Long Shadow*, p. vii.
43 Joint Task Force Odyssey Dawn Public Affairs. (20 March 2011) *International Coalition strikes Libyan air defenses*, US Navy. Online. Available: www.navy.mil/submit/display.asp?story_id=59196 (accessed 15 February 2013). See also Engelbrekt's Chapter 2 in this volume.
44 BBC News. (21 March 2011) *Libya revolt as it happened: Sunday*. Online. Available: http://news.bbc.co.uk/2/hi/africa/9431045.stm (accessed 19 February 2013).
45 This strike against Libyan forces marked the first time that an Ohio-class guided-missile submarine launched a TLAM in conflict. The USS Florida was converted from a strategic missile submarine (SSBN) to a cruise missile submarine (SSGN) in 2006. Besides the equipping with Tomahawk missiles, *USS Florida* was configured to launch Special Forces from stowage canisters and with improved intelligence, surveillance and reconnaissance ability. This specialization of naval power projection capability demonstrates how important the US views this ability.
46 BBC News, *Libya revolt as it happened: Sunday*.
47 BBC News, *Libya revolt as it happened: Sunday*.
48 BBC News, *Libya revolt as it happened: Wednesday*.
49 BBC News, *Libya revolt as it happened: Thursday*.

50 BBC News. (29 March 2011) *Libya and Mid-East crisis as it happened: Monday.* Online. Available: http://news.bbc.co.uk/2/hi/africa/9439215.stm (accessed 15 February 2013).
51 Joint Force Odyssey Dawn Public Affairs. (29 March 2011) *US Navy P-3C, USAF A-10 and USS Barry engage Libyan vessels,* US Navy. Online. Available: www.navy.mil/submit/display.asp?story_id=59406 (accessed 19 February 2013).
52 *Jane's Fighting Ships 2010/2011.*
53 BBC News, *Libya revolt as it happened: Tuesday.*
54 JFC Naples. (23 March 2011) *Press Conference,* NATO. Online. Available: www.jfcnaples.nato.int/page1147714.aspx (accessed 8 October 2012).
55 Allied Maritime Command Naples Factsheet. (23 March 2011) *NATO arms embargo against Libya Operation UNIFIED PROTECTOR,* NATO. Online. Available: www.manp.nato.int/operations/unified_protector/Background.html (accessed 19 February 2013).
56 NATO Public Diplomacy Division. (21 October 2011) *Operation UNIFIED PROTECTOR Facts and Figures,* NATO. Online. Available: www.manp.nato.int/operations/unified_protector/oup_facts_figures%2021_Oct-11.pdf (accessed 19 February 2013).
57 Notice to Mariners is an internationally recognized system of informing civilian shipping of dangers at sea.
58 Allied Maritime Command Naples News Release. (29 April 2011) *Mines discovered in the approaches to Misrata,* NATO. Online. Available: www.manp.nato.int/news_releases/mcnaples/pressreleases11/NR_16_11.html (accessed 19 February 2013).
59 Allied Maritime Command Naples News Release, *Mines discovered in the approaches to Misrata.*
60 Allied Maritime Command Naples News Release. (2 May 2011) *NATO minehunters sweep approaches to Misrata harbour,* NATO, Online. Available: www.manp.nato.int/news_releases/mcnaples/pressreleases11/NR_17_11.html (accessed 19 February 2013).
61 Allied Maritime Command Naples News Release, *Mines discovered in the approaches to Misrata.*
62 Allied Maritime Command Naples News Release. (13 May 2011) *NATO ships thwart attack on Misrata harbor,* NATO. Online. Available: www.manp.nato.int/news_releases/mcnaples/pressreleases11/NR_21_11.html (accessed 19 February 2013).
63 Allied Maritime Command Naples News Release. (16 May 2011) *NATO Maritime assets thwart another attack on Misrata by pro-Qadhafi forces,* NATO. Online. Available: www.manp.nato.int/news_releases/mcnaples/pressreleases11/NR_23_11.html (accessed 19 February 2013).
64 UK Ministry of Defence Announcement. (20 May 2011) *RAF strikes Gaddafi's Navy.* Online. Available: https://www.gov.uk/government/news/raf-strikes-gaddafis-navy (accessed 19 February 2013).
65 NATO Public Diplomacy Division. (2 November 2011) *Operation UNIFIED PROTECTOR Final Mission Stats.* Online. Available: www.nato.int/nato_static/assets/pdf/pdf_2011_11/20111108_111107-factsheet_up_factsfigures_en.pdf (accessed 19 February 2013).
66 Till, *Seapower,* p. 257.
67 MoD, *British Maritime Doctrine,* pp. 2–7. This terminology is inspired by earlier theorists, such as Eric Grove (*military, constabulary and diplomatic*) and Ken Booth (*military, diplomatic and policing*).

6 Fragments of an army

Three aspects of the Libya collapse

Karl Sörenson and Nima Damidez

Introduction

The events of 2011 in North Africa and the so-called Arab Spring are frequently portrayed by both Arab and Western media as events that had common causes, goals and trajectories.[1] Yet while the people in Tunis and Cairo managed to successfully oust their former leaders through protests, sit-ins and demonstrations, the Libyan nation was thrown into a civil war.[2] The Libyan civil war, although a relatively brief conflict and confined to certain areas of the country, was sustained and much nourished by 'Colonel Muammar al-Quadaffi's four-decade-long effort to consolidate his power and rule by patronage to kin and clan'.[3]

The notion that tribal loyalties and kinship played a major role in the events that unfolded in Libya during the ensuing civil war is supported by the fact that Colonel Gaddafi's (Muammar al-Quadaffi's)[4] unpredictable rule had resulted in a deeply rooted suspicion among the Libyan people toward the government and its institutions. Furthermore, prior to Gaddafi's fall and death, the Libyan armed forces was an oversized and archaic organization that desperately lacked the personnel needed to fill its ranks. As with many other Libyan governmental institutions it was severely hampered by the Colonel's constant reorganization attempts and his own eccentric decisions. Many forms of military training were banned due to Gaddafi's fear that they might enable disloyal elements of the armed forces to stage a coup against his rule. These security precautions also entailed rotating officers in order to prevent units of the armed forces from being too attached to their commanding officers.[5]

Ironically, it was the above mentioned measures taken by Gaddafi and those close to him that contributed to the rapid collapse and following disintegration of the Libyan armed forces. As the sizeable Libyan armed forces crumbled through interior fragmentation and external pressure new structures emerged. How can this rapid breakdown of a military organization be explained? What were the inner workings behind the collapse? Although the fabric of Libyan society is complex and there certainly were many contributing factors, internal as well as external, this chapter investigates three aspects which often are taken into account when explaining the political culture of North Africa; patrimonialism, militarism and islamism.

The chapter starts out by offering a general description of North Africa through the prism of these three categories. It then turns to examining the status of the Libyan armed forces prior to the popular uprising. The next part provides a brief summary of the major events which shaped the Libyan civil war in 2011. The chapter then returns to the three aspects of Libyan political culture to assess which of these were more influential as the Libyan armed forces fragmented. Hence, the overarching idea is to identify which of these three aspects is most prominent in an explanatory effort aiming to deconstruct the dynamics that so quickly reshaped the military and political landscape of Libya.

Status of current research

This chapter investigates the period from the inception of the Libyan uprising until the day when the National Transitional Council (NTC) declared Libya liberated, on 23 October 2011. Given the security situation in Libya during this period, reliable sources are notoriously difficult to come by. Hence, most of this chapter's factual claims rely on newspaper articles, reports and internet publications in Arabic, English and French. With regard to the period during Gaddafi's rule in Libya the status of research is considerably better, although Libya never seems to have been the focus of attention for scholars interested in North Africa or the Middle East. This chapter draws heavily on Dirk Vanderwalle's book *A History of Modern Libya* for a backdrop to Libya's political structure and history, while Anthony Cordesman and Aram Nerguizian's presentation of Libya in the North African military balance furnishes the account with rich information about the status of the Libyan armed forces prior to the popular uprising in 2011. For the chapter's theoretical framework we rely on James Bill and Robert Springborg's *Politics in the Middle East*.

Political culture in North Africa

When examining the political context of the North African states, it becomes apparent that the colonial legacy has left a deep imprint on their respective histories. The European colonial venture in North Africa constitutes a major factor in North African state-building and the formation of a national identity. Not only did the Arab people have to succumb to the idea of a fragmented Muslim Nation or 'Umma', but it also posed difficulties for the independent Arab governments in their efforts to generate loyalties to the new states among their citizens, Arab or non-Arab. However, not all of the North African states faced the same mountainous task as nations such as Iraq or Lebanon. Egypt, for example, had enjoyed periods of governmental autonomy, a factor which undoubtedly worked as adamantine glue among the Egyptians.[6] Other North African states, e.g. Algeria, had a burdensome time successfully integrating minority communities into a post-colonial structure. In the case of Libya, the federal system was abolished in 1963, but the unified state with its centralized government never became a natural choice during its state formation.[7]

As mentioned above we approach our topic along three different lines of North African political culture: patrimonialism, militarism and Islamism. These three strains of political development, as proposed by James Bill and Robert Springborg in *Politics in the Middle East*, can be understood as forming important elements of the political landscape.[8] Bill and Springborg stress that to assume that the political culture in North Africa is confined only to these aspects is a generalization with the weaknesses that this entails. Other political ideologies, such as democracy, nationalism and pan-Arabism, are also valid terms when describing the political developments that have emerged in contemporary North Africa. The concepts proposed by Bill and Springborg are, however, especially selected for the purposes of this chapter and aim at reviewing the quick disintegration of the Libyan armed forces and bring a better understanding of the mechanisms that were in play during the turbulent months in 2011, ultimately leading to the fall of the Qaddafi regime.

Patrimonialism

A prevalent characteristic in North African political leadership is the strong presence of patrimonial rule. Patrimonialism often denotes authoritarian rule, characterized by a number of components. These characteristics are personalism, proximity, informality, balanced conflict, military prowess and religious rationalization. Personalism can be explained as governance through a network of personal relationships. Thus, the majority of political decisions reside in the said networks. Personalism was a common trait in the courts of the old Islamic dynasties, though its presence is still tangible in modern-day Arab bureaucracy and authoritarian rule.[9] In patrimonial societies physical proximity often entails political influence and power. First and foremost these are often close family members, such as brothers and sons. The concept of proximity is evident in a number of North African countries, e.g. Libya and Egypt, where the sons of the former leaders were set to sustain their fathers' legacies.[10] The above-mentioned patrimonial characteristics promote informality. Personal relations and proximity to the ruler encourage informal decision making rather than cementing formal political formal institutions. This becomes apparent in the Libyan case where formal decision making was, and to a degree still is, non-existent.[11]

Informality has the 'added benefit' of sowing the seeds of distrust among those involved in the networks.[12] This in turn creates fertile soil for balanced conflict. To echo the assessment of Bill and Springborg: 'In a Middle-Eastern context, the dictum "divide and rule" takes on a special meaning.'[13] Several North African leaders have been especially apt at nourishing existing rivalries and creating new ones. The Gaddafis, the Bourguibas, the Nassers and the Moroccan monarchs have all utilized the tactic of balanced conflict to their advantage. In order to consolidate their political power many of the North African leaders also assume the role of the benevolent knight, a culture that has deep roots in the Middle-East and North Africa (MENA). Military prowess is thus yet another tool used by the patrimonial leader, often permeated by an emphasis on personal courage and skill as a military commander. Abdel-Aziz Bouteflika, the current Algerian president, embodies this ideal as he joined the resistance movement against the French during Algeria's struggle for independence.[14] Muhammad Gaddafi is another North African leader who illustrates the point, holding the title of Colonel since the days of the Libyan revolution of 1969.[15]

As regards religious rationalization, North African rulers tend to opt for a largely secular approach to their power. This does not stop individual leaders in the region from seeking to bolster their legitimacy and power by capitalizing on religion. For example, the Moroccan monarchy has long claimed a genealogic connection to the Prophet Mohammed. From time to time, Libyan leader Muammar Gaddafi also adopted an Islamic rhetoric, most notably during his visits to the sub-Saharan states.[16]

Militarism

In the post-colonial era of the North African states, the military has been generously endowed with resources and few constitutional reins. Thus, the armed forces have managed to acquire a role as a major player on the political scene. There are several explanations for this: the perceived threat from their former colonial masters; regional rivalries; the perceived threat from Israel; the fact that many of the North African leaders have military backgrounds.[17] Furthermore, the military is also regularly cast as a bulwark against political opponents and hostile internal elements, be they chimerical or actual.[18] The military is thus not only used to counter and expel foreign threats but also to effectuate and perpetuate the prevailing political rule.

However, the patronage of the military establishment also poses an inherent danger for the ruling elites. In many North African states the threat of a military *coup d'état* cannot be disregarded by current leaders. A number of techniques have therefore been employed in order to pre-empt the perceived threat. Rotating officers and creating a satisfied military corps are two of the more predominate ones. Of course, this threat varies greatly from state to state and has little to do with the size of the respective country's armed forces, as in the case of Mauritania.[19] A particularly pertinent example of military rule in North Africa is Gaddafi's Libya until 2011. Gaddafi himself was a former soldier: a graduate from the military academy in an era when universities were closed to lower and middle classes, he quickly rose to Captain and was finally promoted to the rank of Colonel.[20] Unlike his North African contemporaries – Mubarak in Egypt and Bouteflika in Algeria – Gaddafi, in a gesture that may be construed to appear as modesty, settled for the rank of Colonel, whereas the former leaders promoted themselves to General and Chief of the Armed Forces, respectively.[21]

Nonetheless, North African Militarism as a political concept also assumes different shapes and forms. In Algeria, for example, the military establishment has manoeuvred itself into a position from whence it can rule but not be burdened by the day-to-day administration of governing a country.[22] As there are few discernible boundaries between the government and the military, its symbiosis can easily be capitalized on, and ultimately controlled by, the politico-military elite. The Algerian example demonstrates that militarism, like many other types of political rule, is constantly evolving and adapting to different circumstances in North Africa.

As a final remark on militarism in the region, there were few signs indicating that this phenomenon was declining in the Maghreb region before the so-called 'Arab spring'. Between the years 1988 and 2006 military expenditure increased by a huge 109 per cent, which in that period made North Africa the record holder for the largest increase in military expenditure in the world by region.[23] On the one hand, the regional rivalries and domestic tensions are likely to sustain this trend; yet, on the other hand, the nascent democracies, in combination with demographic pressure caused by the 'young bulge' in the region, might in the coming decades weaken the hitherto powerful influence of military elites in the Maghreb.[24]

Islamism

Considering the large gap between state and society, and the scarcity of political options in North African states, Islamism has emerged and strengthened its foothold in the entire Maghreb.[25] Islamism in North Africa has many faces; it can entail a moderate and constitutional orientation such as in the case of the Muslim Brotherhood (MB) in Egypt which officially denounces violence,[26] while other groupings, e.g. Al Qaeda in the Islamic Maghreb (AQIM), opt for a militant and violent approach to political rivals.[27] Whichever form Islamism takes on it has been, and to a degree still is, perceived as a real threat by the higher echelons of the North African governments.[28] This with due reason, since Islamism from time to time has posed a tangible challenge to contemporary North African rulers. In the case of Algeria, the challenge from the Islamists culminated in a decade long civil war. The prelude to the war was marked by the electoral victory of the Islamist party, *Le Front Islamique du Salut (FIS)*, in the parliamentary elections of 1991. This was a fact that was hard to accept for the military-backed Algerian government, which gave the order to suspend the electoral process in the beginning of 1992. Armed resistance ensued and the country was plunged in a civil war that lasted for almost a decade and cost almost 150,000 lives.[29]

Not all North African states have had the same history of violence in their confrontations with Islamists as Algeria. Nonetheless, Islamism, both in its constitutional and violent manifestations, has indeed proven to be a political force to be reckoned with in post-revolutionary North Africa.

As mentioned previously, religious rationalization is a key aspect of patrimonialism. In the case of Libya, Islam has never been disregarded as a political tool by Gaddafi. Even in the beginning of his career the former Libyan leader made sure to infuse his political program with references to Islam.[30] However, modern-day Libya was never spared the threat of Jihadism (i.e. Islamism through violence) and, as a political leader in North Africa who throughout his reign battled a variety of Islamist factions, Muammar Gaddafi had his fair share of religiously inspired adversaries. In a sense, Libyan Islamism can best be said to have been a reflection of the rather idiosyncratic political landscape that Gaddafi himself formed and reshaped during his time in power. The lack of a national parliament or any political institutions, other than on a local municipal level, rendered the idea of an Islamist reform party on Libyan soil impossible. In addition, much of what would have been the political language of an Islamist agenda had been thwarted by Gaddafi's political mixture of Islam, Arabism, anti-Western sentiments, and his own brand of Arab socialism, all expressed in his so-called Green Book.[31]

Islamism in Gaddafi's Libya has therefore mainly been represented by the Libyan Islamic Fighting Group (LIFG). Founded in 1990 the group went through most of the alternative stages of a resistance movement's political life: it numbered over a 1,000 members; at one point it pledged allegiance to al-Qaeda; it was disbanded; its leaders renounced its former ways; and finally, in 2011 many of its former members joined the popular uprising against Gaddafi.[32]

The Arab Jamahiriyyah's armed forces

In 2003 the Arab Jamahiriyyah (Great People's Republic) came in from the cold, diplomatically speaking. Before that Libya had made a name for itself as the outcast of the North African countries, a development largely due to the eccentricities and political caprice of the country's leader, Muammar Gaddafi. Militarily, Libya was never entirely disconnected from the rest of the world. Although Gaddafi subjected the Libyan armed forces to a state of perpetual reorganization attempts, he also furnished the military with new weapon systems and platforms. As a result, on paper the Libyan defence looked quite impressive. With vast quantities of equipment, Libya had a formidable military apparatus for a country of roughly 6 million inhabitants, even if a large proportion of this equipment was kept in storage or was poorly maintained. The latter point is highlighted by Cordesman and Nerguizian, who in 2009 referred to Libya as 'the world's largest military parking lot'.[33]

Libya began its military build up in the 1970s and subsequently nurtured a militaristic mindset which resulted in an undermanned and oversized military organization. Until the domestic uprising broke out in February 2011, the Libyan army consisted of 50,000 men, half of whom were poorly trained conscripts (see Table 6.1). The conscripts were organized in units which lacked reasonably dimensioned tasks in relation to their actual capability. To put this problem into perspective, in 2010 Libya possessed 25–33 per cent of the manpower required to fill the needs of existing military units. The army's development was also hampered by widespread nepotism and Gaddafi's own security precautions, which involved rotating officers to prevent coup attempts. Gaddafi had also disallowed certain types of training believing that they might come to threaten his personal security.

Occasionally there were reports of the existence of a few elite units, such as the 32nd Brigade, the People's Cavalry, or the Revolutionary Guard Corps, supposedly better trained and equipped compared to other formations. According to some observers however, these units should be viewed as representative of Gaddafi's transient military ideology rather than genuine attempts at improving the quality of the existing military organization. Moreover, the Jamahiriyyah's capacity for logistics, combat support and services were similarly poor. In particular, the Libyan military leadership's rather whimsical approach to arms and equipment acquisitions made maintenance a horrendously difficult task. All things considered, the combat efficiency of the Libyan armed forces was, already well in advance of 2011, very low, and would never have been able to fight a war, especially not if confronted with a modern military, or even a well-organized asymmetrical enemy.[34]

The above can be said to be true for the Libyan Navy as well. In early 2011, certain crews were regarded to have moderate capacity to operate effectively. However, deficiencies could frequently be found in logistics, support as well as combat training. Libya's naval capacity was restricted to patrol and coastal missions.[35] Nonetheless, a couple of modernization projects were underway, as Libya was to receive patrol vessels to improve the Navy's ability to intercept smuggling and trafficking. New vessel acquisitions were also in progress which could update the country's search and rescue capacity. Libya naval vessels had on a couple of occasions also partaken in NATO-led maritime exercises.[36]

The Libyan Air Force retained an impressive fleet of aircraft, some of which can be considered to be of an advanced type. The majority of the

Table 6.1 Status of Libyan Armed Forces, 2010

Army	25,000 plus an estimated 25,000 conscripts: total 50,000
Navy	8,000
Air Force	18,000 (374 combat-capable aircraft)
Reserves (People's Militia)	Estimated 40,000
Conscription period 1–2 years	

Source: *The Military Balance 2010*, International Institute for Strategic Studies, London: Routledge, 2010, pp. 262–263.

Libyan aircraft were, and are, of Russian origin.[37] Libya's armadas of attack and fighter aircraft, transport and fuel crafts, as well as its moderate support and intelligence capabilities, should have enabled the Libyans to operate an air force to be reckoned with. This, however, was not the case; inadequate pilot training, poor maintenance and a general lack of personnel plagued the air force, for a long period of time in the same manner as the rest of the military branches. In fact, a large proportion of the air force missions were flown by North Korean, Pakistani, Syrian and former Soviet pilots and instructors. In 2010, it is possible that up to 50 per cent of Libya's aircrafts were grounded or unfit for operational service.[38]

Countdown to the fall of Gaddafi

In order to understand the events which finally led to the fall of Gaddafi it is necessary to trace the major events which came to reshape the political landscape in Libya. Well aware that any description of the events during 2011 will be incomplete, something still needs to be said about the chronology of the Libyan conflict during 2011. Although insufficient as a full description of what transpired during the popular uprising, a backdrop in the form of a sequenced narrative is deemed appropriate to set the scene for our forthcoming discussion of Libya's political culture. The idea is to give the reader a brief review of events in order to connect it to the analysis which follows in the next section of this chapter.

As described in the introduction to this volume, an uprising in Tunisia was set off on 19 December 2010 by the confiscation of a young fruit seller's goods in Tunis, Tunisia. The young man, Muhammed Bouazizi, later set fire to himself in apparent frustration over his situation and that of young fellow Tunisians facing rampant unemployment subsistence incomes and few prospects of real improvement. About a month later, on 16 January 2011, Muammar Gaddafi appeared on Libyan state television and condemned the events that unfolded in Tunisia in the aftermath of Bouazizi's one-man protest. Gaddafi finished his speech by listing what he viewed as the benefits of the Libyan system of government to the Tunisian people.[39]

On 16 February 2011, the first protests erupted in Benghazi, Libya's second largest city and located in the eastern part of the country. Beginning as a response to the reports of the arrest of a human rights campaigner, the protests set off a chain of three consecutive days of demonstrations in the city of Benghazi. The Gaddafi regime responded with more riot police, military intervention and by rallying supporters in televised events. As the clashes between the anti-Gaddafi movement and forces loyal to the Colonel continued to intensify, the United Nation Security Council unanimously voted on 26 February to refer Gaddafi to the International Criminal Court.[40] Meanwhile, Britain announced that it had revoked diplomatic immunity for Gaddafi and his family. Just a couple of days later, on 28 February 2011, the rebels seized control of the town of Zawiyah, only 30 miles from the capital Tripoli. On 8 March 2011, as the fighting around the town of Zawiya exacerbated, the British Prime Minister, David Cameron, and the President of the United States, Barack Obama, began seriously weighing the option of imposing a no-fly zone over Libya. On 18 March 2011, the UN Security Council passed a resolution in favour of a no-fly zone and directed the commencement of air strikes in Libya.[41]

Meanwhile, in Benghazi, the resistance continued. The fact that the uprising broke out in the eastern provinces of Libya is hardly surprising. Libya's eastern provinces are made up of several tribes of which the Abu Llail, the Misurata and the al-Awaqirs may be identified as the dominant three. The Misurata tribe, which has taken its name from a region in the east, joined the uprising early and is considered to be one of the largest and most influential tribes in Libya, particularly in the Benghazi area. Members in the Abu Llail were also quick to activate its resistance and contributed to the anti-Gaddafi movement. The Al-Awaqir tribe, like the Misurata, has in the past held several ministerial positions; it is based in the Barqah region in Cyrenaica, and also played a central role in Libyan politics during the country's struggle for freedom under both the Ottomans and the Italians.[42] While all of these tribes at times have had important representation in Tripoli, they have also frequently been marginalized.

On 19 March 2011, when operation Odyssey Dawn was launched, the NATO forces primarily targeted al-Gaddafi's air defences and the cities where the rebels were fighting to hold off the Gaddafi forces. The bulk of the assaults on Gaddafi-controlled Libya were executed in the following three days, during which Muammar Gaddafi's compound was targeted. On 26 March, a week into the establishment of a no fly zone by the coalition, the strategically important town of Ajdabiya was captured by the anti-government rebels. Fuelled by the backing of the Western powers, the rebels' offensive gained momentum. As Gaddafi troops defected they set their sights on the coastal cities and towns between their position and the capital Tripoli. Within a day towns like Brega, Ras Lanuf and Bin Jawad all fell to the rebel advance. Sirte, Gaddafi's hometown and stronghold, rapidly came within their range.[43]

On 30 March 2011, Moussa Koussa, one of Muammar Gaddafi's closest allies and the acting Foreign Minister of Libya, resigned and then fled to the United Kingdom. His escape to Britain was arranged by the British intelligence services. To add insult to injury, the person that was supposed to fill Mr. Koussa's shoes, Deputy Foreign Minister Abdul Ati al-Obeidi, left for Greece. The cracks in Gaddafi's regime were becoming all the more apparent. However, on 10 April, the Colonel's army seemed to have turned the tide and Ajdabiya was wrested out of the rebels' hands. Gaddafi forces then pressed on, reinforced by the 32nd Brigade, towards the heart of the rebel command, Benghazi. In the days that followed, heavy fighting continued over key strategic towns and cities such as Misrata and Ajdabiya. On 1 May 2011, Muammar Gaddafi's son, Saf ul-Arab, and three of the leader's grandsons were killed in a NATO airstrike. The Colonel himself was in the building but managed to escape unharmed.

Although Gaddafi had set up elite units such as the 32nd Reinforced Brigade, led by his own son Khamis, it was rumoured that mercenaries needed to be recruited from Libya's sub-Saharan neighbours to boost the numbers of those forces.[44] The rest of the Libyan army, and the governmental structure supporting it, virtually fell apart during the nine-month long conflict. Starting with the defection of the Libyan Minister for Foreign Affairs, Moussa Koussa, the pace at which those formerly close to the Libyan leader abandoned ship soon accelerated. By the end of May 2011, more than eight generals and an entire brigade had either left the country or joined the opposition in the fight against their former benefactor. Moreover, defecting generals reported in the same month that Gaddafi's army was only operating at a 20 per cent level.[45]

It appears that the Libyan leader was growing more and more desperate during this period. One indication was the steady stream of odd statements made by Gaddafi in which he threatened to send Libyan 'martyrs' to Europe to 'liberate' territories such as the Canary Islands, Andalusia and Sicily (under Arab control in medieval times). A month later Muammar Gaddafi's son, Saif ul-Islam, announced that he had formed a pact with the Islamists (previously charged by him to be the instigators of the civil war). A few weeks later the rebels advanced progressively on Tripoli, as several important towns fell into rebel hands.[46]

The overthrow of Gaddafi appeared inevitable as the rebels sacked his personal compound in the country's capital, Tripoli. However, Gaddafi himself refused to admit defeat as he reportedly proclaimed 'Martyrdom or victory!' and fled his former seat of power. Within two days the NTC announced that it was moving the cabinet from Benghazi to the capital. Gaddafi nevertheless continued to issue messages proclaiming that he would never leave the land, and urged those loyal to him to continue fighting. The search for the former Libyan leader was extended to the town of Bani Walid, where Gaddafi and his son, Saif ul-Islam were rumoured to have taken their refuge.[47]

Gaddafi and forces loyal to him concentrated their efforts to the western provinces, especially the area between Tripoli and Sirte. The major tribes in the west are comprised of the Qadhafah, the Magariha, the Zuwaya and the Warfalla. The Qadhafah is Muammar Gaddafi's own tribe and hence the one from which he recruited his most trusted soldiers. Historically, the Qadhafah tribe has not been considered to be one of the more influential tribes in Libya. After the Colonel's ascension to power the tribe's influence and political clout nonetheless grew. Also located in the West, the Magariha is the tribe of the convicted Lockerbie bomber, Abdel Baset al-Megrahi, and the country's second largest. For decades, the tribe's head, Abdel Sallam Jalloud, was considered to be Muammar Gaddafi's closest associate, and the tribe remained well positioned in the government apparatus and the security services even after he fell from grace.

Two other tribes deserve mention. The Zuwaya is a smaller tribe from the central costal region and also the tribe of the former Libyan minister of justice, Abdulqasim Zwai. The Warfalla has traditionally been aligned with Gaddafi's own tribe, the Qadhafah. At the same time, the Warfalla were among the first tribes to join the movement against Gaddafi. The tribe's adherents amount to approximately one million and their secession from the Colonel's camp in early 2011 dealt a severe blow to his authority.[48]

It was perhaps when the Warfalla tribe abandoned Colonel Muammar Gaddafi that his downfall was accelerated, as the inter-tribal rift suddenly opened up a second flank, now to the west. Several military leaders similarly changed sides, not only to refrain from becoming engaged in direct armed struggle, but so as to actively support the popular uprising. In addition, numerous marginalized and suppressed individuals and communities who had suffered under the Gaddafi regime took up arms and joined the opposition. In the beginning of the uprising, that is, before the influential clans changed sides, this was a particularly dangerous position to adopt for the indigenous Berbers. Primarily located in the western and southern provinces, they were often an easy target for loyalist forces, though always adamant that they would refuse to back down in their struggle against the Libyan leader.

For these and other reasons Sirte became the last key battle ground as NATO forces and the forces of the new Libyan government escalated the search for Gaddafi and his son. The siege in Sirte lasted for roughly two weeks, yet it took an additional week before Colonel Muammar Gaddafi was captured alive. He later died as a result of injuries sustained to his head and legs, caused by his agitated capturers. On 20 October 2011 footage of a body being dragged through the streets resulted in unconfirmed rumours that Muammar Gaddafi had indeed been killed. His body was later taken to the town of Misrata where large crowds gathered. On 19 and 20 October respectively, Saif ul-Islam and the former head of Intelligence Abdullah al-Senussi were also captured while attempting to flee to the country of Niger.[49]

Explaining the collapse: which aspect of Libya's political culture was most significant?

The previous section offers a rudimentary summary of the events leading up to the fall of the Gaddafi regime. Although it is important to understand the major events taking place, what perhaps is most striking is how quickly the situation unfolded. From inception to the end of the crisis less than a year passed. However, the timeline itself does not offer any specific insight into how these events can be understood: perhaps a year is less of a research puzzle if the underlying dynamics can be better understood. Returning to the three political aspects proposed by Bill and Springberg, we shall try to examine if indeed these came into play, and if they did, in what form they can be traced in the rapid succession of events of 2011.

Revolutionary Islamism in Libya

As previously mentioned, like most of its North African neighbours Libya has not been left untouched by jihadism or revolutionary Islamism. After the fall of Gaddafi there were initial fears that the country might become a safe haven for al-Qaeda inspired jihadists. Furthermore, as the elections in Egypt and Tunisia –Libya's geographic and revolutionary neighbours – resulted in parliamentary seats and victories for Islamists of different political and religious persuasions, some observers believed that the political trajectory in Libya might develop along the same lines.

As the prelude to the demise of Colonel Gaddafi was an all-out military conflict, Libya had caught the interest of militant Islamists who thrive in environments that give rise to popular uprisings in the Arab world.[50] During the relatively brief conflict of 2011, jihadist elements did indeed take advantage of the opportunity to participate in the fighting and thus gain more influence. Moreover, there were reports indicating that a smaller number of jihadists and veterans from the conflicts in Iraq, Afghanistan and Pakistan had joined the fighting. At the same time, the jihadists in Libya seemed to exert limited influence during the conflict. Although the jihadists' fighting experience was in demand, the majority of the Libyan population appears to have taken a 'more secular approach' to the uprising and its ultimate objectives. The main reason for the jihadist failure to establish a foothold in Libya seems to be Muammar Gaddafi's policies. The Colonel's persecution of the country's home-grown Islamists, the creation of a relatively secular educational system, and the launching of a reconciliation programme with the remaining hardcore jihadists, severely weakened the Islamist position in Libya.[51]

Overall in North Africa, jihadist movements have proven adept at exploiting the situation in politically unstable Arab states to their own advantage. Libya is no exception, as demonstrated in September 2012 when the United States consulate in Benghazi was attacked by what was described as a 'pro-al-Qaeda group'.[52] Still, it can be argued that the course of the armed conflict in 2011 indicates that the fear of a sanctuary for jihadists on Libyan territory might be exaggerated anyway.[53] As regards the non-revolutionary, constitutional brand of Islamism on Libyan soil, for instance practised by the local branch of the Muslim Brotherhood, they went so far in reconciliatory politics and rapprochement with the Colonel's son, Saif ul-Islam, that their credibility among the Libyan population suffered severely.[54]

Hollowed-out militarism

As the popular uprising in Libya unravelled into an all-out military conflict, the armed forces controlled by Gaddafi were put to their first real test. Ironically, the very system that the Colonel had taken great effort to organize, divide and control in order for it not to pose a threat to his power eventually failed to protect him. Muammar Gaddafi had created a system in which the armed forces, like many other apparatuses of the state, were divided in accordance with tribal, ancestral and clan ties. The armed forces were arranged in such a manner that personal connection, favouritism, proximity and perceived loyalty came to be the chief reason for recruitment and ensuing grants. In a sense, it was an intricate system based on 'divide and rule', but it was a system not only confined to pitching tribe against tribe, or even within the tribes: Gaddafi's scheme went as far as pitching families against each other. The divide and rule concept also included a physical approach where the regime spread mutually isolated military units to garrison towns across Libya.[55]

The deficiencies in military organization, training and equipment maintenance, presented above in this chapter, contributed to the fragmentation accepted, and even cultivated, by the regime. Gaddafi's military structure thus had an extraordinarily difficult task when facing an uprising backed by Western military forces. The militarism that Gaddafi had struggled to uphold was hollowed-out, as he himself was forced to retreat to tribal positions and loyalties. Gaddafi was also forced to rely on pan-military units, such as his Revolutionary Guard and pan-African corps, which consisted of mercenaries recruited during his various campaigns in Africa.[56]

The tribal fragmentation that contributed to Gaddafi's fall is also likely to be one of the largest challenges facing the post-revolutionary government of today. As the armed forces and security services arranged themselves in accordance with pre-existing or new loyalties and allegiances, no real system was poised to consolidate and protect the new political leadership of Libya.[57] It is too early to analyse fully the effects of nearly 40 years of Gaddafi's rule on the security apparatus of Libya. However, efforts to bridge the gaps put in place by the former regime will probably be an important dimension in stabilizing the country's forces and filling the ranks with individuals whose primary loyalty is to the state rather than to ancestral tribes. The restructuring and rebuilding of the Libyan armed forces will present a formidable task from this vantage point, as armed groups may hesitate to relinquish control of military equipment and hardware remains widely scattered around the country.

Patrimonialism and the role of the Libyan tribes

The tribal system in Libya has always played a major role in Libyan society, politically, socially and economically. With Muammar Gaddafi's ascent to power the role of the tribes was further cemented and augmented. Historically, the engagement of the Libyan tribes in the state's political affairs has accompanied the country's conflicts against their colonial adversaries. Ottomans, Italians and other colonial powers have all met with resistance from the Libyan tribes.[58]

During Muammar Gaddafi's reign, Libya made strides towards becoming a more urban society. This is largely due to vast increases in revenue as a result of the country's expanding oil export sector. In recent years Colonel Gaddafi's rule made Libya undergo a modernization process, socially and economically.[59] It could be argued that these relatively rapid changes in the independent Libyan state's fundamental structure should also have presented the prerequisites for demographic shift within the social fabric of the country. Nevertheless, many Libyans continue to identify themselves with a tribe or a clan.

Even in modern times the number of tribes, or their salience, has not diminished. Before Colonel Gaddafi's demise there were roughly 140 tribes, of which around 30 had enough authority to significantly influence the actual politics of the Great People's Republic.[60] A political concession by the Colonel to the tribes, as a social entity, they went from being described and denounced as primordial and archaic to being acknowledged as currency in the political arena of Gaddafi-run Libya. However, it was not until the 1990s, when the revolutionary aspects of Gaddafi's rule were beginning to diminish, that he was forced to rely on the tribes for his own political domination.[61] It was also during the 1990s that the Colonel experienced several coup attempts. These were planned and carried out by officers belonging to the Warfalla tribe and also by the LIFG.

Even though the tribal system is still prominent in Libya, Muammar Gaddafi had masterfully honed his skills in managing and controlling the tribes. This became apparent in the armed forces where, as the BBC reported in February of 2011: 'Fostering rivalries among the various tribes in the army through selective patronage has not only strengthened his control over the military, but has also worked to draw attention away from Colonel Gaddafi and his regime.'[62] Furthermore, it was in different governmental and administrative organizations that tribal associations and kinship became apparent and important. Although the central importance of the tribal communities in modern Libyan politics occasionally has been questioned, their role was highlighted by Saif ul-Islam Gaddafi himself during the initial phases of the Libyan uprising. Fearing civil war Saif ul-Islam noted that 'Unlike, Egypt and Tunisia, Libya is made up of tribes, clans and alliances.'[63] In fact, the words of Saif ul-Islam were not only a reminder to the tribes to remain loyal but presumably also weighed heavily on his own awareness that not even he had complete influence over all the segments of his own father's complex governmental organization.[64]

Although the political authority of tribes and clans may not be as extensive as in the days of Libya's anti-colonial struggle, the evidence suggests that they remain central. Nowhere else was this more evident than within the Libyan armed forces. The constant process of favouring of certain tribes and families over others, as well as the perpetual rotation of officers in order to avoid the bond between officer and soldier growing too strong, ironically appears to have helped to undo the Libyan armed forces, as it was tasked to fight an enemy many times stronger. The patrimonial card had been played consistently and repeatedly, very much at the expense of national and institutional loyalty, so when push came to shove many instantly did precisely what they had been trained to do: they promptly turned to their clan.

Conclusion

In his book *A History of Modern Libya,* Dirk Vandewalle describes the manner in which Muammar Gaddafi ran Libya:

> In principle all authority belonged to the people … In reality, criticism and grievances were only allowed to be expressed in a highly scripted form that served Qadhafi's intentions to keep the political system unbalanced and unpredictable.[65]

The patrimonialism that Colonel Gaddafi exercised was ostentatious, though in many respects effective for the purpose of sustaining his authoritarian regime. The Libyan leader managed to employ a number of patrimonialist tricks to his advantage for over 40 years. However, constant use of the same patrimonialist recipe created a system in which 'everyone was cooking the same soup'. Every sector of Muammar Gaddafi's government, state institutions and protectors was seriously weakened by the Libyan leader's constant changes of will, projects and whims.

The Libyan armed forces, as guardians of the Libyan state, equally suffered under the Colonel's policies. Considering the fact that building operational capacity for any army is usually a time-consuming endeavour, the Colonel's paranoia, caprice and nepotism rendered the armed forces little more than a paper tiger. Plagued by poor maintenance, constant changes in the leadership, faulty or obsolete equipment and a rampant lack of personnel, the Libyan army under Gaddafi was not prepared, trained or motivated to fight an inspired rebel force backed by Western military powers. In fact, the Libyan armed forces had previously also proven to be spectacularly inept at fighting a determined rebel force. This became painfully apparent during the Libya-Chad conflict during the 1980s, when lightly armed Chadian fighters managed to repel Libyan forces, delivering a heavy blow to an already demoralized cadre.[66]

To attribute the collapse of the Libyan army entirely to Gaddafi's version of a patrimonial system through constant manipulation of the tribal system would be unfair, as it ignores other important impulses in Libyan society. Most notably, of course, is the Libyan people's longing for a different system, seemingly a democratic society, in some shape or form. Yet the patrimonial power structures created by the Libyan leader were indeed helpful in shaping an opposition against him based – not solely but to a considerable degree – along tribal lines. Gaddafi's patronage of the tribal system encouraged loyalty towards tribe and clan rather than to a government. This is largely due to the fact that admittance to the inner circles of the government, bureaucracy, security and armed forces was based on a system that essentially operated in accordance with tribal lineage. Thus, Colonel Muammar Gaddafi, like his contemporaries in Egypt and to a degree in Tunisia, eventually became a victim of the very machinations he engineered.

Notes

1 See for example, *al-Jazeera*. Online. Available: www.aljazeera.net/pointofview/pages/4ded82f8–58a3–4db1-a4de-9627366a5047; and F. Ajami, 'The Arab Spring at one: A year of living dangerously', *Foreign Affairs*, March/April 2012. Online. Available: www.foreignaffairs.com/articles/137053/fouad-ajami/the-arab-spring-at-one (both accessed 20 January 2013).
2 L. Anderson, 'Demystifying the Arab Spring', *Foreign Affairs*, May/June 2011.
3 Anderson, 'Demystifying the Arab Spring'.
4 The correct spelling used by professional arabists is Muammar al-Quaddafi. In this book we use the commonly established spelling Muammar Gaddafi.
5 N. Damidez and K. Sörenson, *To Have and Have Not – A Study on the North African Regional Capability*, 2009 FOI-report.
6 J.A. Bill and R. Springborg, *Politics in the Middle East*, 5th edition, New York: Addison Wesley Longman, 2000, pp. 27–31.
7 D. Vandewalle, *A History of Modern Libya*, Cambridge: Cambridge University Press, 2006, pp. 48–49.
8 Bill and Springborg, *Politics in the Middle East*, pp. 101–112.
9 Ibid., p. 120.
10 *All Business*, 'Libya's political leadership, the system', July 2007; *The Trumpet*, 'Concerns mount over a Mubarak dynasty', September 2006. Online. Available: www.thetrumpet.com/article/2708.0.86.0/middle-east/egypt/concerns-mount-over-a-mubarak-dynasty (accessed 20 January 2013).
11 Anderson, 'Demystifying the Arab Spring'.
12 Bill and Springborg, *Politics in the Middle East*, p. 122.
13 Ibid., p. 123.

14 R. Mortimer, 'State and Army in Algeria: the Bouteflika effect', *The Journal of North African Studies*, 11, 2006.
15 R. Fisk, *The Great War for Civilization*, London: Harper Perennial, 2006, p. 199.
16 Fisk, *The Great War for Civilization*, p. 126.
17 A.H. Cordesman and A. Nerguizian, *The North African Military Balance*, CSIS, 2009, p. 3. Online. Available: http://csis.org/publication/north-african-military-balance (accessed 16 December 2012); Bill and Springborg, *Politics in the Middle East*, pp. 168–177.
18 Bill and Springborg, *Politics in the Middle East*, p. 173.
19 See Chapter 4 for further information.
20 Vanderwalle, *A History of Modern Libya*, pp. 79–82.
21 *Al-Sharq al-Awsat*, 'Mubarak has reverted in military rank', 19 January 2012. Online. Available: www.asharq-e.com/news.asp?section=1&id=28159 (accessed 20 February 2013); *Algeria Press Service*, see all results for this publication. Browse back issues of this publication by date 5 July 2011, 'President Bouteflika chairs military-rank ceremony at Defence Ministry'. Online. Available: www.highbeam.com/doc/1G1-260809494.html (accessed 20 February 2013).
22 S.A. Cook, *Ruling but not Governing: The Military and Political Development in Egypt, Algeria, and Turkey*, New York: Johns Hopkins University Press, 2007.
23 A.S. Rönnbäck, *Regional Co-operation in North Africa: Success or Failure?*, Umeå University, 2007.
24 Cordesman and Nerguizian, *The North African Military Balance*, p. 88.
25 Middle-East Policy Council, *Transcript from Symposium on North Africa*, Blackwell Publishing, September 2007.
26 Muslim Brotherhood, 'Dr. Morsi: MB has a peaceful agenda'. Online. Available: www.ikhawanweb.com (accessed 2 July 2009).
27 J. Kirschke, 'The al-Qaeda we don't know: AQIM the North African Franchise', *World Politics Review*, October 2008. Online. Available: www.scribd.com/doc/16929801/AQIM-The-North-African-Franchise (accessed 20 February 2013).
28 Middle-East Policy Council, *Transcript from Symposium on North Africa*.
29 L. Martinez, *The Algerian Civil War 1990–1998*, New York: Columbia University Press, 2000.
30 Vanderwalle, *A History of Modern Libya*, pp. 80–81.
31 Ibid., pp. 97–138.
32 I. Black, 'Libyan Islamic Fighting Group – From al-Qaeda to the Arab Spring', *The Guardian*, 5 September 2011. Online. Available: www.guardian.co.uk/world/2011/sep/05/libyan-islamic-fighting-group-leaders (accessed 20 January 2013).
33 Cordesman and Nerguizian, *The North African Military Balance*, p. 60.
34 Ibid., p. 64.
35 See also Chapter 5 by Wollert in this volume.
36 Cordesman and Nerguizian, *The North African Military Balance*, p. 67.
37 *Jane's Intelligence*, 'Russia prepares to sell weapons worth $2.5 billion to Libya', April 2008, Jane's Information Group.
38 Cordesman and Nerguizian, *The North African Military Balance*, p. 72.
39 *The Military Balance 2010*, International Institute for Strategic Studies, London: Routledge, 2010, pp. 262–263.
39 M. Weaver 'Muammar Gaddafi condemns Tunisian uprising', *The Guardian*, 16 January 2011. Online. Available: www.guardian.co.uk/world/2011/jan/16/muammar-gaddafi-condemns-tunisia-uprising (accessed 20 February 2013).
40 See Chapter 2 by Engelbrekt in this volume.
41 *Le Monde*, 'Guerre en Libye: la chronologie des événements', 20 October 2011. Online. Available: www.lemonde.fr/afrique/article/2011/08/17/la-guerre-en-libye-chronologie-des-evenements_1559992_3212.html (accessed 12 september 2012).

42 Abdulsattar Hatitah and Asharq al-Awasat, 'Libyan tribal map: network of loyalties that will determine Gadaffi's fate', 24 February 2011. Online. Available: www.cetri.be/spip.php?article2102&lang=en (accessed 20 October 2012).
43 *Le Monde*, 'Guerre en Libye: la chronologie des événements'.
44 V. Vira and A. Cordesman, *The Libyan Uprising: An Uncertain Trajectory*, Center for Strategic and International Studies, 20 June 2011. Online. Available: http://csis.org/files/publication/110620_libya.pdf (accessed 20 February 2013).
45 Ibid., pp. 17–21.
46 *The Guardian*, 'Timeline: Libya's Civil War', 19 November 2011. Online. Available: www.guardian.co.uk/world/2011/nov/19/timeline-libya-civil-war (accessed 7 September 2012).
47 Ibid.
48 Notably, members of the Warfalla tribe unsuccessfully attempted a coup against the al-Qaddafi regime in 1993, probably due to the tribe members' perception that they were poorly represented in government. Gaddafi later appointed members of the Warfalla to positions in his security apparatus; see S. Kurczy and D. Hinshaw, 'Libya tribes: Who's who?', *The Christian Science Monitor*, 24 February 2011. Online. Available: www.csmonitor.com/World/Backchannels/2011/0224/Libya-tribes-Who-s-who/(page)/2 (accessed 16 December 2012).
49 Ibid.
50 B. Riedel, 'Al Qaeda in Syria: Jihadists use chaos in Arab Awakening', Brookings. Online. Available: www.brookings.edu/research/opinions/2012/08/28-al-qaeda-syria-jihadists-arab-awakening-riedel (accessed 27 November 2012).
51 Vira and Cordesman, *The Libyan Uprising*.
52 N. Robertson, P. Cruickshank and T. Lister, 'Pro-al Qaeda group seen behind deadly Benghazi attack', *CNN*, 13 September 2012. Online. Available: http://edition.cnn.com/2012/09/12/world/africa/libya-attack-jihadists/index.html (accessed 20 February 2013).
53 Vira and Cordesman, *The Libyan Uprising*.
54 Ibid.
55 *Divided We Stand: Libya's Enduring Conflicts*, Middle East/North Africa Report No. 130, 14 September 2012, International Crisis Group. Online. Available: www.crisisgroup.org/~/media/Files/Middle%20East%20North%20Africa/North%20Africa/libya/130-divided-we-stand-libyas-enduring-conflicts.pdf, pp. 2–8 (accessed 20 February 2013).
56 Saïd Haddadt, *The Role of the Libyan Army in the Revolt against Gaddafi's Regime*, Al Jazeera Centre for Studies, 16 March 2011.
57 *Divided We Stand: Libya's Enduring Conflicts*.
58 Vandewalle, *A History of Modern Libya*, pp. 16–23; Hatitah and al-Awasat, *Libyan Tribal Map*.
59 Mohamed Hussein, 'Libya crisis: what role do tribal loyalties play?', 21 February 2011. Online. Available: www.bbc.co.uk/news/world-middle-east-12528996 (accessed 20 February 2013); Vandewalle, *A History of Modern Libya*, pp. 1–9.
60 Hatitah and al-Awasat, *Libyan Tribal Map*.
61 Vandewalle, *A History of Modern Libya*, p. 6.
62 Hussein, 'Libya crisis'.
63 Kurczy and Hinshaw, 'Libya tribes'.
64 Vira and Cordesman, *The Libyan Uprising*.
65 Vandewalle, *A History of Modern Libya*, p. 145.
66 Vira and Cordesman, *The Libyan Uprising*, p. 22.

Part III
Auxiliary measures and arrangements

7 Managing perceptions

Strategic communication and the story of *success* in Libya

Rikke Bjerg Jensen

The Libya mission highlighted the challenges that the constantly evolving, rapidly changing communication environment holds for NATO forces; and, once again, it questioned the extent to which the British military really 'get it'.[1] As will be demonstrated below, the UK's involvement in NATO's operation in Libya was the first *real* campaign fought by the UK military with the support of strategic communication. This is not to say that employing communication tools as central components of military operations was new to the British military.[2] However, the Libya campaign was the first campaign in which the British military adopted dedicated strategic communication doctrine, streamlined with NATO communication policy.[3] The UK military's approach to strategic communication and their formulation of a campaign narrative thus serve as clear examples of the communication processes in place within Western militaries in general, and within NATO in particular.

For the UK, the Libya campaign presented an attractive opportunity to test the newly established cross-government approach to strategic communication. Framing the mission as a 'liberation' exercise helped promote messages and catchphrases that met the expectations of target audiences at home. Yet while it helped convince domestic audiences that the campaign was worthwhile by painting images of heroes – as well as villains – it generally failed to influence the attitudes and behaviours of local audiences. Importantly, this narrative was not confined to the UK military. In fact, the Libya campaign showed remarkable unity of output among NATO forces involved in the mission, indicating that the strategic narrative was not exclusive to the British armed forces. Rather, the narrative was formulated through recurrent processes within contributing NATO forces, most notably the United States and France, with the latter having politically led the drive for international intervention. The UK approach thus represents a case through which further questions about NATO strategic communication can be raised and analysed. And, as with any case study, understanding an event through the examination of a particular case allows us to draw broader conclusions. Here, it allows us to engage with the overall vehicles and discourses that drove the Libya *storyline*.

However, the specific UK strategic narrative on Libya was also important in its own right. Not only was it essential for generating support among home audiences, it was critical to the creation of a transnational narrative. There are a few reasons for this. First, the key role played by the British armed forces during the Libya campaign positioned the UK storyline centre stage. Second, at a global level (and European in particular), the UK narrative contributed to the formation of strategic narratives within other participating nations, which ultimately meant that similar storylines were adopted across the coalition.[4] And, finally, due to the fact that English as a language continues to be a dominant player on the world stage, narratives emerging from the UK political sphere, and promoted through UK national news outlets, are more likely to influence politicians, policy advisors, decision makers and opinion formers of other NATO countries.

In this chapter, therefore, NATO's 2011 Libya campaign serves as a key to understanding the drivers of military communication efforts and the mechanisms in place to promote particular campaign narratives, in an environment where public opinion sways political will. Engaging with military motivations for and processes of strategic communication during the Libya campaign is thus critical precisely because it problematizes how military-specific systems are employed to fulfil political objectives. This is important as the degree to which the military constitutes an independent organization, motivated by its own internal goals and politics, is largely overlooked.

Particular attention is paid to the UK military's understanding of strategic communication as a critical aspect of Operation Ellamy, the UK armed forces' contribution to NATO's Operation Unified Protector. Drawing on empirical data centred round observations and textual analysis,[5] the chapter argues that the strategic narrative played an essential role for the British military and for NATO forces in Libya. During the Libya campaign the military acknowledged that 24-hour media and digital communications technology had a critical impact on campaign activity. And from a UK military perspective, '[e]ffective strategic communications work was central to the conduct of the campaign, especially in a 24/7 media context.'[6]

The chapter concludes that in order to understand the military driven communication structures, vehicles and discourses in place to 'inform' audiences during operational activity in general and during the Libya campaign in particular, it is important to recognize that new frameworks of understanding may be needed. From a NATO perspective, such frameworks increasingly incorporate the use of strategic narratives as an integrated element of strategic communication.

The problem of multiple audiences and the changing nature of communication

Historically, militaries within democratic systems have always been concerned with the communication of military operations and defence issues, in the same way as they have aimed to generate messages that reach specific audiences. What is new in relation to current campaigns, including Libya, are the increasingly dynamic processes of communication. Non-linear communication models have driven the military communications structure into new territories. Furthermore, Western militaries increasingly understand the perception of campaign activity, as well as its communication, to be as important as the campaign itself.[7]

In line with this, both academics and practitioners refer to *mediatized wars*,[8] which, according to British General Sir Rupert Smith, means that a separate military sphere no longer exists: 'We fight amongst the people, a fact amplified literally and figuratively by the central role of the media. We fight in every living room in the world as well as on the streets and fields of a conflict zone.'[9] And to reinforce this point, he uses the 'theatre' as a metaphor:

> We are conducting operations now as though we are on stage, in an amphitheatre or Roman arena. There are two or more sets of players – both with a producer, the commander, each of whom has his own idea of the script. On the ground, in the actual theatre, they are all on the stage and mixed up with people trying to get to their seats, the stage hands, the ticket collectors and the ice-cream vendors. At the same time they are being viewed by a partial and factional audience, comfortably seated, its attention focused on that part of the auditorium where it is noisiest, watching the events by peering down the drinking straws of their soft-drink packs – for that is the extent of the vision of a camera.[10]

In his much cited article *The Mediatization of Society* Stig Hjarvard describes this form of media*tization* as a process that transforms institutions to adapt to the growing influence of the media.[11] Therefore, applying this concept to the military allows us to understand the institutional practices that have led to increasing military concerns about the role of the media in future conflicts. In Libya, this meant that the incorporation of strategic communication, standardized through a doctrinal note, became a defining factor in mobilizing home support in particular. The mediatization of military practice matters because public perceptions – local, national and intra-military perceptions – of campaigns matter to military success.

Yet the abilities of the military to control the flows of information and, in turn, public perceptions have become increasingly complicated. Messages do not travel uninterrupted from sender to receiver. And modern communication processes, executed through the increasingly complex media and warfare landscapes, have made this yet more difficult. In fact, from a military perspective, technology-savvy adversaries, media-aware international and home audiences, 'plugged-in' soldiers and 24-hour news streams have resulted in an increasingly messy process of communication.[12] What is being communicated is influenced by an array of external factors, including: competing messages; unforeseen incidents; and military action. Against this backdrop, the message being transmitted has to compete with numerous outside interferences, and how this communicated message is received is influenced by the personal attitudes, behaviours and expectations of the audience.[13] Effectively communicating the *right* message to the *right* audience, who interprets the message in the *right* way, and at the *right* time, is thus more the exception than the norm. Therefore, for scholars, it is critical to recognize the military understanding of *audience*. Similarly, for the military it is critical to understand the composition of such audiences; to understand their values, expectations and patterns of communication.

In the case of the UK, target audiences for whom the military construct strategic narratives exist as a dynamic entity in doctrine. Here, audiences comprise three distinct categories: UK audiences (including opinion formers, dependant audiences and the general British public); international audiences (made up of Joint Operations Area (JOA) regional audiences and Joint Operations Area (JOA) local audiences); and internal audiences (military members at home and on deployment).[14] Whereas UK doctrine labels the British domestic audience as the principle target, NATO strategic communication policy is driven by influencing regional and local audiences. Yet according to doctrine, any of these groups hold the power to affect how military communication efforts are conceptualized and implemented during operations. Hence, managing audience perception becomes an important element in relation to strategic communication. The military strive to target each audience sub-category individually so as to exert maximum influence. From a military perspective, therefore, effective strategic narratives are made up of messages that hold the ability to target audiences at both the regional and local levels (enemies and allies), and at the national and international levels (enemies and allies). From the perspective of the Alliance, this also means that the overall strategic narrative must be broad enough to accommodate a range of particular messages that will resonate with diverse audiences; messages that will generate support among allies while neutralizing enemy propaganda. This, as will be demonstrated below, was not the case in Libya.

Organizing structures of communication ahead of and during the Libya crisis

In a politico-military context, it was the attacks of 9/11 that stimulated increased interest in the elusive term of strategic communication as it emphasized the importance of shaping audience perceptions of campaign activity.[15] Yet it is safe to argue that the integration of strategic communication into military structures has not been without problems. Not least in a British context, where the concept has developed in parallel with the emergence of 'influence', which military members now claim is the key to operational work. Influence activity has taken hold in the British military and has gained renewed relevance in military doctrine:

> Within formation headquarters and at unit level, dedicated staff officers are required to support commanders and principal staff officers in balancing kinetic and non-kinetic activity to achieve desired effects on the insurgent, the affected population and, indirectly, wider audiences.[16]

Developing in conjunction with strategic communication, and increasingly endorsed by UK commanders, influence activity functions as a vehicle for strategic communication, in the sense that it involves media operations, information operations and psyops as effective communication tools at the tactical level. To this end, the integration of both strategic communication and influence activity is indicative of a shift in Western military thinking from exclusively focusing on kinetic effects to incorporating *non*-kinetic effects – to 'reassure', 'influence' and 'inform' target groups.[17] Recognized in the 2011 discussion note on military contributions to strategic communication (detailed below), the change in attitudes has been advocated by Royal Navy Commander Steve Tatham in particular. Along with Major General Andrew Mackay, he has pushed for stronger focus on Target Audience Analysis (TAA)[18] so as to 'effect properly constructed influence campaigns, perhaps dislocating the urge to apply force, as the primary activity, from the epicentre of military thinking to the periphery'.[19]

As a result, in April 2011, the Defence Concepts and Doctrine Centre (DCDC), a UK Ministry of Defence think-tank, weighed in with a doctrine note, which defined strategic communication as: 'Advancing national interests by using all Defence means of communication to influence the attitudes and behaviours of people'.[20] As noted by Mackay and Tatham, the document also set out the main forms of communication:

> ... informational, attitudinal, and behavioural. Informational communication seeks to simply impart [...] Attitudinal communication seeks to positively influence people's opinion on a particular issue [...] Behavioural communication seeks to induce a particular type of behaviour, either reinforcing or changing it [...] The three types of communication can be linked together but are not necessarily dependent upon each other.[21]

Evidently, this is important in the sense that it recognizes that strategic communication is driven by psychological means that aim to change attitudes and behaviour. However, the timing of this document was equally important. Launched during the initial phase of the Libya campaign, JDN 1/11 was a result of extensive discussions within both the UK Ministry of Defence as well as among war and communications specialists. This meant that when United Nations Security Council Resolution (UNSCR) 1973 was put into action, strategic communication was already a 'hot topic' within British defence structures; how strategic communication could potentially contribute to political and military success and how the military machinery could potentially contribute to its implementation, had been widely debated among military strategists.

Largely by coincidence, therefore, the Libya crisis not only became the first new crisis involving British troops since the launch of the UK National Security Council (NSC),[22] British involvement in NATO's operations in Libya also became the first *real* campaign fought by the UK military with the support of strategic communication. Therefore, what was particularly new in relation to Libya was the organized structure of strategic communication and how already established components of the military communication process, including information operations, media operations and psyops, were harnessed to support the strategic narrative. Yet according to available doctrine, the distinction between media operations, information operations and psyops was clearly maintained in the UK military approach to Libya. Media operations were specifically targeted at influencing the attitudes and perceptions of domestic as well as wider international audiences by dealing directly with independent, national and international media through daily media updates on air strikes and campaign progress. On the other hand, information operations were the key vehicles for the military communication capability at the tactical level and were primarily concerned with influencing local civilians and countering enemy propaganda, corresponding to military influence policy. To this end, the strategic communication system in place in Libya exploited individual communications vehicles such as media and information operations to target particular audiences through particular means, while still adhering to the principles outlined in military communications doctrine.

Media operations were perceived as being effective in constructing a narrative that met the expectations of the home audience.[23] Yet in a NATO context, information operations faced a more difficult task in attuning their messaging to the values of local civilians. Without a ground-level communications component (UNSCR 1973 strictly prohibited foreign forces on Libyan soil), which could directly influence local attitudes on the one hand and feed local information back to headquarters on the other, addressing the local population proved challenging. During NATO air strikes, it was the task of information operations to ensure that the right messages reached the right audience. Because of the nature of these operations, which meant that the civilian population was at risk, limiting collateral damage through information provision was seen to be critical. More specifically, as has traditionally been the task of information operations staff in recent campaigns, leaflets and radio messages were generated not only to gain local support through influence activity, but to ensure that local civilians stayed away from military infrastructures being bombed by NATO allies.[24] Furthermore, the allied forces sent military advisors to Libya to help the rebels improve their communications systems.[25] Even as it has later been reported that NATO had specialized troops on the ground, which played a central role in the outcome of the campaign,[26] it was important that UK ground-level activities were not seen as an attempt to train or arm the rebels.[27] These efforts thus purely centred round communications endeavours, which meant that strategic communication capabilities not only provided the alliance with a strategically sound narrative, it also helped the rebels spread their message.

> For its part, the NTC [National Transitional Council] increasingly realised the importance of strategic communications and the FCO [Foreign and Commonwealth Office], with MOD support, led HMG [Her Majesty's Government] efforts, in response to NTC requests, to build their capability in Benghazi and outside of Libya.[28]

These UK specific communication vehicles, designed to communicate targeted messages to target audiences, were supported by NATO run YouTube channels, media briefings as part of daily press conferences and a 24-hour media response service. However, it is important to note that despite these individual vehicles, and even as NATO communication units implemented sophisticated and carefully planned structures to explain their Libya campaign, allied forces were largely unable to compete with regime or rebel processes of communication in influencing local perceptions and attitudes. For instance, the rebels were very quick in setting up their own television station *Libya Ahrar* (Free Libya), which allowed them to promote their cause – their rebellion – in an effective and time-efficient manner. Almost paradoxically, therefore, and largely due to the traditionally hierarchical nature and slow paced military organizational structures, the processes of communication within NATO and accompanying communication vehicles essentially failed to meet the demands for speed, flexibility and adaptability demonstrated by rebel communication structures.

However, despite the fact that the UK military strategic communication approach, in line with that of the Alliance, was not effective in keeping up with adverse propaganda and largely failed to tap into local sentiments (demonstrated in greater detail below), communications units across the military institution, across government departments and across the coalition were generally effective in justifying the operation, *in the eyes of the British home audience.* Furthermore, in order to establish a communications structure synchronized across all levels of defence, the British Government put in place the Libya Communications Team (LCT) and the Cross Government Strategic Communication Synchronisation Group (SCSG). These units responded to several hundred media requests, throughout the day. Within this structure, the LCT was tasked with coordinating all communications work across the UK Government and with NATO allies:

> This team co-ordinated production of a daily script and communications activity grid to support our wider objectives through effective communications. It also provided a point of contact for the NATO media operations centre, international allies and internal and external partners with regular calls to key NATO and regional allies to share scripts and co-ordinate communications activity.[29]

While the LCT was physically based at the heart of Whitehall, at No 10, the government-wide SCSG was located in the Ministry of Defence so as to ensure cohesion across all government departments. It had access to NATO operational command and was able to shape the alliance's overall approach to communication. More specifically, the Group was tasked with identifying target audiences for whom themes and messages could be produced. Unity of purpose and common goals were thus essentially secured through the sophisticated organization of strategic communication. The UK approach to and organization of strategic communication was thus a strong driving force behind the transnational strategic narrative on Libya, outlined below. This organizational structure in place to direct or manage the strategic narrative during the Libya mission demonstrated the extent to which communication has moved up the military agenda and into the heart of military operations. Evidently, this can be seen as an indicator that the military have begun treating communication as an integral part of campaign planning and execution; a key component of their operational activities.

Strategic narrative: a story of liberation shaped for the *home audience*

As has been the case in a number of recent military campaigns involving allied forces, one of the challenges in 'communicating Libya' was how to legitimize a campaign of *choice*. In general terms, it meant constructing messages that supported the overall strategic narrative, while anchored in a military hierarchical structure that required synchronization across strategic, operational and tactical levels. To this end, the military's communications strategists also faced the difficult task of constructing a narrative that promoted military success while simultaneously adhering to political objectives and legal boundaries, as determined by UNSCR 1973.[30]

Against the backdrop of the above discussion, Western militaries increasingly rely on the capacity of strategic communication to generate popular support for campaign activity. Yet it is clear that such communication efforts have generally failed to make real and long-lasting contributions to success, as demonstrated in Iraq, and more so in Afghanistan.[31] Still, aimed at synchronizing information flow across national and international command and political structures, strategic communication formulated and coordinated NATO's strategic Libya *narrative;* a narrative founded upon the notion that 'perception becomes reality'[32] and a narrative primarily aimed at targeting home audiences. Conducted in the shadow of Afghanistan, which has generally failed to provide a coherent and credible campaign narrative, the weight and wider influence of the Libya message was important. Thus at a time of strategic uncertainties, the Libya mission served as an opportunity for the military to regain public confidence. But popular domestic support for the Libya operation was neither a given nor a matter which the military took lightly. This was not a conflict from which either British or NATO forces had much to gain. Instead, reputation was at stake. The strategic narrative was thus engineered to generate positive home perceptions from which the military institution as a whole stood to gain, in both the short and the long run.

Therefore, from a UK military perspective, designed to generate support among the British home audience, the strategic narrative on Libya was driven by the aim of proactively drawing attention to favourable aspects of the operation, while obscuring less favourable events. The UK message – and indeed the coalition message – centred round the political storyline of protecting Libyan civilian lives, as determined by UNSCR 1973. Enabling the 'liberation of the Libyan people'[33] was promoted as the underlying reasoning for military intervention. In turn, the aim of military intervention was generally defined as: 'protect Libyan civilians from the threat of attack from Regime forces for as long as is necessary'.[34] As such, the evidence suggests that by *selling* UK involvement in the NATO operation as a humanitarian intervention and a liberation exercise the British military managed to generate domestic support. This was particularly demonstrated by the fact that half of the UK population, according to one national survey,[35] favoured British military involvement, at the outset of the campaign. This can be taken as an indication of the effectiveness of the British military's communications efforts, in the sense that the public *mood* in Britain was largely in favour of the operation.[36]

This may be due to the fact that even before the launch of NATO's Operation Unified Protector, the British military introduced a proactive strategic communication campaign employed not only to explain the circumstances and the grounds for military intervention in Libya, but to justify the campaign in the eyes of domestic population. When the first NATO air strikes hit Libya the UK public was already attuned to the messaging generated through the strategic narrative. In addition to the Libya-specific messaging, discussed here, the UK public had already been accustomed to military and political *storytelling*, in the sense that the events in Egypt, Tunisia, Afghanistan, and elsewhere had demonstrated the nature of such narratives and political reasoning. Resembling previous military constructed campaign narratives, the Libyan regime, personified through the figure of Colonel Muammar Gaddafi, was already depicted as an oppressing power with Gaddafi portrayed as a tyrant.[37] That way, the *need* for 'humanitarian intervention' was seen as imminent, not only from an alliance perspective (led by France) but from a *home audience* perspective as well. This notion of a *need* for intervention also directed the strategic narrative. Since backed by a UN resolution, which allowed member states to not only impose a no-fly zone over Libya but to use 'all necessary measures' to protect local civilians, this narrative appeared legit to most audiences. The messages, designed to generate support among home audiences, were rhetorical in format and criticizing them would effectively mean accepting a tyrant oppressing the Libyan people. Driven by this clear-cut and straightforward storyline of good vs. evil (the stuff fairy tales are made of), the campaign was framed through value-laden and humanitarian political objectives. Although this narrative resembled a fairy tale with good and bad lead characters, unlike fairy tales, the reality was a lot more complex.

Throughout the campaign, the UK military managed to maintain a standardized 'line to take', which centred round the repeated use of words such as 'liberation' and 'freedom'. Hence, phrases like 'protecting the lives of civilians', 'the liberation of the Libyan people' and 'coalition action has [...] prevented Gaddafi from regaining power over Libya' were reiterated as key components of the campaign. Similarly, messages promoting military action were encapsulated in reassuring and positive connotations in statements such as: 'Coalition actions have saved thousands of lives in Benghazi, Misratah and elsewhere in Libya.'[38] In line with this, one of the dominant narrative features voiced by the UK military in the aftermath of the campaign centred on 'liberation': 'Royal Navy, Royal Air Force and Army Air Corps strikes have played a significant role in the enforcement of the UNSCR, the destruction of former regime forces and in enabling the liberation of the Libyan people.'[39]

By framing the operation as a liberation exercise, these messages remained powerful as they supported the dominant, international, political line used to justify the overall mission, as mentioned above. Moreover, by repeating such words and phrases, the military managed to generate cohesion and a strong unison of output on the UK home front, among NATO allies and within political spheres. Therefore, the reasons behind the military use of strategic messaging to *sell* an operation are manifold. They are critical to the generation of support among home audiences. They simplify and reduce the military mission to easily digestible statements that most audiences are unlikely to contest. Because of their universal appeal they enable the military to generate a cohesive strategic narrative that holds the capacity to meet the expectations and values of most target audiences, simultaneously. They boost internal morale. And because of their generic nature, they can easily be adapted to different military scenarios and adopted by multiple allied forces.[40]

Not surprisingly, therefore, and which has already been alluded to above, the strategic narrative of 'liberation' and 'freedom' dominated much of the operation:

> Since the start of military operations, Royal Navy, Royal Air Force and Army Air Corps strikes have damaged or destroyed some 1000 former regime targets which posed a threat to the Libyan people, ranging from secret police and intelligence headquarters, to several hundred tanks, artillery pieces and armed vehicles.[41]

Promoting the humanitarian aspects of the Libya campaign was also critical to the strengthening of public and political endorsement for the campaign:

> Communication of the international humanitarian response was important in maintaining confidence in the ability to manage the situation. An inclusive humanitarian response and effective communication of this approach also supported the core HMG [Her Majesty's Government] message that the purpose of the international intervention in Libya was to protect civilians. Moreover, it helped to bestow confidence and legitimacy in the NTC [National Transitional Council] and its ability to respond fairly and effectively to the needs of the Libyan people.[42]

In light of this, political objectives provided the military with a storyline that generated widespread support, at the outset. Domestic audiences were *sold* the case for international military intervention in Libya as a necessity because of Gaddafi's alleged torturing and killing of his own people, on a large scale. And from the outset of the operation, as well as during the lead-up to international intervention, the strategic narrative remained largely straightforward with Western media reiterating the themes and messages coming from the military. At this stage, news reports in the UK were thus generally in line with the official messaging. In early March 2011, news broke that Gaddafi was expected to kill half a million people and was planning to move into Benghazi to defeat the rebels who had taken hold of the city.[43] During the lead-up to the UN imposed no-fly zone, Western media reported that Libyan regime forces were bombing 'peaceful' rebels. These news media narratives echoed some of the underlying political reasoning given for international intervention in the war. The violence and supposedly imminent attacks on local civilians by Gaddafi and his supporters, who reportedly had 'tanks sitting outside Benghazi' ready for an invasion, were brought into the official messaging and provided a plausible backdrop for the strategic narrative. Moreover, in April when media reports broke of Gaddafi supplying his troops with Viagra to promote rape of women and children,[44] the *mood* of the UK media, helped legitimize the operation by stimulating the need to protect the civilian population from regime repressions 'by all means necessary' (as formulated in UNSCR 1973).

In essence the strategic narrative thus became a key factor in deflecting attention from more critical aspects of the mission so as to minimize the impact caused by the less favourable and more controversial stories emerging from Libya. Yet as the operation progressed, the unambiguous rhetoric that had dominated the beginning of the campaign gradually faded and was replaced with one characterized by caution and compromise. In line with this, the strategic narrative of a *clean* air and sea campaign, as set out in UNSCR 1973 and which dominated the initial phase of the operation, was increasingly seen by Western audiences as flawed. Even though UK forces did not suffer casualties and even as NATO refrained from disclosing any casualty figures, the Royal United Services Institute (RUSI) stated that 'the precision of the attacks kept the number of civilian casualties [...] extremely low (certainly less than 100)'.[45] As the military campaign continued for 204 days and given the fact that the future of Libya is still very much unknown, there is reason to argue that the people of Libya as well as rebel forces paid a heavy price. The image of the campaign as a clean mission and the promise of a clean war gradually deteriorated among UK home audiences. Within four months of the beginning of the operation, one opinion poll suggested that the public mood in Britain went from supporting the operation to thinking that the operation was going 'badly'.[46]

The *local audience* and the challenges of perception

The fact that the strategic narrative in Libya was designed primarily to justify the operation in the eyes of the home audience meant that constructing clear and consistent messages that met the expectations of the local civilian population in Libya became a difficult task; and not only was it a demanding task, it was perhaps even the biggest obstacle to *successful* strategic communication in Libya. This view is based on the evidence which suggests that reaching the local and regional audiences proved the biggest challenge in generating favourable perceptions of the mission.[47] Particularly, given the fluid nature of the communication environment, messages designed to influence home audiences were quickly distributed among a much bigger slice of the global population, including local civilians in the theatre of conflict (traditionally the target of information and psychological operations). This meant that messages that were attuned to the expectations and values of domestic publics within participating NATO countries rapidly found their way to audiences whose expectations and attitudes were very different from those of the intended home audience. Such characteristics of modern communication and information provision thus became an obstacle rather than a vehicle for influencing local attitudes and behaviours.

Yet they were not unique to the Libya mission. Today, both scholars and military strategists are pointing to the fact that while the fight is increasingly concerned with the *will of the people*, as noted by Smith,[48] advances in communications technology make influencing diverse audiences a challenging task. The military and politically constructed narrative as well as its supporting themes and messages are constantly rivalled by competing and compelling storylines promoted through the increasingly seamless information system. For UK and NATO messaging, competing Libyan storylines presented difficulties in the sense that they held the power to potentially result in rumours and media speculation. Moreover, they posed a challenge because they directly contradicted the strategic campaign narrative communicated by allied forces. Therefore, in Libya, as in most military interventions involving international forces and multiple audiences, the evidence suggests that while the 'new', non-linear and fast-moving processes of communication proved effective in mobilizing home support, it became as much an obstacle as a support for the alliance in reaching theatre-level audiences and influencing local sentiments.

However, recognizing the importance of changing attitudes and behaviours within the local population, the UK Ministry of Defence decided to dispatch a small communications team to the NATO Joint Force Command headquarters in Naples, Italy, in April 2011. The main focus was to ensure that timely information reached the intended audiences on the ground.[49] Bearing in mind that allied forces were not allowed to communicate directly with rebel forces, as determined by UNSCR 1973, direct communication with local-level audiences was at a minimum.[50] This was made even more complicated by the fact that, while the UK communications unit understood the civilian Libyan population to be the primary audience, the NATO public affairs team was primarily tuned into Gaddafi's military forces, and not to local civilian sentiments.[51] Initially, as noted by Mackay and Tatham,[52] this meant that internal disagreements within the NATO communications cell largely concerned *target audiences*. As well as resulting in a lack of understanding of the local audience, it also clearly reflected the difficult task of synchronizing communications efforts across international coalitions.

And as noted by Flight Lieutenant Charles Sudborough, during a ten-day exercise prior to deployment to command headquarters in Naples: 'We have to get the right information to the right people at the right time.'[53] Yet in the increasingly messy communication system, determining who 'the right people' are and what 'the right information' consists of is, as we have seen, not straightforward. Moreover, the fact that intra-coalition disagreements on target audiences and communication approaches became a reality during the campaign, demonstrates the challenges inherent in synchronized strategic messaging. The evidence thus also suggests that the military were largely unable to determine the composition of their target audiences with any degree of accuracy. It demonstrates the difficultly in understanding audiences for whom strategic narratives are designed. And it shows how intra-military views on audiences has become a high-profiled component of international operations. Since 'understanding the audience is the beginning and end of all military influence endeavours',[54] a fundamental weakness of current strategic communication policy, therefore, is that it builds false expectations, because it promises success where success may not be achievable.

As such, while the UK military were seen as being effective in *branding* the campaign in ways that met UK home audience expectations, to a large extent, at the local level allied forces generally failed to attune their messaging to the values of the Libyan people and to the dominant media profile in the region.[55] This is supported by scholars and communication practitioners, who, in the aftermath of the campaign, have highlighted the failure of NATO forces to put in place culturally aware systems of operations as one of the biggest problems inherent in the Libya campaign.[56] In line with the views of these scholars, and in the context of strategic communication, tactical-level themes and messages aimed at local civilians were generated based on, at best, limited knowledge of this audience. The expectations and values of the different tribes (the Berbers and Gaddafi supporters) were thus not fully understood. Effectively, this meant that behavioural change at the local level – the cornerstone in strategic communication policy – was non-existent. Or rather, the military systems in place to ensure attitudinal and behavioural change were non-existent. And as noted by Florence Gaub in a NATO Defense College report on the *Strategic Lessons learned from Libya:*

> While NATO continues to deal with nations and cultures very different from those of Europe or North America, it is rather slow in acknowledging the importance of having an accurate grasp of local conditions outside the purely military field.[57]

And if we are to return to Smith, it is clear that where the fight is for the will of the people tactical successes will mean nothing if 'the people do not believe that you are winning'.[58] In this 'battle of wills', Smith contends that the media hold great importance;[59] they are indispensable as the means of conveying narratives about war in what is not so much the global village 'as the global theatre of war, with audience participation'.[60]

Another challenge to successful strategic communication is connected to recent and ongoing developments in the news media. Coupled with advances in communication technology, the news media are now able to obtain a diverse array of information about campaign activity and, therefore, do not always have to rely on storylines generated through the military strategic narrative. In Libya, citizen-led storylines and images were widely used by mainstream media outlets to support the reports coming from the limited number of journalists who reported from the country during the campaign. In light of this, and as a result of such increased patterns of access, strategic communication mechanisms function as information providers on the one hand, and as a control system on the other.

Yet because military organizational structures require all communications activity to be simultaneously synchronized at the strategic, operational and tactical levels, the military are largely unable to compete with the speed of the media and of modern information technology. To this end, NATO's Libya campaign demonstrated the weaknesses of incorporating strategic communication into international coalitions. Messages had to be aligned across coalition partners: 'While the campaign underlined the need to ensure that actions and words were closely aligned across all national means of communication, communications activity also included co-ordination with NATO and other Allies.'[61] Ensuring a coherent output, synchronized at all levels, takes time. Conducting effective communications activity that meets the media's need for speed is thus not a simple matter. This not only refers to the advances in communication technology, which have meant that campaign events and incidents are reported as they happen. It also refers to the fact that the institutional processes of the media are designed to react immediately, whereas inherent military processes run through traditionally slow organizational structures.

In Libya these processes came under enormous pressure as the UK military, along with NATO communications cells, were forced to account for and deal with extensive state and rebel propaganda. In practical terms this meant that strategic communication initiatives were designed to constrain the efficiency and impact of regime propaganda, while supporting the NTC of Libya. In so doing, the messaging was directed towards weakening the publicity campaign launched by the Gaddafi regime. But as demonstrated by *UK lessons learned* from the campaign, limiting this form of propaganda was challenging:

> Qadhafi and his regime used state media for propaganda and inciting attacks on civilians. The UK worked with international partners to limit broadcast of such programmes. Action included listing Libyan State TV under EU sanctions and lobbying local authorities via diplomatic channels to stop transmission. This proved a lengthy, complex and difficult process as many satellite broadcasters had complex ownership structures.[62]

In this context, regime and rebel storylines posed challenges for NATO communication efforts as it forced them to counter such stories, especially in relation to the messaging coming from Gaddafi supporters. While Gaddafi propaganda was described as being openly untruthful about civilian casualties in particular, the rebels were seen to employ a more conventional method of propaganda, which painted a black and white picture of the two opposing forces: good vs. evil.[63] In the Gaddafi camp, and as noted in the above quote, state television – particularly Al-Rai which continued to broadcast during the campaign – showed civilian victims who regime officials claimed had been killed by NATO air strikes. Competing storylines thus continued to challenge the strategic narrative promoted by the coalition, as the messaging stemming from such opposing storylines often directly contradicted the strategic narrative communicated by the allied forces.

Another key obstacle in the military communication structure in Libya was the over-simplification of complex matters. While constructing a strategic narrative founded on key concepts and promoted through set catchphrases, the complexities inherent in joint military operations were left largely unresolved. This approach meant that emergent stories that did not comply with the outlined strategic narrative were omitted in military communication efforts. One example from Libya of the use of over-simplified messages relates to the general belief that Gaddafi would not be able to withstand large-scale opposition; that he would topple within days and that the operation would live up to the promise of a 'clean' mission. As scholars have later found, this narrative failed to make an impact.[64] In their attempt to over-simplify a complex situation, the allied forces unintentionally generated a competing narrative themselves. Not only did it take until October 2011 for the coalition to remove Gaddafi and his supporters from their last strongholds, but by simplifying the situation the strategic narrative built false expectations and thus proved increasingly counter-productive.

In essence, to gain maximum influence from simplified catchphrases NATO as well as individual alliance members are forced to recognize and understand the expectations and values of multiple audiences. Yet given their indirect relationship with these audiences it is inherently difficult to predict which themes and messages will generate popular support through changes in attitudes and behaviours. This often means that dominant, politically generated narratives are adopted. In the Libya campaign, however, the politico-military storyline was, on the one hand, complicated because of a lack of local audience awareness. On the other hand, *selling* the campaign as a 'liberation' exercise through a military constructed strategic narrative, which was supported by a UN resolution that made no legal provisions for regime change, became increasingly difficult as the political leadership – in the form of Foreign Ministers from NATO nations – decided to 'strongly' support Gaddafi's resignation.[65]

The military narrative of an operation carried out to 'liberate the people of Libya' was thus forced to compete with a politically generated storyline, which, for many, cemented the understanding that the joint mission was aimed at removing Gaddafi from power. These contrasting messages made military messaging difficult.⁶⁶ Framing an operation through military constructed messaging becomes increasingly difficult if that messaging has not been properly integrated, realized or accepted at the political level.

Lessons from Libya: re-evaluating strategic communication

The demanding task of targeting diverse groups of people simultaneously, during periods of strategic pressure requires a sophisticated understanding of audience, as noted above. And it requires the ability to control a message in a communication environment that is largely uncontrollable. In other words, efficient communication of a strategic narrative is essential to any military operation and yet, because of the difficulties involved, it is a task more likely to fail than to ensure strategic and tactical level successes. It is thus paradoxical that the British military along with their NATO partners continue to base their communication methods on the instinctive notion that their efforts will result in *successfully* communicating intended messages to target audiences. As noted by Tatham: 'In part this is due to an immature understanding of the manner in which communication is undertaken.'⁶⁷

Strategic communication is still a relatively new, high-profile concept in military strategic thinking. Originally coined as a system for attuning communication processes to the preferences of the consumer, commercial strategic communication has grown in the civilian world as a linking together of advertising, branding and marketing strategies.⁶⁸ Not surprisingly perhaps, and because of the challenges – and indeed opportunities – posed by the rapidly developing information system, this method of promoting and *selling* a brand as a means of targeting audiences has gradually been adapted by Western militaries to suit campaign activity; to increase the opportunity of success. However, in the same way as commercial branding may result in failure, constructing messages and identifying target audiences does not necessarily result in public support, nor does it guarantee military and political campaign success. Nonetheless, the strategic communication mind-set is precisely one of success and the aim is

> to put information strategy at the heart of all levels of policy, planning and implementation, and then, as a fully integrated part of the overall effort, to ensure the development of practical, effective strategies that make a real contribution to success.⁶⁹

Effectively, this means that it fails to account for the complex nature of the current communication system.

Against this backdrop, therefore, it is wrong to assume that strategic communication will always result in what the military term *success*. As we have discovered, strategic communication relies on sophisticated understandings of audience and message in order to be effective, for which the military may not be equipped. Moreover, the process of strategic communication is always based on understandings of best practice; there are no generic step-by-step guidelines and there are no guarantees. Getting the message wrong or misinterpreting public perceptions can have devastating human consequences in a military context; consequences that are incomparable to the business sector's financial risk-takings for example.[70]

It is thus important that, in this, as in other aspects of military media activity, military strategic communication is understood as inherently distinctive from commercial marketing strategies. Yes, it is possible to find traces of civilian branding and advertising initiatives in the strategic communication remit. Strategic communication has also been talked about as a process of 'spin', an expression employed to explain how information is being framed to generate desired audience reactions.[71] And notions of 'propaganda', 'deception' and 'manipulation' continue to colour discussions on military communication, and as a result determine the position authors take.[72] There is thus a danger that while Western militaries struggle to find functional and appropriate communication structures, through which to *tell their story*, strategic communication is increasingly being associated with terms that result in negative connotations; terms which rely on stereotypical understandings of military communication and which fail to advance new frameworks of understanding. At the same time, the processes of military communication have taken on a variety of forms, in recent years, largely determined by the contrasting viewpoints adopted by practitioners and scholars who perceive their roles differently. As noted by Tatham:

> In the UK military environment we are confident with terms such as Information and Media Operations, whilst in military staff colleges Influence and Persuasion are debated. Civilian academics may speak of Soft Power and Public Diplomacy and cynics might prefer the use of Propaganda.[73]

Not surprisingly, therefore, academics and practitioners alike continue to search for alternative ways of explaining the continuous information battle. Different interpretations of how 'strategic' should be defined in the context of strategic communication continue to emerge. Yet whereas it tends to be seen as either the anchoring of an activity at the strategic-political level or as communication that supports military strategic goals,[74] NATO documentation points to a convergence of the two: '[strategic communication] should be integrated into the earliest planning phases – communication activities being a consequence of that planning'.[75] In this sense strategic communication is seen as driven by both military and political objectives which require synchronization across a number of command and political levels. Communication is thus recognized as an important function at the strategic level, in ensuring that communication is incorporated into policy development. We might, therefore, argue that strategic communication has become critical to security policy development and indeed is seen as not merely close to military objectives but actually part of them.

In addition, the practical incorporation and employment of strategic communication 'enablers',[76] the vehicles in place to operationalize the conceptualized notion of strategic communication include: media operations, information operations and psychological operations (psyops).[77] According to doctrine, a vital difference between media and information operations is that 'while media operations cannot control a message once it is in the hands of the media, information operations will attempt to control a message at all stages of its delivery to the target audience'.[78] In line with information operations, psyops are employed to influence the will of the people. It is a tool used strictly to target the local population in the campaign area. So, while it has links with information operations it is distinct from media operations, which the military claim are fact-based and are driven by providing the media with the *truth*.[79] To this end, strategic communication can be seen as an umbrella term, which incorporates a range of practical communications vehicles that seek to preserve, influence and enhance the credibility and favourable conditions of an operation, and to advance the interest, policies and objectives of the military. It is driven by both military and political objectives, which require synchronization across government departments as well as coalition forces. Effective strategic communication thus involves an integrated politico-military effort that stretches beyond what militaries have traditionally been designed to do: take, hold and destroy.

Conclusion: strategic communication as an integral part of military operations

Today, military operations have more to do with information management and public perception than ever before. The communication efforts of NATO forces generate messages and simplified catchphrases designed to meet the expectations of target audiences. Strategic narratives are constructed to tell a story of campaign success. And audiences are being proactively targeted through strategic and tactical level components. Yet at the same time, processes of communication are messier and more complex than ever before. Notions of mediatization are being eagerly discussed among scholars and practitioners. Access to information about military activity can be obtained through multiple platforms. Advances in communication technology allow for information to be distributed simultaneously throughout the information system, and communication exists through non-linear channels. Strategic communication processes thus rely on increasingly uncontrollable communication systems.

Still, strategic communication has moved up the military agenda and into the heart of military campaigns. Shifts in Western military thinking have led militaries to develop increasingly sophisticated strategic communication facilities, which, in a specific UK context rely on 'influence' as the ultimate driving force. Perhaps not surprisingly, therefore, controlling the *message* has become central to military strategic and tactical thinking and is indeed seen as not merely close to military objectives but actually part of them. Audiences, and their perception of campaign activity, have moved into an ever more dominant role in NATO strategic thinking. To this end, military interventions are clearly no longer activities that take place outside of the communication system. Rather, as we have seen, communication mechanisms have become an integral part of strategic military planning, to the point where future operations cannot be understood without accounting for this communication role.

As Western militaries increasingly understand public perception as having a critical and possibly long-term effect on the success or failure of military activity, the Libya campaign clearly demonstrated how *selling* favourable strategic narratives has been institutionalized in the UK military, and attempted and synchronized across strategic communication structures throughout the Alliance. Ultimately, marketing and advertising campaigns (commercial or military) rest upon the existence of an attractive and saleable product.[80] In this analogy, whereas the Libya campaign proved an attractive product to the domestic audience, it failed to attract positive attention from local audiences. And while the UK military managed to sell the operation as a 'liberation' exercise at a national level, through the uses of simplified catchphrases, at an international level NATO strategic communication failed to attune such catchphrases to Libyan sentiments. Therefore, if anything, the Libya mission proved that there are no guarantees in strategic communication. With multiple target audiences, increasingly transparent media systems and independent media organizations, military communication strategists are faced with considerable challenges to control and to communicate messages. At the same time, strategic communication is becoming increasingly integrated in military operations.

There is thus a growing need for new frameworks of understanding among military practitioners as well as war and media scholars. From a military point of view, it may be important to recognize that the overall strategic narrative must be broad enough to accommodate a range of particular messages that will generate support among allies while neutralizing enemy propaganda, as argued above. Above all, we need to recognize the underlying factors that drive military communication efforts and understand them as products of the current media and warfare landscapes. Within such a framework, there is no *one* audience. There is no *one* message. There is no *one* approach. Communication is not simple, nor is campaign activity.

Notes

1 L. Rowland and S. Tatham, *Strategic Communication and Influence Operations: Do We Really Get It?*, Defence Academy of the United Kingdom, 2010.
2 Already in the 1982 Falklands campaign, the UK military realised that they needed to develop sophisticated media and information management structures. Particularly, however, in the aftermath of the 2003 Iraq War, the UK Ministry of Defence inaugurated extensive media and communications systems so as to account for the role of *modern* media in military affairs. This resulted in, for instance: the Defence Media Operations Centre (DMOC); the Directorate Media and Communication (DMC); the Directorate of News (D News); the Defence Online Engagement Strategy (2007); the Defence Communication Strategy (revised March 2009); and the Defence Information Strategy (October 2009).
3 A wide range of doctrine publications, discussion notes and reports have emerged from within NATO communication and public affairs institutions on the topic of strategic communication, in recent years: NATO, *NATO Strategic Communications Policy*, 2009, MCM-0164-2009; NATO, *Military Concept for NATO Strategic Communications*, 2010, MCM-0085-2010; NATO, *NATO ACO Strategic Communications Directive*, 2009, AD 95–2; and NATO, *NATO Strategic Communications Capability Implementation Plan*, 20 April 2011.
4 This was not solely a result of the UK strategic narrative on Libya. As discussed in greater detail below, the nature of military intervention and the legal underpinnings allowed for clear and concise messaging from the outset.
5 Data was collected through observations and textual analysis. While observation work was carried out within the UK-led public affairs office in NATO's Allied Rapid Reaction Corps (ARRC) for two weeks during the lead-up to the Libya campaign, it did not deal specifically with Libya strategic communication considerations. Rather, it provided an 'on-the-ground' understanding of the structures and practices of military communications. This aspect of the methodology was substantiated by doctrinal texts specifically dealing with UK and NATO strategic communication policy during the Libya campaign. Observations were particularly useful as they allowed for understandings of what the military do, rather than what they say they do. Military strategic texts helped validate data collected in the field and were useful in providing citations and a contextual basis. Combined, the methodological choices are believed to reveal institutionally derived military practices in relation to strategic communications activity.
6 P. Ricketts, *Libya Crisis: National Security Adviser's Review of Central Co-ordination and Lessons Learned*, UK Cabinet Office, 2011, 18.
7 S. Badsey, 'Media war and media management', in G. Kassimeris and J. Buckley (eds), *The Ashgate Research Companion to Modern Warfare*, Surrey: Ashgate, 2010, 401–18.
8 For a broader discussion on *mediatized wars* and the *mediatization* of military activity see, for instance: S. Cottle, *Mediatized Conflict*, Berkshire: Open University Press, 2006; S. Hjarvard, 'The mediatisation of society: a theory of media as agents of social and cultural change', *Nordicom Review* 29, 2008, 105–34; and A. Hoskins and B. O'Loughlin, *War and Media: The Emergence of Diffused War*, Cambridge: Polity Press, 2010.
9 R. Smith, *The Utility of Force: The Art of War in the Modern World*, London: Allen Lane, 2005, 19.
10 Smith, *The Utility of Force*, 284–5.
11 Hjarvard, 'The mediatisation of society'.
12 Notions on the role of the media in *modern* wars have been widely examined. See, for instance: S. Allan and B. Zelizer, *Reporting War: Journalism in Wartime*, London: Routledge, 2004; S.L. Carruthers, *The Media at War: Communications*

and *Conflict in the 20th Century*, London: Macmillan, 2000; T. Thrall, *War in the Media Age*, New Jersey: Hampton Press, 2000; D. Thussu and D. Freedman, *War and the Media*, London: Sage, 2003; and H. Tumber and F. Webster, *Journalists under Fire: Information War and Journalistic Practice*, London: Sage, 2006.
13 S. Tatham, *Strategic Communication: A Primer*, Shrivenham: Defence Academy of the United Kingdom, Advanced Research and Assessment Group Special Series 08/28, 2008.
14 Defence Concepts and Doctrine Centre, *Media Operations*, UK Ministry of Defence, Joint Doctrine Publication (JDP) 3-45.1, 2007. A deeper discussion on 'target audiences' in a UK military context can be found in doctrine concerning media operations as well as strategic communication principles.
15 This has been documented in a number of recent scholarly works. See, for instance: D. Betz, 'Communication breakdown: strategic communications and defeat in Afghanistan', *Orbis* 4, 2011, 613–30; T. Elkjer Nissen, *Strategisk Kommunikation – en nødvendig konceptuel og strategisk udfordring*, København: Forsvarsakademiet, 2011; and Tatham, *Strategic Communication*.
16 Ministry of Defence, *British Army Field Manual: Countering Insurgency*, January 2010, 6–3.
17 T. Farrell, 'Dynamics of British military transformation', *International Affairs* 84, 2008, 795.
18 In *Strategic Communication and Influence Operations*, Lee Rowland and Steve Tatham call for an integrated military approach to TAA as they place the *audience* at the heart of military operations.
19 A. Mackay and S. Tatham, *Behavioural Conflict: Why Understanding People and their Motivations will Prove Decisive in Future Conflicts*, Saffron Walden: Military Studies Press, 2011, 135.
20 Defence Concepts and Doctrine Centre, *Strategic Communication: The Defence Contribution*, UK Ministry of Defence, Joint Discussion Note (JDN) 1/11, April 2011.
21 Quoted in Mackay and Tatham, *Behavioural Conflict*, 133.
22 The UK National Security Council (NSC) was launched in May 2010 as a Cabinet Committee. It was created to manage all national security concerns relating to the United Kingdom. It coordinates defence strategy and is integrated at the strategic (highest) level of the British government in regards to national security issues.
23 For a wider discussion on the effectiveness of NATO media operations in Libya see, for instance: F. Gaub. *Six Strategic Lessons Learned from Libya: NATO's Operation Unified Protector*, NATO Defense College, March 2012; and RUSI, *Accidental Heroes: Britain, France and the Libya Operation*, September 2011.
24 Gaub, *Six Strategic Lessons learned from Libya*.
25 Ricketts, *Libya Crisis*.
26 See Chapter 8 by Mohlin in this volume, as well as RUSI, *Accidental Heroes*.
27 On 19 April 2011, the MOD announced that they would send a team of military advisors to Libya to help the rebels with their organization and communications. See: Ricketts, *Libya Crisis*, 27.
28 Ricketts, *Libya Crisis*, 19.
29 Ricketts, *Libya Crisis*, 18.
30 For instance, the agreed UN resolution did not call for regime change or the toppling of Gaddafi, which also meant that military constructed narratives had to frame the operation within the legal boundaries determined by UNSCR 1973.
31 Betz, 'Communication Breakdown', 613–30.
32 Mark Laity, head of NATO Strategic Communication, October 2011.
33 Ministry of Defence, *MOD Top Level Message*, November 2011.

34 Ministry of Defence, *MOD Top Level Message*, October 2011.
35 In a YouGov Opinion poll from 21 March 2011, almost half of all Britons asked said that they believed the UK – along with coalition partners – was right to take military action in Libya. And a couple of days later, as many as 60 per cent of all Britons asked said that they thought the operation was going 'well'.
36 It important to note that this political reasoning for the military intervention, which effectively provided the basis for the strategic narrative, was not exclusive to the UK military. In fact, the notion of 'liberation' was reiterated throughout the coalition.
37 There are many historical precursors to this kind of demonization; most recently, the depiction of Saddam Hussein in the lead up to the 2003 Iraq War.
38 Such words and phrases can be found in the *MOD Top Level Messages*, both during and after the campaign. See, for instance: Ministry of Defence, *MOD Top Level Message*, April–November 2011.
39 Ministry of Defence, *MOD Top Level Message*, November 2011.
40 These reasons are also found in British military doctrine on Defence Concepts and Doctrine Centre, *Media Operations*.
41 Ministry of Defence, *MOD Top Level Message*, October 2011.
42 Ricketts, *Libya Crisis*, 21.
43 See, for instance: C. McGreal, 'Gaddafi's army will kill half a million, warn Libyan rebels', *The Guardian*, 12 March 2011. Online. Available: www.guardian.co.uk/world/2011/mar/12/gaddafi-army-kill-half-million (accessed 18 February 2013); M. Townsend, 'Benghazi attack by Gaddafi's forces was "ploy to negate air strikes"', *The Guardian*, 19 March 2011. Online. Available: www.guardian.co.uk/world/2011/mar/19/benghazi-gaddafi-military-air-strikes (accessed 18 February 2013); Reuters, 'Libya jets bomb rebels', *Reuters*, 14 March 2011. Online. Available:www.independent.co.uk/news/world/africa/libya-jets-bomb-rebels-2241707.html (accessed 18 February 2013).
44 When this *alleged* news broke, most media outlets carried the story. See, for instance: E. MacAskill, 'Gaddafi "supplies troops with Viagra to encourage mass rape", claims diplomat', *The Guardian*, 29 April 2011. Online. Available: www.guardian.co.uk/world/2011/apr/29/diplomat-gaddafi-troops-viagra-mass-rape (accessed 18 February 2013); Daily Mail Reporter, 'Fuelled "by Viagra", Gaddafi's troops use rape as a weapon of war with children as young as EIGHT among the victims', *Daily Mail*, 25 April 2011. Online. Available: www.dailymail.co.uk/news/article-1380364/Libya-Gaddafis-troops-rape-children-young-eight.html (accessed 18 February 2013); and BBC, 'Libya: Gaddafi investigated over use of rape as weapon', *BBC News*, 8 June 2011. Online. Available: www.bbc.co.uk/news/world-africa-13705854 (accessed 18 February 2013).
45 RUSI, *Accidental Heroes*.
46 A YouGov poll from 21 July 2011 indicated that almost half of all Britons asked thought the coalition's military action in Libya was going 'badly'; a 25 per cent increase from 21 March 2011. In comparison, almost 60 per cent of everyone asked thought the campaign was going 'well' on 1 April 2011. This percentage had dropped to less than 30 by 21 July 2011.
47 For a brief discussion on how the allied forces failed to understand the sentiments present in the local population, see: Gaub, *Six Strategic Lessons learned from Libya*.
48 Smith, *The Utility of Force*.
49 Ricketts, *Libya Crisis*.
50 In Afghanistan, for instance, information operations teams on the ground communicate directly with local Afghans.
51 Mackay and Tatham, *Behavioural Conflict*, 216.
52 Tatham, *Strategic Communication*.

53 Ministry of Defence Announcement (28 July 2011) *Air Force Communicators Prepare for Operational Role*, Ministry of Defence. Online. Available: www.mod.uk/DefenceInternet/DefenceNews/TrainingAndAdventure/AirForceCommunicatorsPrepareForOperationalRole.htm (accessed 18 February 2013).
54 Rowland and Tatham, *Strategic Communication and Influence Operations*, 2.
55 See, for instance: Gaub, *Strategic Lessons Learned from Libya*.
56 See, for instance: RUSI, *Accidental Heroes*.
57 Gaub, *Strategic Lessons Learned from Libya*, 4.
58 Smith, *Utility of Force*, 285.
59 Tatham, *Strategic Communication*.
60 Smith, *Utility of Force*, 285.
61 Ricketts, *Libya Crisis*, 18.
62 Ibid.
63 Ibid.
64 Gaub, *Strategic Lessons Learned from Libya*.
65 NATO, *Statement on Libya*, 14 April 2011.
66 Gaub, *Strategic Lessons Learned from Libya*, 5.
67 Tatham, *Strategic Communication: A Primer*, 6–7.
68 Ibid.
69 Mark Laity, NATO Chief Strategic Communication, October 2011.
70 Betz, 'Communication breakdown'.
71 See, for instance: D. Miller, J. Kitzinger, K. Williams and P. Beharrell, *The Circuit of Mass Communication*, London: Sage, 1998; and B. McNair, *An Introduction to Political Communication*, London: Routledge, 2003, 3rd edition.
72 Thomas Rid discusses this in: T. Rid, *War and Media Operations: The US Military and the Press from Vietnam to Iraq*, Abingdon: Routledge, 2007.
73 Tatham, *Strategic Communication*, 5.
74 Nissen, *Strategisk Kommunikation*.
75 NATO, *NATO Strategic Communications Policy*.
76 In *Behavioural Conflict*, Mackay and Tatham conceptualize the notion of strategic communication 'enablers'. They understand such 'enablers' – including media operations and information operations – to be practical drivers of military strategic communication. However, for the purpose of this discussion, the term 'vehicle' has been adopted for consistency and as a linking together of 'enabler' and 'driver'.
77 NATO, *NATO Strategic Communications Policy*.
78 Ministry of Defence, *Army Field Manual*, 6–4.
79 For more information about the distinction between media operations, information operations and psyops, see, for instance: Defence Concepts and Doctrine Centre, *Media Operations*; and Defence Concepts and Doctrine Centre, *Strategic Communication*.
80 Betz, 'Communication breakdown', 629.

8 Cloak and dagger in Libya

The Libyan *Thuwar* and the role of Allied Special Forces

Marcus Mohlin

Introduction

In March 2012, the Human Rights Council (HRC), a UN intergovernmental body, released an advance version of its report on the situation in Libya in the aftermath of the 2011 war.[1] The report listed and dealt with three constellations of actors involved in the conflict: the Gaddafi forces and loyalist troops; the Libyan freedom fighters (also known as the *Thuwar*); and NATO forces. According to the HRC report, which can be said to be reflective of the conventional view of the Libya campaign, the latter was composed of naval and air assets from a variety of different NATO and non-NATO countries.[2] The reality on the ground was, however, somewhat more complex than that: nowhere in the report is there any mention of the fact that some participating countries also sent in military advisors, Special Forces (SF) and para-military intelligence officers to support the *Thuwar*. Importantly, particularly because this volume focuses on the UN-mandated NATO-led operation in Libya, many of the special operations forces (SOF) deployed to Libya were in fact not associated with the NATO-led Operation Unified Protector (OUP).[3] These forces are therefore of particular interest. Not only is there reason to argue that they played a key role for the NATO campaign, but many of the SOF worked outside the NATO chain of command.

As we have seen in previous chapters (especially Chapter 2 by Engelbrekt and Chapter 3 by Holst and Fink), the UN Security Council Resolution 1973 had specifically authorized Member States, 'to take all necessary measures [...], to protect civilians and civilian populated areas under threat of attack in the Libyan Arab Jamahiriya [...], while excluding a foreign occupation force of any form on any part of Libyan territory'.[4] In short, the use of ground forces was disputed and some argued that they were not to be used at all in the Libyan campaign. However, several countries dispatched contingents of Special Forces to assist the rebels in their fight against Gaddafi. In the United Kingdom (UK) this question was specifically addressed in a memorandum written by the International Affairs and Defence Section of the House of Commons. Their conclusion to this memorandum was that the paragraph in the resolution designed to restrain governments from deploying boots on the ground could be interpreted to mean that 'ground forces can be used as long as they do not exercise effective control over the territory'.[5]

British Prime Minister Mr. David Cameron, when asked whether he could guarantee that no ground forces would be used in Libya, told the Commons:

> What I can guarantee is that we will stick to the terms of the UN resolution, which absolutely and specifically rules out an occupying force. We have to be clear: we are not talking about an invasion; we are not talking about an occupying force; we are talking about taking action to protect civilian life, and I think that is the right thing to do.[6]

On that occasion, the position of Mr. Cameron was questioned by several members of parliament who had interpreted the resolution as to rule out any use of troops inside Libya. A few weeks prior to this statement, however, early in March 2011, a team of eight British Special Forces soldiers dressed in civilian clothes had already been caught and taken prisoner by Libyan rebels on the outskirts of a small village some 40 kilometres south of Benghazi. As far as is known today, the soldiers were part of E-Squadron, a highly secretive unit comprising soldiers from both the famous Special Air Service (SAS) and Special Boat Squadron (SBS) as well as operatives from the British Secret Intelligence Service (SIS, aka MI6). Allegedly they were sent to protect a group of diplomats sent to liaise with the rebels in the area.[7]

While information of such activities exist in the public domain, so far scholars have not tried to assess the overall pattern of covert and semi-covert operations associated with the broader NATO campaign. The aim of this chapter is to examine the strategic and operational roles of such foreign Special Forces sent into the interior of Libya, not as constituent parts of the NATO-led operation but as a shadow Land Component of the latter. This will be accomplished first by describing some of the tactical and operational functions performed by these forces, and second by showing how these activities can be connected to larger operational needs and strategic goals. Finally I will discuss some theoretical and policy-relevant implications of this covert use of special operations forces in humanitarian interventions such as the one in Libya. The aim will largely be achieved through an analysis of media reports and official documentation available at the time of writing.

It should be noted that at the time of writing, not many official reports were readily available, something that means that the chapter primarily relies on secondary sources such as press clippings and news reports. There were a few attempts by journalists to provide more detailed accounts, for instance Samia Nakhoul and Mark Urban, but most of the reporting is anecdotal and therefore problematic. I have tried to overcome this by using many different sources and by cross checking them. For instance, I have spoken to two former staff officers that participated in OUP, and one researcher who was embedded with rebels in Misrata, to verify or refute parts of my argument, but some important gaps still remain in this puzzle.

An immediate conclusion that can be drawn from this work, it will be argued below, is that research into the use of SOF in humanitarian interventions has been neglected. One reason for why it is important to study this phenomenon closer is that there is a risk that we will continue to rely on one-sided analysis focusing on air power as the deciding component in current interventions unless we do so. Air power may have laid the foundation for victory in Libya, but in the end it was supplemented by a significant contribution by special operations forces. In essence, it will be argued, the Libyan resistance movement, the *Thuwar*, was supported by a comprehensive and unconventional warfare programme staged by France, Italy, the United Kingdom and the United States in concert with a few allied Arab nations, especially Qatar, Jordan and the United Arab Emirates (UAE). Another reason for examining these nationally organized, military activities is that this systematic and covert use of SOF in humanitarian intervention operations might reflect a new way of conducting warfare by Western countries.[8]

Quite clearly, the covert use of SOF in humanitarian interventions is problematic in that democratic oversight is typically jeopardized by covert operations. Furthermore, we may want to ask some probing questions about the political rationale for deploying covert operations forces in a military mission defined as a humanitarian intervention, but also into the likely repercussions of the particular dynamics of warfare that this use implies. It is tempting to believe that it was a precision bombing campaign, with surgical strikes against Libyan military infrastructure, which finally felled Colonel Gaddafi. In reality, however, the Libyan resistance movement, the *Thuwar*, was supported by a number of foreign SOF teams with, as David Sanger says, a very 'light footprint'.[9] This of course raises several questions that need to be addressed. First, is the West really serious when they advocate the responsibility to protect (R2P) and the need for humanitarian interventions, or are they intervening in conflicts for other reasons? The chapter will therefore address the strategic rationale for entering Libya with covert operations forces. It will also tentatively address some implications of such use. Second, the chapter will also touch upon questions relating to the new dynamics and logic of warfare that this use implies.

Full circle: coming back to Libya

It is almost ironic that non-conventional forces were used during the UN sanctioned intervention against Gaddafi in 2011, because exactly 71 years earlier the concept of SOF was virtually invented in that same region. At the time, the Long Range Desert Group (LRDG) and the Special Air Service (SAS) were founded in order to meet specific strategic demands in Libya and

Egypt: to carry out deep penetration of German and Italian lines and to conduct covert reconnaissance patrols; intelligence missions; and raids, in exactly the same desert as Operation Unified Protector (OUP).[10] The LRDG and the SAS are today regarded as the forerunners of all modern Special Forces, so with Operation Unified Protector, the use of SOF came full circle.

Interestingly, but not surprisingly since covert operations seem to trigger widespread fascination and curiosity, some details of the use of special operations forces in Libya have leaked out. Much of the information is, as mentioned briefly above, somewhat anecdotal, and sometimes even conspiratorial. Yet, the sheer wealth of information available through a variety of sources eventually provides us with a relatively clear picture of the actions of non-conventional military units.

What we do know is that at least the United States, United Kingdom, France, Qatar, Jordan, the United Arab Emirates (UAE) and Italy deployed Special Forces on Libyan soil. What we do not know in detail is which units were actually sent there. From media reports it is reasonable to infer that the United States for instance deployed elements of the Special Activities Division of the CIA, that the British sent elements of their famous Special Air Service (SAS), Special Boat Squadron (SBS) and Special Reconnaissance Regiment (SRR) as well as the Secret Intelligence Service (SIS). Italy dispatched around 40 operatives from the 9th Regiment *Col Moschin*, a crack unit of the Folgore Parachute Brigade.[11] Very little has been reported about UAE and Qatari SF units, except for the fact that they deployed SOF personnel in some numbers.[12]

Below I will briefly describe some of the activities undertaken by foreign Special Forces units deployed in Libya, and the tactical roles they fulfilled on the ground. I will then show how these roles can be connected to operational needs and higher strategic goals. The aim is to contribute to a better understanding not only of the direct role SOF played in the NATO-led Libyan intervention, but also their role in a wider military effort that included a number of auxiliary units and missions. It will be shown that OUP comprised the naval and air wings of what indeed constituted a larger operation that went beyond the immediate and direct control of NATO. That larger operation notably included a covert programme, consisting of a set of interconnected missions, aimed at enhancing the likelihood that the rebels would be successful in toppling Colonel Gadaffi. In the shadows of OUP, the ground component was primarily built around the Libyan rebels, with tacit support from foreign special operations forces of several different participating nations.

The role of Special Operations Forces

Special Operations Forces (SOF) are small units of highly trained military personnel, often recruited from among the best soldiers of conventional military forces or sometimes from military intelligence organizations. They are frequently organized outside the usual chain-of-command in order to underscore their special status and unconventional character. Such forces regularly operate covertly far behind enemy lines, avoiding direct combat and therefore detection by the enemy.[13] Often, SOF have been used with the intention of gaining immediate strategic effects to change the course and outcome of a conflict. Operation Gunnerside in 1943 for instance is a famous example. The operation, aimed at destroying a German heavy water production facility in Rjukan in Norway, was planned by British Special Operations Executive (SOE) and executed by six Norwegian resistance fighters trained as commandos in the UK.[14] Some nevertheless argue that SOF work best when used as a complement to conventional forces for the purpose of strategic attrition, rather than producing a strategic paralysis whereby the opponent is quickly brought to his knees following a sudden, major blow.[15]

Principally, SOF can undertake a number of different tasks; Table 8.1 illustrates the most common tasks given to SOF. Even though the table is based on US Special Operations Command (SOCOM) Joint Doctrine 3–05 which provides overarching doctrine for special operations, it can be used as a general description of such forces and the tasks designated to them.[16] The British may have invented Commando units during the Second World War, and the use of specialized military forces goes back even further than that,[17] but it is the United States that has refined the concept into the flexible and useful tool they constitute today. Today US Special Operations Forces are the trendsetters and stand at the forefront when it comes to the training and utilization of Special Forces worldwide. Many countries that develop such forces seek to directly emulate American units and numerous foreign SF components go there as part of military exchange programmes and training. For this reason, it is not unreasonable to start with Table 8.1, based on US doctrine, as a way of identifying tasks assigned to SOF during the 2011 Libya intervention.

The execution of special operations in parallel with Operation Unified Protector

Using Table 8.1 as a way of organizing empirical evidence found primarily in accounts from journalists, and in some recent academic reports, this section will describe tasks apparently assigned to foreign SOF during the first six months or so of 2011. Because of the limited purpose of this chapter, I will only discuss Direct Action (DA), Special Reconnaissance (SR), Unconventional Warfare (UW) and rescue operations as part of a task other than core activities. The reason is that I find it implausible that SOF were used in any of the other roles. Both Counter Insurgency (CI) and Counter Terrorism (CT), as well as Foreign Internal Defense (FID), have other strategic aims than the aforementioned tasks. In essence, CI, CT and FID are activities aimed at supporting friendly governments while the former are used to destabilize governments.

Table 8.1 Special Forces core activities

Task	Meaning
Direct action (DA)	• Offensive operations in the deep battle space • Infrastructure disruption • Capture or assassination of high-value targets
Special reconnaissance (SR)	• Covert reconnaissance • Long-range reconnaissance of the deep battle space • Human intelligence (HUMINT) collection (Reconnaissance can be terrain, force-, or civil-oriented)
Counterterrorism (CT)	Actions taken directly against terrorist networks
Counterinsurgency (CI)	Assisting a friendly state to defeat an insurgency
Unconventional warfare (UW)	Activities designed to support a resistance movement to coerce, disrupt or overthrow a government
Foreign internal defence (FID)	Activities conducted in support of a friendly state building its internal defence capabilities
Close protection (CP)	Providing personal security details to important personnel
Hostage rescue (HR)	Freeing hostages taken by states, armed groups or criminal organizations
Other tasks	SF are also used for a variety of different tasks for which they are not necessarily useful or effective but which they undertake due to other reasons such as secrecy and availability

Source: partially based on *JP 3–05*, USSOCOM, 2011, Figure II-2, p. II-6.

Direct action: directing air strikes and bounty hunting?

Direct action (DA) activities perhaps constitute the quintessence of Special Operations Forces, at least in the public imagination. Nightly raids, executed by a few select, highly trained and determined soldiers, often against enemy command centres and supply lines (like those carried out by the LRDG and the SAS in Libya during the Second World War) have captured our imagination and built the reputation that epitomizes Special Forces. Such offensive operations in deep battle space include not only infrastructure disruption, but also the capture, or at times assassination, of high-value targets. Contrary to popular belief, in Libya DA was presumably a SOF task during the very early stages of the intervention only, and then as part of the degrading of Libyan air defense (AD) systems.

On 24 March NATO Secretary General Anders Fogh-Rasmussen announced that the Alliance had started enforcing the no-fly zone (NFZ) over Libya, and that they now had fighter jets conducting combat air patrols (CAP) in Libyan air space.[18] The primary function of the NFZ was to prevent Muammar Gaddafi's Air Force from operating over Libya and from targeting the civilian population. But, in order to be able to execute the CAP, NATO had first to deal with a major threat to all Allied air operations: the supposedly highly efficient Libyan air defense systems (AD). During the 1980s the Libyan military had bought several such systems from the Soviet Union, and they were now organized both within the Army and within the Air Defence Command, one of the military branches. According to some sources, in 2011 Libya had 'the most robust air defense network on the African continent, falling second only to Egypt in terms of coverage and operational systems'.[19]

The Libyan Air Defence Command was indeed one of the most prioritized defence functions and served two vital military strategic roles: first, to protect the country from foreign air attacks, and second to make it resistant to strategic coercion similar to the operation executed by NATO against Kosovo in 1999.[20] The Libyan experience of the US air attacks in 1986 probably served as a reminder of how vulnerable they were and must probably have served as a driver of the development of a robust air defence organization.[21] The Libyan approach to theirs was clearly inspired by Soviet Cold War doctrine and built on a system-of-systems approach, whereby units with long-range surface to air missiles (SAM) (for instance SA-3 GOA) overlapped with neighbouring units with shorter-range systems (for instance SA-2 GUIDELINE).[22] The Air Defence Command also possessed a very long-range high-altitude system, the SA-5A GAMMON, which constituted the greatest threat to Allied aircraft. The idea was for the different systems to provide cover for each other, thereby increasing their effectiveness against enemy aircraft.[23] In fact, during the initial stages of Operations Odyssey Dawn and Unified Protector, the Libyan air defences must have seemed fairly impressive to NATO military planners.

Given that one of the tasks assigned to the British SAS during the first Gulf War in 1991 was to search for and destroy Saddam's Scud batteries,[24] it is not surprising that some observers and war correspondents believed that teams of Special Forces had been sent behind the lines to knock out Gadaffi's AD systems in the same fashion. Apparently, as early as the very initial phase of Operation Odyssey Dawn, the predecessor to OUP, both the United States and the United Kingdom did in fact deploy SOF teams on the ground to direct air strikes on Libyan AD.[25] Their task was to locate Gaddafi's Russian-made SAM systems and send their coordinates to national headquarters, which could then transfer detailed information for the Air Component Commander to use in his targeting process; while another task would have been to paint targets with laser designators so attack aircraft could then knock them out.[26] Missions of this type seem to have been given primarily during Operation Odyssey Dawn, when NATO was not yet involved.

From 31 March, when NATO ultimately took command, it would have been difficult to continue giving SOF teams such tasks due to the covert nature of their operations. Directing air strikes against Gaddafi's air defence systems from the ground was probably still considered an operational necessity among many in the NATO staff in Naples, but using covert SOF teams to do it became much more difficult in this multinational setting. Usually, any Combined Air Operations Cell (CAOC – the command and control centre for all air and space operations) would comfortably handle even the most sensitive parts of an operation. However, in this case, the mere deployment of SOF teams on the ground would by some countries have been seen as a violation of the UN Security Council mandate, and therefore a feature that could have politically undermined the entire operation.

Furthermore, given the complexity of ground-led air targeting, and all the processes needed for coordination between Special Forces and attack aircraft releasing their missiles, it is doubtful that SOF teams were used for this specific role during OUP.[27] Many journalists have speculated about SOF teams directing air strikes,[28] but from an operational security and legal perspective this would have been hazardous.[29] Illuminating targets with hand-held laser designators would have required considerable interaction between SOF and the CAOC, and such interaction could easily have compromised the covert SOF teams operating in Libya.[30]

However, there are other, simpler ways of leading and directing air strikes. For instance, foreign SOF teams deployed in theatre provided coordinates of Libyan AD systems, units and other vital infrastructure, such as command posts and ammunition depots, by radio. Reconnaissance prior to air strikes and reporting of battle damage were also missions for the SOF teams of different nationalities deployed. I will return to this below.

Two other classical DA tasks assigned to Special Forces are hostage rescue operations and the capture, and sometimes assassination, of subjects of interest. In the first category, Lieutenant Colonel Otto Skorzeny's raid on the Gran Sasso in 1943 to rescue Mussolini stands out as a classic example. In the latter category, the killing of Usama bin Ladin in 2011 by a team of US Navy SEALs stand out as a clear case of how Special Forces can be used to further national agendas by attacking political and military leaders. Reportedly, the US has on at least three different occasions attempted to assassinate foreign heads of state:[31] Congolese Prime Minister Patrice Lumumba, Cuban President Fidel Castro and Iraqi Prime Minister Abdul Karim Kassem.[32] Many more attempts have been made by other intelligence services, and since operations like these have so often been part of the drama and myths surrounding SOF and intelligence agencies it is not surprising that some journalists suggested that SOF teams were specifically deployed in order to track down and capture Gaddafi and his family at the height of the armed conflict.[33] However, such tasks were probably not in the mandate of any Western country due to the political and legal constraints cited above.

Special reconnaissance: gathering intelligence and liaising with rebels

One important aspect of all military operations is the need for timely and accurate information regarding the situation on ground. This intelligence is preferably gathered by trained troops in the theatre of operations and not only from Signals Intelligence (SIGINT) or other technical intelligence and surveillance systems. The need for such information was by no means less in this intervention when compared to any other military campaign, rather the contrary. The reason was that the operation was aimed at protecting civilians and that incurring significant collateral damage in terms of numerous civilian casualties would both have jeopardized the political process and directly contradicted the notion of operational success.

In SOF terms, this type of intelligence and information gathering is called Special Reconnaissance (SR) and 'entails reconnaissance and surveillance actions conducted as [special operations] in hostile, denied, or diplomatically sensitive environments to collect or verify information of strategic or operational significance, employing military capabilities not normally found in [Conventional Forces]'.[34] Activities such as these are supposed to provide an additional collection capability for both operational as well as strategic staffs and are meant to supplement other reconnaissance and information gathering techniques.

The reconnaissance tasks given to SOF teams in Libya would have had at least two dimensions: the first, as hinted at above, to pinpoint the Libyan AD systems, especially the long-range SA-5s,[35] and the second would have been to provide the different planning and intelligence elements with updated information on rebel activity. The second task would also have included liaising with rebel forces.

Conducting air operations in a situation as complex as it was during the early part of 2011, requires intelligence and information of a quality not always obtainable by satellites, technical signal intelligence (SIGINT) or airborne reconnaissance systems. For instance, target acquisition demands that targets are identified and confirmed by observers on the ground, especially in a situation where the operation is designed to protect civilians. During Operation Unified Protector such operational support activities were not available to the military planning staffs because of the restrictions in the Security Council's mandate. Instead, several different nations decided to support their operations on a national basis by sending in smaller SOF teams.

The amount of SR activities that actually involved foreign SOF is impossible to estimate at the time of writing. It is fair to assume, however, that over time the task would have been expanded to include not only locating AD systems, but also establishing the positions of all pro-Gaddafi forces. This latter task most likely concentrated on locating command centres, ammunition depots and military staging areas.

Reconnaissance is very important in an area of operations, but it can never provide all the critical information requirements of operational or strategic commanders. This is especially true if there are also friendly forces on the ground with whom a certain degree of coordination is necessary.[36] In Libya, this amounted to the absolute necessity of establishing liaison with the many different rebel groups.

The group of eight British SOF operatives caught on the outskirts of Benghazi almost certainly had such a task. Their mission included to 'keep an eye on the humanitarian situation' as well as 'protecting diplomats' sent from the UK on a diplomatic mission to the rebels.[37] In addition, it was imperative for Her Majesty's Government to coordinate operations with the rebels, and to get firsthand knowledge of what was going on among them. Forging links and to open up communication with the rebel leadership was a top priority, and sending in SOF teams was – it can be assumed – the preferred course of action. The task included the establishment of contact, assessment of the operational situation and facilitation of the transition of power from Gaddafi to the rebels.[38] Similarly, the French Special Operations Command (*Commandement des opérations spéciales – COS*) allegedly deployed a few dozen operatives to coordinate operations with rebels,[39] and the CIA did likewise.[40] In this sense, the SOF teams sent to liaise with the rebels were used, one can confidently infer, as conduits of information between the Western powers and the rebels. But there was also an operational requirement that they could provide: namely de-conflicting operations between NATO and the rebels. By exchanging information regarding on-going and planned activities the risk for inadvertent blue-on-blue exchange of fire between NATO and rebel forces could be reduced.

Unconventional warfare: providing support to the rebels

Unconventional Warfare (UW) is a Special Operation that denotes several different activities,[41] all with the overarching goal of undermining and overthrowing a foreign government. Principally, it can be executed in numerous ways, but training and arming, or equipping, insurgent groups are often the centre pieces of such programmes. In contrast to official accounts from NATO and coalition member states, the Libyan *Thuwar* received a substantial amount of such support from foreign states during the intervention in 2011, and this section will briefly describe the two central elements of the UW program staged by the Western powers (outside NATO operations or in parallel to NATO operations). The first entailed a carefully tailored training programme executed primarily by Arab states, while the second was a clandestine equip programme emanating chiefly from France and Qatar, and using Tunisia as a conduit for arms.

According to the NATO spokesperson, Oana Lungescu, the Alliance never took part in any formal coordination on the ground, and did not support the rebels, nor did they provide weapons or instructions to them. In fact, 'NATO [had] no special troops and NATO [had] no ground troops or any sort of ground forces under NATO'.[42] Yet, during the armed conflict it was obvious that the rebels developed a fighting quality and capability they did not have from the beginning. Colonel Burkhard Thierry, spokesman for the French General Staff, claims that the *Thuwar* learnt from their battlefield experience and became a better force over time.[43] However, Eric Dénécé, Director of the French Centre for Research on Intelligence (*Centre Français de Recherche sur le Renseignement*), does not agree: '*Foutaises!*', he says, 'With all the respect I have for the Libyans, the insurgents were totally incapable of doing anything militarily.'[44] Indeed, much points to the fact that several nations sent advisors specifically to train and mentor the *Thuwar*, and that it was this training that eventually and finally turned the tide of war against Gadaffi.

On Saturday 20 August, at around 8 p.m., Operation Dawn Mermaid, the rebel attack on Tripoli, was launched. In several ways, it resembled the well-known CIA sponsored attack on the Bay of Pigs in Cuba in 1961,[45] only it was much more successful. It had all the same ingredients as Operation Zapata, the CIA code name for the attack on the Bay of Pigs: exiled Libyans flown in from many countries to plan and execute the attack; foreign para-militaries participated in both the planning and the execution phase; training and arms were provided by outside powers; and extensive military support in the shape of NATO air and naval forces.[46] Given that forces loyal to Gadaffi were targeted by NATO and subjected to air-strikes, these components helped make Dawn Mermaid a successful: one in which covert foreign SOF teams had an essential part to play.

The foundation for the assault on Tripoli had been laid more than six months previously when the United Arab Emirates (UAE) deployed at least one SOF team on the ground in the Nasuf Mountains, western Libya. From there they supplied the rebel forces with equipment and provisions, and at a later stage they also provided training on the same location.[47] The training covered many different topics and capabilities, but one essential aspect is most likely to have been connected to the central tenet of all military campaigns: namely learning how to plan and coordinate military movements within a larger body of forces. These are skills that are very difficult to obtain without prior and adequate military training, and not something that you learn from a few months of irregular warfare. Commanding a smaller force comprising a handful of rebels can of course be done on a personal and intuitive basis, but executing command and control over several different units in a combined and coherent fashion demands organization and rigorous methods. Educating and training officers to become part of a staff and to learn the necessary staff procedures is the core task of military universities worldwide, and a detailed knowledge of planning and guiding military operations is what makes a military force efficient and sustainable in combat. Besides mentoring the staffs in such basic skills, there were most certainly weapons drills, live firing exercises and communications. All focused on getting rebel soldiers to operate as units and not as individuals. Without adequate knowledge of critical topics like this, especially planning and logistics, all fighting would eventually have ceased and trickled away altogether.

If training is one essential feature in developing an efficient military rebellion, another is arms. The *Thuwar* obtained most of theirs from defecting Gaddafi loyalists and from military stores and depots abandoned during the fighting,[48] but some also came from foreign sources as parts of substantial foreign-sponsored support programmes.

British Foreign Secretary William Hague said on 3 April 2011, that Her Majesty's government had 'taken no decision to arm the rebels', and a subsequent report of the House of Commons Library's research and information service concluded that the UN Libyan sanctions committee would probably not approve arms transfers to the rebels.[49] In France, Qatar and the UAE, however, the resolution seems to have been interpreted differently in that all three countries provided arms to many of the rebel factions in Libya. According to some commentators, Qatar was 'unsparing in its political, financial and military support in favor of Libya's insurgency',[50] and the cornerstone of that support seem to have been equipping and training the rebels from camps in the mountains of western Libya. Parts of the weapons transfers were first flown to Tunisia, and then smuggled into the western part of the country,[51] where they were then handed out to various rebel groups.

Another aspect of this close assistance to the rebels was the need to convey information and intelligence to the leadership and the different rebel groups. Most likely, such information came from the different participating states, as well as from NATO. There were many different critical information requirements that had to be forwarded to them, and the best way of doing this would have been to send small teams composed of operatives from both the SOF and intelligence communities. The group of men from E-Squadron mentioned earlier was such a team, and because it included soldiers as well as intelligence para-militaries, they were able to provide the rebels with highly sophisticated information regarding the locations and strengths of Gaddafi loyalist forces.

There were also occasions when foreign SOF teams actually joined the *Thuwar* in battle. In June 2011, at least four SOF operatives equipped with radios were observed with a group of rebels firing heavy machine guns mounted on light pick-ups.[52] Their mission was most likely to liaise with the rebels, but it could also have been to train the rebels into an efficient fighting force. According to the British foreign secretary, William Hague, the UK would send military advisers to advise the rag-tag rebel forces so they could improve their military organizational structures, communications and logistics: 'The rebels will be trained in the communications, logistics and intelligence skills used by a modern military.'[53] In a speech one day later, Italian Defense Minister, Ignazio La Russa, said that Italy too would send advisers to support the rebels. Even though the mandate of the Italian SOF mission had not yet been determined, he noted that they would 'not be on the battlefield'. Instead, they would act as mentors slightly behind the front lines.[54] Rumors and speculation notwithstanding, it is wholly unlikely that international SOF teams assisted the rebels with air strikes and participated in combat, also partly because of their small numbers they could not really have accomplished much. The fact that they acted behind the lines and were training troops in all likelihood contributed much more than single squads of SOF operatives could have done, even if they had directed the odd air strike here and there. In other words, the training and mentoring may very well have produced much greater military value in that they modified, modernized and enhanced the battle effectiveness of the Thuwar.[55]

So, while Tunisia served as a conduit for French arms shipments into Libya,[56] Qatar and UAE took on the training role and sent several SF operatives into the Nasuf Mountains. Simultaneously, British and American SF operatives and intelligence case officers provided detailed intelligence and information to rebel commanders. All in all this constituted a neat and comprehensively tailored programme using unconventional warfare for the purpose of overthrowing Gaddafi and transferring the power to the rebels. Significantly, a programme such as this can easily be prolonged once the new regime has been put in place, thus laying the foundations for a long-term military support of the new government. As will be illustrated below, one important element of the support to the rebels, especially from a Western perspective, was establishing close cooperation with a post-Gaddafi regime in order to prevent al-Qaeda from gaining influence in the country. Thereby, the foundations were laid for what in US terminology often is referred to as Foreign Internal Defense (FID) operations.[57]

Rescue operations: evacuating civilians caught in the armed conflict

The missions mentioned above are the most commonly tasked to SOF, but at times such forces are used in situations where conventional forces could have been as easily used. The reasons for choosing SF units over conventional forces may depend on their usual high readiness and availability. Thus, Special Operations Forces are at times used for tasks other than the ones they are traditionally designed for.

The first signs of international SF units on Libyan soil were in conjunction with a non-combatant evacuation operation (NEO) executed by the British Foreign Office, a task not usually given to such units. On 26 February, the Royal Air Force (RAF), using two military C-130 Hercules aircraft, flew about 150 oil workers, many of them British nationals, from several different locations in the desert to safety on Malta.[58] Similarly, many foreigners were also evacuated through the harbour in Benghazi and onto HMS Cumberland and HMS York and then brought to safety in Valetta on Malta.[59] These operations were supported by SOF teams.

During the initial turmoil in what would become a civil war in Libya, hundreds of foreign workers were trapped in various locations around the country. Some of them were flown out on what may have been British aircraft commonly used for special operations purposes, though these efforts were led by the British Foreign and Commonwealth Office (FCO) instead of the Ministry of Defence (MoD) or NATO. Even though supporting a NEO is not usually a task given to SOF, the crews of the aircraft were reportedly reinforced with SAS or SBS troops for security reasons. According to one source, 'about two dozen men from C Squadron of the Special Boat Service (SBS)' accompanied one flight.[60] Their primary task was presumably restricted to that of close protection while landing, receiving evacuees and taking off. The SOF personnel were surely prepared for ambush scenarios, but none of the teams appear to have become engaged in any fire fights while evacuating the civilians.

Anyway, the reason SAS or SBS operatives were used in the first place was probably because they were available at short notice, otherwise it would be wasteful to use such an exclusive asset in support of a NEO.

Humanitarian interventions, unconventional warfare and strategy

The activities mentioned in the previous section did not materialize without a plan. The fact that all these activities and actions took place in concert, and that participating states almost systematically shared the burdens, reflect well on the internal cohesion of the wider campaign. It is only when viewed together like this, in the strategic context where they ultimately belong, that such SOF missions make sense. This section will systemize and try to explain how the activities described above can be connected to a strategic plan, one that went beyond the tactical, *Bravo Two Zero*-like level.[61]

Via inductive reasoning based on the tasks conducted by international Special Forces it can be credibly argued that the SOF strategy for Libya rested on three pillars and that international SOF activities were associated to the Libyan civil war in three different ways. First, they were executed in direct support of national needs and NATO operations; second, they were staged in an effort to strengthen the rebels so they themselves could organize a resilient and successful resistance to Gaddafi forces; and finally, SOF teams were used indirectly to thwart any machinations by al-Qaeda in the Islamic Maghreb (AQIM) to gain ground and influence in a post-Gaddafi Libya. Table 8.2 illustrates the three pillars and how the different tasks assigned to SOF can be connected to each of the three pillars.

Deconflicting OUP: supporting national needs and NATO operations

In March 2011, there were wild speculations regarding the activities of the British elite unit, the Special Air Service (SAS) in Libya. It was said that they had deployed so called 'Smash' squads and that their mission was to 'paint targets' with laser beams so that attack aircraft could drop laser guided precision bombs onto Gaddafi loyalist targets.[62] As explained above, such tasks may have been given to British and French Special Forces teams during the early stages of the conflict, but the main mission of SOF changed character as soon as NATO took command of the operation in March. From that point onward, the French and British teams

Table 8.2 Strategic goals and operational tasks

Strategic and operational goals	Tasks of SOF in Libya
Supporting NATO and national functions and operations	• Non-combatant evacuation • Liaison with rebels • Intelligence gathering • Suppression of Libyan air defences
Strengthening the Libyan rebels	• Training and mentoring • Providing arms and equipping rebels • Providing intelligence to rebels • Coordination between rebels groups
Denying access of foreign and competing external powers	• Building ties with the rebel militia • Training and mentoring of the *Thuwar*

focused on, above all, intelligence gathering (even though they almost certainly relayed positions of certain pro-Gaddafi forces and command centres to national intelligence cells). It has also been mentioned that one of the first tasks included evacuating foreign nationals stranded in the conflict. A third task, given to SOF teams to fulfil national and Alliance needs, was to liaise with the different rebel groups in an effort to acquire an overall picture of the resistance. The latter was primarily aimed at providing decision makers in Paris, London and Washington with necessary information, but also for NATO to monitor movements within and between various insurgent groups in an effort to de-conflict rebel and NATO operations.

Supposedly, some of the international SOF teams, especially British, US and French, had the important operational task of liaising with rebels in order to reduce the danger of fratricide (the risk of Western friendly aircraft and other Western forces being fired upon)[63] and to ensure that OUP did not jeopardize rebel activity, or vice versa. In essence, the SOF teams facilitated both rebel and NATO operations and reduced the risk of inadvertent fire on friendly forces.

Avoiding a quagmire: strengthening the Libyan rebels

The second pillar of the SOF strategy concerned active military support to the various rebel groups and to the National Transition Committee (NTC). It was given in the form of a vast train and equip programme, and included mentoring and advice as well as a de facto arming of the rebels. The latter was primarily carried out by the governments of Qatar and France, with tacit approval by the Tunisian government which allowed the transit of weapons through its territory. Tunisia also allowed rebels to set up training bases and intelligence cells in the country.[64]

When the Libyan uprising started, the anti-Gaddafi forces consisted mostly of various groups lacking a central command structure and effective equipment. To make matters worse the rebels were on their own, unlike Gaddafi who partly relied on the assistance of foreign fighters and mercenaries.[65] With the arrival of international SOF teams, who mentored and supplied the rebels, the tide of war gradually turned in their favour.

A primary motive for supporting the Libyan rebels in such a comprehensive unconventional warfare programme was most likely because no Western government wanted to become bogged down in the quagmire of another prolonged war, like Afghanistan and Iraq. According to a senior US intelligence official, the military setbacks of the rebels were 'hardening the U.S. view that the poorly equipped opposition [was] incapable of prevailing without decisive Western intervention'.[66] So in March 2011, when the US administration realized the *Thuwar* were about to lose the ground war, the only feasible option was to train the rebels and let them wage war against Gaddafi. By supporting the rebels in this way, and indirectly supporting them with training, intelligence, mentoring and certain equipment, NATO could focus on providing combat air patrols and act as air cover for the rebellion.

War on terrorism: denying foreign influences access to Libya

None of the two strategic ideas mentioned above has escaped the attention of commentators on the armed conflict in Libya, albeit indirectly since the focus has been on the tactical tasks rather than how the activities of a few hundred foreign SF operators met larger operational or strategic requirements. There is however a third function that has gone unnoticed, yet it is one of immense strategic importance in any zone of conflict. In the current era, and because of the type of recent conflicts, the possible entry of competing outside powers into the war theatre is an issue that politicians, strategists and decision makers must always factor in. This was true during the Cold War, and it is still true today. In a conflict such as the civil war in Libya, similar to what happened in the aftermath of the US victory over Saddam Hussein in Iraq in 2003, there is always a danger that outside powers, or global terrorist groups, will try to use the ensuing power vacuum to further their own agenda and pursue their ulterior goals.

In Libya, and the entire Maghreb, the presence of Islamic militant groups has been a challenge for some time.[67] This problem became more acute when al-Qaeda members were spotted at various locations in Libya. At the beginning of the uprising, fears were raised that 'The Arab spring [would represent] a strategic pivot for al-Qaeda',[68] and that 'spiraling violence in Libya may provide militant Islamist groups future opportunities in the country'.[69] Given that Security Council resolution 1973 only mandated NATO to provide for security to civilians threatened by the Gaddafi war machine, it indirectly created conditions for al-Qaeda in Maghreb (AQIM) to enhance its power and influence. Had the Western powers decided not to enter Libyan territory, al-Qaeda could very well have used the power vacuum as an opportunity to provide the only well organized military wing of the rebellion. Western leaders and intellectuals have argued that 'Al-Qaida [was] branching out' to Libya, and that al-Qaeda might become a destabilizing force and a strategic rival to the West. Hence, it was 'imperative to work to prevent al-Qaeda from sabotaging transitions in the Middle East'.[70] The solution was thus seen to lay, at least in part, in replacing the need for al-Qaeda support by sending in covert military assistance in the form of coalition teams of SOF operatives and para-military intelligence officers, and thereby 'pleas[e] the likely winners of the current conflict'.[71]

In the spring and summer of 2011, the NATO-led military operation in Libya was portrayed as a case of humanitarian intervention, and Security Council Resolutions 1970 and 1973 reinforced this general understanding of the situation. Both documents expressed grave concerns about heavy civilian casualties and the escalation of violence, and demanded that the

Libyan authorities protect its population (see Chapter 2). At the outset the international community may have been content with a cease-fire and the restoration of law and order in Libya. However, when the situation deteriorated into a civil war the strategic options for the Western nations were more limited. The strategic stakes had been raised: not only was the civilian population now threatened by a dictator bent on attacking his own people, but the same dictator, had he crushed the rebellion, might have resorted to his old habit of sponsoring non-state armed groups and terrorists in Europe and elsewhere.[72] Some saw a risk that al-Qaeda would move into the country and either find sanctuary there,[73] or commit its forces to a pitched battle for power and influence in the country. Others, such as Senator John McCain, Obama's 2008 presidential rival, did not take this as seriously and 'shrugged off suggestions that al-Qaeda may have a role to play in the rebellion'.[74] Right or wrong, the mere prospect of al-Qaeda influencing the transitional process meant that the Western powers had to be cautious in terms of whom they armed and trained. For this reason, sending covert forces into the Libyan hinterland became imperative for political and military success.

The coalition could have chosen a strategy resembling that of NATO in Kosovo in 1999, where they relied on air power alone to coerce the political leadership into adhering to the demands of the international community.[75] However, the Western leaders felt they could not risk having the young rebellion crushed, leaving an even more powerful Gaddafi in power. Nevertheless, the resolution made no mention of either toppling the dictator or imposing democracy in the country. Therefore, the only viable strategy for the Coalition was to interpret Security Council resolution 1973 liberally and provide substantial military assistance to the rebels. That was the sole way to 'reconcile the sound humanitarian and strategic reasons for preventing the rebels' defeat' Shashank pointedly argues.[76] Denying al-Qaeda influence became a top priority and something that could be accomplished by training, mentoring and equipping the rebels. By infiltrating and building long-lasting ties with the nascent rebel militia, it was believed that AQIM would be denied access and become redundant in Libyan politics.

Components of a shadow war: SOF and strategy

One might well go as far as to argue that the tide of the entire armed conflict turned when a few foreign countries sent in advisors and trainers to the Libyan rebels. It has been claimed that NATO and the coalition constituted 70 per cent of the effort during the first half of the rebellion while the rebels stood for the rest, but after March or April the reverse was true.[77] It was only when the rebels received foreign sponsored military training and arms that they were able to organize themselves and to offer a substantial military opposition to the unpopular regime. Up until that moment they had primarily been organized in small and disparate groups, individual brigades, security committees or military councils taking local initiatives to fight Gaddafi loyalists wherever they could.[78] The most important contribution of the foreign ground element, was however in the strategic realm, where SOF teams were used to discourage the al-Qaeda terrorist network and its operatives from gaining ground in and among the many disparate Libyan rebel factions.

A central paradox of the utility of SOF is that their use may have serious ramifications for the side accepting support from such forces. First, there is a question of trust. For instance, when the members of E-squadron were taken prisoner by the *Thuwar* south of Benghazi the rebels were highly suspicious about who they were, who they represented and why they had come there. This was probably further emphasized because the group arrived disguised like thieves in the night, instead of openly seeking to establish contact. Second, there is a question of legitimacy. Sending in advisors to rebels struggling to gain consent and political legitimacy from the civilian population can seriously hamper any such mission. The situation was quickly resolved this time,[79] but had it gone awry the Gaddafi side might have pointed to the presence of UK Special Forces in Libya and exploited it to de-legitimize the rebels and brand them as pawns of the former colonial powers.[80]

Eventually, all or most of the activities presented above contributed to the goals of the participating nations: the controlled overthrow of Gaddafi in favour of the NTC and the denial of Libya as fertile ground for al-Qaeda influences. Using covert action based on the principles of unconventional warfare for the furtherance of foreign policy goals is nothing new (even though some may have thought so in the immediate wake of the Cold War).[81] Considering the intervention fatigue prevalent in many Western states there are reasons to believe that this may be the recipe for the future, and that covert operations therefore will be used on a larger scale in other operations.

The present build-up of Western intelligence agencies is a clear indicator of this development.[82] The use of SOF in Libya, as well as in the crises in Syria and Mali during 2012 and 2013,[83] illustrates two separate yet intertwined dimensions of future Western interventions. The first is that Western nations may feel tempted to use covert action to a greater degree than during previous interventions and operations, and the second is that friendly Arab nations are likely to be used as stooges to support Western sponsored insurgencies in the Arab world.

International SOF teams and intelligence operators may not have been deployed in large numbers, but the quality of their contribution was apparently crucial to the outcome of the NATO-led multinational intervention. Most of what we know about these covert operations transpired through the reporting by war correspondents, and not via official channels, and this opens up a discussion on the use of SOF and covert operations as important pillars in Western-led humanitarian interventions.

Optimizing the trajectory: on the strategic utility and inutility of SOF

The utility of SO and SOF is a contested subject,[84] though we can rest assured that their use will continue, not only because they seem able to deliver decisive blows to the enemy at a bargain price but also because of their covert nature. Whether or not there is truth to this set of claims, SOF embodies a strategic value that goes beyond their tactical and material effect. Simply put, SOF brings something else to the table besides the specific tactical tasks assigned to them. Essentially, they operate in the strategic realm almost by definition. The Libyan campaign has constituted a litmus test for the use of SOF working alongside secret intelligence case officers in covert teams specifically created for the purpose. These teams have been used, in line with the principles of unconventional warfare, as replacement for conventional high-visibility forces.

At the operational level the presence of foreign SOF meant that the rebels were able to 'wrest the military initiative from the regime'.[85] Alas, there may be a major fallacy behind the idea that surrounds the use of unconventional warfare in parallel to operations such as Unified Protector. Notably, what are the implications of the use of SOF, despite the fact that a UN Resolution seems to have been written in an effort if not to rule out, but at least to limit boots on the ground?[86] Was it because of a weak mandate, or does the use of SOF show that some of the participating countries already at the outset had loftier ambitions than the rest of the international community? Or, does the use of covert operations on this scale reflect a new, largely covert, form of Western warfare? Are we in fact witnessing a shift towards a new type of global covert warfare waged in the shadows of international law and the Laws of Armed Conflict? Is this global shadow warfare the Western governments' recipe for conflicts in the post-Iraq and post-Afghanistan era and the logical response to the intensified media scrutiny of current operations? Are covert and combined teams of SF and intelligence operatives the interventionist's silver bullet? Strategically, as a matter of course, it makes perfect sense to send in SOF and it is definitely in line with the ideas of the indirect approach as recommended by Basil Liddell-Hart,[87] but is this an acceptable route for democracies to follow in the long run, and what does it imply for transparency and accountability in connection with military action?

The wars in Iraq and Afghanistan went on for more than a decade, and especially in the US, many are deeply skeptical as to whether the West should continue to intervene on such a large scale.[88] Chris Gibson (Rep), Senate House Representative from New York and a US army veteran of four tours in Iraq, stated when the Libya issue rose to prominence: 'I think we have so much on the plate right now that [what] we need to do [before embarking on another military adventure is] to bring closure with regard to Iraq and Afghanistan.'[89] The worsening crisis in Syria and Mali in

2011–2013 and the reluctance of international leaders to seriously engage may be seen as a further indicator of this fatigue.

However, from the point of view of Western leaders there will always be a need for military interventions. Be it for ideological, moral, economic or geopolitical reasons, the West cannot stand idly by and watch competing powers, either organized armed groups or states, gain ground in the aftermath of tumultuous conflict, especially when this takes place on the doorstep of democratic states. This is especially so if there are potentially major consequences for Western security, Western economies or a pending genocide. Still, if popular support for military intervention is low in the West and the political risks are too big when it comes to committing troops to foreign wars, our politicians could resort to covert operations.

If contemporary covert operations, characterized by their seamless integration between elite Special Forces and the intelligence community,[90] represent one feature of the new way of Western warfare, the global shadow war, another is the 'regionalization' and containment of conflicts. While the activities of Qatari and UAE SOF are not known in any detail, both countries provided 'considerable discreet political and military support to the rebels'.[91] Even though the exact operational quality of the assistance is difficult to assess, the real value of having them as partners in the coalition lie in their function as factors limiting the wars to specific regions rather than spreading beyond them. Without Qatar and UAE the entire intervention could easily have been portrayed as Western neo-colonialism and would in fact have worked against the NTC, had the Gaddafi loyalists been successful in their strategic communications. The intervention could have backfired and might have resulted in a wave of terrorist attacks across Europe and the US. In this sense, Qatar and UAE acted as Western proxies that worked to contain the armed conflict in Libya.

The use of covert operations and unconventional warfare either as substitute for, or as a complement to, traditional military interventions raises not only practical questions such as the one above, but also illustrates that there may be even more pressing questions that need to be addressed theoretically as well as philosophically. On a moral and philosophical level, Western leaders must once again revisit the problem of legitimacy. If the West continues to use covert operations to achieve goals, while conducting traditional military interventions, the credibility of Western political and military leaders will likely decrease. As is already the case in some quarters, international norms such as that of 'responsibility to protect' will then be seen as a cover for the promotion of Western interests.

Conclusions

The use of foreign special operations forces during the Libyan Civil War has not yet been properly analysed. The limited information readily available today comes from the reporting of war correspondents and in the form of somewhat anecdotal pieces of information about the presence of a few SOF operators in the country. What they did and the strategic impact they may have had on the conflict as such has not been disclosed by the respective governments. The aim of this chapter has been to examine the role and utility of foreign special operations in Libya, in particular, during the first part of 2011. However, it was not only the difference these operations made to the course and outcome of the direct conflict that was discussed here; rather, the primary subject of discussion has been the utility of Special Forces in Western foreign policy.

Interestingly, Western special operations forces have traditionally been used to support the governments of friendly nations in their respective efforts to counter rebels and insurgents.[92] Such tasks have often, in the US military context, been referred to as Foreign Internal Defense, Counter Terrorism and Counter Insurgency (see Table 8.1), the purpose being to strengthen and stabilize friendly governments. However, those same Western nations are now increasingly using SO and covert operations forces in line with the principles of Unconventional Warfare to overthrow governments, a purpose that is exactly the opposite of traditional military assistance which seeks to strengthen them. Yet, in the end both types of operations works 'to enhance [the sending states'] position in the world and to limit [the] other's expansion'.[93] Unconventional Warfare might therefore be seen as a viable strategic alternative to Military Assistance in the sense that both can be employed toward achieving the same goal. Still, serious ethical and moral considerations separate the two, and require that decision makers – at least intermittently – discuss their use openly.

Whilst it may be tempting to believe that a precision bombing campaign brought about Gaddafi's downfall, in reality, the Libyan resistance movement, the *Thuwar*, was supported by a comprehensive and unconventional warfare programme staged by France, the United Kingdom and the United States in concert with a few Arab allies. This chapter has suggested that the systematic and covert use of SOF in Libya could very well augur a new Western approach to contemporary war: one in which military activities will be characterized by relatively inexpensive low-profile forces, and where non-disruptive use of force is seen as preferable to massive, costly and contentious deployment. Over time, however, the legitimacy of humanitarian interventions may be jeopardized by the expanded use of covert or semi-covert operations, in turn threatening to throw a spanner into the political system underpinning the global security system.

Notes

1. Human Rights Council, *Report of the International Commission of Inquiry on Libya*, 2 March 2012.
2. Similarly, an article published in *Foreign Affairs*, Spring 2012, also neglected the fact that the intervention comprised forces other than just air and naval assets: I.H. Daalder and J.G. Stavridis, 'NATO's Victory in Libya', *Foreign Affairs* 2, 2012, pp. 2–7.
3. C. Ziedler, 'Elitesoldaten liefern Nato Daten für Luftangriffe', *Der Tagesspiegel*, 30 August 2011.
4. UN Security Council, Resolution 1973 (2011), SC/10200, 17 March 2011.
5. International Affairs and Defence Section, *Interpretation of Security Council Resolution 1973 on Libya*, House of Commons, SN/IA/5916, 6 April 2011.
6. See Hansard Documents, column 700, House of Commons (21 March 2011) *Oral Answers to Questions*. Online. Available: www.publications.parliament.uk/pa/cm201011/cmhansrd/cm110321/debtext/110321-0001.htm#1103219000001 (accessed 19 February 2013).
7. BBC News (6 March 2011) *SAS members 'captured near Benghazi'*. Online. Available: www.bbc.co.uk/news/world-middle-east-12658054 (accessed 19 February 2013).
8. For an extended discussion of the US 'light-footprint' strategy, see D.E. Sanger, *Confront and Conceal. Obama's Secret Wars and Surprising use of American Power*, New York: Crown Publishers, 2012.
9. Sanger, *Confront and Conceal*, pp. 243–5.
10. J. Keegan, 'Introduction', in D. Lloyd Owen, *The Long Range Desert Group 1940–1945: Providence Their Guide*, Barnsley: Pen & Sword, 2000, p. xiii.
11. G. Gaiani, 'Tra le forze speciali in Libia 40 uomini del Col Moschin', *Il Sole 24 Ore*, 15 October 2011.
12. C. Gouëset, 'Ce que l'on sait sur les forces spéciales en Libye', *L'Éxpress*, 26 August 2011.
13. C.S. Gray, *Explorations in Strategy*, Westport: Praeger, 1996, pp. 149–52; J.D. Kiras, *Special Operations and Strategy. From World War II to the War on Terrorism*, London: Routledge, 2006, pp. 4–8.
14. Kiras, *Special Operations and Strategy*, p. 1.
15. Kiras, *Special Operations and Strategy*, p. 115.
16. *Joint Publication 3–05, Special Operations*, McDill Air Force Base: USSOCOM, 2011.
17. See for instance T.E. Lawrence, *Seven Pillars of Wisdom. A Triumph*, New York: Anchor Books, 1991, first published in 1926.
18. NATO Press conference (24 March 2011) *NATO Secretary General's Statement on Libya No-Fly Zone*. Online. Available: www.nato.int/cps/en/natolive/news_71763.htm (accessed 19 February 2013).
19. Global Research (21 March 2011) *The Libyan Air Defense System. Libya's Surface to Air Missile (SAM) Network*, Global Research. Online. Available: www.globalresearch.ca/the-libyan-air-defense-system-libya-s-surface-to-air-missile-sam-network (accessed 19 January 2013).
20. D. Byman and M. Waxman, *The Dynamics of Coercion: American Foreign Policy and the Limits of Military Might*, Cambridge: Cambridge University Press, 2002, pp. 101–2.
21. This refers to Operation Eldorado Canyon. M. Codner, 'Military doctrine and intervention', in *Short War, Long Shadow. The Political and Military Legacies of the 2011 Libya Campaign*, London: RUSI, 2011, Whitehall Report 1–12, p. 27.
22. *Military Balance 2011*, London: IISS, 2011.
23. Global Research, *The Libyan Air Defense System*.

24 A. McNab, *Bravo-Two-Zero, The Harrowing True Story of a Special Forces Patrol behind the Lines in Iraq*, New York: Dell Publishing, 1993.
25 Defence Correspondent, 'SAS "Smash" squads on the ground in Libya to mark targets for coalition jets', *Daily Mail*, 21 March 2011.
26 M. Mazzetti and E. Schmitt, 'C.I.A. agents in Libya aid airstrikes and meet rebels', *The New York Times*, 30 March 2011.
27 Admittedly, NATO established a Special Operations Headquarters in 2007 (NSHQ), tasked to coordinate the execution of tasks directly with the appropriate command or nations. But it is not known whether or not they were involved during OUP.
28 See for instance M. Urban, 'Inside story of the UK's secret mission to beat Gaddafi', *BBC News*, 19 January 2012.
29 Interview with a former OUP staff officer. He strongly denied any such cooperation existed inside his staff in Naples.
30 LTG David A. Deptula, in Mazzetti and Schmitt, 'C.I.A. agents in Libya aid airstrikes and meet rebels'.
31 It must however be stressed that on 4 December 1981, President Ronald Reagan issued Executive Order (E.O.) 12333, 'United States Intelligence Activities', explicitly prohibiting assassinations. Section 2.11 of the order provides: 'Prohibition on Assassination. No person employed by or acting on behalf of the United States Government shall engage in, or conspire to engage in, assassination.' Section 2.12 of the order prohibits indirect participation in activities prohibited by the order, stating: 'Indirect participation. No agency of the Intelligence Community shall participate in or request any person to undertake activities forbidden by this Order.' E.O. 12333 is still in force. See E.B. Bazan, *Assassination Ban and E.O. 12333: A Brief Summary*, CRS Report for Congress, 2002.
32 J.J. Nutter, *The CIA's Black Ops. Covert Action, Foreign Policy and Democracy*, New York: Prometheus Books, 2000, p. 114.
33 M. Giannangeli, 'Special Forces hunt for last of the Gaddafi clan', *Express.co.uk*, 22 April 2011.
34 JP 3-05, II-7.
35 The Mirror, 'Crack SAS troops hunt Gaddafi weapons inside Libya', *The Mirror*, 20 March 2011.
36 E. Quintana, 'The War from the Air', in *Short War, Long Shadow*, p. 35.
37 BBC News, 'Libya unrest: SAS members "captured near Benghazi"', *BBC News*, 6 March 2011.
38 T. Judd, K. Sengupta and A. Grice, 'British special forces team released after botched mission', *The Independent*, 7 March 2011.
39 C. Gouëset, 'Ce que l'on sait sur les forces spéciales en Libye', *L'Express*, 26 August 2011.
40 Mazetti and Schmitt, 'C.I.A. agents in Libya aid airstrikes and meet rebels'.
41 JP 3–05, II-9–II-10.
42 O. Longescu, at NATO press briefing on 30 August 2011. NATO (30 August 2011) *Press Briefing on Libya*. Online. Available: www.nato.int/cps/en/natolive/opinions_77480.htm (accessed 19 February 2013).
43 S. Diffalah, 'Libye: une victoire des forces spéciales de la coalition?', *Le Nouvel Observateur*, 24 August 2011.
44 Diffalah, 'Libye: une victoire des forces spéciales de la coalition?'.
45 Nutter, *The CIA's Black Ops*, pp. 14–18.
46 The latter in the guise of OUP.
47 S. Nakhoul, 'Colonel Muammar Gaddafi's regime was delivered by a caterer, on a memory stick', *Reuters*, 6 September 2011; M. Phillips, 'The ground offensive: the role of Special Forces', in *Accidental Heroes: Britain, France and the Libya Operation*, London: RUSI, Interim RUSI Campaign Report, 2011.

48 M. Landler, E. Bumiller and S. Lee Myers, 'Washington in fierce debate on arming Libyan rebels', *The New York Times*, 29 March 2011.
49 International Affairs and Defence Section, *Interpretation of Security Council Resolution 1973 on Libya*, pp. 6–7.
50 Maghreb Confidential, 'Qatar's murky role in the transition', Maghreb Confidential No. 985, 15 September 2011.
51 Nakhoul, 'Colonel Muammar Gaddafi's Regime was Delivered by a Caterer, on a Memory Stick'; Phillips, 'The Ground Offensive'; Shashank Joshi, 'The Feasible Option for Libya', *RUSI*, 14 March 2011.
52 'Qatari Special Forces, British SAS and Americans fighting in Libya'. Online. Available: www.youtube.com/watch?v=8DRhicpr_qg (accessed on 16 January 2013).
53 BBC News (19 April 2011) 'British military officers to be sent to Libya', *BBC News*, 19 April 2011. Online. Available: www.bbc.co.uk/news/uk-13132654 (accessed 19 February 2013).
54 A. Cowell and R. Somaiya, 'France and Italy will also send advisers to Libya rebels', *The New York Times*, 20 April 2011.
55 L. Gelfand, 'Rebels ride wave of momentum towards Ghadaffi's homwtown', *Jane's Defence Weekly*, 31 August 2011, 5.
56 Nakhoul, 'Colonel Muammar Gaddafi's Regime was Delivered by a Caterer, on a Memory Stick'; Phillips, 'The Ground Offensive', p. 11.
57 Joint Chiefs of Staff, *Foreign Internal Defense*, US Government, Joint Publication 3-22, 2010.
58 BBC News, 'Royal Air Force airlifts 150 in second Libya rescue', *BBC News*, 28 February 2011.
59 Channel 4 News (26 February 2011) *RAF planes in Libya desert rescue*. Online. Available: www.youtube.com/watch?v=7nX25t2JlPY&feature=relmfu (accessed 19 February 2013).
60 Urban, 'Inside story of the UK's secret mission to beat Gaddafi'.
61 The analogy is based on the stories of the Scud hunting SAS teams deployed to Iraq in 1991, as told by McNab in *Bravo Two Zero*.
62 Defence Correspondent, 'SAS "Smash" squads on the ground in Libya to mark targets for coalition jets'.
63 For a short discussion of fratricide see *Dispatches: Lessons Learned for Soldiers on Fratricide*, Kingston: The Army Lessons Learned Centre, 2005.
64 Phillips, 'The Ground Offensive', p. 11.
65 B. Barry, 'Libya's Lessons', *Survival* 5, 2011, p. 5.
66 Associated Press, 'CIA operatives reportedly on the ground in Libya', *Associated Press*, 30 March 2011.
67 B. Mendelsohn, 'Al-Qaeda's Franchising Strategy', *Survival* 3, 2011.
68 J.C. Zarate and D.A. Gordon, 'The battle for reform with Al-Qaeda', *The Washington Quarterly*, No. 3, 2011, pp. 107–17.
69 P. Cruickshank, 'Libya: An opportunity for al Qaeda?', *CNN.com*, 25 February 2011.
70 Mendelsohn, 'Al-Qaeda's Franchising Strategy', p. 46.
71 Mendelsohn, 'Al-Qaeda's Franchising Strategy', p. 72.
72 Shashank, 'The Feasible Option for Libya'; J.A. Builta, *Extremist Groups: An International Compilation of Terrorist Organizations, Violent Political Groups, and Issue-Oriented Militant Movements*, Chicago: The University of Illinois at Chicago, 1996, pp. 360–7; A. Sabasteanski, *Patterns of Global Terrorism, 1985–2005. Vol. 1*, Great Barrington: Berkshire Publishing Group, 2005, p. 177; See also M. Mohlin, *The Strategic Use of Military Contractors. American Commercial Military Service Providers in Bosnia and Liberia: 1995–2009*, Helsinki: National Defence University, 2012, p. 16.

73 Cruickshank, 'Libya: An opportunity for al Qaeda?'.
74 Associated Press, 'CIA operatives reportedly on the ground in Libya'.
75 Byman and Waxman, *The Dynamics of Coercion*.
76 Shashank, 'The Feasible Option for Libya'.
77 Conversation with Brian McQuinn who spent the second half of the war embedded with rebels in Misrata.
78 B. McQuinn, *After the Fall: Libya's Evolving Armed Groups*, Geneva: Small Arms Survey, 2012.
79 Judd *et al.*, 'British special forces team released after botched mission'.
80 This was essentially what the Angolan government did during the so-called 'Luanda trials' in 1975, when they charged a group of American citizens for a crime called 'mercenarism'; A. Mockler, *The New Mercenaries: The History of the Mercenary from the Congo to the Seychelles*, London: Guild Publishing, 1985, pp. 210–31.
81 Nutter, *The CIA's Black Ops*, p. 330.
82 G. Miller, 'CIA seeks to expand drone fleet, officials say', *Washington Post*, 19 October 2012.
83 In mid-January 2013, it seemed as if the United States were about to deploy both drones and intelligence assets to Mali in support of French Operation Serval there. 'Jihad in the Sahara', *The Economist*, 19–25 January 2013.
84 See for instance Kiras who argues that SF and SO works best when applied in a role where they support strategic attrition rather than executing traditional direct action tasks in order to create a sort of strategic paralysis. Kiras, *Special Operations and Strategy*.
85 Barry, 'Libya's Lessons', p. 6.
86 See for instance Sanger, *Confront and Conceal*, on the 'light footprint' strategy of the Obama administration.
87 B.H. Liddell-Hart, *Strategy*, New York: Meridian, 1991 (1954).
88 D.H. Allen and E. Jones, *Weary Policeman. American Power in an Age of Austerity*, London: Routledge, 2012.
89 Associated Press, 'CIA operatives reportedly on the ground in Libya'.
90 M. Ambinder and D.B. Grady, *The Command: Deep Inside the President's Secret Army*, Hoboken, New Jersey: Wiley, Kindle Edition, 2012.
91 Barry, 'Libya's Lessons', p. 5.
92 E.M. Pettersen, 'Military assistance for the "Little Wars" of the Third World', in C.M. Brandt, *Military and Foreign Policy*, Wright-Patterson AFB: Air Force Institute of Technology Press, 1990, p. 265.
93 S. Neuman, 'Dependence, power, and influence: the role of military assistance', in C.M. Brandt, *Military assistance and foreign policy*, p. 23.

9 Conclusion

Lessons and consequences of Operation Unified Protector

Robert Egnell

While most eye-catching events on the international stage merit careful attention from scholars and analysts, some events – particularly wars – stand out as especially significant. In a recent analysis, Karl Mueller argues that wars are often particularly noteworthy 'because they are very large, politically consequential, or catastrophic'. Mueller then goes on to assert that the 2011 armed conflict in Libya lacked each of these characteristics. In fact, the NATO-led Operation Unified Protector (OUP) was small, short and low-cost.[1]

NATO's 2011 Libya campaign was nevertheless one of many 'firsts', an outlier, and its peculiarities are what make it significant for both scholars and policy makers. In political and legal terms, it was the first international intervention inspired by the doctrine behind the Responsibility to Protect (R2P). The campaign in Libya was also the first serious Western intervention in the wake of the large-scale quagmires in Afghanistan and Iraq – with the subsequent 'Iraq syndrome' hampering the appetite for international interventions. In military strategic and operational terms, the intervention nevertheless signified a vastly different approach to stabilization and regime change than those applied in Afghanistan and Iraq – a limited aerial campaign that arguably achieved impressive results within a relatively short time. The limited campaign not only protected civilians, which according to UNSCR 1973 constituted the primary task, but also toppled Gaddafi's regime after 40 years of tyranny. At the tactical and strategic levels, the operation saw a successful symbiosis of air assets, Special Forces, and indigenous fighters. In short, there are several features of the Libyan intervention that make it important, and not just 'politically consequential', despite its relatively small size and low cost.

This volume has produced an impressive range of questions, observations and findings that support the notion that the military campaign in Libya is worthy of serious study and further discussion. Trying to summarize the rich analyses of the chapters in this concluding discussion would not only risk unnecessary repetition, but would surely fail to do them justice. The purpose of this chapter is therefore to draw out a number of important questions and findings from the chapters in order to discuss broader lessons and consequences of the intervention. What does OUP tell us about the future of NATO? Is air power the strategic silver bullet that will allow policy makers to respond to complex emergencies on the cheap? To what extent can and should we use OUP as a blueprint for future military interventions in civil wars or in support of civilian protection? Are there any likely long-term legal or normative consequences in the wake of the operation?

Libya and the future of NATO

The intervention in Libya provides an opportunity to assess NATO's effectiveness and limitations in pursuit of broader peace and security, as well as the future of what primarily used to be a collective defence organization. Since the 1999 Washington Summit, the members of the Alliance have sought to create a 'new' NATO, capable of operating beyond the European theatre to combat emerging threats such as terrorism and the proliferation of weapons of mass destruction. The new vision was presented in the 2010 Strategic Concept, which declares that the Alliance must effectively fulfil three core tasks: collective defence, crisis management and cooperative security. Most importantly in relation to OUP and similar conflicts, NATO would, according to the Concept,

> actively employ an appropriate mix of those political and military tools to help manage developing crises that have the potential to affect Alliance security, before they escalate into conflicts; to stop on-going conflicts where they affect Alliance security; and to help consolidate stability in post-conflict situations where that contributes to Euro-Atlantic security.[2]

The Concept also highlighted the importance of enhancing international security through partnership with relevant countries and other international organizations – a more inclusive and multilateral approach beyond the boundaries of the organization itself.[3]

As NATO took over command in Libya, it was still heavily engaged in its first 'out-of-area' mission beyond Europe – in Afghanistan. The Alliance had in fact been in command of the International Security Assistance Force (ISAF) for almost a decade – tackling the challenging tasks involved in stabilizing and reconstructing Afghanistan. Thus, to make sense of NATO's intervention in Libya, it also needs to be placed within the broader context of ISAF in Afghanistan and the legacy of that commitment.

Arguably, the most frequently discussed contextual factor in Libya has been that of the 'Iraq syndrome' – the idea that the large-scale and unsuccessful interventions in Iraq and Afghanistan subsequently reduced both public and political interest in international expeditions for the sake of peace and stability. Within that context, the willingness to intervene in

Libya is surprising. Kjell Engelbrekt's contribution to this volume (Chapter 2) convincingly describes the national interests and political processes involved that led to the relative speed and resolve of the intervention as a set of circumstances that seemingly offset the Iraq syndrome, which of course mostly befell the United States. John Mueller, who first coined the term in a 2005 *Foreign Affairs* article, notably argued that the Iraq syndrome would eventually make America more sceptical of unilateral military action, especially in places that presented no direct threat to it, but was less inclined to dismiss Europeans and other well-meaning foreigners as cowardly or unhelpful: 'The United States may also become more inclined to seek international co-operation, sometimes even showing signs of humility.'[4] The multilateral American approach, including the readiness to pave the way for and undergird the efforts of the European Allies rather than vice versa, seems to corroborate this prediction.

Whether the supporting though decisive role of US forces in Libya was a symptom of the Iraq syndrome or a cost-saving approach to a conflict where no serious American interests were involved is, of course, debatable. But regardless of which comes closer to the truth, an important Libyan lesson for NATO and its member states is that the United States has now demonstrated that it actually can choose to place more of the operational burdens on its European allies and relinquish a leading military role. Given the limited capabilities of the European armed forces, the defence cuts on both sides of the Atlantic and the US 'rebalancing' toward Asia, this may have serious consequences for NATO's future capability to fulfil its ambitious aims in terms of broader peace and security. Where US national interests are not directly involved, the European allies could in the future either be on their own, or be offered very limited direct assistance in order to fulfil military objectives.

Some of the biggest challenges of coalition operations concern how allies and partners agree on mutual aims and approaches to operations, as well as how they coordinate a multitude of actors and activities via an appropriate (preferably single) chain of command. In its command of the complex operations in Afghanistan, for the most part NATO has proved itself capable of mastering such challenges. Also in the Libyan case the Alliance and the larger international community struggled to arrive at a political consensus, and therefore never managed to agree on the strategic aims of operations.

The experience of the ISAF mission in Afghanistan is important, though in several respects troublesome, when it comes to reaching unity of strategic aims and a coherent command structure. In effect, three separate operations were conducted at the same time with essentially different missions: the American-led counterterrorism effort to hunt down any remaining al-Qaeda and Taliban fighters; the NATO-led ISAF operation with a mandate to provide security and to enable a third mission – UNAMA; the latter was led by the UN and entirely devoted to political and economic development. Furthermore, the core of the mission changed over time. Starting out as a counter-terror strike against the perpetrators of the 11 September 2001 attacks, the campaign morphed into a state-building effort intended to prevent al-Qaeda's return and to build a democratic Afghanistan in the calm years after the fall of the Taliban regime. The campaign then evolved into a counterinsurgency campaign as the security situation deteriorated from 2004 onward and as the Taliban regained its strength. Finally, as the coalition started focusing on managing the 'transition' and withdrawal from Afghanistan, a full circle was completed in that the more ambitious aims of state-building and counterinsurgency were replaced by a narrow counterterrorism framework.[5]

The failure in reaching political consensus at the initial stage was repeated in Libya. In the case of OUP, as Jeffrey Michaels shows in this volume (Chapter 1), the political problems were exacerbated by the fact that key allies did not even support a military intervention in Libya (Germany), originally opposed the idea of a NATO framework for operations (France) or raised objections to the notion of targeting ground forces (Turkey). Moreover, many allies failed to contribute to the operation or did so with small numerical commitments and highly limiting national caveats regarding roles and operational areas – making them largely ineffectual. Among the contributing nations of the NATO-led coalition, the aims of operations were also very different – with some seeking regime change while others saw the protection of civilians as the only legitimate aim.

In order to overcome the challenges of managing a coalition of Allies and partners with differing aims and agendas, NATO displayed a surprising amount of flexibility and pragmatic ingenuity in the case of Libya (and, some would say, disingenuousness, as will be discussed below). First, the Alliance has clearly learned some command lessons over the past decade and so could avoid the need for constant consensus within the Alliance by holding the vast majority of Brussels meetings in OUP-format – meaning that troop contributions rather than Alliance membership determined access. To maximize the utility of each of the OUP partners, all information (open and classified) was also shared from the very beginning – in stark contrast with the operations in Kosovo and Afghanistan.[6] A number of more or less formal groups and 'coalitions' were thereby formed within the Alliance, and the politically cumbersome North Atlantic Council (NAC) often became the secondary framework where operational decisions were made. Instead, the most important forum was the 'group of eight', which included the countries that conducted strike missions in Libya. Other forums during OUP were the 'inner-circle' (UK, US and France), as well as the traditional 'two [pairs of] eyes' and 'five [pairs of] eyes' – the Anglophone communities of either both the UK and US, or of the UK, US, Canada, Australia and New Zealand.[7]

The traditionally problematic aspect of separate national chains of command was utilized in OUP to get around the restrictions of UNSCR

1973, which did not allow deployment of ground forces, and to partner with the National Transitional Council (NTC) with the purpose of regime change. Jeffrey Michaels (Chapter 1) and Marcus Mohlin (Chapter 8) have in their respective chapters in this volume described how many of the more sensitive operations were conducted at the national level *alongside* the Alliance operation. Since NATO was not officially providing air support to the rebels, it was problematic to be receiving targeting information from them directly, and the indirect route through national intelligence chains allowed the Alliance to claim 'plausible deniability'; General Bouchard's 'denial' of coordination with the NTC while at the same time acknowledging that 'nations have got their own rights to do certain actions that may not necessarily be shared with the Alliance itself' is telling in this regard.[8]

Another contemporary challenge of NATO that became painfully obvious in Afghanistan was the fact that, despite the relatively limited commitments of many Allies, the campaign still put great pressure on the financially constrained and ever-dwindling armed forces of the European allies. Given the ambitious set of tasks related to a broad view of the security threats facing the transatlantic area, as laid out in the Strategic Concept from 2010, the operation in Afghanistan illustrated that the Alliance faces a significant gap between ambitions and resources. These shortcomings were equally obvious during the intervention in Libya – partly in the form of the limited number of member states which committed resources and partly in the limited contributions of those who did, along with the challenges to maintenance and logistics that evolved among those countries during the course of the operation.

Michaels (Chapter 1) highlights that a lesson from Libya, as well as from Afghanistan and Kosovo, is that non-Allied partnerships matter, not only for what they can do as part of the military mission, but also for what they can achieve in terms of legitimizing political support for that mission. OUP constituted another substantial step towards integrating the partners in the actual decision-making procedures, operational planning and information sharing. Staff members at the Delegation of Sweden to NATO, for instance, confirm that the integration of partnership countries exceeded expectations as soon as the operation was underway.[9] The fact that the vast majority of meetings in Brussels were held in OUP-format and that all information (open and classified) was shared amongst the OUP partners from the outset underscores this observation.[10] To further facilitate partner integration, officers from these countries were based at SHAPE and at the Joint Forces Command (JFC) in Naples. That being said, one may speculate that NATO used access to meetings as leverage to persuade partners to step up their respective contributions and soften national restrictions.[11]

Whether this will be a successful method in future operations remains to be seen. We now turn to other potential lessons from Libya that may be transferrable to future scenarios.

Is 'aerial intervention' the future silver bullet?

At the heart of this choice between approaches lies the more fundamental questions of what determined the outcome of operations in Libya, and whether that lesson can be transferred to other scenarios. At the time of intervention, the rebels were clearly incapable of defeating Gaddafi's forces without external support. The international campaign was therefore an indispensible factor in determining the outcome of operations. The air campaign, in combination with important special operations capabilities provided by a number of coalition members, tipped the scale in favour of the rebels.[12] Operating in coordination with the NTC but without ever deploying regular ground forces, NATO and coalition partners therefore assisted in the gradual weakening and defeat of the Libyan government. Most of the support came from the sky, with aerial targeting of vital government installations and forces. The war raged on until 20 October 2011 when, during the Battle of Sirte, NTC forces captured Gaddafi and subsequently beat him to death. Despite NTC requests that NATO stay on until the end of the year, the death of Gaddafi marked the beginning of the end of the latter's operation in Libya, which was formally terminated the following week.[13]

The intervention was heavily air-centric, as Anders Nygren (Chapter 4) details in his comprehensive account, but its success was not a victory by airpower acting alone, nor was it intended to be so by the airmen leading the operation. In their respective chapters, Christian Wollert (Chapter 5) and Marcus Mohlin (Chapter 8) show that coalition naval operations and Special Forces also played significant roles in the campaign. Even more importantly, while the aim of protecting civilians was achieved by air power alone, the defeat of Gaddafi's regime was ultimately accomplished through a combination of air and land forces, supplemented by naval manoeuvres.[14] In the end, it was the rebel advance towards government-controlled areas, and their capture and killing of Muammar Gaddafi, that ended the war. Therefore, declaring victory by air power alone would be disrespectful of the contributions of rebel fighters who fought their way from Benghazi, Misrata and the Nafusa Mountains to Tripoli; it further downplays the fact that neither party would have been successful without the support of the other. Without the rebels on the ground, a coalition victory in Libya would have come at a much higher price not only in the forms of treasure and ground forces' blood, but also in the forms of violations of the UN mandate and a consequent international political crisis, national political investment and post-conflict responsibilities.

From that vantage point the NATO-led intervention in Libya in 2011 has somewhat simplistically been portrayed as being in stark contrast to the costly and drawn-out campaigns in Iraq and Afghanistan. As an example, air power expert Christina Goulter briefly acknowledges the contribution of indigenous fighters but finds OPU to be a vindication, above all, of air power:

Operation UNIFIED PROTECTOR was a very clear demonstration of the flexibility and effectiveness of air power as a tool of domestic and international policy. After nearly a decade of counter-insurgency campaigns in Iraq and Afghanistan, it provided a useful corrective to those who have argued that counter-insurgency warfare will be the norm for the foreseeable future.... OUP proved that an air campaign, focused and driven by ISR [intelligence, surveillance, reconnaissance], can win a war when combined effectively with irregular ground forces.[15]

In this sense the Libya campaign largely built on, and validated, the so-called 'Afghan model', tried and tested during the combat phase of Operation Enduring Freedom and perceived as a particularly effective means of applying Western military might.[16] Then as now, the model saw Western powers ply their advanced combat capabilities – precision-guided munitions in particular – in support of a local ground force reinforced by a small number of special operations forces to ensure proper coordination. The prototype for the approach was first tested in the Balkan campaigns of the 1990s, in which NATO conducted precision-guided bombings from a virtually risk-free altitude and let local allies (the Croat forces in Bosnia and the Kosovo Liberation Army in Kosovo) conduct ground operations. When refined in Afghanistan with the addition of special operations forces acting as a bridge between land and air, this approach was embraced as a possible way of circumventing the typical pitfalls of 'unconventional' or irregular wars.[17]

The basic concept employed in Libya was that of the Afghan model of warfare, using indigenous allies to replace Western conventional ground troops and exploiting US and coalition airpower and small numbers of special operations forces. Stephen Biddle notes that there are some who argue that this model is widely applicable and that it thereby would enable major restructuring of the US military and considerable freedom for American military intervention.[18] However, Biddle himself provides a more thorough analysis of the experience in Afghanistan and Iraq and finds the model's applicability to be rather limited. Where the indigenous allies 'have had skills and motivation comparable to their enemies', the Afghan model has proven lethal even without the support of Western conventional ground forces. But where the local allies have lacked these skills, they have also proven unable to exploit the potential of American airpower.[19] Biddle's conclusion is that the Afghan model can be a powerful tool, but that it requires a number of important preconditions before it can be successfully employed.[20]

Robert Farley similarly finds that the military victory that the Afghan model envisions is limited, and that larger questions revolve around the post-conflict political settlement and peace-building processes in Libya after the international withdrawal.[21] While the initial assessment of the campaign in Libya is one of unambiguous success, it is certainly too early to arrive at a final verdict regarding the long-term outcomes of the operation. It is worth noting that the campaign in Afghanistan is hardly remembered today for the 'Afghan model' used in 2001, since it was superseded by a violent insurgency. In that light one could deduce that the 'Afghan model' represents no real improvement on previous approaches in that it, too, neglects the ability to manage post-conflict environments – the reconciliation processes and the political settlements, as well as the economic reconstruction and development processes that are necessary for long-term peace and stability.

That being said, the Libyan campaign presents some remarkable advantages in comparison to the manner of intervention seen in Iraq and Afghanistan. First, the operation did achieve the intended aims within a few months and kept the costs to a fragment of those accrued in Iraq and Afghanistan. Second, as Anders Nygren reminds us (Chapter 4), in the NATO-led air campaign over Libya, like that over Kosovo in 1999, coalition and civilian casualties were kept very low. Indeed, NATO was able to intervene in Libya without incurring a single fatality of its own. Third, while some ambiguity surrounded the coalition's actual aims in Libya, the results of the intervention appear far more promising than those likely to be seen in Afghanistan when the last troops eventually withdraw. Finally, for some key participants – not least the UK and France – the operation strengthened the perception of these countries being capable of playing a key role in diplomacy and making a substantial military contribution to international peace and security.[22]

Still, while the merits of this mode of intervention are extolled, it remains important to carefully appreciate the preconditions that rendered it effective (or even applicable). Indeed, the campaign in Libya was in many ways exceptional, a *sui generis* case, which undermines its status as a precedent for future wars. First, Muammar Gaddafi's crude threats against his own citizens, in combination with the backdrop of the recent democratic revolutions in Northern Africa, provided the campaign with unprecedented international political support, as well as a sense of urgency to 'do something' (see Introduction and Chapters 1 and 7 by Engelbrekt and Wagnsson, Michaels, and Jensen, respectively). Second, NATO was aided by the simple fact that the war was largely fought in the desert, which made targeting from the air relatively easy and effective (see Chapters 3 and 4 by Holst and Fink, and Nygren, respectively). Third, there was clear opposition to Gaddafi in the NTC and the rebel troops that served as its proxy force on the ground (see Chapter 8 by Mohlin). Fourth, Libya's geographic location, at Europe's backdoor, not only meant a greater sense of urgency but also made the conduct of operations much easier in terms of basing and logistics (see Introduction and Chapter 5 by Engelbrekt and Wagnsson, and Wollert, respectively). In fact, for the first time since the Second World War, Britain was able to launch a bombing strike directly from the British mainland. Fifth, another important precondition for success in Libya was the sudden collapse of the Libyan army not only as the result of the war itself, but also of the North African political culture of patrimonialism, militarism and Islamism (see Chapter 6 by Sörenson and Damidez). This culture created dynamics within the regime leadership and the Libyan Armed Forces that made them poorly prepared to withstand the uprising and, more obviously, the international intervention.

Furthermore, while the designated enemy in Libya adapted too late, there were signs even here that 'the enemy has a vote' in choosing how the war will be fought – not least by reacting to and exploiting the strategic and tactical preferences of coalition forces. In particular, the obvious response to stand-off weapons – seen also in the Balkans and Afghanistan – is concealment. In the early phases of the war in Libya, government forces were operating and moving in large uniformed units across the desert. Following the initial air attacks, however, this behaviour promptly changed: as Brigadier Ben Barry has explained, Gaddafi's forces 'dispersed heavy weapons in populated areas and made extensive use of armed 4x4 vehicles, similar to those used by the rebels', something that 'greatly complicated NATO's ability to identify and attack them'.[23] While concealment was not as successful in Libya as it had been in Kosovo more than a decade earlier, there are good reasons to anticipate more wily adaptation on the part of future adversaries. This may also limit the effectiveness of Western air power as the main route for winning wars.

There are clearly cases in which air power can have a tremendous strategic effect on its own or in conjunction with special operations forces on the ground. Still, it is important to not lose sight of the many specific enabling conditions present in Libya that made this model work. Proper analysis of these conditions should also give pause to any hasty conclusions regarding how future wars will and will not be fought. In fact, the conditions that made the emphasis on air power possible and successful in Libya are unlikely to present themselves very often in other contexts.[24]

Legitimacy, accountability, and control of future interventions

While the international community responded with remarkable speed to the emergency in Libya, serious concerns can be raised about the ambitions of the intervening coalition to topple Gaddafi's regime rather than to simply protect civilians, as well as about the manner in which this was achieved. A formidable international constituency with Russia and China at the forefront advocates less permissive interpretations of the principles of state sovereignty and non-intervention in general, and specifically when it comes to implementing a Security Council mandate to use force. For these actors, Resolution 1973 allowed the coalition to establish and maintain a no-fly zone, enforce the arms embargo and use 'all necessary measures' short of foreign occupation to protect civilians only in conjunction with the specified constraints, which were thought to delimit the infringement of Libya's rights as a sovereign state. However, in the view of this constituency the intervening coalition violated that understanding in at least two significant ways.

First, despite the seemingly impartial commitment to protect civilians, as outlined in UNSCR 1973, the intervening coalition eventually took sides by actively seeking regime change by coordinating with and supporting the NTC rebel forces, and by aiming to decapitate the Gaddafi regime. The idea of protecting civilians by targeting the command and control centres from which military orders to target civilians emanate is obviously a departure from the mandate provided by the UN – especially given the broad interpretation of what a command and control centre actually is. The view expressed by General Sir David Richards on this issue shows the extent to which the coalition was prepared to stretch the rules to fit operational (and political) needs instead of strictly implementing the outcome of Security Council deliberations: 'We are not targeting Gaddafi directly, but if it happened that he was in a command and control centre that was hit by NATO and he was killed, then that is within the rules.'[25]

A second example of an expansive interpretation of Resolution 1973 was the use of Special Forces in separate national chains of command, as well as the use of 'unofficial partners' on the ground, to get around these limitations of impartiality and non-use of ground forces. The idea that the resolution's restrictions still meant that 'ground forces can be used as long as they do not exercise effective control over the territory', as argued in the memo of the International Affairs and Defence Section of the British House of Commons,[26] would seem to constitute a rather creative and legalistic notion.

To be sure, the nature and content of international and humanitarian law and UNSC Resolutions are often subjected to questionable or apparently disingenuous interpretations that promote national agendas. The American and British debates regarding the legality of the intervention in Iraq 2003 is an obvious case in point. Indeed, the malleability of international law, and the difficultly of enforcing it without coercion or direct military action, generates a sizeable 'damned if you do, damned if you don't' dilemma. Relevant is not exclusively whether the intervention was perceived as legal by government and international legal scholars, but whether it was understood as legitimate in the broader international community and public opinion. As we now know, the intervention in Libya had fairly strong international popular support, and the relative success of the campaign reinforced the view that it was indeed legitimate.[27] As indicated by Rikke Bjerg Jensen (Chapter 7), part of this success is presumably due to the effective strategic communication devised by NATO and countries such as Britain in making it an integral part of military operations.

Does OUP provide a milestone in the normative development of a Responsibility to Protect?

In this volume Fredrik Holst and Martin Fink (Chapter 3) provide a well-informed account of the legal and normative frameworks that shaped the intervention in Libya. A core part of their analysis deals with the challenges involved in implementing the UN mandate to protect civilians and the normative concept of Responsibility to Protect (R2P). Elsewhere, Alex Bellamy has argued that since the 2005 UN World Summit R2P has shifted from a mere 'concept' to a 'principle' in international politics. Treating R2P as a principle implies that it is being elevated to the level of a 'shared understanding and that there is enough consensus to allow it to function as a foundation for action'.[28] Recognizing it as a principle in international politics does not, however, mean that R2P is not contested, and commentators point to the fact that it has only been implemented once – in Libya. On one side in this debate a number of Western states have been promoting the R2P agenda in order to improve the international community's ability to prevent and react to the all-too-common cases of genocide and other mass atrocities. The opposing constituency is made up of a mixture of developing countries and nascent, expanding and rebounding great powers such as Brazil, China and Russia that view R2P as a problematic framework that may enable Western intervention in the internal affairs of sovereign states.

The fact that the language of R2P was invoked in the discussions leading up to Security Council Resolution 1973, and that the resolution entailed a mandate to protect civilians 'with all necessary measures short of ground invasion', is potentially a milestone in the history of R2P. Is the Libyan intervention therefore a sign that R2P is indeed being recognized as a principle, backed up by a consensus that would allow it to function as a foundation for action? Was this the beginning of a new era in which state sovereignty is circumscribed by the obligations inherent to R2P? Even though we should acknowledge that humanitarian concerns were the primary driver of the 2011 Libya intervention, such a conclusion would seem premature, for the following reasons:

First, the Libyan uprising, civil war, and subsequent international intervention took place at the very edges of Europe, in an oil-rich country known for its previous support of international terrorism. Muammar Gaddafi was a notorious human rights violator who had severed or strained relations with most countries in the world and, while being in a period of détente with the West, was always going to be seen as a serious liability for international peace and stability. There were, in other words, plenty of countries with interests in seeing Gaddafi removed. Therefore, as Engelbrekt (Chapter 2) demonstrates, R2P can be seen as a justification rather than a motive for intervention. To make that argument we nevertheless have to highlight the national interests at stake beyond the obvious issue of energy resources, which is where humanitarian norms and national interests begin to overlap. The international community – not least the European governments – were subjected to immense pressure from their own populations to intervene for humanitarian purposes.

Second, the conduct of operations in Libya indicates that regime change rather than protection of civilians was, or successively became, the main concern of key coalition members. Libyan army units were targeted to an extent beyond the need for 'mere' civilian protection, as were leadership headquarters of the regime. Holst and Fink (Chapter 3) note that while civilian protection and activities beyond protection – such as regime change – may theoretically be seen as very distinct and clearly separated activities, in practical terms they are not. Although the UN mandate hardly meant to include regime change in its support of civilian protection, it was possible for coalition members to argue that toppling the morally corrupt Gaddafi regime was indeed necessary to protect civilians, as were the wider 'decapitation efforts' and the targeting of command and control centres. Reaffirming the one-sidedness of the intervention, NATO did not act against rebel units when they posed threats to civilians in government-controlled areas, even (after the regime change) when reports of human rights violation by the NTC started to appear.

Third, one of the main benefits of the R2P framework is that it avoids 'all or nothing choices' – between sending in the Marines and doing nothing. R2P rests on three legs: (1) the responsibility of the state to protect its own citizens from genocide, war crimes and other atrocities; (2) the commitment of the international community to assist states in meeting these obligations; and (3) the responsibility of UN Member States to respond in a timely and decisive manner using chapters VI and VII in the UN Charter as appropriate, when a state is manifestly failing to provide such protection.[29] R2P also embraces a broader range of tools than traditional humanitarian intervention, namely prevention, reaction and rebuilding. However, none of those broader R2P frameworks or tools were used in Libya, reaffirming the impression that protection of civilians was not the overwhelmingly important objective (at least a few months into the operation).

Fourth, the spread of this 'concept turned principle' cannot be measured with reference to isolated interventions. If it is indeed a norm beyond the mere justification of national interests, it should at least hypothetically apply to analogous challenges elsewhere. Bellamy notes that while R2P balances between attempting to limit unilateral action and guiding 'genuine' collective measures, 'the problem nowadays is not that there are too many humanitarian interventions but too few – as Rwanda and Darfur attest.'[30] The selective use of R2P – both in terms of which conflicts to intervene in, and the tools to apply – risks producing an à la carte approach to R2P that largely replicates the activities previously conducted and criticized under the banner of 'humanitarian intervention'. Although the discretionary use of R2P is inherent to the official documents adopted in the UN context (see Engelbrekt in Chapter 2), the perceived arbitrariness of international interventions authorized by the UN Security Council could have a crippling effect on the continued diffusion of R2P.

And the rest is hardly silence...

Even if it fails to become a 'model' in its own right, the intervention in Libya is remarkable for a number of reasons. Politically, the international community responded with unusual speed to prevent a humanitarian disaster in the Libyan civil war. Militarily, the noteworthy success, in terms of shifting the balance in the war and eventually toppling the dictatorial regime of Muammar Gaddafi with an operation mainly conducted from the air, costing 'only' a few billion dollars and leading to no coalition deaths or serious injuries, stands in stark contrast to the enormous costs and limited successes in Iraq and Afghanistan.

The campaign is thereby a reminder that intervention does not necessarily have to involve vast military and civilian efforts. In circumstances conducive to such military campaigns, limited interventions can have great impact – as also displayed by the British intervention in Sierra Leone's civil war in 1999. In many ways, however, this volume shows that the international intervention in Libya was an outlier rather than a useful blueprint for action. Libya was politically and operationally a perfect storm that allowed the international community to intervene with limited investment and reap seemingly large returns. We should at the same time remind ourselves, as pointed out by Engelbrekt and Wagnsson (Introduction), that the jury is still out on the long-term outcomes and consequences of the intervention in Libya.

Indeed, that the processes of political reform and economic development would constitute long and bumpy roads was almost a given regardless of the type of intervention approach employed. On the one hand, Iraq and Afghanistan provide a useful illustration of the insight that masses of men and money do not necessarily solve the problems of post-conflict reconstruction. On the other, the rocky political processes seen in Egypt and Tunisia remind us of the major challenges involved even after relatively peaceful transitions of power. We simply do not have a formula or a silver bullet for the socially and historically complex processes of state formation, democratization and economic liberalization. If Libya does not quickly evolve to a stable, liberal democracy, it will hardly be solely the fault of the limited intervention approach chosen by the coalition in the spring of 2011.

In the face of complex emergencies, overall, a large dose of humility would serve the international community well.[31] Overreaching by creating aims that no set of actors are willing to commit appropriate resources for will never be in the interest of the host country either. In that sense the intervention in Libya is a useful blueprint for future international engagement in terms of its pragmatic stance; a rapid, albeit limited, response aimed at avoiding the worst possible outcome of a crisis in the end achieved more than what was envisioned. Legally and morally, though, that pragmatism also renders the Libya intervention problematic. The legitimacy of the operation was partly undermined because of the coalition's seemingly disingenuous interpretations of UNSCR 1973, in that they supported the rebels in toppling Gaddafi, targeted the regime leadership, and even committed small numbers of special forces on the ground, the latter being specifically precluded in the resolution. In addition, the perceived legitimacy of humanitarian interventions, as well as the principle of R2P, rest not only on just causes of intervention, but also on the conduct of operations and the long-term responsibility towards the host country. In that sense, the intervention in Libya may have negative consequences for the possibility of convincing sceptics of R2P to support future resolutions with a civilian protection mandate.

Clearly, the chapters in this volume have all provided important elements of a more comprehensive understanding of the intervention in Libya. Equally important, this volume has raised important questions about the future of military interventions, the nature and future of NATO, legal and political trends in the international system as well as tactical best practices in the pursuit of peace and security. Indeed, the quality of research should not only be measured in terms of the number of answers provided, but also in relation to the number of new questions raised and areas for research highlighted. By any measure, this volume is a significant contribution to the study of contemporary interventions generally and a milestone in understanding the NATO-led intervention in Libya in particular. The quest for improved knowledge and understanding will certainly continue, since, judging by the civil war in Syria, the shocking levels of violence in the eastern parts of DRC, the failing states of the Sahel and the Horn of Africa as well as the instability of the Middle East and Central Asia, we are hardly close to a peaceful 'end of history' or to the last military campaign with the purpose of averting an even greater human tragedy.

Notes

1 K. Mueller, 'Examining the Air Campaign in Libya', in K. Mueller (ed.), *Precision and Purpose: Airpower in the Libyan Civil War*, Santa Monica, CA: RAND Corporation, forthcoming 2013, p. 5.
2 NATO (20 November 2010) *Active Engagement, Modern Defence: Strategic Concept for the Defence and Security of the Members of the North Atlantic Treaty Organization*. Online. Available: www.nato.int/cps/en/natolive/official_texts_68580.htm (accessed on 18 February 2013).
3 Ibid.
4 J. Mueller, 'The Iraq Syndrome', *Foreign Affairs* 6, 2005.
5 D. Ucko and R. Egnell, *Counterinsurgency in Crisis: Britain and the Challenges of Modern Warfare*, Columbia University Press, forthcoming 2013.
6 Interview with officials at the Delegation of Sweden to NATO, 20 May 2012.
7 Ibid.
8 General Charles Bouchard (14 February 2012) *Coalition Building and the Future of NATO Operations*, talk at the Atlantic Council. Online. Available: www.acus.org/event/libya-revisited-coalition-building-and-future-nato-operations (accessed on 18 February 2013).

9 Interview with officials at the Delegation of Sweden to NATO, 20 May 2012.
10 Ibid.
11 Ibid. As an example, while the Swedish contribution provided the most sought-after recce operations, they were also given access to the meetings of the 'inner-circle' and to deliberations of 'two eyes' and 'five eyes'. At the opposite end of the scale, during the early period in which the Swedish contribution was of limited utility due to the Swedish unit's strict legal interpretations of its political mandate, NATO reportedly kept the Swedish contingent out of the loop at all levels of command.
12 K. Mueller, 'Victory through (not by) airpower', in K. Mueller (ed.), *Precision and Purpose: Airpower in the Libyan Civil War*, Santa Monica, CA: RAND Corporation, forthcoming 2013, p. 338.
13 Ucko and Egnell, *Counterinsurgency in Crisis*.
14 See also Mueller, 'Victory through (not by) airpower', p. 338.
15 Christina Goulter, 'The British Experience: Operation Ellamy', in K. Mueller (ed.), *Precision and Purpose: Airpower in the Libyan Civil War*, Santa Monica CA: RAND Corporation, forthcoming 2013, p. 143.
16 The original formulation of the 'Afghan model' can be found in S.D. Biddle, 'Allies, Airpower, and Modern Warfare: The Afghan Model in Afghanistan and Iraq', *International Security* 3, 2005/06, pp. 161–76. For the Libyan revival of this model, see for example R. Farley, 'Over the Horizon: Libya and the Afghan Model', *World Politics Review*, 23 March 2011. Online. Available: www.worldpoliticsreview.com/articles/8277/over-the-horizon-libya-and-the-afghan-model.html (accessed 19 February 2013).
17 To George W. Bush, Enduring Freedom offered a 'proving ground', showcasing how 'innovative doctrine and high-tech weaponry can shape and then dominate in an unconventional conflict'. See White House, 'President Speaks on War Effort to Citadel Cadets', 11 December 2001. Online. Available: http://georgewbush-whitehouse.archives.gov/news/releases/2001/12/20011211-6.html.
18 Biddle, 'Allies, Airpower, and Modern Warfare', p. 161.
19 Ibid.
20 Ibid.
21 Farley, 'Over the Horizon'.
22 C. Goulter, 'The British Experience', p. 164.
23 B. Barry, 'Libya's Lessons', *Survival* 5, 2011, p. 6.
24 Ucko and Egnell, *Counterinsurgency in Crisis*.
25 C. Coughlin, 'Nato must target Gaddafi regime, says Armed Forces chief Gen. Sir David Richards, *The Telegraph*, 14 May 2011. Online. Available: www.telegraph.co.uk/news/worldnews/africaandindianocean/libya/8514034/Nato-must-target-Gaddafi-regime-says-Armed-Forces-chief-Gen-Sir-David-Richards.html (accessed 19 February 2013).
26 UK House of Commons, *Interpretation of Security Council Resolution 1973 on Libya* (SN/IA/5916), 6 April 2011, International Affairs and Defence Section, House of Commons.
27 German Marshall Fund (2011) *Transatlantic Trends 2011*. Online. Available: www.gmfus.org/publications_/TT/TTS2011Toplines.pdf (accessed 19 February 2013).
28 A.J. Bellamy, *Responsibility to Protect: The Global Effort to End Mass Atrocities*, Cambridge: Polity Press, 2009, p. 6.
29 Bellamy, *Responsibility to Protect*, p. 97.
30 Ibid., p. 18.
31 R. Egnell, 'The organized hypocrisy of international state-building', *Conflict, Security and Development* 4, 2010, pp. 465–91.

Select bibliography

Accidental Heroes: Britain, France and the Libya Operation, Interim RUSI Campaign Report, London: RUSI, 2011.

Adams, S., *Libya and the Responsibility to Protect*, Global Centre for the Responsibility to Protect, Occasional Paper Series, No. 3, October 2012. Online. Available: www.globalr2p.org/media/pdf/LibyaAndR2POccasionaPaper.pdf (accessed 10 December 2012).

Allen, S. and Zelizer, B., *Reporting War: Journalism in Wartime*, London: Routledge, 2004.

Allen, D.H. and Jones, E., *Weary Policeman. American Power in an Age of Austerity*, London: Routledge, 2012.

Ambinder, M. and Grady, D.B., *The Command: Deep inside the President's Secret Army*, John Wiley and Sons, Kindle edition, 2012.

Amnéus, D., *Responsibility to Protect and the Prevention of Genocide: A Right to Humanitarian Intervention?*, edited by Charlotte Haider, Stockholm: The Living History Forum, 2008. Online. Available: www.levandehistoria.se/files/A%20right%20to%20humanitarian_final.pdf (accessed 31 August 2012).

Amnéus, D., *Repsonsibility to Protect by Military Means: Emerging Norms on Humanitarian Intervention*, LL.D. Dissertation, Stockholm: Stockholm University, 2008.

Barry, B., 'Libya's Lessons', *Survival*, Vol. 53, No. 5, 2011.

Bazan, E.B., *Assassination Ban and E.O. 12333: A Brief Summary*, CRS Report for Congress, Washington DC: US Congressional Research Service, 2002.

Bell, J.P. and Hendrickson, R.C., 'NATO's Višegrad Allies and the Bombing of Qaddafi: The Consequence of Alliance Free-Riders', *The Journal of Slavic Military Studies*, Vol. 2, No. 5, 2012.

Bellamy, A.J., *Responsibility to Protect: The Global Effort to End Mass Atrocities*, Cambridge: Polity Press, 2009.

Bellamy, A.J. and Williams P.D. 'The New Politics of Protection? Côte d'Ivoire, Libya and the Responsibility to Protect', *International Affairs*, Vol. 87, 2011.

Berridge, G.R., Keens-Soper, M. and Otte, T.G., *Diplomatic Theory from Machiavelli to Kissinger*, Basingstoke: Palgrave, 2001.

Biddle, S.D. 'Allies, Airpower, and Modern Warfare: The Afghan Model in Afghanistan and Iraq', *International Security*, Vo. 30, No. 3, 2005/06.

Bill, J.A. and Springborg, R., *Politics in the Middle East*, 5th edition, New York: Addison Wesley Longman, 2000.

Blanchard, C.M. 'Libya: Unrest and US Policy', CRS Reports for Congress, Washington: CRS, 2011.

Booth, K., *Navies and Foreign Policy*, New York: Holmes & Meier, 1979.
Bosco, D.L., *Five to Rule Them All: The UN Security Council and the Making of the Modern World*, Oxford: Oxford University Press, 2009.
Brandt, C.M. (ed.), *Military Assistance and Foreign Policy*, Wright-Patterson AFB: Air Force Institute of Technology Press, 1990.
Bring, O., *FN-stadgan och världspolitiken – om folkrättens roll i en föränderlig värld*, 4th edition, Stockholm: Nordstedts juridik, 2002.
British Army Field Manual: Countering Insurgency, London: Ministry of Defence, January 2010.
British Maritime Doctrine, Shrivenham: Ministry of Defence, DCDC, 2011.
Buckley, C.A. 'Learning from Libya, Acting in Syria', *Journal of Strategic Security*, Vol. 5, 2012.
Builta, J.A., *Extremist Groups: An International Compilation of Terrorist Organizations, Violent Political Groups, and Issue-Oriented Militant Movements*, Chicago: University of Illinois at Chicago, 1996.
Byman, D. and Waxman, M., *The Dynamics of Coercion: American Foreign Policy and the Limits of Military Might*, Cambridge: Cambridge University Press, 2002.
Cable, J., *Gunboat Diplomacy 1919–1991: Limited Applications of Naval Force*, 3rd edition, New York: Palgrave Macmillan, 1994.
Carruthers, S.L., *The Media at War: Communications and Conflict in the 20th Century*, London: Macmillan, 2000.
Clapham, A., *Human Rights: A Very Short Introduction*, Oxford: Oxford University Press, 2007.
Cook, S.A., *Ruling but Not Governing: The Military and Political Development in Egypt, Algeria, and Turkey*, New York: Johns Hopkins University Press, 2007.
Corbett, J.S., *Some Principles of Maritime Strategy*, Annapolis, MD: Naval Institute Press, 1988.
Corn, G.S. and Corn, G.P., 'The Law of Operational Targeting: Viewing the LOAC through an Operational Lens', *Texas International Law Journal*, Vol. 47, No. 2, 2012. Online. Available: www.tilj.org/content/journal/47/num2/Corn337.pdf. (accessed 8 October 2012).
Cottle, S., *Mediatized Conflict*, Berkshire: Open University Press, 2006.
Daalder, I.H. and Stavridis, J.G., 'NATO's Victory in Libya: The Right Way to Run an Intervention', *Foreign Affairs*, Vol. 91, No. 2, March/April, 2012.
Dinstein, Y., *War, Agression and Self-Defense*, 3rd edition, Cambridge: Cambridge University Press, 2001.
Farrell, T., 'Dynamics of British Military Transformation', *International Affairs*, Vol. 84, 2008.
Fenrick, William J., 'Targeting and Proportionality during the NATO Bombing Campaign against Yugoslavia', *European Journal of International Law*, Vol. 12, No. 3, 2001.
Fink, M.D., 'UN-mandated Maritime Arms Embargo Operations in Operation Unified Protector', *Military Law and the Laws of War*, Vol. 50, No. 1–2, 2011. Online. Available: http://dare.uva.nl/document/456665 (accessed 21 January 2013).
Fisk, R., *The Great War for Civilization*, London: Harper Perennial, 2006.
Fleck, D., *The Handbook of International Humanitarian Law*, New York: Oxford University Press, 2008.
Foreign Internal Defense, Joint Publication (JP) 3–22, US Army, 2010.

Gill, T.D. and Fleck, D. (eds), *The Handbook of the International Law of Military Operations*, Oxford: Oxford University Press, 2010.

Gordon, J., Johnson, S., Larrabee, F.S. and Wilson, P.A., 'NATO and the Challenge of Austerity', *Survival*, Vol. 54, 2012.

Górka-Winter, B. and Marek M. (eds), *NATO Member States and the New Strategic Concept: An Overview*, Polish Institue of International Affairs, 2010.

Gow, J. and Michalski, M., *War, Image and Legitimacy*, London: Routledge, 2007.

Gray, C., *International Law and the Use of Force*, 3rd edition, Oxford: Oxford University Press, 2008.

Gray, C.S., *Explorations in Strategy*, Westport: Praeger Publishers, 1996.

Henckaerts, J.M. and Doswald-Beck, L., *Customary International Humanitarian Law, introduction to ICRC study, Volume I: Rules*, xxv-li, Cambridge: Cambridge University Press, 2005.

Henderson, C., 'International Measures for the Protection of Civilians in Libya and Côte d'Ivoire', *International and Comparative Law Quarterly*, Vol. 60, 2012.

Hoskins, A. and O'Loughlin, B., *War and Media: The Emergence of Diffused War*, Cambridge: Polity Press, 2010.

Hurd, I., *After Anarchy: Legitimacy and Power in the United Nations Security Council*, Princeton: Princeton University Press, 2007.

Hvidt, N. and Mouritzen, H., *Foreign Policy Yearbook*, Copenhagen: Danish Institute for International Studies, 2012.

Ikenberry, J.G., 'Institutions, Strategic Restraint, and the Persistence of American Postwar Order', *International Security*, Vol. 23, No. 3, Winter, 1998–1999.

International Humanitarian Law and the Challenges of Contemporary Armed Conflicts, 31IC/11/5.1.2 (31–10–2011 Report), Geneva: ICRC, 2011. Online. Available: www.icrc.org/eng/resources/documents/report/31-international-conference-ihl-challenges-report-2011–10–31.htm (accessed 18 January 2013).

Jakobsen, P.V. and Moller, K.J., 'Good News: Libya and the Danish Way of War', in *Danish Foreign Policy Yearbook 2012*, Copenhagen: Danish Institute for International Studies, 2012.

James, G.K., Holcomb, L. and Manske, C.T., 'Joint Task Force Odyssey Dawn: A Model for Joint Experience, Training, and Education', *Joint Forces Quarterly*, Vol. 64, 2012.

Jentleson, B. and Whytock, C., 'Who "Won" Libya? The Force-Diplomacy Debate and Its Implications for Theory and Policy', *International Security*, Vol. 30, 2005/2006.

Johnson, A. and Mueen, S. (eds), *Short War, Long Shadow: The Political and Military Legacies of the 2011 Libya Campaign*, London: RUSI, 2012.

Kassimeris, G. and Buckley, J., *The Ashgate Research Companion to Modern Warfare*, Surrey: Ashgate, 2010.

Kiras, J.D., *Special Operations and Strategy. From World War II to the War on Terrorism*, London: Routledge, 2006.

Kolb, R. and Hyde, R., *An Introduction to the International Law of Armed Conflicts*, Oxford: Hart, 2008.

Kreps, S., 'Elite Consensus as a Determinant of Alliance Cohesion: Why Public Opinion Hardly Matters in Afghanistan', *Foreign Policy Analysis*, Vol. 6, 2010.

Lawrence, T.E., *Seven Pillars of Wisdom. A Triumph*, New York: Anchor Books, 1991.

Lehmann, J.M., 'All Necessary Means to Protect Civilians: What the Intervention in Libya Says about the Relationship between the Jus in Bello and the Jus ad Bellum', *Journal of Conflict and Security Law*, Vol. 17, 2012.

Lessons Learned for Soldiers on Fratricide, Dispatches, Vol. 11, No. 1, Kingston: The Army Lessons Learned Centre, 2005.

Lindley-French, J., 'Welcome to NATO Operation Protecting Disunity', *Atlantic Council*, 15 April 2011.

Lloyd Owen, D., *Providence Their Guide: The Long Range Desert Group, 1940–1945*, Barnsley: Pen & Sword, 2000.

Mackay, A. and Tatham, S., *Behavioural Conflict: Why Understanding People and Their Motivations will Prove Decisive in Future Conflicts*, Saffron Walden: Military Studies Press, 2011.

Mann, J., *The Obamians: The Struggle inside the White House to Redefine American Power*, London: Viking, 2012.

Martinez, L., *The Algerian Civil War 1990–1998*, New York: Columbia University Press 2000.

McLaughlin, R., 'The Legal Regime Applicable to Use of Lethal Force when Operating under a United Nations Security Council Chapter Vii Mandate Authorizing "All Necessary Means"', *Journal of Conflict and Security Law*, Vol. 12, No. 3, 2007. Available: doi: 10/1093/jcsl/krn003 (accessed 17 January 2013).

McNab, A., *Bravo-Two-Zero. The Harrowing True Story of a Special Forces Patrol Behind the Lines in Iraq*, New York: Dell Publishing, 1993.

McNair, B., *An Introduction to Political Communication*, London: Routledge, 2003.

McQuinn, B., *After the Fall: Libya's Evolving Armed Groups*, A Small Arms Survey, Geneva: Small Arms Survey, 2012.

Media Operations, Joint Doctrine Publication (JDP) 3–45.1, US Army: Defense Concepts and Doctrine Center, September, 2007.

Mendelsohn, B., 'Al-Qaeda's Franchising Strategy', *Survival*, Vol. 53, 2011.

Menon, A., 'European Defence Policy from Lisbon to Libya', *Survival*, Vol. 53, 2011.

Meron, T., 'Geneva Conventions as Customary Law', *American Journal of International Law*, Vol. 81, 1987.

Milanovic, M., 'Al-Skeini and Al-Jedda in Strasbourg', *European Journal of International Law*, Vol 23, No 1, 2012.

Military Balance 2011, London: IISS, 2011.

Military Concept for NATO Strategic Communications, NATO, MCM-0085–2010, 11 August 2010.

Miller, D., Kitzinger, J. and Beharrell, P., *The Circuit of Mass Communication*, London: Sage, 1998.

Mockler, A., *The New Mercenaries: The History of the Mercenary from the Congo to the Seychelles*, London: Guild Publishing, 1985.

Mohlin, M., *The Strategic Use of Military Contractors. American Commercial Military Service Providers in Bosnia and Liberia: 1995–2009*, Helsinki: National Defence University, 2012.

Moskos, C.C., Williams, J.A. and Segal, D.R., *The Postmodern Military: Armed Forces after the Cold War*, Oxford: Oxford University Press, 2000.

Mueller, J., 'The Iraq Syndrome', *Foreign Affairs*, Vol, 84, No. 6, November/December 2005.

NATO ACO Strategic Communications Directive, NATO, AD 95–2, November 2009.

NATO Strategic Communications Capability Implementation Plan, NATO, 20 April 2011.

NATO Strategic Communications Policy, NATO, MCM-0164–2009, 29 September 2009.

Nissen, T.E., *Strategisk Kommunikation – en nødvendig konceptuel og strategisk udfordring*, Copenhagen: Forsvarsakademiet, 2011.

Nutter, J.J., *The CIA's Black Ops: Covert Action, Foreign Policy and Democracy*, New York: Prometheus Books, 2000.

Olsen, J.A., *John Warden and the Renaissance of American Air Power*, Dulles: Potomac Books, 2007.

Orford, A., *International Authority and the Responsibility to Protect*, Cambridge: Cambridge University Press, 2011.

Pape, R., *Bombing to Win: Air Power and Coercion in War*, Ithaca: Cornell University Press, 1999.

Parker, K. and Neylon, L.B., 'Jus Cogens: Compelling the Law of Human Rights', *Hastings International and Comparative Law*, Vol. 12, 1988–89.

Payandeh, M., 'The United Nations, Military Intervention, and Regime Change in Libya', *Virginia Journal of International Law*, Vol. 52, No. 2, 2011. Online. Available: www.vjil.org/assets/pdfs/vol.52/issue2/Payandeh_Post_Production.pdf (accessed 18 January 2013).

Pippan, C., 'The 2011 Libyan Uprising, Foreign Military Intervention, and International Law', *Juridikum: Zeitschrift für Kritik–Recht–Gesellschaft*, No. 2, 2011.

Quartararo Sr., J., Rovenolt, M. and White, R., 'Libya's Operation Odyssey Dawn: Command and Control', *PRISM* 3, 2012.

Report of the International Commission of Inquiry on Libya, Human Rights Council, 2 March 2012.

Rid, T., *War and Media Operations: The US Military and the Press from Vietnam to Iraq*, Abingdon: Routledge, 2007.

Ringsmose, J. and Børgesen, B.K., 'Shaping Public Attitudes towards the Deployment of Military Power: NATO, Afghanistan and the Use of Strategic Narratives', *European Security*, Vol. 20, 2011.

Robert, E., 'The Organized Hypocrisy of International State-Building', *Conflict, Security and Development*, Vol. 10, No. 4, 2010.

Roberts, A. and Guelff, R. *Documents on the Laws on War*, 3rd edition, Oxford: Oxford University Press, 2000.

Rogers, A.P.V., *Law on the Battlefield*, 2nd edition, Manchester: Manchester University Press, 2004.

Rönnbäck, A., *Regional Co-operation in North Africa: Success or Failure?*, Umeå University, 2007.

Rowland, L. and Tatham, S., *Strategic Communication and Influence Operations: Do We Really Get It?*, Defence Academy of the United Kingdom: Strategic Series, August 2010.

Sabasteanski, A., *Patterns of Global Terrorism, 1985–2005. Vol. 1*, Great Barrington: Berkshire Publishing Group, 2005.

Sanger, D.E., *Confront and Conceal: Obama's Secret Wars and Surprising Use of American Power*, New York: Crown Publishers, 2012.

Smith, R., *The Utility of Force: The Art of War in the Modern World*, London: Allen Lane, 2005.

Special Operations, Joint Publication (JP) 3-05, McDill Air Force Base: USSOCOM, 2011.

Stewart, J.G., 'Towards a Single Definition of Armed Conflict in International Humanitarian Law: A Critique of Internationalized Armed Conflict', *International Review of the Red Cross*, Vol. 85, No. 850, 2003. Online. Available: www.icrc.org/eng/assets/files/other/irrc_850_stewart.pdf (accessed 5 November 2012).

Stuart, A. and Zelizer, B., *Reporting War: Journalism in Wartime*, London: Routledge, 2004.
Tangredi, S.J., *Globalisation and Maritime Power*, Washington: National Defence University Press, 2002.
Tatham, S., *Strategic Communication: A Primer*, Shrivenham: Defence Academy of the United Kingdom, Advanced Research and Assessment Group Special Series 08/28, December, 2008.
Thrall, T., *War in the Media Age*, New Jersey: Hampton Press, 2000.
Thussu, D. and Freedman, D., *War and the Media*, London: Sage, 2003.
Tichenor, M.A., 'Bombers over Libya', *Air Force Magazine*, July 2011.
Till, G., *Seapower: A Guide for the Twenty-First Century*, London: Frank Cass, 2004.
Tumber, H. and Webster, F., *Journalists under Fire: Information War and Journalistic Practice*, London: Sage, 2006.
Ucko, D. and Egnell, R., *Counterinsurgency in Crisis: Britain and the Challenges of Modern Warfare*, Columbia University Press, forthcoming 2013.
United Nations, *A More Secure World: Our Shared Responsibility. Report of the Secretary-General's High-Level Panel on Threats, Challenges and Change*, New York: United Nations, 2004. Online. Available: http:www.un.org/secureworld/report2.pdf (accessed 20 June 2012).
United Nations, *The Law of the Sea – UNCLOS*, New York: United Nations, 1997.
van Creveld, Martin, *Air Power and Maneuver Warfare*, Honolulu: University Press of the Pacific, 2002.
Vandewalle, D., *A History of Modern Libya*, Cambridge: Cambridge University Press, 2006.
Voeten, E., 'The Political Origins of the UN Security Council's Ability to Legitimize the Use of Force', *International Organization*, Vol. 59, 2005.
Volker, K., 'Don't Call It a Comeback: Four Reasons Why Libya doesn't Equal Success for NATO', *Foreign Policy*, 23 August 2011.
Wagnsson, C., 'A Security Community in the Making? Sweden and NATO post-Libya', *European Security*, Vol. 20, 2011.
Warden III, J.A., 'The Enemy as a System', *Air Power Journal*, Spring 1995.
Weiss, T.G., 'R2P after 9/11 and the World Summit', *Wisconsin International Law Journal*, Vol. 24, No. 3, 2006.
Wheeler, N., *Saving Strangers: Humanitarian Intervention in International Society*, New York: Oxford University Press, 2000.
Wilmshurst, E. (ed.), *International Law and the Classification of Conflicts*, Oxford: Oxford University Press, 2012.
Zarate, J.C. and Gordon, D.A., 'The Battle for Reform with Al-Qaeda', *The Washington Quarterly*, Vol. 34, No. 3, 2011.

Index

Page numbers in *italics* denote tables, those in **bold** denote figures.

AAR *see* air-to-air refuelling (AAR)
Abdel-Jalil, Mustafa 20
Abu Llail tribe 159
Afghanistan 10, 106, 222, 223–4, 225, 227
Afghan model 227–8
African Union 45
aid, humanitarian 131–2, 136, 139, 142
airbases, attacks on 114, 115
aircraft: B-2 Spirit bombers 105, 115; F-15 crash 116–17, 138; helicopters 76, 109, 119; Libyan 108–9; naval 138, 139, 141; P-3 Orion 106, 141; reach 104–5; restrictions on use 28–9, 84–5; shortage of ground attack 28–31; unmanned aerial vehicles 76, 106, 122; *see also* air operations
aircraft carriers 105, 116, 138–9
air defence systems: attacks on 22, 78, 113–15, 138; avoiding 105; Libyan capability 107, 109–11, 201
air operations 103–4, 111–18; chase of Khamis Brigade 119–20; coalition airpower 104–6; importance of control of the air 122; lessons learned 120–3, 226–9; Libyan airpower 107–11, 157–8, **158**; shortage of ground attack aircraft 28–31; sorties carried out 76, 103; as strategic tool 104–6; *see also* no-fly zone
air-to-air refuelling (AAR) 104–5, 107, 122
air-to-ground attacks 22, 78–9, 111–12, 113, 114, 116; Gaddafi family members killed 160; numbers carried out by NATO 76, 103; shortage of aircraft for 28–31; Special Forces direction of 202; stand-off weapons 105
Ajdabiya 4, 20, 119, 159, 160
Al-Awaqir tribe 159
Algeria 50, 153, 154, 155–6
Al Khums naval base 139–40, 143
ambivalent interventionism 49–51, 52
ammunition dumps, attacks on 78, 103
Annan, Kofi 44–5
anti-aircraft artillery (AAA) 109, 115
AQIM *see* al-Qaeda in the Islamic Maghreb (AQIM)
Arab League *see* League of Arab States
Arab Spring 4–6, 18–19, 49, 151
armed conflicts, determination of 71–5
arms, supplied to rebels 206
arms embargo: enforcing 24, 76, 85–8; Resolution 1970 52, 69, 135; Resolution 1973 85, 137; Resolution 2009 70, 85
arms related materials, embargo 86–7
arrest warrants 69, 79
assassination missions 202–3
assertive interventionism 47–8, 52
asset freeze 52, 69
audiences: domestic 174, 176, 177–82; local 174, 176–7, 182–7; multiple 174; Target Audience Analysis 175; *see also* strategic communications
Australia 48

B-2 Spirit bombers 105, 115
Bab-al-Aziziyah, Tripoli 80
Bahrain 5
balanced conflict tactic 154
Ban Ki-Moon 47
Belgium 34, 141
Bellamy, Alex 231, 232

Ben Ali, Zine El Abidine 4
Benghazi 5, 19, 20, 117, 159; attack on US consulate 162–3; battles of 106, 112–15; evacuation of civilians from 135, 208; snipers 120
Berbers 161
Berlusconi, Silvio 29
Biddle, Stephen 227
Biden, Joe 29
Bill, James 153
blue-on-blue *see* friendly fire incidents
Bosnia and Herzegovina 57, 227
Bouazizi, Muhammed 4, 158
Bouchard, Charles 24, 32, 80, 141, 225
Bouteflika, Abdel-Aziz 154, 155
Brazil 50–1, 55, 57, 59–60, 231
British maritime doctrine 129, 147
burden-sharing issues 25–7, 28–31, 33–4, 35

Cameron, David 20, 23, 27, 48, 53, 80, 113, 196
Canada 111, 136, 137–8, 143
canals, protection of 79
capture and assassination missions 202–3
carpet bombing 106, 107
Chad 166
Charles De Gaulle (aircraft carrier) 116, 138–9
chemical weapons 19
China 51, 53, 54–5, 57, 60, 229, 231; oil companies 3
CIA 198
civilians: casualties 81, 89–90, 118, 182; evacuations 132, 135, 136, 208; increasing focus on 42; used as human shields 119; warnings to 82, 177; *see also* protection of civilians
civilian vehicles, use by Libyan forces 79, 119
civil wars 71, 72–4, 75; Algerian 155–6
Clapham, Andrew 67, 69
Clinton, Hillary 20–1, 24, 27, 49, 113
coalition of the willing 22, 23; *see also* Operation Odyssey Dawn (OOD)
collateral damage 104, 119, 177
Col Moschin 198
Colombia 70
colonial legacy, North Africa 152–3
combat search and rescue (CSAR) 108, 122, 138
command-and-control centres, attacks on 78, 113–14, 138, 230

command and control issues, coalition forces 24, 112, 117, 123
communications: changing nature of 173–4; Libyan regime 185–6; over-simplification 186; rebel 177, 185, 186; *see also* strategic communications
concealment, by Libyan forces 79, 119, 229
conflict prevention, law of 64
constructive abstention 54, 55, 60
Council of Europe 88
coups d'état, threats of 154, 157
covert operations *see* Special Forces
cruise missiles 105, 113–14, 138
CSAR *see* combat search and rescue (CSAR)

Dabbashi, Ibrahim 50, 53
defections: leading politicians 160; Libyan forces 5, 19, 113, 115, 160
defence budgets, decline in 8, 18
Defence Concepts and Doctrine Centre (DCDC), UK 175
Denmark 19, 29, 34, 112
Di Paolo, Giampaolo 31–2
direct action, Special Forces *200*, 201–3
disaster relief 131–2
divide and rule tactic 154, 163
dual use objects 78–9

Egypt 4–5, 136, 151, 152–3, 155, 162
Erdogan, Recep Tayyip 24, 27, 112
European Court of Human Rights (ECtHR) 66
European NATO allies: burden-sharing issues 25–7, 28–31, 33–4, 35; dependence on United States 7, 8, 27; divisions over role of NATO 8–9; objections to NATO involvement 20, 23–4
European Union 3, 23, 45, 50
evacuations, non-combatant 132, 135, 136, 208
Evans, Gareth 48
expeditionary operations 132–3, 137, 140, 144, 145

F-15 crash 116–17, 138
Falklands 132
5 ring model 104
force, international law on use of 66–7
Foreign Affairs Committee, UK 67
Foreign and Commonwealth Office (FCO), UK 208

foreign occupying force, ban on 54, 55–6
France 22; air operations 22, 105, 111–12, 113, 116, 117, 121–2; leadership role 54, 117; naval operations 136, 138–9, 141; objections to NATO involvement 20, 23, 24; Operation Harmattan 111, 137; Special Forces 198, 204, 209–10; supply of weapons to rebels 206; support for intervention 19, 20, 21, 47–8, 70
Frattini, Franco 88
friendly fire incidents 79, 113, 118; reducing risk of 32, 204; risk of 31, 107, 111, 117

G8 (Group of Eight) 49, 53, 54, 224
Gabellini, Claudio 80
Gaddafi, Khamis 119–20, 160
Gaddafi, Moammar: arrest warrant for 69; capture and death 32, 161; cause of deficiencies in own forces 163, 165–6; family members killed 160; flees 160; Green Book 156; military background 154, 155; notoriety 231; speech on Tunisian uprising 158; targeting of 79–81, 114, 115; travel ban and asset freeze 52
Gaddafi, Saif al-Arab 160
Gaddafi, Saif al-Islam 69, 160, 161, 163, 165
Gates, Robert 8, 20, 27, 29
Gaub, Florence 184
Geneva Conventions (1949) 44, 55, 71, 72–3, 74, 77
Germany: concerns about intervention 21–2, 50, 55, 57, 59–60; evacuation of civilians 136; lack of participation 24, 26, 28, 29; objections to NATO involvement 23, 25
Ghardabiya airbase 115
Gibson, Chris 214–15
global financial crisis 18
Goulter, Christina 226–7
Gray, Christine 67
Greece 141
Green Book (Gaddafi) 156
ground attack aircraft, shortage of 28–31
ground attack missions *see* air-to-ground attacks
ground forces 54, 55–6, 76, 230; *see also* Special Forces

Group of Eight (G8) 49, 53, 54, 224
Gulf Cooperation Council 49–50, 53

Hague, William 28, 206, 207
Ham, Carter 137
helicopters 76, 109, 119
Hillen, Hans 27, 28
HMCS Charlottetown 136, 138, 143
HMS Cumberland 135, 138, 208
hostage rescue 202–3
humanitarian constituency 48, 52, 56, 59
humanitarian intervention, in international law 67–8
humanitarian operations, naval 131–2, 133, 137, 140, 144
humanitarian organizations 136, 139
Human Rights Council, UN 48, 73–4, 75, 81, 195
human rights law *see* international human rights law (IHRL)
human security 42
human shields, civilians used as 119
Hurd, Ian 41

IAC *see* international armed conflicts (IAC)
ICC *see* International Criminal Court (ICC)
ICISS *see* International Commission on Intervention and State Sovereignty (ICISS)
ICJ *see* International Court of Justice (ICJ)
ICRC (International Committee of the Red Cross) 73, 74–5
IHL *see* International Humanitarian Law (IHL)
IHRL *see* international human rights law (IHRL)
incidental harm, taking account of risk 81
India 50–1, 55, 57, 59–60
influence activity 175
information operations 175, 176–7, 182–7
intelligence activities 19, 31–2; and rebels 206–7; special reconnaissance 200, 203–4; tactical reconnaissance 112, 122
internally displaced persons (IDPs) 135
international armed conflicts (IAC) 71, 72, 73, 74–5

Index 245

International Commission on Intervention and State Sovereignty (ICISS) 43, 45, 60
International Court of Justice (ICJ) 44, 73
International Criminal Court (ICC) 44, 52, 69–70, 79
International Criminal Tribunal for Former Yugoslavia (ICTY) 71–2
International Humanitarian Law (IHL) 65, **65**, 71–5, 76–82
international human rights law (IHRL) 64, 65
international law 44–5, 64–75, **65**, 230; applied to Libyan crisis 69–71, 73–5, 76–82; International Humanitarian Law (IHL) 65, **65**, 71–5, 76–82; international human rights law (IHRL) 64, 65; *ius ad bellum* 65, **65**, 66–71; *ius in bello* 65, **65**, 71–5, 76–82; of the sea 64, 65, 88
International Security Assistance Force (ISAF) 222, 223–4
interventionism: ambivalent 49–51, 52; assertive 47–8, 52; moderate 48–9, 52; reluctant 51, 52; *see also* non-interventionism
Iraq 6, 79
Iraq syndrome 221, 222–3
ISAF *see* International Security Assistance Force (ISAF)
Islamism 155–6, 162–3
Israel 46
Italy: air operations 28, 29, 105; naval operations 28, 141; refugees 88, 136; Special Forces 198, 207; support for NATO involvement 24; tactical reconnaissance 112
ius ad bellum 65, **65**, 66–71
ius in bello 65, **65**, 71–5, 76–82

Jibril, Mahmoud 20–1
jihadism 162–3
Jordan 6, 31, 112, 198
Juppé, Alain 27, 28, 54

Khamis Brigade 108, 119–20, 160
Kosovo 10, 78, 227
Koussa, Moussa 160
Kuwait 6

Lampedusa, Italy 88, 136
land forces *see* ground forces
La Russa, Ignazio 207

law, international *see* international law
law of peace 64–5, **65**, 66–71
law of the sea 64, 65, 88
Laws of Armed Conflict (LOAC) *see* International Humanitarian Law (IHL)
laws of war *see* International Humanitarian Law (IHL)
LCT *see* Libya Communications Team (LCT)
leaflet drops 82, **83**, 177
League of Arab States 6, 20, 21, 49–50, 53, 107; role recognised in Resolution 1973 54, 56
Lebanon 70
legitimacy 229–30, 234; of rebel forces 213; and regional support 6, 49–50, 112, 215
lessons learned 1–2, 17; air operations 120–3, 226–9; future of NATO 222–5; legitimacy 229–30; naval operations 145–7; political 33–5; Responsibility to Protect 231–3; Special Forces 213, 214–15; by United States 7
liberation of Libyan people, as justification 179, 180–1, 186
Libya-Chad conflict 166
Libya Communications Team (LCT) 178
Libyan forces 156–8, *158*; Air Force 107, 108–9, 115, 157–8, *158*; airpower 107–11; air strikes on 22, 111, 112, 113, 116; Army 108, 157, *158*; defections from 5, 19, 113, 115, 160; deficiencies causes by Gaddafi 163, 165–6; Navy 107–8, 116, 118, 139–40, 143, 157, *158*; radio messages to 82, 116; Special Forces 118, 143; use of concealment 79, 119, 229; *see also* air defence systems
Libyan intervention: build-up to 18–22; sequence of events 158–61; take over by NATO 22–5; as unique case 6–7, 221, 228–9, 233; *see also* air operations; naval operations; Operation Odyssey Dawn (OOD); Operation Unified Protector (OUP); Special Forces
Libyan Islamic Fighting Group (LIFG) 156
Lisbon Treaty 48
live video feed 122
Lockerbie bombers 3, 161
Locklear, Sam 137

logistical problems 7
Long Range Desert Group (LRDG) 197–8
Longuet, Gerard 27

Mackay, Andrew 175, 183
Magariha tribe 161
Maizière, Thomas de 25
Mali 59, 213, 215
Malta 108, 115, 135, 208
maritime operations *see* naval operations
maritime patrol aircraft 106, 141
maritime security operations 133, 135, 141, 144, 146
maritime surveillance area (MSA) 85–6
media, news 181–2, 184–5
media operations 175, 176, 177–82
mediatization of war 173
al-Megrahi, Abdel Baset 161
mercenaries 86, 119–20, 160, 163
Merkel, Angela 22
MI6 *see* Secret Intelligence Service (SIS), UK
militarism 154–5, 163–4
military advisors 31, 177, 195, 207
military necessity 57, 77–8
mine-laying 88, 118, 142
Misrata 19, 20, 86, 160; aid shipments to 139, 142; friendly fire risk 117; Libyan forces attacks on 117, 119, 120, 142–3; mine-laying 88, 118, 142
Misurata tribe 159
mobile surface-to-air missile systems 115
moderate interventionism 48–9, 52
Morocco 31, 154
MSA *see* maritime surveillance area (MSA)
Mubarak, Hosni 4–5, 155
Mueller, Karl 221
Muslim Brotherhood 155, 163

NAC *see* North Atlantic Council (NAC)
Nafusa mountains 19, 206
national level operations 22, 23, 34–5, 225; *see also* Operation Odyssey Dawn (OOD); Special Forces
National Security Council (NSC), UK 176
National Security Council (NSC), US 21
National Transitional Council (NTC) 5, 19, 20, 74, 75

NATO: conditions for engagement 53; future of 222–5; Strategic Concept (2010) 8, 222; take over of intervention 22–5; *see also* European NATO allies; Operation Unified Protector (OUP)
natural gas, Libyan reserves 3
Naval Cooperation and Guidance for Shipping (NCAGS) 142
naval diplomacy 129, 131, 132–3, 136, 140–1, 144–5, 147
naval forces 128–33; coalition 137–8, 141; Libyan 107–8, 116, 118, 139–40, 157, *158*
naval gunfire support 88, 107, 116
naval operations 85–8, 134–47; attacks on Libyan Navy 118, 139, 143; cruise missiles 113–14, 138; early phases 134–7; non-combatant evacuations 132, 135, 136, 208; Operation Odyssey Dawn 137–41; Operation Unified Protector 85–8, 112, 141–5; *see also* arms embargo
necessity, military 57, 77–8
negotiated settlement, calls for 27
Netherlands: limited commitment 25, 28, 29, 84–5, 112; naval operations 141; objections to regime change 27; on responsibility for refugees 88
news media 181–2, 184–5
NIAC *see* non-international armed conflict (NIAC)
no-fly zone: enforcing 76; first mentioned 50; problems establishing 107–8; proposals 19, 20, 53, 54; in Resolution 1973 21, 56; take over by NATO 24
non-combatant evacuations 132, 135, 136, 208
non-international armed conflict (NIAC) 71, 72–4, 75; *see also* civil wars
non-interventionism 51, 71, 229–30; *see also* interventionism
North Atlantic Council (NAC) 19, 24, 84
Norway 24, 28, 29, 34, 112, 199
Notice to Mariners 142
NSC *see* National Security Council (NSC), UK; National Security Council (NSC), US

Obama, Barack 21, 24, 27, 29–30, 80
offshore patrol vessels (OPVs) 128
oil 3–4; attacks on infrastructure 78;

embargo of refined products 86–7; Libyan reserves 3
oil companies 3
Olson, Peter 80
OOD *see* Operation Odyssey Dawn (OOD)
Operation Dawn Mermaid 205
Operation Ellamy 111, 137, 172
Operation Gunnerside 199
Operation Harmattan 111, 137
Operation Mobile 111, 137
Operation Odyssey Dawn (OOD) 22, 63, 111–12, 137–41, 202
Operation Unified Protector (OUP) 25–32, 75–88, 117, 226; command meetings 224; end goals 75–6; and international law 76–82; naval operations 85–8, 112, 141–5; rules of engagement 83–5; special operations 202; targeting process 82–3
opposition forces *see* rebel forces
Organization of Islamic States 49–50
OUP *see* Operation Unified Protector (OUP)

P-3 Orion 106, 141
partnership countries 31–2, 34, 222, 225
patrimonialism 153–4, 164–5
peace, law of 64–5, **65**, 66–71
personnel recovery *see* combat search and rescue (CSAR)
petroleum embargo 86–7
pilots, Libyan 109, 115, 158
pirates 135, 146
Poland 25, 26, 28–9
political culture, North Africa 152–6, 162–5
political will, lack of 23–4, 25–7, 28–31, 35
Pommier, Bruno 68, 78
popular support: consequences of low 215; gaining 174, 176, 177–82; Iraq syndrome 222–3; in NATO states 9
precautionary measures 82, **83**
precision guided munitions 105; *see also* cruise missiles
propaganda: Libyan regime 185–6; rebel 177, 185, 186
proportionality 81–2
protection of civilians 6, 76, 87, 88; evacuations 132, 135, 136, 208; in international law 44–5; as justification to public 179, 180–2; in Resolution 1973 21, 55–6, 70; *see also* no-fly zone; Responsibility to Protect (R2P)
psychological operations 82, 116, 175, 176, 189
public opinion *see* popular support

Qadhafah tribe 161
al-Qaeda 223, 224
al-Qaeda in the Islamic Maghreb (AQIM) 155, 208, 209, 211–12
Qatar 6, 31, 112, 198, 206, 215

R2P *see* Responsibility to Protect (R2P)
radar 114, 115, 116
radio messages 82, 116, 177
Rasmussen, Anders Fogh 8, 9, 24, 25, 30, 53
rebel forces 120–1; arming 21, 206; attack on Tripoli 205; building relationships with 31–2, 35, 137; communications 177, 185, 186; early successes 19, 20; importance of contribution 226; legitimacy of 213; Special Forces support 204, 205–7, 210–11, 212–13; training 31, 206, 207; *see also* friendly fire incidents
reconnaissance *see* intelligence activities
refineries 4
refugees 88, 135, 136, 144
regime change 27, 32, 71, 80, 229–30, 232; *see also* liberation of Libyan people
regional collateral damage 59
regional support 51, 53, 54; and legitimacy 6, 49–50, 112, 215
reluctant interventionism 51, 52
rescue operations 132, 135, 208; civilian evacuations 132, 135, 136, 208; combat search and rescue 108, 122, 138
Resolution 1970 45, 51–2, 69–70, 74, 135–7
Resolution 1973 6, 21–2, 45, 55–8, 63; and air operations 106–8; drafting of 54; expands arms embargo 85, 137; permissive interpretation of 195–6, 230; and Responsibility to Protect 54, 55, 57–8, 70–1
Resolution 2009 70, 75, 85
Resolution 2016 70, 85
Responsibility to Protect (R2P) 6, 42, 43–5, 46; extra constraints due to 81–2; in international law 65, 68–9; lessons learned 231–3; and Resolution 1973 54, 55, 57–8, 70–1

revolutionary Islamism 162–3
Rice, Susan 43, 49
Richards, Sir David 80, 230
ROE *see* rules of engagement (ROE)
Royal Air Force (RAF) 105, 143, 208
Rudd, Kevin 48
rules of engagement (ROE) 83–5
Russia 51, 53, 55, 57, 60, 229, 231

SACEUR (Supreme Allied Commander Europe) 84
SAM *see* surface-to-air missile (SAM) systems
sanctions 51–2, 69, 70, 86–7, 135; *see also* arms embargo
Sanctions Committee 69
Sands, Philippe 79
Sarkozy, Nicolas 20, 27, 48, 80, 113
SAS *see* Special Air Service (SAS)
SBS *see* Special Boat Squadron (SBS)
Schmitt, Eric 83
SCSG *see* Strategic Communication Synchronisation Group (SCSG)
sea, law of the 64, 65, 88
sea, operations at *see* naval operations
SEAD *see* suppression of enemy air defences (SEAD)
Secret Intelligence Service (SIS), UK 196, 198
al-Senussi, Abdullah 69, 161
Shalgham, Abdel Rahman 47
Sirte 119, 159, 161
SIS *see* Secret Intelligence Service (SIS), UK
Smith, Sir Rupert 173, 184
snipers 120
sovereignty, state 47, 51, 229–30, 231
Spain 28, 29, 138, 141
Special Air Service (SAS) 196, 197–8, 208
Special Boat Squadron (SBS) 196, 198, 208
Special Forces 195–216, *200*; capture of British team 196, 204; countries deploying in Libya 198; direct action *200*, 201–3; evacuation of civilians 208; implications of use 213, 214–15; Libyan 118, 143; special reconnaissance *200*, 203–4; strategic context 208–13, *209*; support of rebel forces 204, 205–7, 210–11, 212–13; unconventional warfare *200*, 205–8
special reconnaissance *200*, 203–4
Special Reconnaissance Regiment (SRR) 198

Springborg, Robert 153
stand-off weapons 105, 229
state sovereignty 47, 51, 229–30, 231
stealth bombers 105, 115
Stewart, James G. 72–3
strategic communications 171–90; defined 175; domestic audiences 174, 176, 177–82; lessons 187–9; local audiences 174, 176–7, 182–7
Strategic Communication Synchronisation Group (SCSG) 178
supply problems 7
suppression of enemy air defences (SEAD) 113–14, 122; radar jamming 115, 116
surface-to-air missile (SAM) systems 107, 109–11, 115, 201; *see also* air defence systems
surveillance 106, 122
Sweden 31, 70, 84–5, 112
Syria 33, 50, 213, 215

tactical reconnaissance 112, 122
Taliban 223, 224
tanks, attacks on 79, 103, 105
target acquisition 32, 204
Target Audience Analysis (TAA) 175
targeting policy 77, 115
targeting process 82–3
Tatham, Steve 175, 183, 187, 188
television stations: attacks on 78–9; Libya Ahrar (Free Libya) 177
terrorism 208, 209, 211–12
Thakur, Ramesh 58
Thuwar *see* rebel forces
Till, Geoffrey 131, 132–3
Tomahawk Land Attack Missiles (TLAMs) 105, 113–14, 138
training, rebel forces 31, 206, 207
travel ban 52, 69
tribes, Libyan 159, 161, 164–5
Tripoli 32, 80, 114, 205
tsunami, Indian Ocean (2004) 132
Tunisia 4, 151, 158, 162, 206, 210
Turkey 23–4, 26, 28, 29, 51, 117, 141
Tusk, Donald 25

UAVs *see* unmanned aerial vehicles (UAVs)
unconventional warfare *200*, 205–8, 210–12, 213
unilateral action 22, 23, 34–5, 225; *see also* Operation Odyssey Dawn (OOD); Special Forces

United Arab Emirates 6, 31, 112, 198, 206, 215
United Kingdom: air operations 104–5, 111–12, 113–15, 116, 117, 143; British maritime doctrine 129, 147; evacuation of civilians 135, 208; Foreign Affairs Committee 67; interpretation of ground force exclusion 195–6; naval operations 135, 138, 141, 143; Operation Ellamy 111, 137, 172; Special Forces 196, 198, 204, 207, 208, 209–10; support for intervention 19, 21, 47–8, 54; task force to Falklands 132; *see also* strategic communications
United Nations 2005 World Summit 44
United Nations Charter 41, 55, 64–5, 66–7, 71
United Nations General Assembly 42, 48
United Nations Human Rights Council (UNHRC) 48, 73–4, 75, 81, 195
United Nations Security Council 41–3, 45–7, 66–7; Resolution 1970 45, 51–2, 69–70, 74, 135–7; Resolution 2009 70, 75, 85; Resolution 2016 70, 85; *see also* Resolution 1973
United Nations Support Mission in Libya (UNSMIL) 70
United States: air operations 29, 104–6, 111–12, 113–17; attack on Benghazi consulate 162–3; costs of intervention 22; criticism of Europeans 27, 29; European dependence on 7, 8, 27; naval operations 135–6, 137–8; reduction in contribution 26–7, 29–30; Special Forces 198, 199, 203, 210; support for intervention 21, 48–9; supporting role only 7, 33, 48, 223; use of veto to protect Israel 46
unmanned aerial vehicles (UAVs) 76, 106, 122
UNSMIL *see* United Nations Support Mission in Libya (UNSMIL)
USS Kearsarge 108, 114, 116, 135, 137, 138

Vandewalle, Dirk 165
Veri, Rinaldo 141, 142
video feed, live 122
Viotti, Maria Luiza Ribeiro 46

Warden, John 104
Warfalla tribe 161, 164
warnings to civilians 82, 177
weapons: chemical 19; costs to United States 22; European shortages of 7, 27; of mass destruction 3; numbers used by NATO 76, 114; supplied to rebels 206
weapons depots, attacks on 78
Wilmshurst, Elizabeth 73
World Summit 2005 44

Yemen 5
YouTube 177

Zuwaya tribe 161